AF744270

The Development of Intellectual Property Regimes in the Arabian Gulf States

Infidels at the Gates

This book examines the development of national legislative regimes for the protection of intellectual property rights in the Arabian Gulf states: Bahrain, Kuwait, Oman, Qatar, Saudi Arabia, the United Arab Emirates and Yemen. David Price analyses IP rights in these states in the context of WTO membership and consequent compliance with the requirements of the WTO's TRIPS Agreement. The challenges of domestic enforcement of the states' IP laws receive critical attention.

A particular focus of the book is on foreign forces which have shaped or influenced the character of the states' IP protection regimes. It includes commentary on the contribution of foreign states, the WTO and WIPO in the pre-TRIPS and TRIPS-compliance stages, and the US bilateral trade strategy for pursuing IP protection standards that exceed those enshrined in TRIPS, and the impact of these forces upon the states' enforcement performance. The role of the Office of the United States Trade Representative (USTR) and the Special 301 provisions as powerful tools in the US's bilateral strategy receive particular attention.

The intellectual property laws of these states have been developed virtually in the span of a single generation, and the process of change is continuing. As such, this book will interest practitioners both in and outside the region, and those with an interest in intellectual property law, comparative law, Middle East legal systems and affairs, and international trade.

Dr David Price is Senior Lecturer in Law and Leader of the Law Research and Consultancy Group at Charles Darwin University, Australia.

Routledge-Cavendish Research in Intellectual Property

Other titles in the series:

Re-thinking Intellectual Property:
The Political Economy of Copyright Protection in the Digital Era
YiJun Tian

Forthcoming books:

Intellectual Property, Community Rights and Human Rights:
The biological and genetic resources of developing countries
Marcelin Tonye Mahop

The Development of Intellectual Property Regimes in the Arabian Gulf States

Infidels at the Gates

David Price

Routledge
Taylor & Francis Group
LONDON AND NEW YORK

LLYFRGELL PRIFYSGOL BANGOR UNIVERSITY LIBRARY

First published 2009
by Routledge-Cavendish
2 Park Square, Milton Park, Abingdon, Oxon OX14 4RN

Simultaneously published in the USA and Canada
by Routledge-Cavendish
270 Madison Avenue, New York, NY 10016

Routledge-Cavendish is an imprint of the Taylor & Francis Group, an informa business

© 2009 David Price

Typeset in Sabon by
Florence Production Ltd, Stoodleigh, Devon

All rights reserved. No part of this book may be reprinted or reproduced or utilised in any form or by any electronic, mechanical, or other means, now known or hereafter invented, including photocopying and recording, or in any information storage or retrieval system, without permission in writing from the publishers.

British Library Cataloguing in Publication Data
A catalogue record for this book is available from the British Library

Library of Congress Cataloging in Publication Data
A catalogue record for this book has been requested

ISBN10: 0–415–47576–7 (hbk)
ISBN10: 0–203–87894–9 (ebk)

ISBN13: 978–0–415–47576–1 (hbk)
ISBN13: 978–0–203–87894–1 (ebk)

BU Main Library
KMC370. P75 2009
30110008172661

The development of intellectual property regimes in the Arabian Gulf states

Contents

Preface

This book examines the performance of the Arabian Gulf states in protecting intellectual property rights, in the context of their accession to the World Trade Organisation and consequent compliance with the requirements of the WTO's Agreement on the Trade-Related Aspects of Intellectual Property Rights (TRIPS), and accession to the international conventions upon which TRIPS has been built.

In the span of a single generation, the legal systems of those Gulf states that are also members of the Gulf Cooperation Council (GCC) – Bahrain, Kuwait, Oman, Qatar, Saudi Arabia and the United Arab Emirates – have undergone dramatic change and development – and that change is continuing. The change has been characterised by a major trend towards codification of domestic laws, entailing increasing substitution of institutionalised procedures for the former discretionary exercise of personal authority largely based on local application of *Shariah* law. Nevertheless, the states' intellectual property laws still contain characteristics peculiar to themselves and to the Gulf, such as the status of *Shariah* law and its relationship to intellectual property protection. Yemen, the other Gulf state included in this study, is seeking membership of both the WTO and the GCC. It remains a generation behind the GCC member states in terms of the standard of its intellectual property protection regime.

The driving force for the development of each state's intellectual property regime has been primarily external and hence a dichotomy has arisen between the formal expression of the legislation and its practical application through enforcement efforts. The dichotomy arises in major part because of the external pressures upon the states to adopt laws for which they do not possess fully the expertise, infrastructures or cultural mores to effectively execute to the level of satisfaction sought by the more demanding developed countries.

Even though the states have regimes that are largely TRIPS-compliant, and have demonstrated a general willingness to address the complex issue of enforcement – albeit with mixed success – they face additional pressures from developed countries, notably the United States, to adopt even higher standards of protection – TRIPS-plus standards. The greater pressures are applied through bilateral investment treaties and free trade agreements, which are then being promoted by the developed countries as representing the new international consensus on intellectual property protection standards.

There are some contentious areas of intellectual property rights of particular concern within the region that are not yet adequately protected, such as traditional knowledge and cultural heritage, and indigenous biodiversity. Accordingly, intellectual property protection regimes in the Gulf states are still undergoing a TRIPS-plus phase of construction. Hopefully, future developments will change its character more in favour of the states' interests themselves – Insha'allah.

Acknowledgements

During the year 2000, the Sultanate of Oman embarked on the ambitious venture of enacting a full suite of intellectual property laws and attaining membership to the World Trade Organisation, an account of which appears in the following pages.

At the same time, I enjoyed the good fortune to be living and working in the Sultanate and being able to follow this ambitious venture at close quarters. I also experienced first hand the exciting challenge of working in an area of national development that was breaking new ground. Issues of intellectual property, particularly in the areas of copyright and trademarks, were everyday challenges. I shall be forever beholden to the Sultanate and the Omani people for providing such tremendous experiences which acted as the catalyst for this project, and for such wonderful memories.

Research for this project has taken me back to the Sultanate and other Gulf states on a number of occasions. On each and every occasion officials in the various ministries I visited in the course of my research showed close interest in the project and its future outcomes, and were generous in their enthusiasm and assistance. To them, I extend my sincere appreciation and gratitude. My good friend Yahya deserves particular acknowledgement and thanks.

In 2003, the Max Planck Institute for Intellectual Property, Competition and Tax Law, Munich awarded me a scholarship to undertake research at the Institute and to interact with other scholars. Those months generated a tremendous boost for the research project and provided me with a marvellous opportunity to interact with other scholars and researchers with similar interests from all around the world. I am pleased to be able to place on record in this place my acknowledgement of the Institute's support.

Particular thanks are extended to Jessica Moody and Katie Carpenter at Taylor & Francis for their expert and astute advice and guidance in the preparation and editing of the manuscript for publication.

This project arose out of research originally conducted for a doctoral dissertation at Charles Darwin University, and I must acknowledge the opportunity provided by my university for my doctoral research and the interest in the project provided by my colleagues.

Finally, I owe an immeasurable debt of gratitude to my wife, Jane, to whom this book is dedicated. Without her undying encouragement, support and forbearance, this project would not have been possible.

David Price
Charles Darwin University
Darwin, Australia

Tables

Abbreviations

ACTPN	Advisory Committee for Trade and Policy Negotiations
AED	Emirati dirham
BD	Bahraini dirham
BIT	Bilateral Investment Treaty
BSA	Business Software Alliance
FTA	Free Trade Agreement
FTAA	Free Trade Agreement of the Americas
GATT	General Agreement on Tariffs and Trade
GCC	Gulf Cooperation Council
ICSID	International Centre for Settlement of Investment Disputes
IDCAS	Industrial Development Centre for Arab States
IIPA	International Intellectual Property Alliance
ITAC-15	Industry Trade Advisory Committee on Intellectual Property Rights
KACST	King Abdul Aziz City of Science and Technology
KD	Kuwaiti dinar
KUNA	Kuwait News Agency
MEFTA	Middle East Free Trade Area
MFN	Most Favoured Nation
NAFTA	North America Free Trade Area
OR	Omani rial
PCT	Patent Cooperation Treaty
PLT	Patent Law Treaty
PhRMA	Pharmaceutical Researchers and Manufacturers of America
QR	Qatari riyal
SR	Saudi riyal
TIFA	Trade and Investment Framework Agreement
TLT	Trademark Law Treaty
TRIPS	Trade-Related Aspects of Intellectual Property Rights
UAE	United Arab Emirates
UCC	Universal Copyright Convention
UNCITRAL	United Nations Commission on International Trade Law
UNCTAD	United Nations Commission for Trade and Development

UPOV	International Union for the Protection of New Plant Varieties
URAA	Uruguay Round Amendment Act, 1994 (US)
USTR	United States Trade Representative
WCT	WIPO Copyright Treaty
WIPO	World Intellectual Property Organisation
WPPT	WIPO Performances and Phonograms Treaty
WTO	World Trade Organisation
YER	Yemeni rial

1 'Infidels at the gates' – introduction and context

1.1 Introduction and context

The primary objective of this work is to examine the development of national legislative regimes for the protection of intellectual property rights in the six states of the Arabian Peninsula that constitute 'The Cooperation Council for the Arab States of the Gulf', otherwise known as the Gulf Cooperation Council (GCC),[1] namely:

- the Kingdom of Bahrain;
- the State of Kuwait;
- the Sultanate of Oman;
- the State of Qatar;
- the Kingdom of Saudi Arabia; and
- the United Arab Emirates (the UAE).

In order to properly provide a full survey of all Gulf states, the work also includes commentary on the development of intellectual property protection in the remaining Gulf state that is not yet a GCC member, namely, the Republic of Yemen.[2]

The work examines the extent to which these legislative regimes and their enforcement both meet the states' international treaty obligations and are congruent with their domestic policy objectives and needs.

As the title suggests, particular attention is given to the foreign forces which have shaped or influenced the character of the Arabian Gulf states' intellectual property legislative regimes. Hence, the work examines the performance of the states in protecting intellectual property rights in the context of their accessions to World Trade Organisation (WTO) membership, the consequent compliance with the requirements of the WTO's Agreement on the Trade-Related Aspects of Intellectual Property Rights (1994) (TRIPS) and the international conventions for the protection of intellectual property rights upon which the Agreement draws and builds, notably the Paris, Berne and Rome Conventions and the Washington Treaty.[3] In brief, TRIPS serves as the benchmark for this study. The work does not attempt to offer a detailed legal commentary on the text of each law, but instead focuses on the salient features of each area of intellectual property protection and its particular idiosyncratic features.

The work also examines the US strategy of using bilateral agreements to achieve standards of intellectual property protection that exceed those enshrined in TRIPS and the impact of this strategy upon the Gulf states' intellectual property protection regimes and their degree of success in effectively enforcing them. The role of the Office of the United States Trade Representative (USTR) and the Special 301 provisions as a coercive tool in the US bilateral strategy receive particular attention.

A secondary objective is to establish a substantive record of the nature of the states' intellectual property laws and the history of their recent development. Previous studies on intellectual property rights protection that have concerned the Middle East region have tended to concentrate either on one type of law, notably copyright, trademarks or patents, or on a few Gulf states only. Selective studies on intellectual property protection in developing countries further afield have tended to pass over the countries in the Gulf region, with the occasional exception of Saudi Arabia, in favour of a selection from a more active and industrially advanced group of developing countries. This work attempts to redress that imbalance. While it focuses primarily upon patent, trademark and copyright protection, since these are the key areas of intellectual property concern, interest and activity within the states and the international community, it also encompasses the other significant areas of intellectual property in the states, such as industrial designs, geographical indications, integrated circuits and undisclosed information (trade secrets), and new plant varieties. It also examines regional initiatives for the protection of traditional knowledge and cultural heritage, being areas of intellectual property which fall outside the parameters of TRIPS, but which are of significant concern to the Gulf states and other developing countries and to which they are giving increasing attention in terms of providing proper protection.

An appreciation of the enforcement and recognition of intellectual property rights in the Gulf would be incomplete without an understanding of the religious, political and cultural forces deeply rooted in Middle East history that shape the protection of intellectual property rights in the Middle East today.[4] Accordingly, the position of *Shariah* law as a major influence upon the intellectual property rights protection and the constitutional and judicial framework in which it resides is reviewed, as background and context for the examination of the region's intellectual property laws. The precedence of Islamic law, or the *Shariah*, as a legal imperative is unequivocal; its status has been described by one commentator thus:

> 'Behind all secular law stands the *Shariah* law of Islam . . . the *Shariah* runs like a golden thread through the legal systems of the Arab Middle East.'[5]

1.2 The Gulf states and the development of intellectual property laws

What makes a study of these six GCC member states and Yemen of current-day relevance and interest is that the emergence of each as a modern state is a very recent and ongoing occurrence and yet they have assumed a not insignificant regional and global influence in international affairs and trade. With the arguable exception of Saudi Arabia, the other five GCC member states have taken quantum leaps in their national development, to emerge from being quasi-feudal or disputative tribal regions under actual or effective foreign domination into stable and sophisticated independent sovereign states, in just two generations or less. Bahrain, Kuwait, Qatar and the seven sheikhdoms of the Trucial States (that later formed the UAE) were still part of the UK Persian Gulf interests until they gained independence in 1961 (Kuwait) and 1971 (Bahrain, Qatar and the seven sheikhdoms). Oman, although long an independent sovereign state, was still under British influence prior to 1970 and deemed the most feudal and withdrawn of all the Arab Gulf countries; it did not start to emerge from this pseudo-feudal state until the present Sultan succeeded his father in a British-backed palace coup in 1970.[6] Prior to 1990, Yemen existed as two separate states, the Yemen Arab Republic (North Yemen) and the pro-Marxist People's Democratic Republic of Yemen (South Yemen, formerly under British control centred in Aden until 1967). The two states formally united to create the Republic of Yemen on 22 May 1990, although armed insurgency and separatist movements continued until 1995. Not surprisingly, therefore, Yemen has lagged behind the other Gulf states in terms of its emergence as a modern state generally, and in respect of the development of its intellectual property protection regimes.

The consequence of this strong British influence, at least in the eastern and southern Gulf region, was that a system of British laws and justice prevailed throughout the Gulf region until 1971 (except for Muslim nationals on matters within the province of *Shariah* law) and this influence, modified and added to by other western influences, continued well after independence.

As part of their ongoing respective political, economic and social metamorphoses, the legal systems of the states have undergone dramatic, radical and progressive change and development over the last 30 years or so and that change is continuing. The major trend has been towards a shift towards greatly increased codification of law and administered regulation which has entailed increasing substitution of institutionalised procedures for the former informal, discretionary exercise of personal authority sometimes based on local interpretation of *Shariah* legal principles.[7] With this movement towards codification of the law and the institutionalisation of the judiciary and government, there has emerged a growing tension between the protection of local and national interests and traditions and the governmental recognition of the need to embrace western-based legal and economic principles, practices and infrastructures.

The work argues that there exists a dichotomy between the formal expression of intellectual property protection through the states' laws and their practical application through the states' respective enforcement strategies and efforts. The dichotomy arises as a consequence of the external pressures upon the states to adopt laws for which they have neither the resources nor the expertise nor the infrastructures to effectively execute to the level of satisfaction sought by the more demanding developed countries. The work speculates on the extent to which the legislative and operational responses of the states satisfy WTO/developed countries' expectations and what further changes might be sought in the future.

Since the late 1960s/early 1970s, when they either gained their independence or emerged from sustained periods of international isolationism, the Gulf states have undertaken a transformation of their intellectual property legislative regimes at an extremely rapid rate – virtually in the time frame of a single generation. The period of this transformation has been marked by three major, but very different, phases in the development of the regimes. Each phase has been characterised by significant degrees of foreign intervention which have directed or at least strongly influenced the construction of the states' intellectual property laws. But this foreign intervention has not necessarily caused the creation of laws which have been congruent with the states' needs or which have enabled the achievement of national objectives and international requirements in terms of their enforcement effectiveness.

The first of these phases, namely the pre-TRIPS period that existed until the mid 1990s, is notable for the dearth of *sui generis* intellectual property laws in place in the Gulf states; the exceptions were few in number and existed in the field of trademarks, patents and industrial designs, but even these laws were subject to foreign design. However, this dearth of *sui generis* laws does not mean that protection for certain types of intellectual property rights was not available; it existed in an overarching perspective in the divine laws of social and moral conduct laid down in the *Qur'an* and the *Hadith* of the Prophet. In a more corporeal and secular sense, and in the absence of any mainstream intellectual property framework, it also existed in the form of laws governing commercial activity and conduct. Protection in pre-TRIPS times was available for the benefit of the foreign merchant or the merchant's local agent, the trader and the consumer, instead of for the holder of an intellectual property right of foreign origin, but on occasion it coincided for the benefit of both groups. However, even these commercial laws were generally subject to foreign influence. In addition, the national frameworks for the control of publishing and public dissemination of printed material, which all states actively enforced, provided some limited protection for certain types of copyrightable material.

The second developmental phase is marked by the establishment of the WTO, the consequent introduction of TRIPS and a post-TRIPS flurry of legislative activity by the GCC states as they attempt to meet their statutory obligations to introduce intellectual property laws or to make their current laws TRIPS-compliant and their enforcement effective. TRIPS heralded a major shift in intellectual property by establishing unprecedented levels of protection to be enforced worldwide. However, the shift took shape by reference largely to the needs of the few leading industrialised nations (and to a lesser extent those of the other major developed countries). The World Intellectual Property Organisation (WIPO), which had already been a significance influence in shaping the states' pre-TRIPS intellectual property laws, continued to play a crucial role in guiding the states in their compilation of TRIPS-compliant laws and in their enforcement, structural and administrative capacity-building efforts. With fluctuating degrees of commitment, the states embarked on reshaping their intellectual property protection regimes during this period.

Hardly have the Gulf states come to terms with the enormity of the dimension of the transformation to their respective intellectual property protection regimes required by the TRIPS and post-TRIPS phase than they are faced with a new round of imposed changes as they enter the third phase – the TRIPS-plus phase. The dominant driving factor shaping the character of their laws during this period is the bilateral agreement strategy pursued by the United States. This new round commenced with a series of bilateral trade and investment agreements from the late 1990s; more recently, the United States has concluded free trade agreements (FTAs) with Bahrain and Oman, both agreements incorporating extensive provisions on intellectual property. The provisions constitute much higher standards of protection than those set by TRIPS and also remove and restrict the limited degree of manoeuvrability that TRIPS permitted developing and least developed countries. The bilateral agreements are reinforced by demands that the signatory states not only adopt higher standards enshrined in the FTAs themselves but also adopt and adhere to a range of multilateral treaties which represents TRIPS-plus standards. Both the FTAs and the multilateral treaties reduce and restrict the flexibilities and exceptions provisions that TRIPS allowed to signatory states to craft their laws to take account of their respective national needs and objectives.

The intellectual property laws of the Gulf states reflect a common heritage. They contain many similarities with each other, indicating an ongoing process of mutual collaboration and borrowings. They have also drawn much from countries in the region which progressed through an earlier modernisation/westernisation process, notably Egypt, and from other Arab states through their influence in regional groups such as the League of Arab States and the GCC itself. However, the major influence in the construction of their legislative regimes and the character of the intellectual property laws has undoubtedly been WIPO and the models it provides through its various draft laws and technical assistance.

Nevertheless, the states' intellectual property laws still contain their own idiosyncrasies, arising from, for example, the status of *Shariah* law and its relationship to intellectual property, regional attitudes towards enforcement, protection of geographical indications, wines and spirits, moral rights and translations of copyright works, compulsory licensing, protection of pharmaceuticals and even the Arab boycott of Israel (for which statutory provision existed in earlier commercial and intellectual property laws, but which has now been generally removed).

1.3 TRIPS and the globalisation of intellectual property rights

1.3.1 The global pressures

A fundamental element of the emergence of the modern Gulf state is the move to gain membership of the WTO and the consequent perceived benefits of being a member of the global trade community (or the negative impact of not attaining membership). One consequence of such membership, however, is that legislation relating to trade and services, and to intellectual property in particular, must conform to the provisions of the international treaties in this area, notably TRIPS and the Paris, Berne and Madrid Conventions and the Washington Treaty. TRIPS sets new international minimum standards of protection for each of the main categories of intellectual property by building on these major conventions and adding a requirement for effective enforcement regimes.

Since its introduction in January 1995, TRIPS has generated considerable ongoing debate concerning the benefits and disadvantages that its standards of intellectual property protection bring to developed, developing and least developed countries. According to some commentators, there exists a powerful lobby representing developed countries which believes that all intellectual property rights are good for business, benefit the public at large and act as catalysts for technical progress.[8] The rights are necessary to stimulate economic growth which, in turn, contributes to poverty reduction; by stimulating invention and new technologies, they increase agricultural or industrial production, promote domestic and foreign investment, facilitate technology transfer and improve the availability of medicines necessary to protect public health. The developed country lobby considers TRIPS to be a useful tool with which to achieve its objectives and it holds that there is no reason why a system that works for developed countries could not work in similar fashion in developing countries.[9]

On the other side, there are those who believe that the protection of intellectual property rights according to the formula of the major industrialised countries is likely to cripple the progress of local industry and technology in developing countries, will harm their local populations and benefit none but the developed world.[10] Intellectual property rights do little to stimulate invention in developing countries, where the necessary human and technical capacity is absent, and they are ineffective in stimulating research to benefit the poor because they will not be able to afford the products, even if developed. They limit the option of technological learning through imitation and they allow foreign firms to drive out domestic competition by enabling these firms to obtain protection to service the market through imports rather than domestic manufacture. Very high standards of protection may be in the public interest in developed countries with highly sophisticated scientific and technological infrastructures, but this does not mean the same standards are appropriate in all developing countries.[11]

Harmonisation of intellectual property rights, whether as a regional or global initiative, is a contentious issue which still has much distance to travel. To its critics, harmonisation is the strategy devised by the leading developed nations to achieve and maintain global domination through control of international trade and to protect their commercial interests in the developing and least developed countries. By that view, intellectual property rights are imposed by developed countries on the developing and least developed countries as a non-negotiable total package, compliance with which is a prerequisite for membership of the international trade community of which WTO is the global representative. International intellectual property standard-setting has been dominated by western states and intellectual property owners, and the dominant mechanism of standard-setting has been economic coercion, of which TRIPS has been the most potent multilateral expression.[12] Some commentators argue that TRIPS principally benefits the developed countries and the credibility of the WTO as an instrument to promote free trade in the interests of all countries is weakened:

> 'TRIPS does not involve mutual gain; rather, it positions the WTO primarily as a collector of intellectual property-related rents on behalf of multinational corporations (MNCs). This is a bad image for the WTO and in the view of many . . . reflects the "capture" of the WTO by the MNCs.'[13]

The Gulf states saw that WTO membership would give them the potential ability to exert some influence on international trade, whereas outside the WTO they would have no such ability. Yet the states have really had little choice but to join the international community which the WTO represents. The perceived significance to the states of membership of the WTO and the requisite intellectual property legislative framework as a key national political and economic strategy is illustrated by Oman's reaction to achieving WTO membership.[14] Quoting senior ministry sources, the local media reported that Oman's accession to the WTO had great implications and importance for the country and paved the way for globalisation of the Omani economy.[15] Protectionism, which had been the catchword of yesteryear, would be a thing of the past and the indigenous business would be open to international competition. The options before the Sultanate were limited; it was, in effect, a game of do or die – either accede to the WTO or face global isolation. The report continued that, despite the opposition to the WTO and the vehement criticism of its policies in certain quarters, it was a well-known fact that remaining outside the WTO would lead to ostracism which would not be in the interests of any country, particularly a developing country.[16]

In both the legal and commercial contexts, global harmonisation is an intrusive process that demands an active re-examination by the state of its laws and regulations. Arab countries are being driven by pressures from a variety of sources, such as the WTO and individual developed countries, to review and upgrade their laws governing a wide range of economic activity and to introduce a widely embracing set of laws where none previously existed.[17] Even the GCC itself has applied pressures for conformity in the intellectual property field, albeit with limited success, in the drive for a degree of regional cohesion and influence.

1.3.2 The Gulf states' response to the pressures

The question arises as to the extent to which the Gulf states have succumbed to this pressure or whether they have managed to maintain their integrity and to some extent outmanoeuvre the developed countries in some instances. Some intellectual property issues that have become of increasing importance to the states, such as the protection of indigenous rights, traditional knowledge and cultural heritage, have not yet been pursued with the same degree of aggression by the industrialised nations as they have moved to protect their rights and interest on copyright, patents and trademarks. In terms of its impact on the direction of standard-setting in global public health, the Doha Declaration, suggests Drahos, is a concrete success to which developing countries can point, although it remains to be seen whether it has generated an ongoing significant shift in the capacity of these countries to influence the global standard-setting process in intellectual property.[18]

Critics of the performance of developing countries in displaying their commitment to the protection of intellectual property rights according to the standards set by TRIPS would argue that the states, as developing countries, are paying lip service to the rightful demands of the developed countries for the effective protection of intellectual property rights.[19] The states may be establishing the legislative regimes by adopting the intellectual property laws as required by the consortia of the developed countries, but they appear unwilling, uncommitted or unable to act as expeditiously and as fully as required with an effective implementation strategy and execution. To substantiate their complaints, the critics point to the perceived delays in introducing the necessary implementing regulations to give practical effect to the laws, the lack of structural reforms in the states' judicial, infrastructural and administrative areas, and enforcement actions which appear erratic, occasional, misdirected and which do not conclude in successful judicial prosecutions and outcomes.[20]

The most challenging element of the TRIPS and TRIPS-plus phases, as perceived by both the Gulf states themselves and the industrialised nations, is the regional enforcement of the states' intellectual property protection obligations consistent with the standards enshrined in TRIPS, the TRIPS-plus treaties and the bilateral agreements to which the states have made commitments. Notwithstanding the presence of comprehensive sets of laws and treaty commitments, there nevertheless exists a dichotomy between the principle of enforcement as enshrined in the various legislative regimes and the practice as exemplified by the degree of effective action. In all states, the practical application of compliance obligations through effective enforcement has been, and continues to be, the most difficult area with which to contend.

The emergence of this dichotomy is also experienced by many other developing and least developed countries. Why and how this dichotomy emerges and what are, and might continue to be, the consequences for each state can be demonstrated by:

- the comprehensive nature of the legislative regimes in light of the TRIPS minimum benchmark and the dimension of institutional and structural reforms being progressively initiated;

when contrasted with:

- implementation actions, as evidenced by policing actions against illegal activities, piracy and counterfeit goods; and
- the nature and frequency of judicial actions and the severity of penalties available and imposed.

One measure of the extent of this dichotomy can be seen in the responses of the developed countries, as evidenced by the United States through the application of its USTR Annual Special 301 Reports, and the influence thereon of the powerful multinational industry lobby groups. For most Gulf states, the principal barriers to the elimination of intellectual property infringements, which lie at the heart of this dichotomy, do not subsist so much in the substantive law as in their practical application. The reasons for these barriers, which this work explores, are many and do not rest solely with the enforcement authorities or the judiciary; entrenched local societal, cultural and commercial attitudes are also major contributing factors.

In the cause of securing membership of the international community, the states have had little option but to adhere to agendas set by the developed countries through the WTO and the major international treaties which they sponsor. While the agendas may not necessarily have yet hampered the development of nationally appropriate intellectual property protection regimes, they are cementing in place conditions which will restrict the future freedom or discretion of the states to develop in directions which best deal with national imperatives or opportunities. Since becoming part of the international community, the states face, and will continue to face, direct pressure from some developed countries (notably the United States) to accept the imposition of further enhanced levels of intellectual property protection, again with the objective of protecting the particular interests of the developed countries.

Arab countries have been exhorted to play a more active role in the international arena by joining forces with like-minded countries.[21] However, they are unlikely to be inclined to do so by their own volition unless there arises the necessity to develop national and regional agendas that pay particular attention and care to their development needs and priorities. The states already have had in existence a regional structure that could serve as the logical springboard for launching a greater presence in international forums, namely the GCC itself. However, the GCC has its own internal dysfunctionality at present that militates against an effective presence on behalf of the Gulf states or in concert with the wider Middle East, the greater Arab world or a major consortium of developing and least developed nations. The states, either collectively as a regional bloc or individually, have not attempted to make their presence felt in the affairs of the WTO or WIPO councils and committees. The lack of active participation reinforces the view expressed earlier that membership of these two bodies, although deemed necessary, has not always been viewed enthusiastically.

1.4 Multilateralism by the backdoor – the strategy of bilateralism

While TRIPS has set the minimum international standards for intellectual property protection, the nature of these standards and universal adherence to them has still created difficulties and challenges for the states, other developing countries and least developed countries. It has also generated a considerable degree of frustration and dissatisfaction for the major industrialised nations. In some respects, TRIPS has become somewhat superseded by the emergence of the new round of intellectual property law-making in the post-TRIPS world. The WTO has stumbled at its recent ministerial meetings on efforts to liberalise global trade and to also inject a greater degree of equity and access into TRIPS. Failure to conclude the Doha Rounds after seven years of largely fruitless negotiations calls into question the WTO's continuing existence as the lead forum for the global trade agenda. At the same time, WIPO has been confronted with its own self-examination debate over proposals and counter-proposals which have the potential to significantly change its position and role in the global intellectual property arena. The new 'international standard' of intellectual property protection in practical terms is fast becoming that which is defined by the terms enshrined in the latest bilateral agreement which the United States and the EU in particular may have concluded, together with the prescriptions of the TRIPS-plus treaties, such as the WIPO 'Internet Treaties'[22] and conventions. The 'highest international standards' have become very much a dynamic formula in a bilateral context rather than the multilateral forums.

While negotiations on intellectual property rights in the WTO are virtually paralysed and the launching of negotiations on investment finds strong opposition, developed countries, notably the United States, have turned to bilateral dealings to advance their industries' economic interests and obtain higher levels of commitment from developing countries.[23] Powerful and influential multinational business interests actively push for progressively escalating standards and carefully monitor the progress and performance of the US government in imposing TRIPS-plus standards on weaker countries. Hence bilateral trade and investment agreements, particularly FTAs, typically contain extensive intellectual property protection provisions which are used to establish TRIPS-plus standards, to remove or reduce the flexibilities provided for in TRIPS and to establish protection in new areas of intellectual property rights which go beyond the parameters of TRIPS.[24]

Bilateral trade and investment agreements are promoted by their advocates as being stepping stones towards full integration of the participants into a global free market economy by ensuring governments implement the liberalisation, privatisation and deregulation measures of the globalisation agenda.[25] However, they have also been described as part of an insidious, fast-expanding and bewildering coercive web, popping up like Hydra's heads throughout the world and constructing in patchwork fashion what the developed nations have not been able to impose through such international forums as the WTO, or through multilateral negotiations.[26] They are seen as insidious because they are invariably conducted in unequal contest in closed session between unequal partners. With the stronger partner having an established objective to protect its own economic and trade interests, and having little or no interest in making allowance for the divergent or conflicting national and developmental interests of the weaker partner, the resultant agreement is both inevitable and predictable.

On intellectual property issues that really matter to it, the United States has utilised webs of coercion, and one of those webs is its strategy of establishing bilateral agreements which include the establishment of standards of intellectual property protection which may far exceed TRIPS standards and extend beyond the scope of TRIPS.[27] Developing countries operate within an intellectual property paradigm dominated by the United States, the European Union and international business; given the track record of the United States and the European Union, developing countries can expect very few concessions on intellectual property issues in either a bilateral or a multilateral context.[28] However, developing countries are prepared to enter into bilateral agreements containing provisions on intellectual property rights in order to gain access to US and EU markets or to avoid losing access to them.

Having introduced intellectual property laws of largely foreign origin to satisfy the requirements to comply with TRIPS, the Gulf states are faced with the issues and challenges of their domestic implementation and enforcement. Even though the states have demonstrated a general willingness to address the complex and contentious issue of regional piracy – albeit with mixed success – they now face additional pressures from the United States to adopt TRIPS-plus standards of intellectual property protection. A crucial tool in the application of this pressure is the use of the USTR's Special 301 Annual Reporting provisions, which identify countries which fail to provide adequate protection of US intellectual property rights or deny market access to US companies and which threaten possible US retaliatory trade actions. Furthermore, the TRIPS-plus treaties are being used to apply the higher standards on the grounds that these treaties represent the new consensus on higher international standards for intellectual property protection. The intellectual property areas which receive the greatest attention under these bilateral actions are those of economic concern to the United States, particularly protection in the broadest sense of patents, pharmaceutical patents, copyright and neighbouring rights in the digital environment. In contrast, little or no effort is being made within these bilateral agreements to introduce protection of the states' traditional knowledge and cultural heritages, geographical indications of non-European origin, plant varieties and traditional agricultural practice.

The United States has declared its intention of establishing a Middle East Free Trade Area (MEFTA) by 2013 as a crucial tool in giving effect to its Middle East Peace Initiative and its global war against terrorism. To achieve the Middle East Free Trade Area, the United States intends to enter into an FTA with each GCC member state, create a regional Gulf bloc and then promote the benefits of this bloc as an incentive to other Middle East countries to participate. The recent completion of FTAs with Bahrain and Oman will be the catalyst for further development change of this regional strategy. These FTAs require each state to make a number of significant concessions and commitments in the area of intellectual property protection which well exceed TRIPS standards and which counter TRIPS flexibility provisions. The Bahrain FTA was based on the US model developed for Jordan; more significantly it was also the first of the GCC agreements. The intellectual property provisions of the Bahrain FTA set a new TRIPS-plus benchmark in terms of intellectual property protection in the Gulf, while the Oman FTA raised it slightly higher. There is no doubt that regional FTA negotiations already in progress with the other states will strive to raise the benchmark even further; what is in doubt, however, is whether these negotiations will eventuate into formal agreements.

This work explores in some detail the intellectual property provisions of the bilateral trade and investment agreements, and particularly the FTAs that the United States has recently concluded with Bahrain and Oman. While the United States has stated that it is pleased with the strengthened protection of intellectual property rights in its most recent FTAs, it has also stated that it will be seeking even higher levels of protection and enforcement standards in agreements under negotiation or preliminary discussion with the UAE, Kuwait and Qatar.[29] However, at the time of writing, these negotiations and discussions appear to have stalled.

1.5 Structure of the work

This chapter has introduced some background to the Arabian Gulf states and briefly explored the paradigm in which the states have been required to operate in the establishment of their legislative regimes for intellectual property protection.

Chapter 2 examines the regional and domestic moral fabric for intellectual property protection in the Gulf states. It explores the idea of *Shariah* law as a 'golden thread' that runs through the constitutional, legal and judicial structures of the states, and the changing nature of its influence as the secular laws of the states have become increasingly codified. The work examines the extent to which the *Shariah* drives or influences the regional protection of intellectual property rights.

Chapter 3 addresses the pre-TRIPS period of this study. It examines the recent history of intellectual property rights protection within the Gulf and in each state. In so doing, it refers to examples of other laws which were outside a fledgling intellectual property framework, but which offered varying degrees of protection to some intellectual property rights by virtue of their common or overlapping objectives. The chapter also examines some of the foreign influences that have been brought to bear, directly and indirectly, on the development of the states' intellectual property laws. It also questions the impetus behind the states' decisions to join the international trade community and discusses the external inputs into the preparation of their legislative regimes as a precursor to their acceding to the WTO and to TRIPS.

Chapter 4 analyses the standards for intellectual property protection enshrined in TRIPS with the provisions of the states' current laws in the major intellectual property areas prescribed by TRIPS. It examines the extent to which they comply with their obligations under TRIPS requirements and standards. It deals with each of the main areas of protection in turn, as presented in TRIPS, from copyright through to unfair competition, and then adds a brief commentary on protection of new plant varieties. The chapter focuses on the salient features of each area of intellectual property protection and its particular idiosyncratic features, rather than offering a detailed commentary on the text of each law.

Chapter 5 continues the review process from Chapter 4 and examines the performance of the states against the enforcement standards and obligations required by TRIPS. It argues that, in the post-TRIPS environment, there exists a dichotomy between the principle of intellectual property protection (as enshrined in the legislation) and the practice (as measured by its enforcement). It questions whether that dichotomy is a reflection of the political and societal commitment to enforcement, of a political and commercial attitude to intellectual property rights that differs from that of the major developed countries, or of the imposition by the major developed countries of inappropriate requirements and standards that are beyond the capacity of the states to effectively implement. It offers some possible reasons for the dichotomy. In so doing, the work examines regional societal and cultural attitudes and obstacles, and the institutional and judicial capacity and limitations to enforcement within the respective states.

Chapter 6 examines the environment in which TRIPS-plus treaties and bilateral agreements are fast overtaking TRIPS as the new benchmark-setting standard for intellectual property protection. It suggests that the strategy adopted by the United States in particular in pursuing bilateral trade and investment agreements with the individual states bypasses the multilateral forums and agreements and thereby constitutes 'multilateralism by the backdoor'. It examines the role of the USTR and its use of the Special 301 provisions as a tool to pressure the states to adopt standards of protection which are much higher than those required by TRIPS and which go beyond the parameters of TRIPS. Finally, it examines in detail the intellectual property provisions of the free trade agreements which the United States recently completed with Bahrain and Oman, and the implications of those provisions for the other Gulf states.

Chapter 7 examines some 'TRIPS-minus' areas of intellectual property rights protection. It discusses some activities by the Gulf states in areas of intellectual property in which there has been little or no foreign interest in establishing standards of protection on behalf of the states or in the states themselves – notably traditional knowledge, cultural heritage and the offshoots of traditional medicines and indigenous plant species. The states have for some years taken a particular interest in these areas and have taken the initiative in introducing some protection standards in these areas.

In conclusion, Chapter 8 suggests that intellectual property protection in the Gulf region is still, in essence, 'work in progress'. It reviews the development of the states' intellectual property protection regimes and reports on the current status of the national laws and accessions to the major international forums and international conventions on intellectual property protection. It suggests some possible courses of action in both the domestic and international contexts and questions whether the states, now that Saudi Arabia has finally achieved WTO membership, may nurture the emergence of a regional bloc to generate influence within the new development agenda that is emerging in the international forums. In closing, the chapter comments on the nature of the relations between the United States and the states in the context of the proposed MEFTA.

Finally, the Appendix lists the intellectual property laws and corresponding implementing regulations and ministerial orders that the Gulf states have issued during the time frame encompassed by this study. The list also includes laws which are associated in one form or another with intellectual property protection, such as civil, criminal and commercial codes, and laws controlling the press and publications. The list of laws is not complete, but is still impressive, and strikingly illustrates just how active the states have been over the last generation, and particularly during the current post-TRIPS decade, with their law-making endeavours in the field of intellectual property protection.

2 'The golden thread that binds' – the *Shariah* and intellectual property protection

2.1 Introduction – 'the golden thread'

In its simplest definition, Islamic law, or the *Shariah*, is the corpus of rules and principles derived from the Holy *Qur'an* and *Sunnah* (Traditions) of the Holy Prophet which is aimed at regulating the spiritual as well as the temporal conduct of the Muslim in his relationship with God, with other Muslims and with non-Muslims. The precedence of Islamic law, or the *Shariah,* as a legal imperative is unequivocal; its status has been described thus:

> 'Behind all secular law stands the *Shariah* law of Islam . . . the *Shariah* runs like a golden thread through the legal systems of the Arab Middle East.'[1]

Islam has been described as the cultural epicentre of identity in Arab Muslim life.[2] There exists an interrelational and reciprocal influence between its legal, religious and ethical aspects. As a divine-sourced religion, Islam, like many other religions, is characterised by:

- divine sources which are the highest primary sources and therefore possess supreme character and authority;
- other sources based on human reasoning which are therefore secondary and must defer to the primary sources, taking account of the settled rules and principles of Islamic methodology;
- divine sources which are free from errors whereas human sources are fallible;
- divine sources which form the framework outlining the general doctrines and principles, according to which the corpus of the detailed Islamic rules can be formulated.[3]

As the *Shariah* is a whole, comprehensive and interrelated corpus of rules, its application is subject to a single set of standards. Hence one does not find a separate discipline of Islamic law called, for example, intellectual property law. Instead, Islam has the *Shariah*, which deals with every aspect of human conduct regardless of its description as a personal, civil or international code of conduct.[4] Islamic jurisprudence (*fiqh*) as the body of rules and principles that is developed by the reasoning of Muslim jurists, then aims to approach as close as possible to the highest ideals of Islamic doctrinal aspiration.[5] The role of the Muslim jurist is to identify the detailed rules of Islamic law to meet the particular needs of time and place. The different views that emerge are seen not so much as an inconsistency or deficiency in the *Shariah* but rather a flexibility in its application which does not lose sight of the *Shariah* but still takes account of the unique time frame and facts of a particular circumstance or instance. Since Islamic law is set within these formulated rules, the doctrine of legal precedence of the common law system does not occupy an important place in the Islamic judicial system. The value of legal precedent in the Islamic context, which is therefore limited, lies in merely aiding consistency.

Almost 30 years ago, William Ballantyne (1980) described what he perceived to be the impasse between *Shariah* law and western law as the classical situation of an 'irresistible force meeting an irremovable object':

> 'The problem is that the Arabs have, to a greater or less degree, in wishing to adopt the existing international world of commerce, come face to face with the classic situation: an irresistible force against an irremovable object. As is not uncommon in these circumstances (not by any means only in the Arab world) the question has been begged on all sides. It will be, to say the least, interesting to see for how long and to what extent this apparent anomaly can continue.'[6]

Ballantyne's 'irresistible force' is the ongoing codification of laws in the Arab states, particularly in the area of commercial activity, while the 'irremovable object' is the Islamic *Shariah*. The conundrum, at least at the time of Ballantyne's writing, was whether the anomaly could be sustained or whether there would be, legislatively at least, a clear domination by western-derived secular law, with Islamic law becoming an irrelevancy in all but personal matters. In the present age, Ballantyne's anomalous situation is being resolved insofar as a domination of western-derived secular laws over the *Shariah* in the commercial context has already arrived. The conundrum has now shifted to being one of whether the position of *Shariah* law in the civil, criminal and other legal contexts may be further eroded, maintained or even re-asserted and enhanced.

Amin argues that, although Islamic law is complete in the sense that it supplies answers to all questions in all times and places, its very content and style leave it to jurists to answer the many questions unanswered in the original textual sources.[7] General and non-specific prescriptions existing in the classic textbooks in Islamic law are inadequate in the contemporary context. At the same time, the general principles and basic structure of Islamic *fiqh* leave ample room to manoeuvre, and jurists are thus given broad and general guidelines to regulate new issues in the contemporary context. New rules of law may also be developed through modern legislation and administrative regulations, incorporating concepts of secular thought and custom as appropriate. Unlike western legal theory, Islamic law and principles of morality in government, business and personal conduct are indivisibly linked.

Stovall suggests that the argument that Islamic law is irrelevant is a myth, as is its sister myth that Islamic law is also inherently unsuitable for modern commercial transactions. Practical minds have developed expedients to overcome these difficulties in most cases and hence Islamic law has continued to be revitalised in the Arabic world.[8] The application of the prohibition upon *riba* (usury, or interest charged upon money lent) is the classic example. Despite the universal prohibition in the *Shariah* upon *riba*, most Arab legal systems draw a distinction that permits interest charges on commercial transactions, at least under specified ceilings, but not on civil transactions. However, such expediency might be viewed as a practical solution or an unprincipled shortcut, depending on one's opinion of the underlying impasse, and such expediency might not offer permanent solutions. Stovall further suggests that this type of fine-tuning is likely to become more common in future throughout the Arab world, both in civil codes and in other laws.

It is thus impossible to talk about a secular legal system in the Gulf states in the real sense, suggests Rayner: legislation may appear to be secular but the sources of reference and the consciences of its interpreters are innately religious.[9]

2.2 The *Shariah* and the Gulf state constitutions

Throughout the constitutions of the Gulf states, or constitution equivalents in the case of Oman and Saudi Arabia, the *Shariah* weaves its influence – as that common golden thread portrayed earlier by Ballantyne. But that weave varies in its paramountcy from state to state. Whilst the *Shariah* is still primary in all states, it is not always paramount.

Based upon their constitutional and political development, the states can be categorised into three groups:

- a largely western style, which is characteristic of the Bahraini, Kuwaiti and Emirati constitutions;
- a combination of quasi western and traditional styles, as epitomised by Qatar's constitution; and
- the more fundamentalist style of the Omani and Saudi Basic Laws, and the Yemeni constitution.[10]

The Kuwaiti, Bahraini, Qatari and Emirati constitutions are based on a common model drawing much from the French, United States and Egyptian constitutions, and the Universal Declaration of Human Rights (on which the

Egyptian constitution was also partially based).[11] Since Kuwait received its constitution a decade before the other three states, its model formed a useful precedent. Kuwait's constitution has remained unaltered since it was first introduced more than 40 years ago, while the other three states have since introduced new constitutions or significant changes in recent times. Oman and Saudi Arabia have each enacted a 'Basic Law', as distinct from constitutions, as a formal recognition of the higher status of the *Shariah* within those statutes, but they essentially serve the same purpose.

The constitutions have very strong common elements, each stipulating that the state is a sovereign independent and Islamic state with a hereditary constitutional monarchy (that is, except for Yemen, being a republic), that Islam is the religion of the state and that Arabic is its official language. However, although the position of the *Shariah* is primary, it is not by any means paramount in every case. The states each place the following degree of primacy on the *Shariah* within their constitutions:

- Bahrain, Kuwait and the UAE provide that the *Shariah* is *a main source* of law;[12]
- Qatar declares that the *Shariah* is *the main source* of laws;[13]
- Oman mandates that the *Shariah* is *the basis* of legislation;[14]
- Yemen declares that the *Shariah* is *the source of all* legislation;[15]
- Saudi Arabia declares that the *Qur'an* and the *Sunnah* of the Prophet are not only *the sole source* of law but are also the constitution of the state.[16]

Hence, only Saudi Arabia and Yemen, and to a slightly lesser degree Oman, make the *Shariah* paramount.

As a main source of law, the *Shariah* has, at best, equal standing with other sources of law. It is neither the sole source nor even the main source of law and thus cannot take general precedence over other sources. The impact is two fold. First, the constitutional position facilitates the implementation of modern codified laws derived from non-Islamic sources. Second, their application replaces the *Shariah* and progressively reduces its general jurisdiction so that it becomes increasingly confined to matters involving personal relationships between Muslims. But absent from the Bahraini, Qatari and Emirati constitutions is any direction or guidance as to when the judiciary should turn to either one source or another for application of the proper law. For this, direction must first be sought from specific legislation and then from general legislation. Only where existing legislation is incomplete shall the *Shariah* prevail.

The Qatari constitution declares that the *Shariah* is *the main source* of laws, though not the sole source. It is thus given more weight in this context than those of Bahrain, Kuwait and the UAE, but still considerably less weight than the Yemeni constitution and the Saudi and Omani constitution equivalents. While no further constitutional guidance as to the application of the *Shariah* is provided, the Oaths of Office of the Emir, the Advisory Council and the Cabinet reinforce the higher status of the *Shariah* in the daily operation of government. Each is required to swear to respect, in order, 'the Islamic *Shariah*, the Constitution, and the Law . . . and people's freedom and interests'.[17] The clear implication here is that, in the first instance, one must turn to the *Shariah*.

The Omani Basic Law of the State asserts that the *Shariah* is *the basis* of all legislation. It is also one of the fundamental pillars of national political policy. The government is required to maintain genuine consultation with the people, 'based on the national heritage, its values and its Islamic *Shariah*, while incorporating such contemporary manifestations as are appropriate'.[18] Hence, Oman's constitutional position is closer to Saudi Arabia than to the other states. However, notwithstanding the constitutional mandate, the degree of *Shariah* control is also being emasculated as Oman, too, moves to a greater codification of its laws.

In slightly stronger terms, the Yemeni constitution declares that Islamic *Shariah* is *the source of all* legislation. This wording was one of the more controversial of a number of constitutional amendments introduced in 1994, in order to reinforce the status of *Shariah* law. The constitution had previously declared *Shariah* law as merely 'the main source' of law, akin to the more liberal Qatari position. The Yemeni constitution further enhances the status of the *Shariah*, providing elsewhere that Islamic social justice is one of the key principles on which the national economy is founded, that women have rights and duties guaranteed and assigned by the *Shariah* and stipulated by law, that inheritance is regulated by the *Shariah* and that defending the religion is a sacred duty. The Oath of Office of the President and other members of government requires them to 'swear by Allah Almighty to adhere to the *Qur'an* and his Prophet's *Sunna* . . .'.[19]

The position of the Saudi Basic Law in respect of the *Shariah* stands in stark contrast to that in the Bahraini, Kuwaiti and Emirati constitutions. Although facing some erosion of its position with the introduction of modern codified laws, the *Shariah* is still paramount and is reiterated throughout the Basic Law as being the fundamental principle underlying the government, the law, the economy and society. The Basic Law in essence ties the very existence of the Kingdom to Islam, declaring that Saudi Arabia is a sovereign Arab Islamic state whose constitution is the Holy *Qur'an* and the *Sunnah* of the Holy Prophet.[20] The government derives its authority from the Holy *Qur'an* and the *Sunnah*, which are the ultimate sources of reference for the Basic Law and for all other laws of the state.[21] Governance must be based on the principles of justice, *Shura* (consultation) and equality in accordance with the Islamic *Shariah*. The state is required to protect Islam, implement its *Shariah* and order the people to do right and shun evil.[22] Property, capital and labour are personal rights which perform a social function in accordance with the Islamic *Shariah*.[23] Legislation, enacted by resolution of the Council of Ministers and ratified by royal decree, must be compatible with *Shariah* law.[24] Although the Basic Law provides for the separation of the branches of government, the King, in principle at least, is still the source of authority and thus the ultimate (mortal) power in the governance of the state.[25] However, the King's powers are not without limit since he is still obliged to observe the *Shariah* and other Saudi traditions in the execution of his office, amongst which is maintenance of *Shura* with the (male) members of the Saudi royal family, the country's religious leaders and the leading members of the Saudi elite.[26]

In all GCC member states, supreme executive, legislative and judicial authority is vested in the central government and ultimately the ruler and his family, although in the UAE authority is divided between the federal government and the seven constituent Emirates.[27] In Yemen, the authority is vested in the President. The states generally separate the executive and legislative branches of government, although the latter does not necessarily enjoy autonomy and independence. In most instances, the executive branch firmly cements in place the authority of the ruling family, since it predominately comprises the royal family's senior male members by virtue of both their blood lineage and the senior government offices they also hold. The distinction between the executive and the legislative branches of government exists more in the principle than in the practice.

2.3 The *Shariah* and the judicature

The constitutions of the Gulf states generally mandate that the courts are independent and that judges shall not be subject to any authority or interference. The Saudi Basic Law, for example, provides that no control may be asserted over judges in the dispensation of their judgments except in the case of the Islamic *Shariah*.[28] Nevertheless, the state executives may still have leverage over the judicial power, since senior members of the judiciary are appointed by the exercise of executive authority through law or royal decree, and the laws that determine their prerogatives may be both initiated and issued by that same executive power. Apart from the UAE, where the constitution contains explicit conditions governing their removal from office, the states' executive authorities (that is the rulers) retain power to appoint and dismiss members of the judiciary, notwithstanding constitutional provisions apparently to the contrary.

While the principles derived from the *Shariah* are still a primary basis for all laws, most states have separate secular courts to deal with civil, criminal and commercial cases for which codified laws have been established or to which the *Shariah* cannot always be applied.

The Bahraini legal system is a mixed system based on English common law models and Sunni and Shia *Shariah* traditions, with influences from British India systems. The Judiciary Law of 1971 divides the judicature into two divisions – the civil courts and the *Shariah* courts with the Sunni and Shia (Jafari) jurisdictions. The civil courts are empowered to settle all commercial, civil and criminal cases and all matters related to the personal status of non-Muslims. The *Shariah* court system is limited to personal status cases of Muslims. It comprises a high court and a high court of appeal, both with Sunni and Jafari divisions. The Kuwaiti and Qatari legal systems are also based upon a number of diverse sources. Commercial and criminal laws derive from Ottoman and several modern Arab sources, notably Egyptian, and also reflect elements of the French legal code and the English common law. But unlike the Kuwaiti legal system, Qatari has maintained a *Shariah* court system which has full jurisdiction in all civil and criminal disputes over nationals and Muslims from other countries.

The Omani legal system is based primarily on the Islamic *Shariah* traditions of the Ibadi school. Custom, tradition and the *Shariah* still occupy important places as guides in judicial decision-making. Oman was the last of the GCC member states to overhaul its judicial system, with major changes in 1999 bringing the judiciary into line with the dictates of its Basic Law. A ternary courts system replaces the earlier separate *Shariah*, commercial courts and criminal courts. The *Shariah* courts, which formerly held competency in all civil and most criminal cases, have had their jurisdiction restricted to personal cases involving Muslims in both parties, and then as a court of first instance. Appeals against decisions of the *Shariah* court are made to the general courts of appeal.

The Saudi judicial system retains the traditional form of *Shariah* courts, with courts of first instance, courts of appeal and ultimately the High *Shariah* Court. Within this *Shariah system* there exists the Board of Grievances, which is effectively a civil court with jurisdiction over commercial matters which fall within the terms of reference of codified laws.

In Yemen, the *Shariah* and Islamic jurisprudence play a larger role in the legal and judicial structure than in most other Arab states, arguably except for Saudi Arabia. Yemen has a unified judicial structure, with courts of first instance, courts of appeal and ultimately the Supreme Court, all as courts of general jurisdiction. Separate specialised courts are prohibited by the constitution, hence the above courts can hear all civil, criminal, commercial and personal status matters. The Supreme Court also serves as a constitutional court. In addition to these established courts a system of tribal adjudication applying customary law or tribal law exists outside the main urban areas for local issues.

The UAE remains unusual for the Arab world because of its federated structure. The Federal constitution permits each Emirate to have its own legislative body and judicial authority, thereby allowing the existence of both federal courts and local courts. Alongside this federal/local structure there exists another division between secular and *Shariah* judiciary, giving the UAE a fairly complex judicial structure. The UAE is essentially a civil law jurisdiction heavily influenced by the Egyptian legal system which in turn had its source in French and Roman law. It has also been influenced by Islamic law codified in the *Shariah* and embodied in the UAE civil, criminal and commercial codes. The Emirates of Abu Dhabi, Dubai and Ras Al-Khaimah have retained their own judicial structures, with Abu Dhabi and Dubai having a system of inferior, intermediate and superior courts. Ras Al-Khaimah possesses inferior and intermediate courts only, with final appeals going to the federal Court of Cassation.

In broad terms, the result is essentially a dual legal system (with lesser or greater degrees of seamless amalgamation) in which a civil law orientation exists in parallel with the Islamic *Shariah*. But in practice the *Shariah* courts and the body of *Shariah* law are becoming increasingly restricted to personal status matters of Muslims – family matters, divorce, inheritance, succession, property and charitable donations, some limited torts and a few criminal matters.[29]

The Kuwaiti and Saudi structures reflect the opposite ends of the judicial spectrum. At one end, Kuwait (which, it will be recalled, holds the *Shariah* as *a main* source of law) avoids the civil court–*Shariah* court dualism extant in some of the other states, having adopted a unified court structure approach rather than establish separate secular and *Shariah* courts. Hence Muslim personal status cases are not assigned to a separate *Shariah* judiciary; instead, sections of the civil courts are designated for hearing personal status cases. The courts rule on the basis of codified Sunni law or Shia (Jafari) law, depending on the school of Islam to which the litigants adhere.[30]

While the Kuwaiti constitution remains silent on the question of the precedence of the various sources of law, the law governing the conduct of the judiciary moves to qualify that flexibility.[31] It requires a judge to proceed first by reference to the civil and commercial laws of the state, then to custom, and finally by reference to the *Shariah*:

> '(a) Legislative provisions apply to the matters to which such provisions relate both expressly and by implication.
> (b) If there is no legislative provision, the judge gives judgment in accordance with custom. If there is no custom, the judge deduces his opinion taking guidance from the dictates of the Islamic jurisprudence (*fiqh*) most in accord with the reality and the interests of the country'.[32]

Hence the order of priority of primary sources of Kuwaiti law is firstly constitutional, then legislative, customary and tribal, and lastly the *Shariah*.

In like manner, the Bahraini constitution provides the same degree of flexibility and its law governing the judiciary also moves to qualify that flexibility.[33] But, unlike Kuwait, it requires that, in the absence of an express statutory legal provision, reference is directed first to the *Shariah*:

> 'In the event that a judge finds no provision of law capable of application, he shall deduce the bases of his judgment from the principles of the *Shariah* and the provisions thereof; in the absence of any such provision,

custom shall be applied. A particular custom shall be preferred to a general custom. In the absence of custom, the tenets of national law and the principles of equity and good conscience shall be applied.'[34]

Like Kuwait, Oman and Qatar also have largely unified systems, but both place a much greater emphasis on the importance of the *Shariah* in judicial decision-making. Both enjoy unified structures integrating the earlier systems of *Shariah* courts, commercial courts and criminal courts. In Oman's case, the former separate *Shariah* courts, which held competency in all civil and criminal cases, have had their jurisdiction restricted to the status of a court of first instance on personal status matters. Appeals against a decision of the *Shariah* court are now brought before general courts of appeal. Qatar has maintained *Shariah* divisions in both the primary and appellate jurisdictions, but retains a unified court of cassation, or supreme court. While these integration actions might be viewed as a weakening of the position of the *Shariah*, it could be equally argued that they constitute a strengthening of its position by keeping it in the mainstream of the judicial system instead of marginalising it.

However, this still raises the issue of whether the general dictates of the *Shariah* should apply in the first instance as general principles, or latterly in respect of the particular circumstances of the case being heard. Since both constitutions are not exclusive in their status of the *Shariah*, it may well have been the intention of the Omani and Qatari legislators to allow some degree of flexibility to avoid direct conflict between the *Shariah* and the secular codes. Where the civil or commercial laws or other laws or sources are silent on the matter of legislative application, there would be little question that it would be appropriate to turn in the first instance to the *Shariah* as the principal source of law. However, where the codes do give voice, they are generally comprehensive and their intentions are clearly prescribed, as the following extract from Qatar's civil commercial code illustrates:

'1. The tenets of this law shall apply to all matters embraced expressly or by implication by the provisions hereof as well as to all commercial acts engaged in or by any person even if not a merchant.
2. In prescribing principles which apply to merchants and commercial acts, regard shall be had to contracts recognised by law . . .
3. If there is no contract, or if there is but it is silent as to a particular provision, or the provisions set out in the contract are void, the legislative provisions contained in this Law shall apply.
4. In the absence of the legislative provision which can be applied, the judge shall adjudicate in accordance with custom, special or local custom taking precedence over general custom, and in the absence of custom the principles of the Islamic Shari'a . . .'[35]

The laws establishing the UAE federal supreme court and the federal courts of first instance require the courts to apply the provisions of the *Shariah* in the first instance:

> 'The Supreme Court shall apply the provisions of the Islamic Shari'a, federal laws, and other laws in force . . . conforming to the Islamic Shari'a. Likewise it shall apply those rules of custom and those principles of natural and comparative law which do not conflict with the principles of the Shari'a.'[36]

Likewise, the courts of first instance are required to adhere to the following directive:

> 'The federal courts shall apply the provisions of the Islamic Shari'a, federal laws, and other laws in force, just as they shall apply those rules of custom and general legal principles which do not conflict with the provisions of the Shari'a.'[37]

Notwithstanding the fact they have retained separate judicial structures, the Emirates of Dubai and Ras Al-Khaimah provide that their respective courts shall exercise their powers, in order of priority, on the basis of the laws in force in the Emirate, on the provisions of the Islamic *Shariah*, on provisions of custom unless these contradict the law or public order or decency, and finally on the principles of natural justice, right and equity.[38]

These positions would appear to give precedence to the *Shariah* over all other sources of law and thereby, in effect, hold it as the principal source of law. As the courts would therefore appear to hold that any measure contrary to the *Shariah* would seem, by express provision, to be invalid, there arises the question of whether the laws establishing these courts contradict a constitutional position which has established that the *Shariah* is but one source of law amongst others.[39] Since the Federal Supreme Court also acts as a constitutional court and would thus rule on such question should it arise, it would presumably uphold the basic constitutional dictate.

At the other end of the above-mentioned spectrum is Saudi Arabia. As the most conservative and fundamentalist Islamic state in the Gulf region, the principles of the *Shariah* maintain a stronger hold in Saudi Arabia than in the other states. The *Shariah* remains the fundamental basis of the legal system, and justice is administered according to the *Shariah* by a system of religious courts. While traces of a hybrid dual system can be discerned in parts of the Saudi legal order by the existence of quasi-judicial administrative tribunals such as the Board of Grievances, the foundation of the Saudi judicial order is still wholly *Shariah*-based.

Having proclaimed the Holy *Qur'an* and the *Sunnah* as the basis of laws and as the constitution, the Basic Law requires the Saudi courts to apply the rules of the Islamic *Shariah*, in accordance with indications 'in the Holy

Qur'an and the *Sunnah*, and then in accordance with the statutes of the Kingdom provided they do not contradict the *Qur'an* or the *Sunnah*'.[40] Thus, the *Shariah* is seen as superior to any positive legal or judicial order, a provision which assumes a unified, *Shariah*-based judiciary independent of the King. Since this system was well established when the Basic Law was introduced in 1992, the Basic Law does not so much establish a new judicial order as describe and codify the prevailing custom and practice.

Hence the Saudi *Shariah* courts have never lost their status as courts of general jurisdiction and there is no special personal status court structure or personal status code as exists in the other states under their dual or integrated systems. However, still within the *Shariah* judicial system, but operating at arm's length from the *Shariah* courts, are the quasi-judicial specialised tribunals which adjudicate on matters which are essentially administrative in nature, or on disputes between government bodies and members of the public over government processes or decision-making (such as disputes over trademark registrations). Although the tribunals address matters which are governed by regulations which do not derive from the *Shariah* or are not easily covered by existing Islamic *fiqh*, they are still required to ensure that they do not conflict with their provisions. One outcome of this structure is that the pure essence of the *Shariah* can be better preserved without the constant diluting effects of introduced secular laws.

While Ballantyne saw the *Shariah* as a golden thread running through the legal and judicial systems of the Gulf and the Arab world beyond, he also suggested that the key characteristic of the *Shariah*'s position within these systems of the Gulf was one of uncertainty.[41] Almost 30 years later, the uncertainty retreats progressively as the secularisation and codification of the laws within each state continues. With the possible exception of Saudi Arabia and Yemen, the *Shariah* may still intervene to a lesser or greater degree in most jurisdictions. The unknown factor in this progression exists outside the legal framework – namely the marked resurgence of Islam domestically and its growth internationally. As it attracts increasing numbers of new followers and appears to become increasingly fundamentalist, Islam may well have an as yet unforeseen impact on the domestic legal, judicial and societal structures – which in turn could stimulate somewhat of a reversal of status towards its former enhanced position within the constitutional, legal and judicial frameworks.

2.4 The *Shariah* and intellectual property protection

The situation of intellectual property law protection, a recent development in the legislative regimes of the Gulf states, illustrates this dichotomy between the *Shariah* and codified laws. The concept of intellectual property and its recognition and acceptability in *Shariah* law has been a subject of ongoing discussion amongst contemporary Muslim scholars.[42] Intellectual property as an intangible object, being the product of one's mental labours, is a recent concept not expressly mentioned in either the Holy *Qur'an*, the *Sunnah* or the early Islamic jurisprudence. Accordingly, its acceptability or otherwise must be inferred from general principles laid down by the *Shariah*. As the views of scholars and Islamic jurists differ on the issue of the application of these principles to new situations, it follows that there are differences of opinion in relation to the ownership and protection of intellectual property.

Some contemporary scholars reject the concept of intellectual property on the grounds that the concept of ownership in the *Shariah* is confined to tangible objects only.[43] They contend that there is no precedent in the *Qur'an*, the *Sunnah* or the views of early Muslim jurists for an intangible object, such as knowledge, to be subject to private ownership or to sale and purchase. They would argue that, since it originates from or owes its origin to God, knowledge (and its expression in all its manifestations) is the common heritage of all mankind.[44] Knowledge cannot therefore become the exclusive property of one individual, nor be prevented from being acquired by others. Accordingly, a concept of intellectual property which leads to a monopoly over knowledge by an individual could not be acceptable by Islam.[45]

Yet other scholars have argued that intellectual property and its exclusive ownership is acceptable, since there is no express provision in the *Qur'an* or in the *Sunnah* which restricts the rights of ownership to tangible objects only.[46] Intellectual property protection does not necessarily hinder the acquisition of knowledge since an intellectual property law does not prevent an individual from accessing or utilising knowledge enjoying some form of protection as offered by that law. On the contrary, the law may prohibit a third party from gaining commercial advantage from the work without the permission of the individual who, by mental labour, has produced the work and is therefore most entitled to enjoy the commercial benefits that derive from it.

Jamar suggests that, although the *Shariah* does not specifically address intellectual property matters, it does not prevent the enactment or enforcement of intellectual property laws.[47] Since intellectual property protection is neither prohibited nor mandated, its legal protection is therefore fully consonant with the *Shariah*. In the Islamic state, every citizen enters into an express or a tacit agreement to abide by its laws to the extent that they do not compel compliance with anything that is not permissible in the *Shariah*.[48] Accordingly, if the state promulgates a law in favour of intellectual property protection without violating a provision of the *Qur'an* and *Sunnah*, then that law is binding on all its citizens and must be respected. In this sense, intellectual property law is no different to criminal law or commercial law in its relationship to the *Shariah*.

Other proponents of this line of reasoning argue that ownership of intellectual property is justified on the basis of 'economic gain through labour'. The creation of intellectual property through the efforts of mental labour brings with it an entitlement to its exclusive exploitation. As is the case with movable and immovable property, any creative idea of a person expressed in written, technical or graphical terms should be respected in Islam.[49] While it may be intangible, intellectual property may still be deemed to have a value quantifiable in a market context and therefore can be traded, transferred and transacted.[50] This is further borne out by writings of Muslim jurists who deal with the prohibition of unjust enrichment and the discouragement of certain types of commercial transactions such as those involving misrepresentation, fraud and trickery.[51]

According to Khoury, some commentators have gone so far as to contend that Islamic law comprises 'enough inconsistencies to [generally] make predictability in certain matters a serious concern'.[52] The disagreements thus arising cut across sectarian lines:

> 'The very nature of Islamic law as a jurist's law and differences of opinion even within individual schools means that it is not possible to provide firm answers to many of the questions that arise. As usual in the *Shariah*, which proceeds by way of example rather than principle, it is only possible to evaluate the general risks involved through isolation and investigation of the particular issues arising in [connection with the legal issue].'[53]

It has been argued that the *Shariah* fails to keep abreast of the needs of increasingly complex economies and commercial practices, and that this failure constitutes a criticism against the functionality of the *Shariah* as a viable intellectual property regime.[54] Consequently, there exists a trend away from *Shariah* law towards modern western-derived law throughout the commercial laws in the Middle East. Indeed, one commentator suggests that the bulk of commercial law in the Middle East reads as a direct transportation of European law, while the case law is perceived as a direct translation of western terminology. This trend is also quite apparent with respect to intellectual property laws generally. The *Shariah* may provide basic principles and rules that promote the protection of intellectual property; however, in view of the lack of comprehensive certainty and agreement, the states appear to opt for a direct adoption of western legal norms and standards of protection.

While some may argue that in reality there is a gulf between *Shariah* concepts and practice in Islam, their arguments, in Khoury's view, ignore the following:

- the *Shariah* includes clear norms and teachings concerning fair trade and rejection of unfair competition;
- while the *Shariah* law is an ancient law which does not provide clear-cut answers to modern legal issues such as those surrounding intellectual property, the answers to these modern questions may still be formulated by religious scholars through reasoning based on the underlying Islamic principles;

- the *Shariah* is not the only legal system not to have a binding precedent system – the civil law system does not have one – and therefore this should not pose an insurmountable hurdle to the development of consistent and fair rules relating to intellectual property protection;
- where conflict does arise it is not in respect of inner conflicts between the principles within Islamic law but rather a balance between principles and conflicting interests.[55]

The *Shariah* may not directly address the issues relating to intellectual property rights, but the principles provided therein clearly indicate that the *Shariah* does not stand neutral on the question of intellectual property protection. Islamic legal and general principles of equity, prohibition of unjust enrichment and of misleading and dishonest representation can still be applied, particularly in respect of passing-off and trademark infringement. Where a state possesses and applies secular laws governing intellectual property protection, traditional Islamic principles would still feature prominently since constitutionally no legislation can be contrary to the provisions of the *Shariah*, and the interpretation of the secular law should be aided and supported in such a way as to support the Islamic legal culture.[56] Where the secular law of the west and the *Shariah* are philosophically opposed on this point is that the secular law is concerned with the rights of the intellectual property right holder and is designed to protect their exploitative interests. The *Shariah*, however, is concerned with obligations and aims at condemning dishonesty by the deceiver and protecting the consumer.[57]

Azmi suggests that the basis of intellectual property rights must be the principles of the *Shariah*, with the standards concerning the availability, scope and use of such rights measured by their compatibility with the *Shariah*.[58] However, some emerging areas of intellectual property do not easily fit with this fundamental criterion and may therefore result in conflict with religious tenets of the *Shariah* – notably patents arising out of biotechnological products and processes. Azmi draws a distinction between patents involving animals and plants and those involving human tissues, genes and body parts. While man has domination over other creatures, this domination does not grant an absolute right to do anything desired without limit. Mankind must act with a sense of stewardship and ultimately be held responsible for its actions and their consequences. Islam still requires animals to be treated with due respect and without cruelty. Accordingly, experimentation on animals and the patenting of the outcomes may be allowed under the *Shariah* provided there is a balancing of the relative harm to the animals and the benefits to mankind. In respect of modification and manipulation of biological materials, the position is not quite so clear. The *Qur'an* reiterates that the universe and all its creations are created with a sense of order and proportion according to a set of laws of nature, which man cannot change. Yet it also recognises science's role in improving what exists in nature for the benefit of mankind. The issue comes to a head in respect of transgenic animals used as xenografts, which Azmi suggests are beyond the limits allowed by the advancement of science and the *Qur'anic* bounds on man's stewardship over other creatures.[59]

In respect of the exploitation of the human material, whether genetic material or body parts, Azmi argues such exploitation is *haram* (forbidden), according to the *Qur'an*.[60] He points out that classical scholars have long held that any transaction involving parts of the human body, whether by sale or donation, is *haram* on the grounds that it demeans the human dignity and the place of man in the fixed order of creation and function of living things. But modern scholars accept circumstances in which transplantation and donation of body parts may be acceptable, namely if:

- the transplant or donation constitutes the lesser of two evils, the benefits outweigh the risks and the potential donation does not cause harm to the donor;
- the process of donation or transplant is assured of success; and
- the transplant, donation or extraction does not impair the function of the human body.

Intellectual property is not the only area of law where the Islamic states need to promulgate civil or secular laws. Indeed, the *Qur'an* is silent, or at least vague, on a wide range of commercial issues, including some modern commercial transactions, financing arrangements and limited liability commercial entities such as corporations. While the *Qur'an* addresses subjects of poverty, conventional commercial transactions, honest dealings, testimony and association, it does not provide systematic rules but rather exhorts the believer with words of wisdom, admonition and guidance amounting to mandatory injunction.

2.5 Concluding remarks

While the *Shariah* is prescribed as at least a major source of law, the increasing codification of the law, particularly in respect of commercial relations, has acted to progressively reduce its former pre-eminence and will likely continue to do so in the future. As commercial law continues to develop along western lines, the position of the *Shariah* will continue to be eroded and the customary laws and remnants of the common law systems will become extinguished.[61]

It could be argued that the *Shariah* need not necessarily hinder the transplantation of intellectual property laws of foreign origin with any great drama or conflict. The drama may arise when the application of the western-derived law conflicts with the principles of the *Shariah*. By incorporating in their intellectual property laws a qualification to the wholesale deference to western-based criteria by at least requiring the practical application of the law to be not inconsistent with the *Shariah*, some Arab Gulf states have not resiled from this potential for conflict. For example, while all states exclude from patentability inventions which, amongst other conditions, are in violation of public order or morals, the GCC patent regulation extends that provision to also exclude inventions which conflict with or violate the principles of the Islamic *Shariah*.[62] The Saudi patent law includes a similar exclusion provision, but narrows it somewhat by confining the exclusion to inventions whose *commercial exploitation* (instead of the invention itself) violates the *Shariah*.[63] Thus the GCC and the Saudi positions would appear to be at odds with the western liberal philosophy established by the US Supreme Court generalisation that 'anything under the sun can be patentable'.[64]

Even more subtle, yet of much greater application, is the reflection of the *Shariah* exhortation against the consumption of alcohol by Muslims, which ultimately becomes manifest in most Gulf states in the prohibition of registration of trademarks and geographical indications relating to wines, spirits and other alcoholic beverages. While the domestic intellectual property laws are generally silent on this matter, the universal practice is that such types of trademarks and geographical indications are not protectable.

One cannot assume that the bastion of *Shariah* preservation in the commercial context is not being continually eroded. The recent decision of the Saudi Board of Grievances to rule against a longstanding *Shariah* prohibition on the registration of trademarks depicting pictures or drawings of living animals, despite strident opposition from the traditionalists, illustrates how that erosion continues on a number of fronts.[65] In arriving at its decision, the Board ruled that the principles on which the original prohibition was based were disputable and, more importantly in this context, that the prohibition was against the public policy of Saudi Arabia and the interests of consumers and owners of the genuine trademarks. Some might suggest that the Board ruling reinforces the argument that the *Shariah* is irrelevant in the modern context when it confronts the commercial/legal imperative. They might also propose that it simply illustrates yet another anomaly pertinent to Ballantyne's conundrum of a generation ago concerning the irresistible and the irremovable. The real test is in the interpretation and application of these respective legal imperatives on the streets and in the courts.

Despite the absence of formal rules within the *Shariah* on intellectual property protection, the *Shariah* has within its primary sources basic principles that do not discourage such protection. The analysis of the underlying principles of fair trade, prohibition of unfair competition and the importance of private property lead to the conclusion that Islam does not stand idle on issues pertaining to intellectual property rights and their protection.[66] Indeed, the underlying principles might appear to be not all that dissimilar to the rationales of intellectual property protection as perceived by modern western legal systems.

It is in this context that one needs to look at the development of intellectual property regimes in the states themselves.

3 Pre-TRIPS and intellectual property protection in the Gulf states

3.1 Introduction

The legal systems of the Gulf states have undergone dramatic, radical and progressive change and development over the last 30 years or so, and that change is continuing. The major trend has been a greatly increased codification of law and administered regulation which entails increasing substitution of institutionalised procedures for the traditional informal, discretionary and often arbitrary exercise of authority.[1]

The pre-TRIPS history of the progressive formulation of intellectual property legislative regimes in the Gulf states illustrates a remarkable cycle of developments over an equally remarkably short period of time.[2] A generation or so ago, the level of effective intellectual property protection was virtually non-existent. None of the states possessed any laws in respect of copyright and neighbouring rights or subscribed to any international or regional convention in respect of protection of literary works or author's rights. The position in respect of trademarks, patents or other areas of industrial property was hardly brighter, although some limited legislation was in place in a few states.

Governmental concern and consequent legislative activity in respect of the protection of intellectual property rights existed primarily in relation to trademarks and trade descriptions, and then only in respect of a state's commercial dealings with expatriate and foreign traders and businesses. There was little, if any, concern in respect of patent protection, and nil concern or activity in respect of author's rights and other areas of intellectual property such as plant varieties, geographical indications and the like.

Three distinct phases can be observed in the development of the states' intellectual property laws in this pre-TRIPS era:

- laws enacted before independence or during a period of effective foreign control, and which are an extension of or subordinate to those foreign sources – the prime example being Bahrain's 1955 omnibus Patents, Industrial Designs and Trade Marks Regulation of 1955, and Kuwait's intended equivalent 1958 regulation;[3]

- laws which were developed as part of a post-independence codification of commercial and civil laws, led by Kuwait as the first of the British-protected states in the Gulf to achieve independence;
- more recent legislation in the late 1980s and early 1990s, generated by the states' recognition of the necessity to become part of the international trade community, and the obligations on compliance with international protection benchmarks that accompanied such membership.

The hallmark of the pre-independence laws was a subordination to, or transplantation of, laws or regulations already in existence in other jurisdictions. The Bahraini 1955 regulation providing protection for patents, industrial designs and trademarks, for example, borrowed much from the Indian pre-independence equivalent statute and was generally dependent upon UK laws and processes to be valid and operable.[4] The laws or regulations were not directed towards purely domestic operation at a local level, except to the extent that they impacted on foreigners' and expatriates' commercial relations with the local populace.

By contrast, the post-independence laws were largely developed by the respective states with domestic needs and applications starting to come to the fore. However, they were still subject to external influences – but the influences were becoming more regional in nature and possessing a greater degree of Arabic character. Sources of laws were also becoming increasingly regionalised – partly as a consequence of the states taking advantage of the opportunities to interact with their fellow Arab countries through their memberships of regional Arab bodies such as the League of Arab States and the GCC. Kuwait's constitution and early laws, particularly its commercial code which incorporated provision for trademark protection, were largely based on Egyptian statutes, which in turn were based on French legal codes.[5] And since Kuwait's codes and laws were already in Arabic and had already undergone a period of extended testing in the context of common usage, it is not surprising that many of them became models for the equivalent laws required by the other states. The inconsistencies that could be observed in the equivalent laws across the other states largely arose as the states adapted the Kuwaiti models for their own perceived needs and use.

As the legislative regimes of the states became increasingly codified, secularised and sophisticated, and as the states themselves moved at their own separate pace towards membership of the international trade community, they were obliged to address the standards and obligations relating to intellectual property protection required by these bodies. New laws were introduced and enhancements were made to laws already in place, presaging the pending creation of the WTO and the introduction of TRIPS – for which WIPO was arguably the major source of influence by virtue of the legislative and other technical assistance it provided to the states. The suite of intellectual property laws enacted by Oman in 2000 is a prime example of this assistance. However, the developed countries with commercial interests in the Gulf region also endeavoured to bring considerable influence to bear upon the states to conform to international standards of protection, particularly in respect of trademarks and copyright and neighbouring rights.

3.2 Early regional initiatives on intellectual property protection

As Table 3.1 so succinctly illustrates, the early 1970s saw little specific provision in place for the protection of intellectual property rights *per se*. Saudi Arabia had introduced a trademark protection law over 30 years earlier, in 1939. But Kuwait was setting the regional benchmark in respect of protection standards, with the introduction in the early 1960s of its patent and industrial design statute, and with its civil, commercial and penal laws which also gave some measure of intellectual property protection. By the mid 1970s Kuwait and Bahrain had already introduced and upgraded trademark protection laws, and Qatar had set plans in motion to introduce its own trademark law. Oman and the UAE, meanwhile, lacked any specific intellectual property legislation and had little else by way of civil or commercial codes. None of the states had any copyright protection provisions, although, as is discussed later, other laws regulating publications and printing, and legal deposit of works, did enable some degree of protection – albeit by association rather than by design.

The Gulf states were also conspicuously absent from the signatory lists of the major international bodies and the conventions on intellectual property rights. Kuwait became a signatory to the WTO's precursor, the General Agreement on Tariffs and Trade (GATT), soon after independence and remained the sole signatory from the Gulf region for over 30 years until Bahrain, Qatar and the UAE also became signatories just prior to the creation of the WTO. Qatar and the UAE joined WIPO in the 1970s, again soon after they each gained independence. Yet none of the Gulf states was a signatory to any of the international treaties and conventions administered by WIPO, and in particular the Berne, Paris and Rome conventions. Nor had they utilised any of the model laws for the protection of intellectual property rights that WIPO had devised specifically for developing countries and which encompassed:

- inventions and know-how;
- marks, trade names and acts of unfair competition;
- industrial designs;
- appellations of origin and indications of source.

All Gulf states were members of the League of Arab States, Saudi Arabia joining in 1945 as a foundation member and the other states joining progressively as they achieved independence. The League, with the assistance of WIPO, had sponsored the development of two model laws for League

Table 3.1 Intellectual property laws and international conventions in the Gulf states in the mid 1970s

		Bahrain	*Kuwait*	*Oman*	*Qatar*	*Saudi Arabia*	*UAE*	*Yemen*
National Laws	Copyright	-	-	-	-	-	-	-
	Trademarks		1961	-	1978	1939	-	1940/76
	Patents	1955/77						
	Industrial designs		1962	-	-	-	-	-
	Plant varieties	-	-	-	-	-	-	-
	Geographical indications	-	-	-	-	-	-	-
	Integrated circuits	-	-	-	-	-	-	-
	Trade secrets	-	-	-	-	-	-	-
	Legal deposit of works	1975	-	-	-	-	-	-
	Printed matter	-	1961	1975	1968	-	1973	-
	Commercial codes	1971	1961	-	1971	-	-	-
Bodies	League of Arab States	1971	1961	1971	1971	1945	1971	1945
	GATT	-	1963	-	-	-	-	-
	WIPO	-	-	-	1976	-	1974	-
	– Berne Convention	-	-	-	-	-	-	-
	– Paris Convention	-	-	-	-	-	-	-
	– Rome Convention	-	-	-	-	-	-	-
	– Other Conventions	-	-	-	-	-	-	-

Source: compiled by the author

Notes: The Emirate of Ras Al-Khaimah introduced a trademark registration statute in 1974 which, by virtue of the registration process, provided some degree of protection for registered marks.

In 1940 the British government issued a simple statute covering the British Protectorate of Aden (southern Yemen); the independent Yemen Arab Republic (northern Yemen) issued a trademark statute in 1976.

Northern Yemen joined the League of Arab States in 1945; southern Yemen was still part of the British Protectorate of Aden.

members, one in 1972 addressing patent protection and the other in 1975 on trademarks, trade names, commercial indications and unfair competition.[6] Again, none of the states had taken advantage of the availability of this set of model laws to introduce or update their legislative regimes, although some of the other Arab countries, which were also members of the Arab League, had done so.

3.2.1 Trademarks

Trademarks have been the form of intellectual property most familiar to the states and to the business communities in the Gulf region. Trademarks lie at the heart of the system of commercial agencies that has dominated the nature and structure of regional and local business. For both practical and legal reasons, foreign merchants have nearly always had to appoint a local commercial agent (who was also a national of the state) if they wished to do business in a sustained way in an Arab state. The agent thereby enjoyed, in effect, a local monopoly to import and distribute the foreign merchant's goods or services, and trademarks provided the means by which those goods and services were identified. Trademark protection was thus actively pursued by the local agent as an essential requirement in the protection of one's own trading territory. Local regulatory authorities, such as ministries of commerce or customs, helped to give practical effect to the local monopoly concept. In fact, many monopolies were (and still are) held by members of 'well-connected' families who often also held dual roles as senior members of the ruling elite. This was not necessarily construed as a conflict of interest, but more an appropriate and reasonable exploitation of position, capacity and available financial resources for the generation of both further wealth and employment for the local community.

Attempts to parallel import goods bearing a foreign merchant's mark or goods which fell within the monopolistic control of the local commercial agent would be implacably opposed by the agent, irrespective of whether the goods in question were authentic or counterfeit. In this way, commercial agency legislation served indirectly as the main instrument whereby trademarks were protected. Trademark infringement cases in the civil courts were relatively rare occurrences. When they did appear, they focused on the protection of commercial rights and the elimination of the threat to monopoly rather than the recognition and protection of intellectual property rights. Hence early litigation arising out of the protection of these interests, such as the *Brylcreem*[7] case in the UAE and the *Dettol*[8] case in Saudi Arabia, were not lodged under the trademark laws then in place but under the laws of commercial transactions.

However, rather than reliance merely on statute, the customary practice throughout the Gulf region to obtain some notional measure of protection for trademarks was through the publication of cautionary notices in the local Arabic and English-language daily press. Whilst the cautionary notices had no legal status *per se*, they served to establish and reinforce claims of prior ownership, useful in a dispute before a *Shariah* court or judicial or administrative authority on commercial conduct involving trademark ownership, rights of usage, or commercial agency rights.

Saudi Arabia was the first Gulf state to introduce any form of statutory protection in any field of intellectual property with its trademark decree of 1939.[9] The decree provided for the local registration of trademarks and protection for a period of ten years with provision for renewal. Significantly, it also provided for both criminal and civil liability, for the ordering of provisional measures and for sanctions that must have been substantial for the region and the time – up to six months' imprisonment and between 5 and 50 guineas (being the official currency in circulation at the time). The decree did not address any other areas of intellectual property.

Bahrain, while still a protected state as part of the British Persian Gulf and Trucial States interests, provided limited trademark protection with the issuance in 1955 of an omnibus patents, industrial designs and trademarks statute.[10] The original form of the statute was made by the British government as a Queen's Regulation issued by its Political Resident in the Gulf (and resident in Bahrain), as part of the British government's extra-territorial jurisdiction in Bahrain.[11] The statute was subsequently translated into Arabic and issued by the Emir as a Bahraini statute.[12] This status was very much reflected in the statute, which was subordinate and supplementary to the then UK trademark law.[13] In effect, it enabled the local registration of trademarks (and industrial designs) which were already protected by virtue of registration in the UK, and extended to them the same level of protection locally as enjoyed in the UK. It also enabled the registration of trademarks of local origin, for which protection applied only in Bahrain, Kuwait and the other regional 'territories' of Qatar, Oman and Muscat (now Oman) and the Trucial States (now the UAE). Bahrain did not entirely remove its 1955 regulation from the statute books until 1991, although in 1977 it introduced a number of amendments to remove references to the UK and UK-related institutions.[14]

The Political Resident issued the equivalent regulation for Kuwait in 1958.[15] However, unlike his Bahraini counterpart, the Kuwaiti Emir did not translate and reissue it as a Kuwaiti local statute. Since Kuwait was moving towards independence in the near future and was well advanced in preparing a constitution and suite of post-independence statutes, it decided against bringing this colonial-era regulation into local effect. Instead it incorporated trademark protection provisions within its new commercial code which, at the time and by regional standards, was well advanced and enlightened.[16]

In the three states which possessed trademark laws (Saudi Arabia, Bahrain and Kuwait) in these early years, the examination of trademark applications was simple – the grounds for rejection being limited to procedural deficiencies or marks which were contrary to public policy or morality, or confusingly similar to armorial bearings and flags, and official signs and marks. Saudi

Arabia extended its examination to include marks which were confusingly similar to international symbols or elements with a religious significance, marks contrary to the traditions or principles of Islam, and marks similar to marks already registered or under application.

Qatar enacted its first intellectual property law and first law on trademark protection late in the 1970s.[17] The law regulated the protection of trade and service marks, group marks, commercial indications, and indications of source and origin, but did not go so far as to encompass industrial designs. The law was largely derived from the League of Arab States' 1975 model law on trademarks, trade names, commercial indications and unfair competition, and was influenced by the corresponding sections of the Kuwaiti commercial code.

Trademarks still lacked any statutory form of protection in Oman and the UAE. Historically, Omani and UAE businesses and local authorities and courts have considered both states to be essentially free markets into which any licensed business may import goods without any form of regulatory control, such as restrictions on the sale of counterfeit merchandise. Accordingly, trademark owners had no real statutory means available to protect their interests from infringing marks. Ras Al-Khaimah (RAK), one of the smallest of the seven Emirates comprising the UAE, independently introduced a decree in 1974 which provided for a trademark registration and protection service administered by the Emirate's Chamber of Commerce, Industry and Agriculture. The protection afforded by registration did not extend outside the Emirate, but it did serve as a useful stratagem for reinforcing claims of ownership in the other Emirates and was therefore utilised by foreign merchants and their agents based in those other Emirates.[18]

The southern part of Yemen that constituted the British Protectorate of Aden reportedly offered a form of trademark protection from 1940, by way of regulation issued as part of the British government's extra-territorial jurisdiction, akin to the trademark protection available in Bahrain. The northern part of Yemen, then constituting the independent Yemen Arab Republic, enacted a simple trademarks and trade names law in 1976.

Information on the level of trademark registration activity in the region during these early years is patchy and uncertain. According to a survey conducted by WIPO and published in 1978 on intellectual property activity in the Gulf region, only Bahrain and Kuwait provided statistics on trademark applications and registrations.[19] The study reported that, for 1974, the latest year for which any statistics were recorded in the study, Bahrain granted 184 trademark registrations and Kuwait approved 372 applications. What is more telling is that only ten of the Bahraini applications and 13 of the Kuwaiti approvals were of Arab/local origin.[20] The pattern in Ras Al-Khaimah in respect of the predominance of trademarks of foreign origin was even greater than that in Bahrain and Kuwait; of the 800 marks registered in Ras Al-Khaimah during the period 1974–8, only two were of Arabic/RAK origin.[21]

3.2.2 Patents

Until a pre-TRIPS flurry of legislative activity in the early 1990s, only Bahrain and Kuwait provided any measure of notional patent protection during the 1970s and 1980s. None of the other Gulf states possessed any patent protection statutes.

Bahrain's omnibus Patents, Designs and Trade Marks Regulation of 1955 also provided a form of protection for patents and industrial designs. Totally subordinate and supplementary to the then UK patents and industrial designs legislation,[22] it required prior registration of a patent with the UK Patent and Trade Marks Office as a pre-condition of eligibility for local registration, and granted local protection only for the duration of the UK period of protection. Bahrain amended the law in 1977 after independence to remove any reference to UK dependency.[23] However, it did not replace it entirely until 2004 when it issued a new law governing the protection of patents and utility models.[24]

Kuwait, meanwhile, issued its original patent law (which also applied to industrial designs and models) in 1962.[25] The law provided for a period of protection of 15 years for patents and five years for designs and industrial models, from the date of application.[26] By virtue of this law, Kuwait was the first state to introduce its own patent law. Although only seven years apart, the Bahraini and Kuwaiti laws were markedly different, with the Bahraini law very much reflecting its then status as a British protected territory and Kuwait's 1962 law reflecting its newly acquired independence.

The level of service available in respect of patents was even more limited than it was for trademarks. Bahrain and Kuwait would accept patent applications, but would limit examination to matters of form and local application procedural requirements, since neither state possessed the means or expertise to carry out substantive or technical examinations. Hence the function of the respective receiving offices was in fact to serve as little more than a mailbox and a record of ownership – fulfilling a similar role to that of cautionary notices in the local media.

Available information on the amount of patent-related activity is even more difficult to identify than that for regional trademark activity. The aforementioned WIPO 1978 Report also recorded that in 1974, 35 patent applications were filed for protection in Bahrain, all of which were of non-Arab origin, while for the same year 115 applications were filed in Kuwait, of which only four were of Kuwaiti origin.[27] However, there is no record of any of these patents having been granted. In any case, judging by the data of recent patent applications from the Gulf region states, it is more than likely that these few applications originated not from Kuwaiti nationals but from foreign expatriate workers in the oil industry and also claimed priority on the basis of another foreign patent.[28]

3.2.3 Copyright

None of the Gulf states possessed any *sui generis* copyright protection legislation until 1989, when Saudi Arabia issued the region's first copyright law.[29]

Most states had in force laws which addressed the control and registration of published works, such as newspapers, journals, pamphlets and books.[30] The primary purpose of these laws was to ensure that all publishers were registered and that all material that they intended to publish or publicly distribute was first approved by the responsible ministry. Hence the laws' main objective was one of censorship and control. As part of the control mechanism, the laws generally required literary works to be lodged in a national repository, registered and approved by a central authority prior to their publication. They also required the publisher to provide written certification of the author's agreement to the publication of the work in the format presented for governmental approval. This was very much a control and censorship function rather than an acknowledgement of, and provision for, the protection of author's rights. Saudi Arabia's printing and publishing law was one which specifically directed that, in addition to meeting the control and censorship elements of the law, publishers must respect the rights of the author, provided he was a Saudi national:

> 'Copyright of literary works, printing, translation and publishing are reserved for their Saudi owners, their heirs and persons whose works are printed . . .
>
> The Ministry must prevent every infringement of the rights stipulated in the above article; a committee . . . shall have jurisdiction to consider every infringement on said rights and award compensation to the interested party for the material and moral damages suffered.'[31]

However, none of the publication and registration control laws offered a definition of an author or of a literary work. It is telling that responsibility for the control of publishing houses, and the printing and public circulation of material, rested with a ministry whose responsibilities also extended to the control and censorship of all material and information entering the public domain and often included the administration of justice and the *Shariah* as a public order and morality issue.

3.3 Early regional intellectual property legislation

The Bahraini 1955 omnibus Patents, Designs and Trade Marks Regulation and the Kuwaiti 1962 Patents Law show in stark contrast the fundamentally different philosophical and structural attitudes between the subordinated pre-independence regulation and the emancipated post-independence statutes. The objective of the Bahraini regulation was to address and protect the commercial and industrial interests of the UK businesses trading in Bahrain and, by association, the interests of their local agents. The patents and designs provisions in particular, by virtue of the UK registration prerequisite, precluded any real opportunity for the encouragement and development of locally generated industrial property and its protection. The provision for a dual system of trademark registration, allowing for the protection of marks of local origin and usage, at least recognised the realities of regional trade.

3.3.1 The Bahraini Patents, Designs and Trade Marks Regulation of 1955

The subordinated status of the Bahraini regulation was established very clearly in the statute's opening definitions, which included the following:

> '"Comptroller-General" means the UK Comptroller-General of Patents, Designs and Trade Marks, and included any person authorized by him or the UK Board of Trade to issue certificates in respect of UK-registered patents, designs or trade marks.
>
> \- - - - - -
>
> "Court" means the Joint Court.[32]
>
> \- - - - - -
>
> "Patentee" means a person or persons for the time being entered on the UK Register of Patents as grantee or proprietor of the patent and the personal representative of a deceased grantee or proprietor.
> "Registrar" means the person appointed jointly by the Political Resident and the Ruler of Bahrain to be Registrar of Patents, Designs and Trade Marks for the Territory...
> "Territory" means the territory for which the 1955 law has been made applicable.'[33]

Bahrain was not specifically identified as the territory in question. However, some guidance was later provided by the description of the territory of a local trademark as constituting 'the territories of Bahrain, Kuwait, Qatar, Muscat and Oman, and the Trucial States'.[34] The law did not distinguish between local or otherwise in respect of the other areas of industrial property protected by the legislation.

To be competent to apply for local registration of a patent or design, the applicant was required to first have his right, title or interest entered on the UK Register of Patents and either be the patentee or designer or otherwise have legal title.[35] The law did not define a patent or describe its characteristics, the fundamental proposition being that an invention or article was a patent by virtue of its registration as such in the UK.

By contrast, the statute drew a distinction between trademarks already registered in the UK and trademarks of local origin and for local use only. In the former case, an applicant was required to first have his right, title or interest entered on the UK Register of Trade Marks and be either the owner or assignee of the mark.[36] In the case of an original local registration only, any person claiming to be the proprietor of a mark was entitled to seek registration.[37]

Some limited degree of protection was provided in respect of well-known marks in that a mark could not be registered if it was identical with, or confusingly similar to, a mark already registered in either part of the local Register in respect of the same goods or description of goods.[38] However, the Registrar might not refuse an application for registration solely on the grounds of being identical or very similar to a locally registered mark if the applicant could demonstrate that his mark was already registered in the UK or had been in regular local use for at least one year before the other mark was first used or locally registered.[39]

The Registrar possessed not inconsiderable discretionary powers. The Registrar could accept or reject any application for registration, or require any modifications or impose such conditions or limitations as he thought fit.[40] The Registrar could reject a mark if it was considered that its use would:

- be injurious to public order, morality, or the interests of the community as a whole;
- be contrary to law or public policy;
- deceive the public;
- hurt or arouse religious susceptibilities of any part of the community; or
- be otherwise inconsistent with any part of that law.[41]

A local mark (but not a UK-registered trademark, to which the following conditions did not apply) could not be registered in whole or in part if it consisted of or contained:

- public or armorial bearings, crests, insignia or decorations of any state or nation, or official hallmarks or signs indicating an official warranty, unless properly authorised;
- marks identical with or similar to national flags, military or naval flags, medals or badges, or the signs of the Red Crescent or Red Cross, or emblems of exclusively religious significance;
- a geographical name or surname, or the name of a sect, castle or tribe in any of the territories;
- marks which were or contained the picture, name or tradename of a person, body corporate, association, without prior consent.[42]

The period of protection for a patent, design or UK-dependent trademark was not granted in terms of a stipulated period of time but existed only as long as the corresponding prerequisite UK registration remained current and valid. Where a term was extended in the UK, the local registration could also be similarly extended.[43] By contrast, the validity of a local origin and use trademark registration was seven years, with provision for renewal for periods up to a maximum of 15 years.[44]

A suit for infringement could be brought only by the registered owner or assignee and then only in respect of a duly registered patent, design or trademark. However, provision existed for the granting of injunctive relief, including the seizure and destruction of infringing goods and any associated materials and equipment, and the award of damages and costs.[45] The nature of the scale of penalties for different types of infringements reflected the commercial imperatives of the statute. Unauthorised use of the [British] Royal Arms or Arms or Emblems of the ruler of the Territory [that is, Bahrain] or of deceivingly similar arms or emblems, or using any sign or title to create the impression of being an employee of, or supplier to, either government carried a fine of only 300 Indian rupees.[46] In contrast, such acts as:

- applying a false trade description to articles or goods protected by a registered patent or trademark;
- forging or counterfeiting a registered trademark, patent or design or possessing equipment for such purpose;
- importing, selling or possessing any goods which infringed a registered patent;
- importing, selling or even possessing any goods which carried a counterfeit or misleadingly similar trademark, design or description, or which were so presented as to enable them to be passed off;

carried penalties in each case of imprisonment for a period not exceeding two years, or a fine of up to 1,500 Indian rupees, or both. The court could also award damages of up to 1,500 Indian rupees for any losses which had been suffered as a direct result of the infringement and which had not already been otherwise compensated.[47]

The 1955 regulation remained unchanged until 1977, when a new law made sweeping changes to reflect and recognise Bahrain's change of status in 1971 from a UK-administered territory to an independent sovereign state.[48] The effect of the 1977 amendments was, in general terms, to:

- remove any subordination or cross-reference to UK patents, design or trade mark legislation, regulation or procedure;
- remove any reference to the UK or UK institutions such as the UK Patents Office or Trade Marks Registry, or 'Comptroller-General', and to any local offices or organisations which were part of Bahrain's former status as a UK-protected state, such as the 'Joint Court', the 'Political Resident' and the 'Crown Prosecutor';
- expand the registrability of marks to include services;
- stipulate provisions and conditions in lieu of the former UK-dependent provisions and conditions for registered patents, designs and non-local trademarks;

- introduce provision for semi-independent review of administrative decision-making, by transferring the quasi-judicial discretionary authority of the Registrar of Patents, Designs and Trade Marks to a semi-independent committee formed by the Minister of Commerce and Agriculture.

The former UK-dependent term of protection for patents and designs was replaced by a period of 15 years for patents and five years for designs, with provision for renewal.[49] Patent protection could be renewed for another ten years if it could be shown that the patent was of special significance and had not returned a financial award proportional to the expenditure incurred by the inventor. Similarly, the former UK-dependent trademark term of protection was replaced by a period of five years with provision for further ongoing renewals for successive periods of five years each. Curiously, although all references to the UK were deleted throughout the new law, the former reference to a two-part Register of Trade Marks (Part II for UK registrations and Part III for local registrations) remained unchanged. Hence the original provision for a seven-year term for local trademarks remained unchanged, thereby creating a contradiction between the two provisions and confusion as to the proper and valid period of protection. Similarly, the description of a local trademark and the territories in which it was applicable, and the reference to trademarks which fell outside its bounds, was also overlooked in the 1977 amendments.

Nor did the 1977 amendments include any changes to either the description of the nature of infringements, or the nature or level of sanctions available. The relief and precautionary measures available to a court in respect of infringements remained unchanged, as did the use of the Indian rupee as the currency of the legislation, notwithstanding the fact that Bahrain since independence had adopted the dinar as the state's legal currency.

3.3.2 The Kuwaiti Patents Law of 1962

By virtue of Law No. 4 of 1962, Kuwait was the second country after Bahrain amongst the Gulf states to introduce its own patent legislation. The law also provided protection for industrial designs and models. National treatment was extended to non-Kuwaitis living in or who had an established business in Kuwait, other foreigners who were nationals of or lived in countries that gave Kuwait reciprocity, as well as companies, public institutions and other legal entities established in Kuwait or of countries which gave reciprocity to Kuwait.[50]

The Kuwaiti law provided for the grant of letters patent for 'any new invention which is utilizable in industry whether it concerns new industrial product, original industrial process and techniques or a new application of known industrial process or techniques'.[51] Excluded from protection by the granting of a patent were:

'1. inventions whose utilisation results in a breach of morality or public policy;
2. chemical inventions relating to foodstuffs, medicines or pharmaceutical formula unless such products are made by special chemical methods or processes. In the latter event, the patent shall not be issued for the products themselves but for the method of their preparation.'[52]

Protection was granted for 15 years from the date of filing of the application, with provision for a single renewal for a further five years. An application for a pharmaceutical patent, being a patent which fell within the scope of the above exemption from exclusion provision (that is, certain types of chemical inventions requiring special chemical methods or processes), could be protected for only ten years without provision for renewal.[53] Protection for a registered industrial design or model was valid for five years and renewable for two additional consecutive terms.[54]

Provision was also made for appeals to independent judicial authority, namely the Kuwait court of first instance, against decisions of the Trade Marks Control Office to reject an application or objection against an application, or non-renewal.[55] The jurisdiction of the court also extended to appeals against decisions of the Office in respect of compulsory licences and compensations and revocation of patent registrations.

Compulsory licensing could be granted in circumstances where the patented invention had not been utilised in Kuwait within three years from the date of grant of the patent, where the patent owner was unable to utilise it adequately to meet the needs of the country or where the utilisation of the invention had ceased for at least two consecutive years.[56] Authority for granting the compulsory licence rested with the Trade Marks Control Office, provided the applicant could demonstrate that the invention would be utilised effectively and the patent owner had received suitable compensation. The decision of the Trade Marks Control Office in respect of a compulsory licence was also challengeable before the courts, but in the 40 years since this law was promulgated, no compulsory licences have been issued in Kuwait.

If the invention was deemed to be of great national importance and its utilisation necessitated use of another invention for which a patent had already been granted, the Trade Marks Control Office could grant a compulsory licence to exploit both patents to either the applicant or to the owner of the previous invention, depending on which invention was of greater importance.[57] An invention could also be expropriated if such expropriation was deemed to be in the public interest or for national defence by the Minister of Finance and Economy.

Infringement of the rights of a patent, design or model holder was limited to the following:

- imitating the subject matter of a patented invention or duly registered design or industrial model;
- knowingly selling or offering for sale or circulation, or importing or acquiring with intent to trade, imitated products or materials bearing an imitated design or industrial model, if the invention or industrial model is registered in Kuwait;
- without right, placing on products, notices, trade marks or packing articles, particulars leading to the belief of his having obtained a patent of invention or a registration of a design or industrial model.[58]

Where a civil or criminal action had commenced, the right holder could request the court to issue provisional orders, particularly seizure of the infringing products or goods and any equipment or machinery used in the infringement. Penalties available to the court included a term of imprisonment for up to two years or a fine of not less than 10 Kuwaiti dinars and not more than 225 Kuwaiti dinars, or both, and seizure and destruction of the offending goods and any tools, machinery and equipment used as part of the infringing activity.

Law No. 4 of 1962 is remarkable for its longevity by regional standards, which stands as testimony to its enlightened and careful construction. Subject to amendments in 1991 and again in 2001, the law is still essentially in force today. In recent years of the present TRIPS-plus era, however, it has attracted criticism because of the flexibility and scope of its patentability exclusion provisions, the perceived gross inadequacy of its sanctions by modern standards, and because of the exclusion from protection of patentable pharmaceutical and agricultural products.

3.4 Protection by association – non-intellectual property sources of protection

Notwithstanding the paucity of intellectual property law in the Gulf states throughout most of the pre-TRIPS era, some degree of protection can be found in sources other than intellectual property-based laws, although the protection granted to rights holders was at times incidental and fortuitous.[59] The primary beneficiary was intended to be the local trader or agent or the consumer and not necessarily the owner or right holder of an intellectual property right. Hence the main objects of the protection were items of a commercial nature such as trademarks, trade names and indications of origin. While provisions existed for the punishment of infringers, the same degree of attention was not available for the award of financial compensation to the owner or right holder or for the payment of damages. In the application of these laws by the courts, the primary objective was to secure the cessation of the infringing activity rather than the imposition of deterrent sanctions.

The UAE Civil Transactions Code of 1985, for example, restates the principle drawn from the *Shariah* that, while an individual may exercise certain rights, it cannot be done so at the expense of the same rights that others are entitled to enjoy. In essence, a right is balanced by an obligation. Damage to, or infringement upon, the rights of others by one's actions must be compensated, but the original damage cannot be offset by another damage – in other words, 'two wrongs don't make a right'. The Code postulates three fundamental principles in respect of causing damage to others in commercial transactions, which can equally be applicable to the protection of intellectual property:

> '1. A person shall be held liable for the unlawful exercise of his rights.
> 2. The exercise of a right shall be unlawful:
>   (a) if there is an intentional infringement of another's rights;
>   (b) if the interests which such exercise of right is designed to bring are contrary to the rules of the Islamic *Shariah*, the law, public order, or morals;
> (c) if the interests desired are disproportionate to the harm that will be suffered by others; or
> (d) if it exceeds the bounds of custom and usage.'[60]

The UAE Penal Code of 1978 addresses misrepresentation in commercial transactions and provides a degree of protection for the consumer in respect of the true nature of goods offered for sale. The Code provides that any person who:

> '. . . resorts to deception or fraudulent means in contracting with another person and disseminates information contrary to the facts as to the nature or essential qualities of his goods or to the elements of its competition or as to the basic description or origin of his goods . . . shall be punishable . . . Any person who imports, purchases or promotes such goods for commercial gain with full knowledge of their reality shall also be liable . . .'[61]

Similarly, the Oman Penal Code of 1974 provides a certain degree of protection for both the commercial agent and the consumer in respect of the use of imitated or confusing similar trademarks and trade names. The Code provides that a person who commits the following acts may be liable to a fine or term of imprisonment or both:

- imitates a registered mark belonging to a third party, or places such mark on any product, or knowingly offers for sale or sells a product bearing such imitated mark;
- uses a mark that is very similar to a registered mark to sell or offer for sale a product, with the intention of misleading a buyer;
- illegally uses, in any way, another person's trade name or a name which is very similar, with the intention of confusing or misleading or creating an association with that other trade name.[62]

Similar provisions can be found in the penal codes and commercial transaction codes of the other states.

The laws governing the operation of commercial agencies generally recognise the exclusive right of a registered commercial agent to deal in the goods or products which are the subject of his agency. In establishing the commercial agent's monopolistic rights, the laws establish a limited form of protection for the marks and indications carried by those goods, providing that both the agency agreement and the associated marks are registered. The net effect of this protection is that other parties are prohibited from importing or trading in those goods, or in goods that are deceivingly similar or which carry deceivingly similar marks. Again, the law is directed at protecting the commercial rights of the agent and less so the rights of the owner of a trademark.

The role that the press and publications laws could play in providing some notion of copyright protection has been mentioned above. The fact that an application by a publisher to the government authority for approval to publish a work had to be accompanied by the author's agreement to publication at least provided the opportunity to clearly establish ownership of a literary work and thereby offered some degree of protection in limited circumstances. However, the approval requirement did extend to literary works that were not published in commercial quantities or works already published outside the state. By the same token, the laws requiring the lodgement of a published work in a repository holding may have established ownership, but the intellectual property protection they provided was almost accidental, where it did occur. Accordingly, the protection provided by the publishing laws and the lodgement laws were at best incidental and could not be considered to represent an unequivocal or adequate means of copyright protection.

The pursuit of the protection of intellectual property rights through the region's judicial systems had been a mixed success – in part due to the deficiency of qualified and experienced judges familiar with the concepts of intellectual property rights and the interpretation of the intellectual property laws.[63] The common law doctrine of *stare decisis* is not recognised under the *Shariah* and thereby is not adhered to in the *Shariah* courts or the civil courts. Consequently, the absence of accepted legal precedent also contributed to problems in respect of consistency in the application of judicial principles and interpretation of the statutes on intellectual property rights and their protection.[64] The following two cases from the Dubai courts illustrate this inconsistency.

In 1977, the owners of the trademark *Brylcreem*, an internationally well-known haircare product, brought an action in the Dubai courts against a local manufacturer of an identical product offered for sale under the trademark *Berylcream*. The Dubai court held that prior use and registration in a foreign country were persuasive elements in confirming ownership of a trademark and that fraudulent use of a well-known and original mark, irrespective of whether the original mark was also used in the UAE, constituted unfair competition. It further held that protection of the original mark should be provided according to the general laws against unfair competition and that the law should not turn a blind eye to the harm done to the rightful owner of the mark simply because of the absence of a law regulating the use of trademarks:

> 'Non-existence of a law regulating the registration of trademarks leads to the fact that this court cannot levy the penalties which are usually provided for in such laws, but that does not prevent the court from granting the necessary protection to the trademark on the bases of general principles of law and the principles of justice and equity.'[65]

It further held that 'as to proving damage and fraud to the public through the use of the imitation trademark, the Court is of the opinion that it is not necessary to prove the actual occurrence of misrepresentation, but it is sufficient to say that there is a probability of such an imitation misleading the public'.

However, in an action brought by the owner of the *TIDE* trademark, against a local manufacturer of a similar product offered under the trademark *TIPE*, the Dubai appellate court held that, without a trademarks law in Dubai, imitating a trademark did not constitute an offence. It further held that, because Dubai was a trading community, it would be 'contrary to the principles of justice and equity' to impose any restriction upon free trade in the absence of government legislation.[66] In so ruling, it overturned the decision of the lower court that had been in favour of granting protection to the *TIDE* trademark. The Dubai Court of Cassation upheld the judgment of the appellate court on the grounds that, in the absence of any statutory trademarks law or customary law or Islamic law protecting trademarks, there was no basis for trademark infringement or unfair competition.[67]

In 1980, the Abu Dhabi Appeal Court held that an internationally known mark did not need to be registered locally in order to be entitled to local protection, since the property right to the mark was established by its first use and not by the act of registration.[68] Registration merely served to confirm rather than establish that right. The Court upheld the decision of the lower court that, although the *McDonald's* trademark was not at that time registered in the UAE, it was so well known internationally that local use of an identical or confusingly similar mark was likely both to be fraudulent and to cause confusion. This same principle was later endorsed by the Sharjah civil court in a similar action brought by the McDonald's Corporation (in fact, against the same defendant).[69] In the absence of any trademark laws in the UAE, the first law not being enacted until 1992, the decision in favour of McDonald's was based on the *Shariah*, the local civil codes and the general principles of justice and equity.

The case of *Reckitt and Colman v Al Jazirah* has been generally recognised as a landmark decision in controlling the production of locally manufactured counterfeit products in Saudi Arabia. The case, the first under the Saudi 1984 trademark law, was brought by Reckitt & Colman as the owners of the *Dettol* trademark against a local producer of *Bettol*, an imitation of Reckitt & Colman's *Dettol* disinfectant. On behalf of the company, the Saudi Ministry of Commerce had successfully appealed the original judgment in favour of the defendant, the local producer. The Ministry further appealed the appellate judgment, even though the decision was in its favour, on the grounds that the Ministry considered that the penalty was not commensurate with the gravity of the infringement. The Board of Grievances reversed the earlier decisions and ordered that the defendant be fined SR50,000, the maximum allowed under the trademark law.[70] It also ordered that all products and other labels, signs and materials bearing the imitation trademark *Bettol* be destroyed. Interestingly, though, the Board of Grievances did not order the defendant to pay any compensation, damages or costs. A civil case was reportedly settled satisfactorily out of court.[71]

However, apparently this was not the end of the matter for Reckitt & Colman in its protection of its *Dettol* trademark. According to one local report, more than 29 imitations of *Dettol* were found in Saudi Arabia in 1993, a year after the conclusion of the landmark decision in its favour.[72] The need to again defend *Dettol* arose in Ras Al-Khaimah where a producer of allegedly counterfeit *Dettol* tried to register the trademark *Dollen.* The application for registration was rejected after the lodgement of an objection by Reckitt & Colman. The local producer reportedly simply moved production to Qatar and subsequently began exporting *Dollen* to the other Gulf states, including the UAE.

3.5 The pre-TRIPS status of intellectual property protection

3.5.1 Trademarks

By the mid 1990s and just prior to the establishment of the WTO and the appearance of TRIPS, all Gulf states had trademark laws in place – some of them long established and in a few instances second- and third-generation legislation. Bahrain, for example, issued a new trademark law in 1991 which eventually replaced entirely the 1955 regulation and the 1977 amendments and thereby provided the opportunity to redress a number of the inconsistencies and contradictions which arose from an unsatisfactory and incomplete amendment of the original 1955 regulation.[73] Similarly, Kuwait over the years issued a number of enhancements to the trademark provisions of its longstanding commercial code.[74]

The most recent versions of the trademark laws of this period showed a high level of consistency and similarity, since most borrowed from the original Kuwaiti provisions, and thereafter continued to cross-fertilise each other as each round of new laws or amendments was introduced. However, most laws also relied quite heavily on the model laws on trademarks that had been prepared by the League of Arab States with the assistance of WIPO. Accordingly, they all contained similar provisions, particularly in respect of protection against counterfeiting and trademark infringement.[75] By the same token, they also all contained similar inadequacies in the eyes of the WTO and WIPO and would require a number of changes to bring them into compliance with TRIPS, notably in respect of:

- protection for well-known marks, including foreign marks;
- provision for licensing;
- existence of sanctions that would act as a deterrent;
- expansion of provisional measures, remedies and relief;
- effective border-control measures
- protection of trade secrets and protection from unfair competition;
- appeal provisions to independent judicial bodies on administrative decisions.

The UAE was the last of the Gulf states to provide some form of statutory trademark protection when it finally issued its first trademark law in 1992.[76] By mutual agreement, the law also superseded Ras Al-Khaimah's trademark registration statute of 1974. A unified Yemen issued a general intellectual property law in 1994, encompassing both copyright and industrial property and replacing the early trademark provisions of the former British Protectorate of Aden (southern Yemen) and the (northern) Yemen Arab Republic's trademarks and trade names law of 1974.

3.5.2 Patents and industrial designs

By the mid 1990s, all Gulf states except Oman and Qatar had introduced their own domestic patent legislation, although implementation and administration systems and services varied from state to state. Oman and Qatar, meanwhile, intended to adopt the regional patent regulations recently approved by the GCC Supreme Council for their own domestic purposes and therefore did not introduce any patent legislation.[77] The major drawback with this strategy was that the GCC statute was intended to be supplementary to domestic laws. In particular, it did not contain any enforcement provisions or sanctions – this being deemed a matter for domestic laws to address.

Where patents laws were in place, the laws contained shortcomings which ensured that they would attract pressure for change. Kuwait's 1962 law as amended, for example, provided protection for only 15 years instead of the conventional 20 years and excluded certain chemical inventions involving foods, pharmaceuticals and medicines from protection.[78] By the same token, the UAE's patent law produced 30 years later contained a similar glaring deficiency – and one that attracted severe criticism from the United States – in that it did not provide any patent protection for pharmaceutical products and only a ten-year term of protection for pharmaceutical processes.[79] Yemen's comprehensive intellectual property law, which incorporated protection for patents, similarly provided protection for patents for only 15 years. Although these states provided for a conventional system of protection through registration and examination, they tended to operate as filing systems or mailboxes only. Saudi Arabia alone provided for a working registration system that allowed for both formal and substantive examination.

Protection for industrial designs was achieved by the Yemeni law by a combination of specific and separate provision and by the application of the law's general provisions. In Kuwait and the UAE the general provisions of their patent laws were extended to encompass industrial designs and models.

With the agreement of all member states, the GCC issued its regional patent regulations in late 1992. The regulations established a scheme for regional protection throughout all member states by allowing the lodgement of a single application with a regional patents office. However, the regional patent regulations were somewhat wanting in respect both of their effective operation and their compliance with TRIPS, because of their:

- exclusion of pharmaceutical and chemical inventions from any form of protection;
- protection commencing from date of grant, instead of date of application;
- protection for only 15 years, contrary to TRIPS Article 33 requirement of 20 years;
- absence of any effective enforcement provisions, or sanctions, remedies or relief;
- prohibition of concurrent applications to national patent offices and to the GCC Patent Office.[80]

The regional patent regulation specifically prohibited the simultaneous lodgement of a patent application, or even the enjoyment of concurrent protection, with the GCC regional office and a national receiving office.[81] The practical implications of this prohibition were that an application to the regional office was required to demonstrate that any former or simultaneous application to a national receiving office had been withdrawn, and any national protection already granted had been surrendered, prior to the GCC regional office accepting the application for regional protection. Also militating against the effective utilisation of the unified patent regulation was the delay by the GCC in issuing the corresponding implementing bylaws, which did not eventuate until some four years later, in 1996. Furthermore, the regional patents office did not come into operation and was not in a position to accept any patent applications until October 1999.

While Kuwait, Oman and Qatar all claimed to ascribe to the GCC unified patent regulations as their national patent law, only Oman enacted a decree prior to 1995 to formally recognise the regulation and to legitimise this arrangement.[82]

In practical terms, patent infringement issues were less likely to arise in the GCC member states than trademark or copyright issues, and patent protection would have been the area in which it would arguably have been easier for the states to satisfy demands from the industrialised countries to improve intellectual property protection. Indeed, the amount of local and original patent generation was so small there was little pressure to test the efficacy of the local laws and organisational structures. The fact that the Kuwaiti patents office, established under its original 1962 patents law, was still not examining or publishing applications or granting patents 30 years after it was established did not appear to have attracted any great concern either locally or internationally (although the lack of provision of a satisfactory patents protection regime, particularly for pharmaceutical products, has still attracted criticism).[83] Even in the immediate pre-TRIPS period of the early 1990s, the primary purpose of the Kuwaiti Patents Office appeared to be that of a repository only, with the issuance by the Office of reminder notices, for the renewal of applications to maintain protection, a common practice.

3.5.3 *Copyright*

The situation in respect of copyright was very different to that in respect of trademarks and patents, with little progress having being made throughout the Gulf region towards the provision of effective national protection regimes. All Gulf states were signatories to the League of Arab States' 1981 Agreement on the Protection of Author's Rights, but only Kuwait, Qatar and Saudi Arabia appear to have issued domestic regulations to formally recognise the provisions of the Agreement at home. This Agreement espoused many of the principles enshrined in the Universal Copyright Convention and some elements of the Berne Convention. However, it limited the term of protection of literary works, performances or broadcasts to the life of the author or date of performance or broadcast plus 25 years. Protection was limited to the works of nationals of the Arab signatory states and foreign nationals resident in those states whose own governments provided reciprocal rights. Further, the Agreement relied entirely on the signatory states to have in place their own national copyright laws to enable the effective implementation and enforcement of the rights enshrined in the Agreement. None of the above states at that time possessed the necessary domestic legislation and hence their adoption of the Agreement was largely symbolic.

By the mid 1990s, four states possessed their own copyright laws, namely Bahrain (1993), Saudi Arabia (1989), the UAE (1992) and Yemen (1994).[84] Saudi Arabia enhanced the copyright protection environment provided by its 1989 law by acceding to the Universal Copyright Convention in 1994.

The UAE introduced its first copyright law in 1992, reportedly after considerable and sustained pressure from the United States for the UAE to issue copyright and neighbouring rights protection legislation.[85]

These copyright laws were deficient in respect of complying with a number of the provisions and minimum standards of copyright protection required by the Berne Convention and which would soon be required by the impending TRIPS, particularly in respect of the following matters:

- inadequate, or in some instances absence of, provision for the protection of neighbouring rights;
- existence of compulsory licensing provisions;
- absence of detailed provision on rental rights, particularly in respect of computer programs and cinematographic works;
- absence of national treatment for the protection of foreign works that had already been published abroad;
- terms of protection of only up to 25 years, much less than the minimum period of 50 years that TRIPS would stipulate;
- little or no provision for independent judicial review of decision-making processes;
- inadequate or no border-control provisions;
- sanctions which were perceived as being inadequate and with little or no deterrent effect.

Protection of foreign works was a matter of particular concern to the developed countries and to the United States in particular. Generally speaking, both the Berne Convention and the UCC require member states to protect foreign works on the same basis as they protect national works. In terms of actual standards of protection that all members undertake to provide, the UCC requirements are few in number, modest and vaguely worded[86]; the Berne Convention, however, prescribes a much more fully articulated scheme of mandatory minimum standards of protection. Adherence could therefore permit a significantly lower level of protection for foreign works than would be allowed under Berne. None of the four Gulf states with domestic copyright legislation had acceded to the Berne Convention, and in any case, their domestic laws did not meet its standards.

Effective implementation of the above laws was hampered by the ongoing non-appearance of the necessary implementing regulations – a pattern of extended delay which often repeats itself throughout the Gulf states. Saudi Arabia's implementing regulations for its copyright law of 1989, for example, did not appear until some three years after the law was enacted. Yemen's implementing regulations for its 1994 intellectual property rights law (which included the provisions for copyright) were not issued until 2007.

This disinterest or disinclination to embrace copyright and neighbouring rights protection can be explained in part by the entrenched attitude by officialdom that copyright was still essentially a mechanism for the control of local press and publications. This attitude is reflected by the pre-publication approval and registration lodgement provisions contained in the Bahraini, Saudi, Emirati and Yemeni copyright laws which, in the case of Bahrain and Saudi Arabia, were still compulsory and carried provision for the imposition of fines for non-compliance.[87]

Other areas of intellectual property for which the forthcoming TRIPS would require WTO members to provide protection – notably plant varieties, geographical indications, layout designs of integrated circuits, undisclosed information and trade secrets – remained largely ignored or overlooked and without targeted or specific protection provisions.

In respect of membership of the multilateral trading system, Kuwait became a contracting party to GATT in 1963, soon after its independence, and remained the only member from the Gulf region for many years. Thirty years later, Bahrain became a contracting party to GATT in 1993, and Qatar and the UAE both followed suit in 1994. Saudi Arabia applied to contract to GATT in 1993, enjoyed observer status at the Uruguay Round of meetings on the new WTO, and continued to seek membership of the WTO. Oman had not expressed any formal interest in contracting to GATT and was not inclined to initiate an application for membership of the WTO until 1996.

Only Qatar, Saudi Arabia, the UAE and Yemen were members of WIPO, the UAE being the first Gulf state to join. The Yemen Arab Republic (northern Yemen) joined in December 1978, while the southern People's Democratic Republic of Yemen acceded to the WIPO convention in December 1989. After unification, WIPO recognition of the two former states was withdrawn and a unified Republic of Yemen was recognised as a member in lieu in December 1990.

None of the Gulf states had yet expressed any intention of acceding to the major international intellectual property protection agreements, such as the Berne, Paris and Rome Conventions. It has been suggested that the long-term reluctance of the states to accede to the major intellectual property conventions was not so much due to a policy of commercial isolationism or ignorance of intellectual property protection but rather an indication of their full appreciation of the commercial implications of intellectual property and its protection, and an understanding of the restrictions upon their current commercial practices that accession to the international conventions would bring.[88] The states had always been aware that their domestic production of the various forms of subject matter amenable to legal protection as intellectual property, although growing, was still far outweighed by the volumes of foreign production that they imported for local use. Accession to the international conventions was perceived as being more likely to restrict that growth than to accelerate it.[89]

One curious anomaly in this picture of general disinterest in the international intellectual property conventions is the accession by Oman (1986) and Qatar (1983) to the Nairobi Treaty on the Protection of the Olympic Symbol (see Table 3.2).[90] In Oman's case, accession took place more than

Table 3.2 Intellectual property laws and international conventions in the Gulf states in the early 1990s

		Bahrain	*Kuwait*	*Oman*	*Qatar*	*Saudi Arabia*	*UAE*	*Yemen*
National laws	Copyright	1993	-	-	-	1989	1992	
	Trademarks	1991	1980	1987	1978	1984	1992	1994
	Patents	1977	1962	-	-	1989	1992	
	Industrial designs			-	-	-		
	Plant varieties	-	-	-	-	-	-	-
	Geographical indications	-	-	-	-	-	-	-
	Integrated circuits	-	-	-	-	-	-	-
	Undisclosed information	-	-	-	-	-	-	-
	Legal deposit of works	1975	-	-	1982	1989	1993	1994
	Printed matter & publication	1979	1961	1984	1979	1982	1980	-
	Arab Agreement on Author's Rights	-	1986	-	1986	1985	-	-
	GCC patent regulation	?	?	1993	?	?	?	-
Bodies	League of Arab States	1971	1961	1971	1971	1945	1971	1945
	GCC	1981	1981	1981	1981	1981	1981	-
	GATT	1993	1963	-	1994	-	1994	-
	WIPO	-	-	-	1976	1982	1974	1990
Conventions	Berne		-	-	-	-	-	-
	Paris		-	-	-	-	-	-
	Rome	-	-	-	-	-	-	-
	Nairobi (Olympic symbol)	-	-	1986	1983	-	-	-
	Universal Copyright Convention	-	-	-	-	1994	-	-

Source: compiled by the author

Notes: The League of Arab States (LAS) formally adopted the Arab Agreement on Author's Rights at the Conference of LAS Ministers of Culture held in Baghdad on 5 November 1981. The Agreement was prepared with assistance and guidance from UNESCO. However, the Agreement did not come into force until 1985, when ratification by the required number of Arab states was achieved. Accession to the Arab League did not necessarily also require formal adoption of the Agreement. It is worth noting that none of the four Gulf states which acceded possessed its own copyright laws to enable it to locally implement the limited protection to copyright provided by the Agreement.

Although all GCC member states had endorsed the GCC Unified Patent Regulation, and had at various times declared that they recognised its validity, only Oman had enacted a statute formally adopting the Regulation as the Patent Law of Oman (Ministerial Regulation No. 219/1993, September 1993). In 2003, Qatar eventually enacted a similar law (Law No. 12 of 2003).

a decade before it achieved membership of WIPO and almost 15 years before it acceded to any of the core intellectual property protection conventions. However, in both cases, accession could be construed more as a reflection of the keenness of the two states to become involved in the Olympic movement, for which adoption of the Nairobi Treaty was an essential political pre-requisite in the absence of an international sporting pedigree, than as a commitment to intellectual property protection.

3.6 The external influences

3.6.1 The Gulf Cooperation Council (GCC)

The Gulf Cooperation Council (GCC) is portrayed by its advocates as the means for the fulfilment of the aspirations of the citizens of the Gulf states for some form of Arab regional unity. Accordingly, they exhort that the decision to create the GCC was not a product of the moment but an institutional embodiment of an historical, social and cultural reality reflecting the deep religious and cultural ties that link the six member states and the strong kin relations that prevail among their citizens.[91] From a more pragmatic perspective, it was also a response to a perceived threat from an Islamic fundamentalist Iran, a Ba'athist Iraq, the state of civil war in Yemen and the recent Soviet intervention in Afghanistan – all of which threatened to destabilise the ruling dynasties in the Gulf region and to involve their states in wider conflicts.[92]

The GCC's advocates further argue that the GCC establishes a cooperative framework for mutual coordination and integration in many fields in order to achieve a strong degree of regional unity.[93] According to the GCC Charter, the underpinnings for this framework are the special relations, common qualities and similar systems founded on the creed of Islam, faith in a common destiny and the sharing of one goal. These noble sentiments have not been mere hollow words; in fact, parallels might be drawn between the movement towards Gulf regional integration and the early character of the European Union before the latter reached its current highly homogeneous state. While the GCC states have established common regional positions on such international political issues as regional security, support for Palestine and the Arab boycott of Israel, the two Gulf wars and the US occupation of Iraq, they have also had differences of opinion on these same issues. But the mixed reactions and acrimony amongst the GCC members that emerged during the GCC Summit of December 2004, in reaction to Bahrain's recent commitment to a free trade agreement with the United States, are a recent and pertinent illustration that the solidarity amongst the GCC members may not be as strong as the GCC's advocates would wish to portray, when self-interest comes to the fore.

Apart from the issuance of its regional unified patent regulations in 1992 and amendments in 2000, and the establishment of a regional patent office in Riyadh, Saudi Arabia, the GCC as a regional body has not produced much in the way of effective contribution to the development of intellectual property protection regimes in its member states. It took the regional patent office, for example, over six years from the time of its approval before it was able to commence operations and receive patent applications from October 1998. Even then, it was not able to undertake any substantive examination of the applications. A much more effective contribution to the development of intellectual property protection regimes has been the ongoing willingness and practice of the government officials with responsibilities for certain elements of intellectual property matters to network with their counterparts in the other GCC states. The networking generally focuses on emerging practical issues relating to intellectual property rights such as legislative drafting, administration and systems, and enforcement practices. There is no doubt that the GCC framework has facilitated this regional networking, but that is not to say that the GCC itself has proactively created or fostered this networking process.

For some 20 years, the GCC has been working on a proposed regional trademark regulation, the genesis of which pre-dates its unified patent regulations. The proposed regional law suffered from frequent review – which in part explains its non-appearance as a formal statute, but also illustrates the fluid state of regional trademark protection perceptions and regional differences of opinion. The proposed regulation was eventually concluded and agreed upon by GCC members in mid 2007, well after each state had constructed its own TRIPS-based trademark law. However, the regulation appears to have been overtaken by other events in the arena of bilateral agreements in the region. Both Bahrain (in 2006) and Oman (in 2008) have introduced new trademark legislation as a consequence of their commitments under the intellectual property chapters of their respective free trade agreements with the United States.[94] Although the Saudi Cabinet has approved the GCC trademark regulation (which, in any case, does not bring it into force domestically), and Qatar and the UAE have reportedly acceded to it, it is now unlikely that the regulation will come into regional effect, even though some states may well adopt it in a display of regional unity. However, in fairness, it did influence the nature of the first round of post-TRIPS trademark laws of Bahrain, Oman and the UAE.[95]

The GCC has also been working for some time on a proposed uniform law on commercial transactions which reportedly will contain a chapter regulating trademarks, trade names and unfair competition. However, the objective of this regulation, if it comes to pass, will be to establish a certain degree of regional harmonisation between the respective GCC states in respect of their trademark registration processes and to establish rules on intra-regional collaboration. It does not seem that it would attempt to compete with the national laws already in place and the international agreements on trademark protection to which the states are obliged to adhere.[96]

It is perhaps not all that surprising, then, that in terms of its contribution towards shaping the character and direction of its member states' intellectual property laws and protection regimes the GCC has been overshadowed by the contributions of other regional organisations, such as the League of Arab States, and by WIPO. In particular, WIPO has had a major influence on the states' intellectual property laws, with input ranging from policy development and legislative drafting through to infrastructural capacity building, systems, staff training and public awareness education.

3.6.2 The Gulf states and the WIPO relationship

The contribution of WIPO, and in particular its Bureau for Arab Countries, to the development of the Gulf states' intellectual property laws has ranged from policy development and legislative drafting through to infrastructure development, staff training and public awareness education. As mentioned earlier, WIPO had input into the early models of intellectual property laws developed by the League of Arab States.

WIPO places its Economic Development Sector division (of which the Bureau for Arab Countries is a part) at the disposal of any state that requests advice on issues of compatibility of existing or planned national intellectual property legislation with treaties administered by WIPO, and with other international norms and trends, including TRIPS.[97] The Bureau is also available to assist developing member countries of either WIPO or the WTO with translations of their intellectual property laws and regulations, and to provide legal and technical advice relating to TRIPS and its enforcement. It is also meant to take into account the unique situation of each country, given that member states have different legal systems and different political and cultural structures. However, WIPO does have a particular agenda.

In relation to the preparation of intellectual property legislation for the implementation of TRIPS, assistance is given in the following ways:

- preparation and submission of draft laws on all areas of intellectual property;
- preparation and submission of draft provisions to amend and update existing intellectual property laws;
- preparation and submission of comments and suggestions on draft laws prepared by (and received from) governments of developing countries.

WIPO has constructed a number of draft or model laws and has utilised these laws in providing legislative advice to countries which seek its assistance.[98] The laws take into account developments in intellectual property at the international level as reflected in meetings of the various WIPO committees, and WIPO used these model laws as its preferred way of implementing the provisions of the various international treaties in each particular field of intellectual property.[99]

The WIPO assistance to the Gulf states included input into the creation and construction of their intellectual property laws and all states have taken advantage of this input. But it has also included assistance with the preparation of responses to questions from members of the WTO Council of TRIPS, both in the pre-accession examination process and in the reviews that the Council conducted during 2000 and 2001 of WTO developing country members which had utilised the TRIPS five-year transition period. Bahrain, Kuwait, Qatar and the UAE went through this review process, and Yemen is currently doing so. So did Oman, even though its intellectual property laws had received close scrutiny from WTO members just a year earlier as part of its WTO accession process.[100]

The following extract from the WTO's working party on Oman's progress towards WTO accession clearly illustrates the close collaboration between Oman and WIPO and the major role played by the latter in the construction of Oman's suite of seven intellectual property laws that was enacted throughout 2000.[101] As the extract states, all seven laws were developed with the assistance of WIPO.

Status of Legislation on Intellectual Property in Oman (June 2000)[102]

Area of TRIPS	Present Position and On-going Program
1 Trademarks	Trademark Law is in place since 1987 and is being implemented. Points of conformity and non-conformity of the existing law with the provisions of the TRIPS Agreement have been identified. Draft amended law has been prepared in consultation with WIPO. It has been examined, translated into English and submitted to WTO for comment.
2 Copyright and related rights	Copyright Law of Oman is in force since 1996 and is being implemented. Points of conformity and non-conformity of the existing law with the provisions of the TRIPS Agreement have been identified. Draft amended law has been prepared in consultation with WIPO and submitted to WTO for comment.
3 Patents	Draft Ministerial Decree adopting the revised GCC Unified Patent System as the law of Oman, together with the amendments bringing it into full conformity with the provisions of the TRIPS Agreement, have been submitted to WTO for comment.

4 Geographical Indications	Draft law on geographical indications of origin has been translated into English and submitted to WTO for comment
5 Industrial Designs	There is no law at present on industrial designs. A draft law prepared by WIPO has been examined, translated into English and submitted to WTO for comment.
6 Plant Varieties	There is no law at present. A draft law has been prepared and submitted to WTO for comment.
7 Layout Design of Integrated Circuits	There is no law at present. WIPO has provided a draft law which has been examined. It has been translated into English and submitted to WTO for comment.
8 Trade Secrets	No law at present. A draft addition to the Trademark Law has been prepared in consultation with WIPO.
9 Abuse of Anti-Competitive Practices.	No law at present. A draft addition to the Trademark Law has been prepared in consultation with WIPO.

What stands out from the above example is that the Gulf states have maintained good working relations with WIPO and its International Bureau. They have relied, and continue to rely, on the Bureau for the formal roles stipulated above as part of the Bureau's brief on technical assistance. Indeed, this close relationship generally continues through the present day and officials in the states' ministries talk of a virtual hotline between their offices and WIPO.[103] This close and positive relationship between WIPO and its member states has been reported by other commentators.[104] The other side of this positive relationship is that the laws prepared and presented by WIPO to these states as their domestic intellectual property protection regimes enshrine the formal position of WIPO as an international organisation 'dedicated to helping to ensure that the rights of creators and owners of intellectual property are protected worldwide',[105] that is, a protectionist policy. WIPO's position, perhaps not unreasonably so from its perspective and charter, is that the incorporation of these higher standards on intellectual property protection into the states' laws at the earliest possible point – that is, at their drafting – will 'resolve problems for the developing countries before they arise'.[106]

3.7 Concluding remarks – a prelude to TRIPS

TRIPS constitutes Annex IC of the Marrakesh Agreement Establishing the World Trade Organization (WTO), which was concluded on 15 April 1994 and entered into force on 1 January 1995. In accordance with the requirements of Article II.2 of the Marrakesh Agreement, TRIPS is binding on all members of the WTO. In terms of its coverage, TRIPS is the most comprehensive multilateral agreement on intellectual property rights, encompassing most types of rights with the particular exception of breeders' rights, utility models and traditional knowledge. It establishes minimum standards of protection in respect of:

- copyright and related rights, including computer programs and databases;
- trademarks, including service marks;
- geographical indications, including additional protection for geographical indications for wines and spirits;
- industrial designs;
- patents, including new plant varieties;
- layout designs of integrated circuits;
- undisclosed information, including trade secrets, and control of anti-competitive practices in contractual licences.

It has been suggested that TRIPS was successfully advocated by the governments of the industrialised world in order to obtain worldwide protection for the innovations and technologies generated by their corporations.[107] Industrialised countries forced developing countries to negotiate an agreement on TRIPS with a clear objective of universalising the standards of intellectual property protection that they had incorporated in their domestic legislation once they had obtained a high level of technological and industrial capacity. Correa suggests that a number of factors that converged during the 1980s/1990s explain the priority given by some countries, notably the United States, to a far-reaching enhancement of the intellectual property system worldwide, namely:

- the growing importance of technology as a factor in international competition;
- elimination or reduction of trade barriers in developing countries, which increased both the opportunity for direct exports from those countries and their attractiveness to multinational companies to gain access to those markets without the obligation for local investment or technology transfer;
- the erosion during the 1980s of the US supremacy in manufacturing and technology by Japan and subsequently Asian 'tiger economies', attributable to too-open policies in respect of technology transfer and innovation imitation.[108]

The perception that this declining American competitiveness was in large part due to losses from overseas piracy and counterfeiting was effectively promoted by US industry lobbies, particularly the pharmaceutical, software and recording industries, which convinced the US government of the need to link trade and protection of intellectual property rights to preserve US technology supremacy and the consequent economic advantage. Thus TRIPS was not conceived merely as an instrument to combat counterfeiting and piracy but also as a component of a policy of 'technological protectionism' by establishing international rules to counter a declining competitive position in world markets.[109] The adoption of TRIPS represented a major victory for industrialised countries and for their most active industry lobbies. It mirrored the standards of intellectual property rights protection that were suitable for industrialised countries at their then prevailing level of development. It thus has several serious and adverse implications for developing countries, as many of its protectionist provisions could place higher obstacles in the path of these countries in their endeavours towards technological achievement.

The economies of the Gulf states were largely driven by products outside the remit of the WTO, namely oil and gas. However, the states also saw that membership of the WTO would give them the potential to exert influence on some areas of international trade, whereas outside the WTO they would have no such ability. Yet the states also realised that they would have little choice but to join the international community which the WTO represents and to become part of the north–south argument, particularly as they tried to broaden and develop their national economic bases. The perceived significance to the states of membership of the WTO and the requisite intellectual property legislative framework as a key national political and economic strategy is illustrated by Oman's reaction to achieving WTO membership. As mentioned earlier, the options before the Sultanate were perceived to be somewhat limited; it was, in effect, a game of do or die – either accede to the WTO or face global isolation. Despite a somewhat lukewarm attitude towards the WTO and the vehement criticism of its policies in some quarters, it was widely accepted that remaining outside the WTO would not be in the interests of any country, particularly a developing country. And with membership of the WTO came, along with a number of other agreements, a requirement to adopt and establish laws and systems to comply with the requirements of TRIPS. While the Gulf states may well have viewed membership of the WTO as a necessity in an international context, TRIPS was more likely perceived as just part of a total package. Even if there were misgivings in some quarters concerning its new minimum protection standards, TRIPS may well have been viewed as being largely irrelevant domestically and hence having little practical impact in the internal marketplace.

Reporting in early 1995, and just after the introduction of TRIPS, the United States Trade Representative reported that the GCC as a whole, as well as its member states, lacked comprehensive sets of laws and regulations to ensure effective intellectual property protection, although some progress had been made in recent years.[110] While all three major areas of intellectual property, namely trademarks, patents and copyright, received critical attention, the report was particularly scathing of the inadequate levels of protection for literary works of foreign origin, for sound and video recordings, and for a wide range of foreign goods imported for domestic consumption. It added that in no case was protection adequate for US works. The report was particularly critical of the absence of patent protection for pharmaceutical products, and of inadequate terms of protection for pharmaceutical processes in Kuwait and the UAE, lack of protection for US copyright works and sound recordings in Bahrain and the UAE, and the widespread copyright and trademark violations in Oman and Qatar. At the same time, the report acknowledged that Bahrain had strong patent and trademark laws, that Saudi Arabia had a complete and adequate patent law and that the UAE had taken very effective steps to eliminate copyright piracy in video products. However, the report focused on the inadequacy of levels of protection for US interests and not on the degree of compliance with TRIPS requirements. In so doing the report reveals the major US corporate influences behind the direction the report takes, namely the pharmaceutical industry and the film, recording and video industry.

Also writing on the status of intellectual property protection in the Gulf at the time of the establishment of the WTO, one expert commentator and long-term expatriate resident of one of the states showed considerable foresight when he suggested that the pre-TRIPS period of the Uruguay round of negotiations represented 'an era of resurgent bilateralism'. He predicted that 'the Gulf states can expect to remain under continuing pressure . . . for legislative and enforcement activity in intellectual property matters'.[111] In fact, the states would enjoy little respite from the US bilateralism for the next five years of transitional period for TRIPS compliance and beyond. If the writer was short of the mark in his forecast, it was only in respect of an underestimation of the timing and duration of the period of US resurgent bilateralism, which continues today under the banner of the US Middle East Free Trade Area (MEFTA) strategy. The states would experience the effects of the increased 'ratcheting up' of US policy in using bilateral trade agreements in the post-TRIPS climate to establish the MEFTA as one of its objectives in attempting to establish a dominating diplomatic and economic influence in the Gulf region as part of its broader international political strategy.

As this chapter has attempted to explore, the history of intellectual property protection in the Gulf states in the pre-TRIPS era shows that foreign influences have continually made their presence felt on the states intellectual property legislation. Sometimes the foreign influences have been obvious and intrusive, as in the case of the Bahrain pre-independence omnibus regulation, and at times the influences have been subtle but even more effective, as illustrated by Kuwait's post-independence introduction of commercial and civil laws based on Egyptian and French foundations. The foreign influences have been of both western and Arabic origin.

However, the next major influence of foreign origin on the development of the intellectual property regimes of the Gulf states, and which would soon confront them, would be the creation of the WTO and the introduction and implementation of TRIPS – as Chapter 4 discusses.

4 TRIPS and the nature of compliance by the Gulf states

4.1 Introduction – the context of TRIPS and its conventions

TRIPS was created not with the view of establishing an entirely new regulation but with the intention of supplementing and developing some sense of cohesion with the then existing major international conventions on intellectual property protection, namely the Berne, Paris and Rome Conventions, and the Washington Treaty. TRIPS is based upon and supplements these conventions by providing additional obligations and a higher level of protection. The supplemented provisions become compulsory, even for WTO member countries that have not ratified the above conventions (except for the Rome Convention which continues to be binding on states that have joined it), by virtue of their WTO membership. However, nothing in TRIPS may derogate from any existing obligations that members may have to each other under the Paris, Berne or Rome Conventions or the Washington Treaty.[1]

The general goals of TRIPS, as enunciated in its Preamble, include the reduction of distortions and impediments to international trade, the promotion of effective and adequate protection of intellectual property rights, and ensuring that measures and procedures to enforce intellectual property rights do not themselves become barriers to legitimate trade. Although the Preamble recognises that intellectual property rights are private rights, the underlying public policy objectives of national systems for the protection of intellectual property, including developmental and technological objectives, are also recognised. The Preamble also acknowledges that least developed countries require maximum flexibility in the domestic implementation of their laws and regulations in order to enable them to create a sound and viable technological base.

The Agreement's public policy objectives are further enunciated in Part I by a declaration on the fundamental objective of TRIPS and on the equally fundamental principles by which members should be guided in formulating their laws relating to the Agreement. Article 7 *Objectives* provides that:

> 'The protection and enforcement of intellectual property rights should contribute to the promotion of technological innovation and to the

> transfer and dissemination of technology, to the mutual advantage of producers and users of technological knowledge, and in a manner that is conducive to social and economic welfare, and to a balance of rights and obligations.'

Article 8 *Principles* recognises that members have the right to adopt measures necessary for the protection of public health and other public interest reasons in sectors of vital importance to their socio-economic and technological development. However, such measures must still be consistent with TRIPS provisions.

TRIPS Part I (Articles 1–8) sets out further general provisions and basic principles governing the protection of intellectual property rights. It establishes minimum standards to be applied by all WTO members, these same standards also being the maximum standards that members are obliged to adopt. However, members are not constrained from adopting more extensive protection than that required by TRIPS, provided that such protection does not contravene the TRIPS provisions. Members are also free to determine the appropriate method of implementing the TRIPS provisions within their own legal systems and practices. Articles 3–5 stipulate the fundamental obligations on national and most-favoured-nation (MFN) treatment of foreign nationals, which are common to all categories of intellectual property covered by the Agreement. These obligations cover not only the substantive standards of protection but also matters affecting the availability, acquisition, scope, maintenance and enforcement of intellectual property rights as well as those matters affecting the use of intellectual property rights specifically addressed in the Agreement.

TRIPS Part II (Articles 9–40) addresses each intellectual property right in succession and sets out the minimum standards of protection to be provided by each member.[2] Each of the main elements of protection is defined, namely the scope of the subject matter to be protected, the rights to be conferred and permissible exceptions to those rights, any particular special provisions (such as the reversal of burden of proof in respect of process patents), and the minimum duration of protection. TRIPS sets these standards by requiring compliance with the substantive obligations of the major pre-existing conventions and by adding a number of obligations on matters where the pre-existing conventions are silent or where they are seen by their proponents as being inadequate.

Part III (Articles 41–61) requires members to have in place enforcement procedures which permit effective action against infringements, with remedies that constitute an effective deterrent to further infringements. The procedures apply equally to all fields of intellectual property covered in Part III. The procedures must be equitable and fair, and must not be unnecessarily complicated, costly or involve unreasonable time limits or unwarranted delays, but their application must not create a barrier to legitimate trade. However, a member is not obliged to put in place a special judicial system for the enforcement of intellectual property rights distinct from that for the enforcement of law in general, nor is a member required to make a preferential allocation of resources to intellectual property enforcement at the expense of the law in general.

Part IV (Article 62) addresses the acquisition and maintenance of intellectual property rights and related *inter partes* procedures. Members may require compliance with certain procedures as a condition of enjoying intellectual property rights within that member's national boundaries, but such procedures and formalities must be reasonable and must not create an unwarranted curtailment of the period of protection of a right. Final administrative decisions in any of these procedures must be subject to review by a judicial or quasi-judicial authority.

Part V (Articles 63 and 64) provides for the establishment of a multilateral mechanism for the settlement of disputes between members, in accordance with the provisions of Articles XXII and XXIII of GATT (1994) as elaborated and applied by WTO's Dispute Settlement Understanding (DSU) – a provision sought in particular by developing countries to counter the perceived likelihood of unilateral action by developed countries in respect of enforced adherence to TRIPS or greater standards.[3] Retaliatory action by one member against another may be taken only after the existence of a violation or non-compliance has been established by the WTO's Dispute Settlement Body. This mechanism is aimed at preventing unilateral actions, such as those undertaken by the United States under Section 301 of its Trade and Tariffs Act.[4]

Part VI (Article 65–67) establishes transitional arrangements for the implementation of the obligations of TRIPS. Developed countries are granted a one-year period to bring their legislation and practices into conformity with TRIPS. Developing countries and countries in the process of transformation from a centrally planned into a market economy are granted a five-year transition period, and least-developed countries are granted eleven years (except for obligations concerning national and most-favoured-nation treatment, to which the standard one-year transition applies). In addition, a further transitional period of five years is allowed for countries which are bound to introduce product patent protection in areas of technology not so protected in their territory on the general date of application of TRIPS for those countries. However, patent applications for pharmaceutical and agricultural chemical products must be accepted for filing from the very beginning of the transition period. Although granting of the patent could be deferred until the end of this period, the novelty of the invention is preserved as of the date of filing the application. If authorisation for the marketing of the relevant pharmaceutical or agricultural chemical product is obtained during the transitional period, the developing country concerned is required to offer an exclusive marketing right for the product for five years, or until a product patent is granted, whichever is the lesser period.

The final provisions and institutional arrangements, as described in Part VII (Articles 68–73), includes provision for the establishment of a Council to monitor the operation of TRIPS and, in particular, members' compliance with their TRIPS obligations. The Council was specifically directed to act in cooperation with WIPO. The Council was also required to review the implementation of TRIPS after the expiry of the five-year transitional period granted to developing countries and again at subsequent two-year intervals.

4.2 TRIPS and the GCC member states

All GCC member states have adopted TRIPS by virtue of their WTO membership. Kuwait became a contracting party to GATT in 1963, just two years after it gained its independence. Thirty years later, Bahrain, Qatar and the UAE became contracting parties to GATT, WTO's predecessor organisation, just prior to the introduction of the WTO. As such they became foundation members of the WTO and signatories to TRIPS, and any scrutiny of their intellectual property regimes by other WTO members was notional. Oman and Saudi Arabia were treated differently, since both were required to undergo a full scrutiny of their intellectual property protection regimes as part of their WTO accession processes. Oman's accession process took just four years to complete, from 1996 to 2000. Saudi Arabia, meanwhile, required more than 12 years of political and diplomatic wrangling before its bid for accession was successful. Saudi Arabia was finally admitted to WTO membership in November 2005, just in time to fully participate in the sixth WTO Ministerial Conference in Hong Kong in December of that year.

Bahrain and Oman have both significantly upgraded their intellectual property protection regimes as a consequence of their obligations under their respective recent free trade agreements with the United States. Their current laws now exceed the minimum standards required by TRIPS.

Yemen is neither a member of the WTO and thereby not a signatory to TRIPS, nor a GCC member state. It currently enjoys Observer status while seeking admission to the WTO, but it may well be another few years or more before it achieves membership. Yemen will need to significantly expand and upgrade its intellectual property regime, which essentially comprises just the single non-compliant law, before it can attain membership. As at June 2008, Yemen's intellectual property regime had not been subject to close scrutiny by WTO members.

4.2.1 National treatment and most-favoured-nation treatment

The national treatment provision of TRIPS forbids discrimination between a member's own nationals and the nationals of other members, and requires the member to accord treatment no less favourable than that accorded to its own nationals. The MFN treatment obligation forbids discrimination between the nationals of other members by requiring that any advantage a member grants to the nationals of another member must be extended immediately and unconditionally to the nationals of all other members, even if such treatment is more favourable than that which the member gives to its own nationals.

Specific provision for both the national treatment and MFN treatment obligations of TRIPS Articles 3–5 is the exception rather than the rule and appears to be somewhat inconsistently applied within a state's various laws. While most provide a general statement addressing national treatment, few make similar provision for MFN treatment.

Hence, Kuwait's copyright law declares that protection is extended to works published for the first time in any WTO member state by authors who are nationals of a WTO member.[5] Yet its patents, designs and industrial models amendment law of 2001 retains the national treatment provisions from the original 1962 law, which restricted the right to submit patent applications to foreigners residing in Kuwait, and nationals or residents of countries which accorded Kuwait reciprocal treatment.[6] It stops short of making any mention of MFN treatment.

Qatar allows the protection of its copyright law to include works protected by international agreement to which Qatar is a party, but limits the protection of its trademarks law to foreign countries which accord reciprocal treatment to Qataris – notwithstanding any international bilateral or multilateral agreement to which it may be party.[7]

Saudi Arabia's 2002 trademark law states that protection may be extended to nationals of any country which treats the Kingdom on a reciprocal basis, as well as to a country which is a signatory to an international agreement to which the Kingdom is also a signatory. Its copyright law of similar vintage extends protection to works copyrighted under international agreements to which the Kingdom is a party. Yet its later industrial-property law of 2004 does not make any reference to either national treatment or MFN treatment.[8]

The UAE's original trademark and patents laws of 1992 make stated provision for reciprocal treatment, the patents law also providing for the application of international treaties to which the state is a signatory (these provisions remaining unchanged in the respective 2002 amending legislation); the copyright law makes no reference to either national treatment or MFN treatment.[9]

Bahrain and Oman, no doubt reflecting the imperatives of their recent free trade agreements with the United States, adopt a slightly different approach. Rather than placing weight on the inclusion of simple declarations on national treatment or MFN treatment, they incorporate throughout their laws a significantly greater degree of detail on prerogatives, conditions and restrictions relating to rights holders which effectively ensures that equal treatment exists regardless of country of origin. Thus, Oman's copyright law alone makes any specific reference to national treatment or MFN treatment.[10]

Likewise, the states whose laws make only passing reference to either national treatment or MFN treatment would argue, as Oman has done before the WTO, that the brevity of any specific provision in their laws does not necessarily preclude the enjoyment of such treatment equally by both nationals and foreign rights holders.[11] They would contend that, since their laws do not impose any nationality conditions or limitations in respect of rights holders to whom the protection of the laws might be extended to the detriment of non-nationals, national treatment and MFN treatment may be assumed; accordingly, they hold that they comply with their obligations under TRIPS Articles 3–5. In any case, brevity or absence of specific provision is more than offset by the increasing degree of obligation by the states to international conventions which themselves require commitment to national treatment and MFN treatment between the convention signatories.

Even Yemen's pre-TRIPS law of 1994 provides a succinct declaration on national treatment to the effect that the rights relating to a work, invention, trademark or design of foreign origin shall be recognised to the extent that the foreign country concerned accords the same treatment to Yemeni works, or accords treatment in accordance with international agreements to which Yemen is a party.[12]

4.3 Copyright and neighbouring rights

4.3.1 TRIPS copyright provisions and obligations (Articles 9–14)

TRIPS utilises and adds to the substantive provisions enshrined in the Berne Convention, as the foundation for its copyright protection standards. TRIPS does not fully elucidate the nature of literary or artistic works entitled to protection, but instead obliges members to comply with Articles 1–21, except Article 6*bis,* and the Appendix of the Convention, which address issues of protectable subject matter, minimum terms of protection, rights to be conferred and permissible limitations to those rights.[13] The Convention Appendix allows developing countries, under certain conditions, to make some limitations to author's rights in respect of the translation and reproduction of copyright works. The provisions for the protection of moral rights, as enshrined in Article 6*bis* of the Convention, are specifically excluded from TRIPS and therefore receive neither acknowledgement nor protection. However, TRIPS Article 2.2 and Article 9.1 still require members to comply with other Convention provisions which address some moral rights elements, namely, Article 10 (3) (right of attribution in quotations of the author's work), Article 11*bis* (2) (moral rights in broadcasting and public communication) and Appendix Article IV (3) (right of attribution in the case of translations or reproductions produced under licence).

TRIPS Article 9.2 confirms that copyright protection shall extend to expressions and not to ideas, procedures, methods of operation or mathematical concepts as such. Computer programs, whether in source or object code, shall be protected as literary works under the Berne Convention and hence only those limitations that apply to literary works may be applied to computer programs.[14] Databases and other compilations of data or other material, whether in machine-readable or other form, are similarly protected, provided that they constitute intellectual creations by reason of the selection or arrangement of their contents.[15] Such protection does not extend to the data or material itself and is without prejudice to any copyright otherwise subsisting in the data or material.

TRIPS Article 11 establishes the existence of rental rights for computer programs and of cinematographic works in certain circumstances. Authors shall be provided with the right to authorise or to prohibit the commercial rental of originals or copies of their copyright works. In the case of cinematographic works, the exclusive rental right is subject to the so-called impairment test: a member is excepted from the obligation unless such rental has led to widespread copying of such works which is materially impairing the exclusive right of reproduction conferred on authors. In the case of computer programs, the obligation to provide rental rights does not apply where the program itself is not the essential object of the rental.

The related rights pertaining to performers, producers of phonograms and broadcasting organisations are stipulated in TRIPS Article 14. Rather than simply refer to the Berne Convention, as it has done in respect of literary and artistic works, TRIPS reproduces the substantive rights recognised by the Rome Convention, albeit in a simplified form. Performers may prevent the unauthorised fixation of their live performance, the reproduction of such fixation and the unauthorised broadcasting and the communication to the public of their live performance, although the right covers only aural and not audiovisual fixations. Producers of phonograms are entitled to an exclusive reproduction right and an exclusive rental right, while broadcasting organisations have the right to prohibit the unauthorised fixation, reproduction and rebroadcasting of broadcasts, as well as any other public communication of their television broadcasts.

TRIPS addresses the question of terms of protection by referring back to the Berne Convention or by reproducing the provisions of the Rome Convention. In the case of an artistic or literary work, photograph or work of applied art, TRIPS defers to the Berne Convention provisions.[16] TRIPS also provides that, except for a photographic work or a work of applied art, where a minimum term is calculated on a basis other than the life of a natural person, the term shall be not less than 50 years from the end of the calendar year in which the work was published or otherwise made.[17] However, TRIPS restates the terms of protection stipulated in Article 14 of the Rome Convention for performances, phonograms and broadcasts, and extends them to 50 years for works by performers and producers of phonograms and 20 years for broadcasting organisations, calculated from the end of the year in which the performance, recording or broadcast took place.[18]

Where members permit limitations or exceptions to exclusive rights, they are required to confine them to certain special cases which do not conflict with a normal commercial exploitation of the work and which do not unreasonably prejudice the legitimate interests of the right holder. In any case, any such limitations or exceptions must remain within the extent permitted by the Berne or Rome Conventions.

4.3.2 Current regional copyright legislation

Although the GCC member states generally have long provided some limited degree of protection to a narrow range of published artistic, literary and scientific works through laws dealing with proper commercial practice and the control of publications and publishing houses, the introduction of regional copyright protection legislation has been a very recent phenomenon. The catalyst for the introduction of specific copyright laws arose more from external pressures from developed countries for frameworks to protect their copyrightable works in the region, rather than a proactive local appreciation of the imperatives for comprehensive copyright protection. As discussed earlier, not all states had copyright laws in force when TRIPS was introduced, and those laws that were in existence fell some way short of the TRIPS minimum protection standards. Hence, most states have been required to revisit their copyright laws with a view to bringing them at least up to the standard of TRIPS and the other major international conventions and somewhat closer to the standards of protection being demanded by the major developed countries.

Bahrain, Oman, Qatar, Saudi Arabia and the UAE have all undergone the process of initially enacting copyright laws and subsequently substantially amending or replacing them, in each case since 2000. Oman underwent this process as part of its WTO accession process, introducing its first copyright law in 1996 at the time of its initial application but subsequently replacing it as a consequence of the WTO legislation examination process, just prior to acceding to the WTO Protocol in October 2000. The Saudi law has been through similar scrutiny. Qatar introduced its current law in 2002, but is reportedly in the process of upgrading it. The UAE's 2002 law retains levels of protection previously provided by its copyright law of a decade earlier, but strengthens the nature of the protection for computer programs and redefines the rights of performers, producers of sound recordings and broadcast organisations. The law reflects a dramatic shift in attitudes towards the protection of all copyrightable material within the UAE government, business and community environments since the original law was implemented.

Bahrain and Oman now represent the benchmark for regional copyright protection, both in terms of the standards and the comprehensive nature of their respective laws. Both have recently upgraded their laws to give effect to the substantially increased levels of copyright protection arising from their obligations under their respective free trade agreements with the United States. Particular attention has been given to protection and enforcement of copyright in the digital environment. Consequently they each possess the most advanced and comprehensive copyright laws in the Gulf region.

Kuwait's post-TRIPS law is now the longest-standing copyright law amongst the GCC member states, dating from 1999 (see Table 4.1). The law contains the lightest penalties of any of the copyright laws, a situation that has caused it to attract considerable criticism from the United States and from the international copyright industry lobby groups. Kuwait reportedly upgraded the law during 2007, but has yet to bring it into effect.

Most states have now acceded to the Berne Convention, although this does not necessarily greatly enhance the level of copyright protection they provide – with the exception of the protection of an author's moral rights, the standards of the Berne Convention have already been largely incorporated into TRIPS. More recently, some of the states have also acceded to the WIPO Internet Treaties, namely the WIPO Copyright Treaty (WCT) and the WIPO Performances and Phonograms Treaty of 1996 (WPPT), both of which aim at providing enhanced levels of protection for technological and internet-based copyright material.

4.3.3 The nature of copyright protection

Amongst the copyright laws of the Gulf states, an author is variously defined as:

> 'except as proved otherwise, any person who publishes a work and claims authorship either by stating his name on the work or by using any other means to claim authorship of the work.'[19]

Or elsewhere, quite simply as:

> 'the natural person who creates the work.'[20]

The declared purpose common to all the copyright laws is to protect the authors of creative works which are of a literary, scientific, artistic and cultural nature in general regardless of the nature of such works, or the type thereof, or the method of expression used therein, or the purpose of writing or creation.[21] The laws generally replicate the range of protectable works as listed in the Berne Convention Article 2, including derived works with creative elements and translated works. As stipulated by the Bahraini and Omani laws (in virtually identical lists), created works of literature, arts and science enjoy protection regardless of their value, type, form of expression or purpose of production. The protected works include:

- books, booklets, articles, pamphlets and other written works;
- computer programs and databases, whether in the source or object code;
- works that are delivered orally such as lectures, speeches, sermons and other oral works of a similar nature;

Table 4.1 Current copyright laws and international conventions in the Gulf states

Bahrain:	Legislative Decree No. 22 of 2006 with respect to the Protection of Copyright. Legislative Decree No. 19 of 2005 ratifying Bahrain's accession to the WIPO Performances and Phonograms Treaty (WPPT) and the WIPO Copyright Treaty (WCT). Legislative Decree No. 30 of 1996 ratifying Bahrain's accession to the Berne Convention for the Protection of Literary and Artistic works.
Kuwait:	Law No. 64 of 1999, governing Copyrights and Neighbouring Rights (issued as Law No. 5 of 1999 during the period of dissolution of Parliament, and reissued by the new Parliament as Law No. 64 of 1999). Law No. 16 of 1986, acceding to the Arab Agreement for the Protection of Author's Rights.
Oman:	Royal Decree No. 65/2008, the Law of Copyrights and Neighbouring Rights. Royal Decree No. 53/2005 ratifying Oman's accession to the WIPO Performances and Phonograms Treaty (WPPT) and the WIPO Copyright Treaty (WCT). Royal Decree No. 63/1998 ratifying Oman's accession to the Berne Convention for the Protection of Literary and Artistic works and the Paris Convention for the Protection of Industrial Property.
Qatar:	Law No. 7 of 2002 in respect of Copyrights and Neighbouring Rights. Law of July 2005 in respect of Qatar's accession to the WIPO Performances and Phonograms Treaty (WPPT) and the WIPO Copyright Treaty (WCT). Law No. 31 of 2001 in respect of Qatar's accession to the Berne Convention for the Protection of Literary and Artistic works. Law No. 50 of 1986 in respect of Qatar's accession to the League of Arab States Agreement for the Protection of Author's Rights
Saudi Arabia:	Royal Decree No. M/41 of 1424 AH (2003) concerning Copyright. Royal Decree No. M/48 of 1424 AH (2003) ratifying Saudi Arabia's accession to the Berne Convention for the Protection of Literary and Artistic works and the Paris Convention for the Protection of Industrial Property. Royal Decree No. M/12 of 1414 AH (1994), assenting to the Universal Copyright Convention.
UAE:	Federal Law No. 10 of 2005, ratifying the UAE's accession to the WIPO Performances and Phonograms Treaty (WPPT). Federal Law of October 2004 ratifying the UAE's accession to the International Convention for the Protection of Performers, Producers of Phonograms and Broadcasting Organizations (Rome Convention). Federal Law of April 2004 ratifying the UAE's accession to the WIPO Copyright Treaty (WCT). Federal Law No. 7 of 2002, concerning Copyright and Neighbouring Rights.
Yemen:	Law No. 19 of 1994 in respect of Intellectual Property. Accession of April 2008 to the Berne Convention for the Protection of Literary and Artistic works

Source: compiled by the author

- dramatic and dramatico-musical works, dances, pantomimes and other works created for theatrical performance;
- musical compositions with or without words;
- audio-visual works such as cinematographic works and works for television;
- line or colour drawings, sculptures, engravings, lithography, printing on fabric, wood or metals, and any similar works in the field;
- photographic works and works analogous to photography;
- works of applied and plastic arts either handcrafted or industrial;
- illustrations, geographical maps, designs, sketches and three-dimensional works related to geography, topography, architecture or science;
- the title of the work if creative.[22]

Also protected are derivative works, such as translations, adaptations and orchestrations, as well as collections of works and expressions of folklore, such as encyclopedias and anthologies, provided there is creativity in the selection or the arrangement of the contents of such works.[23]

By the same token, the copyright laws replicate the Berne Convention's list of works to which protection is commonly not extended, such as legislation, court judgments and administrative determinations, international agreements and treaties, official documents and their translations, or news which is published, broadcast or otherwise placed in the public domain. However, they also generally make provision for the protection to be extended to folklore or works of national culture, which are not mentioned in either TRIPS or the Convention.

With the exception of the Kuwaiti and Yemeni laws, the states provide an added measure of protection for software, with specific attention given to infringements, and penalties in particular being increased in respect of technology-related offences.[24] In respect of the requirement of TRIPS Article 10, computer programs and software are generally included in those works to which protection is extended, and described in sufficiently broad terms to give some degree of flexibility to allow for technological advances. Databases are also protected if they are creative in the arrangement and selection of their subject matter. The extent of the exception to this provision is very limited – such as the Saudi provision for the production of 'one reserve copy of computer programs . . . for the purpose of protecting the original, whilst keeping the original with the user, to show upon request'.[25] The Emirati law covers even more ground than the other states by allowing for further discretion to be granted to the responsible minister to determine what may constitute computer programs and applications, databases and works analogous to them, to which protection may be later extended as further technological advances may require.[26]

In accordance with the exception provision of TRIPS Article 13, the laws allow for a limited range of circumstances and situations in which protected works may be used without the permission of the author or right holder.

They generally include limited reasonable use by libraries and educational institutions, use for teaching and research, use in news or current affairs in print or broadcast media, and personal use.

Except for Bahrain and Oman in one context, and Yemen in another, the states generally adhere to the requirements of TRIPS Articles 12 and 14.5, and the Berne Convention Articles 7 and 7*bis* in respect of minimum terms of protection granted to copyrightable works, with provision commonly existing as follows:

- for the works of a sole author, the lifetime of the author plus 50 years;
- in respect of the works of joint authors, the lifetime of the last surviving author plus 50 years;
- for works published under a pseudonym, anonymously (unless the identity of the author becomes known) or posthumously, 50 years from first publication;
- for cinematographic works, works of applied articles and photographic works, 50 years from first publication;
- in respect of the works of performers, 50 years from the first recording of the performance or, if no recording was made, from the first performance;
- in respect of the works of producers of sound recordings, 50 years from the first production, publication or fixation (if not published) of the sound recording;
- for works whose ownership is vested in a legal entity, 50 years from the first publication or production;
- in respect of broadcasts, 20 years from the date of first broadcast.

The period of protection is generally calculated from the beginning of the year following the year in which the death of the author, or the first publication, production, recording, fixation or broadcast took place, although some exceptions do exist.

The Saudi copyright law distinguishes between the main corpus of artistic works and photographs and works of applied arts. It extends to photographs and works of applied arts a period of protection of only 25 years, which is actually consistent with the standards set by TRIPS Article 12 and Berne Convention Article 7(4).[27] Other states do not bother to make the Saudi or TRIPS/Berne distinction between these and other literary or artistic works, thereby neatly avoiding the necessity of otherwise defining works of applied articles and distinguishing them from other works.

The Bahraini and Omani laws, meanwhile, offer significantly increased periods of protection, to reflect their obligations under the intellectual property protection provisions of their recent free trade agreements with the United States. Hence, Bahrain has extended protection for the above categories for a further 20 years to a total of 70 years, with the exception of broadcasts which still enjoy 20 years' protection.[28]

Oman provides an even further extensive period of protection and in so doing has established a whole new benchmark for the region. In accordance with the terms of its free trade agreement, literary works are protected for the life of the author plus 70 years, while joint works enjoy protection for 70 years following the year of the death of the last surviving author.[29] However, audio-visual works and collective works, anonymous and pseudonymous works, performances and sound recordings are all now protected for 95 years following the year of first publication.[30] Furthermore, if such works are not published or otherwise made public within their first 25 years, protection exists for 120 years following their creation. Broadcasting programmes retain the commonplace 20-year period of protection.

By contrast, the Yemeni law falls far short of TRIPS and Berne Convention requirements. It provides for the following periods of protection:[31]

- literary works: life of creator plus 30 years;
- films or TV productions: 25 years;
- photographs: 10 years;
- broadcasts: 2 years (generally) or 3 years for TV broadcasts.

4.3.4 Moral rights and economic rights

Although TRIPS specifically excludes any provision for the protection of an author's moral rights *per se,* they receive attention in the Berne Convention and are addressed in the copyright laws of all Gulf states. The laws all draw a distinction between an author's moral rights and economic rights and, in some cases, between those of the performer. The laws generally provide that the author's moral rights are inalienable and include the right to decide whether his work should be published and the manner of its publication; the economic rights encompass the right to utilise his work commercially or to authorise others to do so.[32] The scope of the author's moral rights includes the right to:

- have his/her name or pseudonym indicated on his/her work;
- object to any alteration, deformation or any modification of his/her work;
- object to any distortion and to prohibit any other use of the work which would be prejudicial to the author's honour or reputation;
- withdraw the work from publication, under certain circumstances.

Economic rights include the exclusive right of the author to commercially exploit the work by carrying out, or authorising others to carry out, any of the following acts:

- reproduction of the work;
- translation of the work;

- making excerpts, musical arrangement or other transformation of the work;
- distribution to the public of the work through sale;
- rental to the public of audiovisual works or computer programs;
- public performance of the work;
- communication of the work to the public.

The economic rights are transferable to other parties. Such transfer must generally be in writing and be registered and lodged with the relevant ministry for it to be valid and have legal standing. The rights are also transferable wholly or in part by inheritance or by legal action. The Qatari and Saudi laws also stipulate that, where an author dies intestate, the rights devolve to the persons entitled to receive them, according to the provisions of *Shariah* law in respect of inheritance.[33]

The notion of providing any form of protection for neighbouring rights was largely unknown in the Gulf and was therefore conspicuously absent from the states' copyright laws until first incorporated by Oman into its law of 2000.[34] The current laws now generally provide an enhanced level of protection for performers, producers of sound recordings and broadcasting organisations. Saudi Arabia and Yemen, however, generally defer the specification of such rights to their corresponding responsible authorities to detail through ministerial regulation. The laws differentiate between the respective rights of the performer, producer and broadcaster, bringing their laws more into line with the requirements of TRIPS Article 14. They generally provide for performers to have the moral right to be identified with respect to their performances and to object to any distortion, mutilation or any modification of their performances. They also enjoy economic rights to:

- fix or record their unfixed performances;
- broadcast or communicate to the public their unfixed performances;
- reproduce sound recordings containing an unauthorised fixation of their performances;
- rent sound recordings containing their performances;
- make recordings of their performances available to the public.[35]

Producers of sound recordings and broadcast organisations, meanwhile, enjoy only economic rights, such rights being the exclusive right to carry out or authorise the direct or indirect reproduction of their recordings or broadcasts in any form, the rental or sale to the public of copies of the recording, or the rebroadcasting of the original broadcast.[36] Qatar and the UAE place limits on these rights. Qatar restricts the rental right of performers and producers to sound recordings only, without recognising the rental rights of broadcasters; the UAE extends the rental right of performers to audiovisual works, but also does not recognise rental rights for broadcast organisations.[37]

The distinction between the respective rights of the various contributors to joint and collective works receives somewhat briefer attention than that devoted to rights of performers, producers and broadcasters.[38] Where the respective contributions in respect of joint works can be identified and separated, each contributor enjoys his moral and economic rights in respect of his part separately to the other contributors and may exploit his own part provided that this does not prejudice the exploitation of the jointly owned work. But where the respective contributions cannot be separated, all are considered equal partners in the ownership of the whole work, unless they have otherwise agreed, and no partner may solely exercise any rights without the agreement of the other partners.

In the case of a joint musical composition, the composer retains the exclusive right to the public performance, execution, publication or copying of the whole work, but without prejudice to the right of the lyricist to separately publish his own created part.[39] Where the joint musical production involves choreography which has special predominance or elements, such as opera or ballet, the choreographer may utilise a public performance of the whole work, while the composer may utilise the musical element provided that he does not use it as a basis for another musical work, unless otherwise agreed.

In the case of a joint work for cinema, radio, television or other broadcast, contributing partnership includes the scenarist or author, the scriptwriter, the editor or adaptor, the composer, the director and the original author if the joint work is an adaptation or extraction from another prior work.[40] The scenarist, scriptwriter, editor and director are jointly entitled to produce the adapted work, notwithstanding any objections from the author of the original work or musical composer but without prejudice to the rights of these two resulting from their participation in the joint composition. The author and composer are still entitled to publish their respective particles of the work in any other manner, unless otherwise agreed.

Where the respective contributions cannot be distinguished and the work was created under the direction of a natural person or legal entity who also undertakes responsibility for publication, that person or legal entity is entitled to enjoy both the moral and the economic rights involved in creating the collective work.[41]

4.3.5 Translated works and compulsory licensing

Some states take advantage of the provision in respect of the translation of foreign works, as allowed by TRIPS Article II, which provides *inter alia* that a member may grant to one of its nationals a licence to translate and publish a foreign-language work that has not been translated and published in that member within three years of the original publication of the work. This provision, which amounts to a form of compulsory licensing, continues to meet with opposition from some developed countries and particularly the copyright exporting countries, which see it as a form of potential encroachment on the monopolistic nature of their copyright rights and a potential loss of income generation. It is an area which has been discussed in the United States free trade agreements with both Bahrain and Oman. Perhaps not surprisingly, therefore, Bahrain and Oman have removed such provisions from their current laws.

While an author's right to translate his/her work (or to authorise others to do so) is generally acknowledged, Qatar, the UAE and Saudi Arabia make provision for the responsible minister to grant a non-exclusive and non-assignable licence for the translation into Arabic and/or the domestic publication of an Arabic translation of a foreign language work if the author of the original work fails to exercise translation rights within a specified period of time (3–5 years) after its original publication.[42] As a general principle, the ministerial authority is restricted to foreign works which may be desirable or necessary for educational or research purposes, but it may also be exercised where it would be in the public interest to do so. Saudi Arabia extends this right to works that have already been translated and published in Arabic in the Kingdom, but which have gone out of print and the author or translator has failed to authorise further publication.[43]

4.3.6 Management of collective rights

The principle of collective-rights management and practice of creating copyright collection and protection societies goes beyond TRIPS and the Berne Convention. Although the principle and practice is now common in developed countries, it has not yet gained wide acceptance or recognition in the Gulf states. Bahrain, Oman and the UAE have taken some steps towards copyright protection management by including provision for the collective administration of copyright and the neighbouring rights. They give specialised collection societies legal status and enable the holders of copyright and the neighbouring rights to assign their economic rights to them to commercially exploit and administer on the right holders' behalf.[44]

The societies are forbidden to discriminate amongst the right holders with whom they enter into management contracts. They must keep registers including the names of their members, their positions and the jobs they contracted, indicating the type of job, duration and the agreed licensing fees. The societies must be registered and annually licensed by the responsible ministry and must inform the ministry of any change in these registers.

One likely impact of the Bahraini, Omani and UAE provisions is that collective management organisations already established in developed countries may well be encouraged to establish operations or set up regional associations. Such activity would not only improve the enforcement of domestic copyright and neighbouring rights protection but also spearhead the spread of collective management societies to the other states. Such activity would also benefit the right holders and serve as another effective mechanism for the control of unauthorised and counterfeit copyrightable works of all descriptions. Currently, effective copyright collection agencies do not operate in the Gulf region.

4.3.7 Technological protection measures, rights management and internet service provision

Reflecting the changing nature of infringing activity away from traditional print-based acts to electronic and broadcast-based acts of an increasingly technical sophistication, the more recent laws now take cognisance of acts which facilitate or enable the commission of infringements relating to the manufacture or import of electronic deactivation devices, satellite decoding devices, or the illegal modification or removal of such devices or information concerning transmission broadcast rights. These new clauses are directly aimed at confronting the burgeoning industries concerned with the production of counterfeit computer software including games, pirated music and video recordings and downloads. They are also aimed at more recent internet-based material, counterfeit smart cards, and decoders/descramblers for the multitudinous satellite TV channels for which the Gulf region in general is squarely placed within the transmission footprints.

With the exception of Kuwait and Yemen, the region's laws now generally recognise, to a lesser or greater degree, the illicit removal or alteration of any technical protection or rights information intended to regulate or limit public access to any work, performance, recording, broadcast or transmission as an infringing activity.

Each in very similar language, the current Bahraini, Omani, Qatari and Saudi laws now include provision for the prohibition of the following acts related to technological protection measures, rights management information and the retransmission of television signals:

- circumventing without authority any effective technological measure that controls access to a protected work, performance, phonogram or other subject matter;
- manufacturing, importing, distributing or otherwise dealing in any devices, products, components or services which are promoted as being able to circumvent any effective technological measure, or have only a limited commercially significant purpose or use other than circumvention, or are primarily designed, produced or performed for the purpose of enabling circumvention;
- committing any of the following without authority, and knowing or having reasonable grounds to know that it would induce, facilitate or conceal an infringement of any copyright or related right:
  - knowingly removing or altering any rights management information;
  - importing or distributing rights management information knowing that the rights management information has been removed or altered without authority; or

  - importing or distributing, broadcasting or making publicly available copies of works, performances or phonograms, knowing that rights management information has been removed or altered without authority;
- manufacturing, marketing or otherwise distributing a tangible or intangible device or system, knowing or having reason to know that it is primarily of assistance in decoding an encrypted program-carrying satellite signal;
- receiving or further distributing a program-carrying signal that originated as an encrypted satellite signal knowing that it has been decoded without proper authorisation.[45]

Bahrain goes a step further by including detailed provisions concerning the proper conduct of internet service providers, reflecting, again, its obligations under its free trade agreement. The law provides that a service provider shall be held to be a contributory infringer where it is established that the provider knowingly caused, induced or materially contributed to, through his system or network, an infringement of the rights of a copyright holder by another party. However, a service provider who complies with certain conditions shall not be held liable for any damages for infringements that may occur in the course of normal service provision business.[46] The conditions require that the service provider:

- does not receive any financial benefit directly attributable to the infringement;
- does not make any modification to the content of the material during transmission through its network;
- does not select the recipients of the electronic copy of the material, except as an automatic response to a third-party request;
- expeditiously removes or disables access on its network to the material upon receipt of notification of an infringement;
- ensures that, where the material is subject to conditions on user access at the originating site, access is limited to authorised users;
- complies with widely internationally accepted rules concerning the refreshing, reloading or other updating of material when specified by the party making the material available online in accordance with widely internationally accepted standards in respect of data communications protocol for the system or network through which that person makes the material available; and
- does not interfere with technology that is consistent with widely internationally accepted standards on information governing use of the material.

Where a service provider satisfies or complies with these requirements, the injunctive relief which a court may grant against the service provider for infringing activity is limited to orders to disable access to infringing material, link or online location, or to terminate a specified account. The service provider shall then be exempted from liability for any resulting claims. A copyright office is authorised, on complaint by a copyright or related right holder of an alleged infringement, to require a service provider to make available to both the office and the right holder any information in its possession as to the identity of the alleged infringer.

Those laws which give particular attention to infringements in the digital/technological environment also draw a distinction between the scale of penalties that may be imposed in respect of infringing acts across the broad copyright spectrum, with provision for the more severe penalties to be applied to the infringements in the digital/technological environment.[47]

4.3.8 Infringements

The nature of copyright infringement provisions in the earlier copyright laws of the Gulf states dealt mainly with the traditional form of unauthorised reproduction of print material. In the more recent laws, there has emerged a pattern of increasing complexity in the nature of the infringing acts, accompanied by a shift in emphasis away from the more conservative or conventional forms of infringement involving print-based or hard-copy material towards infringing acts within an electronic/digital context.

While the states still recognise the traditional or conventional infringements against a right holder's moral rights, they also recognise infringements against economic rights, such as unlawful alteration, publication, reproduction, translation, performance and broadcast, and importation or promotion of any imitated or forged works. The older laws of Kuwait (1999) and Yemen (1994) do not go any further. The newer laws of Bahrain and Oman now include fairly extensive provisions in respect of infringing acts in the digital context, notably relating to technological protection measures, rights management information and the responsibilities and liabilities of internet service providers.

4.4 Trademarks

4.4.1 TRIPS provisions and obligations (Articles 15–21)

The fundamental principle of trademark protection provided by TRIPS is that any sign, or any combination of signs, capable of distinguishing the goods and services of one undertaking from others must be eligible for registration as a trademark, provided that it is visually perceptible. Such signs may take the form of particular words, including personal names, letters, numerals, figurative elements and combinations of colours as well as any combination thereof. Where signs are not inherently capable of distinguishing the relevant goods or services, members may require, as an additional condition for eligibility for registration, that distinctiveness be acquired through use. Members are free to determine whether to allow the registration of signs that are not visually perceptible, such as sounds or smells. Certain limited exceptions to the rights conferred by a trademark, such as fair use of descriptive terms, may be permitted, provided that such exceptions take account of the legitimate interests of the owner of the trademark and of third parties.

The owner of a registered trademark must be granted the exclusive right to prevent all third parties not having the owner's consent from using in the course of trade signs for goods or services which are identical or similar to those in respect of which the trademark is registered, where such use would result in a likelihood of confusion. In case of the use of an identical sign for identical goods or services, a likelihood of confusion must be presumed.

TRIPS takes the provisions of Article 6*bis* of the Paris Convention in respect of prohibiting the registration or use of a mark which is confusingly similar to a well-known mark that is either already registered or in use for identical or similar goods, and extends them, *mutatis mutandis*, to marks in respect of services. It further takes these provisions and applies them to marks for goods and services which are not similar to goods and services for which a well-known trademark is used or registered if their use would indicate a connection between those goods or services and those of the owner of the well-known mark, to the detriment of the owner's interests.

Initial registration, and each subsequent renewal, of a trademark shall be for a term of not less than seven years, while registration shall be renewable indefinitely. Where use is required as a condition of registration, cancellation on the grounds of non-use can occur only after three years of uninterrupted non-use, unless valid reasons based on the existence of obstacles to such use are shown by the trademark owner. Use of a trademark by another person, when subject to the control of its owner, must be recognised as use of the trademark for the purpose of maintaining registration status.

4.4.2 Regional trademark laws

Trademark laws are the longest-standing intellectual property protection laws in the Gulf states. They have faced scrutiny from both regional and international sources and consequently been subject to review processes which have given them the best opportunity of all intellectual property laws in the states to reach TRIPS compliance. The fact that they also address an area of commercial endeavour which has been longstanding, locally active and financially lucrative for local traders and businesses means that they have also had the opportunity to be tested in respect of their efficacy and practicability.

All GCC member states have upgraded or entirely replaced their early trademark laws since the introduction of TRIPS. Most of the enhancements have been carried out since the expiration in 2000 of the TRIPS-permitted transitional period for developing countries and have thereby brought them generally into compliance with TRIPS requirements. Oman replaced its original 1996 law in 2000 as part of its WTO accession process, but has since incorporated trademarks protection into a single comprehensive law encompassing all areas of industrial property.[48] This was a logical and sensible move, since the year 2000 suite of seven *sui generis* intellectual property laws contained many provisions, particularly in respect of enforcement and sanctions, that were identical across all seven laws. Qatar and Saudi Arabia likewise replaced their original laws in 2001 and 2002. Kuwait and the UAE were content to retain their laws, but introduced a range of amendments – sweeping amendments in the case of the UAE – in 2001 and 2002 respectively.

Bahrain introduced in 2006 a new law to replace what had been the longest-standing and therefore the most conservative trademark law in the region, namely its pre-TRIPS law of 1991. This 1991 law had been created by the excision of the trademark provisions from the original pre-independence omnibus regulation of 1955, as amended in 1977 into a new and specific trademark law. Consequently the law still contained some minor elements from the 1955 and the 1977 amendments. More importantly, it was strikingly deficient in respect of crucial elements such as protection for well-known marks. The new law has provided the opportunity to redress a number of the inconsistencies and contradictions which arose from the past incomplete restructurings of the original 1955 legislation. However, since the implementing regulations for the 2006 law have yet to be issued, the former law with its 1955 and 1977 vestiges is still in effect.

Kuwait, a regional leader in the codification of its commercial laws in the 1960s, has since trailed behind the other Gulf states in the status of all its intellectual property laws, including its trademark law. It still incorporates its trademark protection into a dedicated chapter of its commercial code originally enacted in 1961. The trademark provisions of the commercial code have been amended a number of times, the most recent of any substance being in 1999, although further minor changes were subsequently introduced in 2001. But no changes were made to the nature of infringements, nor increases introduced to the level of penalties that existed in the original law. This situation has caused Kuwait to attract critical attention from within the WTO and from the United States in particular through its Special 301 Reports, for the perceived inadequacy, laxity and non-deterrent character of its trademark protection.

Yemen, however, still relies on its pre-TRIPS omnibus intellectual property law of 1994, which will require substantial changes to bring it to TRIPS compliance as part of Yemen's eventual WTO accession.

Table 4.2 shows Current Trademark Laws and Conventions in the Gulf States.

In the last few years, some of the Gulf states have also shown increasing willingness to commit to or at least follow some of the WIPO-administered international agreements that complement the TRIPS trademark provisions.

Table 4.2 Current trademark laws and conventions in the Gulf states

Bahrain:	Legislative Decree No. 11 of 2006 with respect to Trade Marks. Legislative Decree No. 31 of 1996 ratifying Bahrain's accession to the Paris Convention for the Protection of Industrial Property. Legislative Decree No. 18 of 2005 ratifying Bahrain's accession to the Protocol Relating to the Madrid Agreement for the International Registration of Marks. Legislative Decree No. 17 of 2005 ratifying Bahrain's accession to the Nice Agreement Concerning the International Classification of Goods and Services for the Purpose of the Registration of Marks. Legislative Decree No. 18 of 2007 ratifying Bahrain's accession to the Trademark Law Treaty.
Kuwait:	Law No. 2 of 1961, the Commercial Code, as amended by Law No. 6 of 1980, Law No. 3 of 1999 and Law No. 1 of 2001.
Oman:	Royal Decree No. 67/2008, The Law on Industrial Property Rights. Royal Decree No. 63/1998 promulgating the Sultanate's accession to the Paris Convention for the Protection of Industrial Property and the Berne Convention for the Protection of Literary and Artistic Works. Royal Decree No. 37/2000 promulgating the Sultanate's accession to the Protocol Relating to the Madrid Agreement for the International Registration of Marks and to the Trademark Law Treaty.
Qatar:	Law No. 18 of 2007, adopting the GCC Unified Trademark Regulation in Qatar Law No. 9 of 2002 in respect of Trade Marks, Business Names and Data, Industrial Designs and Geographical Indications. Decree No. 31 of 2001 in respect of Qatar's accession to the Paris Convention for the Protection of Industrial Property.
Saudi Arabia:	Royal Decree No. M/21 of 1423 AH (2002), the Law of Trademarks. Royal Decree No. M/48 of 1424 AH (2003), ratifying Saudi Arabia's accession to the Paris Convention for the Protection of Industrial Property and the Berne Convention for the Protection of Literary and Artistic Works.
UAE:	Federal Law No. 52 of 2007, adopting the GCC Unified Trademark Regulation in the UAE. Federal Law No. 37 of 1992 concerning Trade Marks, as amended by Federal Law No. 8 of 2002. Federal Law No. 20 of 1996, concerning the UAE's accession to the Paris Convention for the Protection of Industrial Property.
Yemen:	Law of February 2007 ratifying Yemen's accession to the Paris Convention for the Protection of Industrial Property. Law No. 19 of 1994 in respect of Intellectual Property.
GCC:	Unified Trade Mark Regulation of December 2006

Source: compiled by the author

Hence, all states except Kuwait, but including Yemen, have now acceded to the Paris Convention, the UAE being the first to do so in March 1996 and Yemen being the most recent when it joined in February 2007. By the same token, most of the states have either formally acceded to the Nice Agreement Concerning the International Classification of Goods and Services, or declared that they adhere to the Nice Agreement without going through the accession process, or at least generally use its classifications for the purpose of categorising goods and services for their domestic trademark registrations. The advantage of adopting one of the two latter options is that the states can retain the flexibility to ignore or prohibit certain classification categories, as discussed further below. Bahrain and Oman have been the most active states in this regard, formally acceding to the Berne Convention, the Nice Agreement, the Protocol Relating to the Madrid Agreement for the International Registration of Marks, the WIPO Trademark Law Treaty, although accession to the latter three agreements has been as a direct consequence of their obligations under their recent free trade agreements with the United States.

In December 2006, the GCC Supreme Council adopted the long-awaited GCC Unified Trademark Regulation, a statute that was over 20 years in the making. The primary objective of the Regulation is apparently to replace the trademark laws of each of the GCC member states, thereby introducing a degree of consistency in regional trademark protection. The main features of the Regulation include provision for:

- extension of the definition of a trademark to include sound and smell marks;
- collective marks;
- claims of priority based on prior foreign applications;
- cancellation of a mark for non-use over a period of five consecutive years after registration;
- protection for marks well known in the GCC, even if not registered;
- civil and criminal action by right holders against infringing parties;
- strengthened sanctions, including terms of imprisonment of up to five years, and fines of up to 1 million Saudi riyals ($US270,000).

However, the Regulation does not offer a unified filing system as is the case with the GCC unified patent regulation, and trademark applications will need to continue to be filed separately in each state for protection. The above penalties are consistent with those prevailing in the Saudi trademark law, but are significantly different from those stipulated in the trademark laws of the other states.

The Regulation will be effective only when, or more likely if, it is ratified by the individual member states and the related implementing regulations are issued. What is also uncertain is whether the Regulation or domestic trademark laws will take precedence where the two are inconsistent – which is certainly the case for most states in respect of sanctions.

By early 2008, only Qatar and the UAE had sanctioned the Regulation. The Saudi Cabinet had approved the Regulation, but a Royal Decree was still required to bring it into force in the Kingdom.

4.4.3 Scope of protection for trademarks

Areas in which the original and pre-TRIPS trademark laws of the GCC states generally fell well short of the minimum standards required by TRIPS included:

- protection for well-known marks, in particular foreign marks;
- protection for geographical indications;
- clarification of licensing and transfer provisions;
- expansion of remedies and relief, and sanctions of a deterrent nature;
- border-control measures;
- appeal provisions to independent judicial bodies on administrative decisions.

In particular, the laws of the 1990s lacked provision for protecting well-known marks; a well-known mark could be refused registration and protection if the same or similar mark was already under application. The post-TRIPS laws have gone a long way in addressing these shortcomings. Except for the widely divergent degrees of severity of their respective penalties for infringements, the texts of the latest laws show remarkable similarities in addressing these shortcomings, an indication of the degree of reliance upon the same source for the construction of the laws, and the degree of interaction and consultation between the states on the general thrust of the laws. In respect of the nature of protectable subject matter, the descriptions of each state are generally consistent with the minimum requirements of registrable matter outlined by TRIPS Article 15.

Bahrain and Oman again provide the leading definition of what may constitute a mark, the primary characteristic being the ability to be graphically represented. Bahrain provides that a trademark shall:

> '. . . mean everything that takes a distinctive form such as names, words, signatures, characters, codes, numbers, signposts, seals, drawings, sounds, smells, pictures, inscriptions, packaging, figurative elements, figures, colours, combinations of colours, or any combination thereof or any other sign or a group of signs if used or intended to be used in distinguishing goods or services of an establishment . . .'[49]

Oman goes one step further, including:

> '. . . words (including personal names), designs, letters, colors or combinations of colors, numerals or the shape of goods or their

packaging, holograms, geographical indications, sounds, scents and tastes. Slogans, where they are not long enough to be protected by copyright, shall be protected as marks.'[50]

The older laws retain the more conservative visual presentation requirement. The Saudi law specifically requires trademarks to take a 'visible form capable of being distinguished' or to be 'recognized by sight', and omits smells and sounds from its trademark prescriptions.[51] The Qatari law appears contradictory in respect of what may constitute a trademark, on the one hand defining both trademarks and service marks as 'any visible sign', yet subsequently allowing both sound and smell to be registrable as marks when having a distinctive form.[52] The subsequent reference in the Qatari law does not require that a sound or smell can be registrable only if used in conjunction with other, visible elements. Kuwait allows colour, sound and/or smell if in combination with other visual elements of marks, while the UAE allows sounds to be registrable under the same condition but not smells.[53]

TRIPS Article 17 permits limited exceptions from registrability provided that a balance is maintained between the legitimate interests of the trademark owner and those of third parties, without providing further guidance as to the nature or limits of those limitations. The states commonly allow that the grounds for exclusion of a sign from recognition as a trademark or from registrability generally include the following:

- marks devoid of any distinctive feature, or which consist of merely generic names or ordinary images on goods, products or services;
- marks identical or confusingly similar to the public emblems, flags and other symbols related to the state, Arab or international organisations or any institutions thereof, or any foreign country;
- symbols of the Red Crescent or the Red Cross and other similar symbols as well as any confusingly similar forms of those symbols;
- marks which are identical or similar to symbols of a purely religious nature;
- geographical names and indications where the use thereof may be misleading as to the origin of the goods or services;
- names, photographs or emblems of a third party, unless with prior consent;
- degrees or awards to which an applicant is not lawfully entitled;
- marks which may mislead the public or which contain false data as to the origin of products or services, or their other characteristics, as well as marks containing an imaginary, imitated or forged trade name;
- marks owned by natural or legal persons, dealing with whom is forbidden;
- a mark, the registration of which for some classes of goods or services may decrease the value of other goods or services distinguished by such mark;

- marks containing the words or phrases: 'Privilege', 'Privileged', 'Registered', 'Registered drawings', 'Copyright' or 'Imitation is forgery' or similar words and phrases;
- national and foreign decorations, as well as currency coins and bank notes;
- a mark which is an imitation, reproduction of an essential feature or translation of a well-known trademark or other prior registered mark if this will cause public confusion as to identical or similar, or even dissimilar, goods covered by the mark.[54]

All states affirm that any sign which is offensive to or a violation of public morals, or is contrary to public order, shall not be considered to be a mark and may not be registered as a trademark.

The exclusion from registration in the above listing of 'marks owned by natural or legal persons, dealing with whom is forbidden' applies in particular to marks owned by Israelis or Israeli companies, as part of the boycott of Israel adopted and implemented by members of the League of Arab States as a by-product of the support of the Arab states for Palestine in the Israel–Palestine conflict.[55] The earlier trademark laws of Kuwait and Qatar specifically excluded from registration 'marks which the boycott of Israel Office decides it is identical or similar to an Israeli, mark, symbol or emblem', while those of Oman included an exclusion similar to that above. Qatar and Oman have since removed any reference to the non-registration of trademarks in the context of the boycott of Israel. The Kuwaiti and Saudi current trademark laws still include a similar exclusion, but the adherence now exists more in the principle than the practice.

4.4.4 Well-known marks

Insufficient or total lack of protection in the Gulf states for well-known marks and signs of foreign origin has been an area of particular contention and concern for the developed countries, and the provisions in the states until recently fell far short of the protection required by TRIPS. Article 16 of TRIPS requires countries to provide a level of protection that prevents third parties from taking commercial advantage of the goodwill associated with well-known marks, irrespective of whether those marks are registered or in use locally. The recently updated trademark laws have paid particular attention to this area, and the protection of well-known marks and signs, particularly foreign signs, has now been considerably strengthened. As a general rule, the laws provide that a mark or sign may not be registered if:

- it is identical with, or confusingly similar to, or constitutes a translation of, a mark or trade name which is well known in the country for identical or similar goods or services of another enterprise; or

- it is not identical with or similar to a well-known mark, but its use would indicate a connection between those goods or services and the owner of the well-known mark and the interests of the owner of the well-known mark would likely be damaged by such use.[56]

A well-known mark does not need to be registered to gain this protection, but it must be well known outside its country of origin, that is internationally or at least regionally. TRIPS Article 16.2 requires members to take account of knowledge of the trademark in their own country, including knowledge obtained as a result of promotion of the trademark, even if in advance of actual use. The states which offer protection to well-known marks stop short of making any stipulation on the nature or degree of a well-known foreign mark's local status or even requiring the application of TRIPS Article 16.2, thus leaving this point unstated and removing a qualification which could limit the conditions for protection. It is not yet clear what standards of evidence the respective courts in the different states will require or accept in adjudicating on whether a trademark is well known locally, but in any case this common provision places significant discretion in the hands of the judiciary to influence or control the introduction of marginal foreign marks. At present, it would appear that a consistent and widespread judicial position on the treatment of well-known marks has yet to make itself manifest, even in the UAE courts, which probably see more cases dealing with trademark infringements than any of the other states. However, the UAE and Dubai courts, in particular, have shown an increasing willingness in recent years to provide protection for internationally known marks.

Some further advantage is given to marks deemed to be well known by the provision in some of the trademark laws of a right of applicants to claim priority on the basis of an earlier application for registration filed either with a member state of the WTO or the Paris Convention (Bahrain and Oman), a co-signatory to another international agreement (Saudi Arabia), or to countries which grant national treatment on a reciprocal basis (Qatar, again Saudi Arabia).[57] The trademark laws of Kuwait and the UAE do not make any specific provision for either national treatment or MFN treatment in respect of trademarks.

4.4.5 Rights of ownership

The basic right to be protected by the registration of a trademark is the exclusive right to use the mark and to prevent other parties from using the mark without consent.[58] The owner of the registered mark can also prevent others from using identical or similar marks on similar, or dissimilar, goods or services if such use may give grounds for confusion by the public. The aged Kuwait law does not include any similar or equivalent statement on rights conferred by registration. Accordingly, such rights must therefore be inferred by the nature of marks excluded from registration, such as a mark similar to one already registered, or by the prescribed acts which attract a punishment under the law, such as use of a counterfeit mark.

All states provide that the person who registers the mark is deemed to be the owner of the mark, unless there is proof to the contrary.[59] However, any claim of ownership cannot be disputed if the owner of the registered mark has used it continuously for five years since registration and no claim has been made against the validity of the original registration during this period. For the purposes of this provision, continuous use includes use by a licensee or assignee.

Saudi Arabia's early trademark law of 1984 established the precedent for a period of protection of ten years (albeit, according to the Hajri or Islamic calendar) for a registered trademark, and the other states have since followed suit (but according to the Gregorian calendar).[60] All accommodate unrestricted renewal, commonly for recurring ten-year periods – thus exceeding by some margin the minimum period of seven years specified in TRIPS Article 18. However, since TRIPS requires, and all states provide, indefinite renewal, the distinction is largely academic.

Arising from concerns expressed in WIPO and the WTO in respect of the inadequacy or absence of licensing and transfer provisions in the earlier trademark laws of the states, provisions addressing licensing and transfers have been strengthened and are now extant across the states' laws. In general terms, the owner of a mark may grant a non-exclusive and non-assignable licence to any natural person or legal entity in respect of some or all of the products or services for which the mark is registered.[61] The licensing agreement must be in writing, specify the terms, conditions and duration of the licence, and be registered with the responsible ministry to have any legal effect. None of the states permits compulsory licensing of trademarks, in accordance with the exclusion stipulated by TRIPS Article 21, although Oman does permit the responsible minister to declare a trademark exhausted and to authorise other parties to use that mark or import goods bearing that mark in instances of unmet demand, anti-competitive practices and unreasonably low-quality standards of goods.[62]

The ownership of a registered trademark may be transferred or assigned with or without the goodwill of the commercial business. Where the marks are deemed to have an established relationship with the business, the transfer of ownership of the business is deemed to include the transfer of the trademarks registered in the name of the transferor, unless specifically agreed otherwise. If the ownership of the business is transferred without the trademark, the transferor may continue to use the mark in connection with the products or services in respect of which the mark was originally registered.[63]

4.4.6 Classifications system for goods and services

Only Bahrain amongst the Gulf states is signatory to the Nice Agreement on the International Classification of Marks for Goods and Services, having adopted the eighth edition of the Agreement in February 2005. The other states either generally follow the Nice Agreement classifications or at least refer to them, as the starting point for categorising goods and services for domestic trademark registrations. The advantage of this strategy is that they can retain the flexibility to ignore or prohibit certain classification categories, as suits their domestic needs and prerogatives. This strategy is not inconsistent with the Paris Convention Article 6*quinquies* allowing signatory states to deny registration to marks that are deemed to be contrary to public order or morality, and the Nice Agreement Article 2 permitting signatory states to reserve the right to use the Nice Classification merely as a subsidiary system.

All states conform to a lesser or greater extent with the Agreement's classification system. The majority provide for the registration of marks for both goods and services in classes in accordance with an 'international classification' system (without specifying the Agreement) as well as in accordance with their respective implementing regulations, thereby allowing some discretion at the ministerial level, on the exclusion or otherwise of certain classes of goods or services. Classes commonly subject to possible exclusion are notably class 32 (beer and stout, as well as mineral and carbonated waters, other non-alcoholic beverages, syrups and other products used to make non-alcoholic beverages) and class 33 (wines and spirits). Generally, there are no restrictions on classes of registration or goods within individual classes in the laws themselves, but the laws make additional allowance for ministerial discretion as to the classes in which marks may or may not be registered. Each stipulates that a trademark may be registered for one or more classes of goods or services as prescribed (which includes the provision to prohibit) by their respective responsible ministers in the corresponding implementing regulations.[64] The Bahraini and Omani implementing regulations allow that applications for the registration of marks shall be submitted in accordance with the international classification of goods and services, including classes 32 and 33, without qualification. The Kuwaiti and Saudi regulations both exclude class 33 in its entirety, and restrict class 32 to 'mineral and aerated water and other non-alcoholic beverages – syrup and other preparations for making drinks', thereby deleting any reference to beers, spirits or alcoholic beverages.[65] Qatar does not make reference to any established classification system and it remains to be seen whether the as-yet-to-be-issued implementing regulations for its current law will provide any guidance and clarification. However, the existing regulations, which actually pertain to the superseded 1978 law, allow only 23 of the 42 classes within the international classification system to be granted in their entirety, with classes 32 and 33 and classes 35–42 concerning service marks amongst those excluded.[66]

However, what may appear to be allowed, or at least not disallowed, in one place may be prohibited in another. Since the consumption of alcohol is generally prohibited in the *Qur'an*, it follows that the registration of marks related to alcohol products would be contrary to public morals. Accordingly, the position commonly espoused both by the respective responsible ministries and by regional trademark registration agents alike is that trademarks in class 32 and class 33, as well as class 29 (meat products) in respect of pork-based products, are not registrable in any of the Gulf states on the grounds that they are contrary to the teaching of Islam, to *Shariah* law and to the respective states' trademark laws.[67] Saudi Arabia, when recently lodging its instrument of accession to the Paris Convention, expressed its objection to and concern with the stipulation of Article 7 of the Convention that 'the nature of the goods to which a trademark is to be applied shall in no case form an obstacle to the registration of the mark', on the grounds that some goods such as alcoholic and pork-based products were prohibited under Islamic law.[68] On an issue of such fundamental religious and social significance to Saudi Arabia, reliance alone on the generality of public order and morality provisions of the Paris Convention and TRIPS to prohibit the registration of offending marks was clearly inadequate.

4.4.7 Infringements

Some states draw a clear distinction between acts of infringement against the private rights of the trademark owner and those against the public rights in respect of representation of the status of a mark. Kuwait, Qatar, Saudi Arabia and the UAE deem infringements against the private rights of the trademark owner, and thereby potentially or actually causing commercial loss, to be the more serious offences. Hence such acts as counterfeiting a registered mark, fraudulently using another person's registered mark, or knowingly and misleadingly imitating a registered mark may attract the severest penalties. Use of an unregistered mark or mark excluded from registrability (except for those marks excluded solely for want of distinctive features), or falsely claiming or indicating that a mark has been registered, may be punishable by penalties that are a fraction of those which can be applied to the former type of infringement. The Saudi law, for example, provides for the imposition of penalties of up to one year's imprisonment and a fine of up to 1,000,000 Saudi riyals, or both, for infringements against the trademark owner's rights, while penalties against the public representational restrictions may attract penalties that are a quarter of the former.[69] At the other end of the scale, Kuwait, which recognises a similar distinction in the nature of infringements, provides for a maximum fine of only 600 Kuwaiti dinars and an unspecified term of imprisonment for similar offences.[70]

In contrast, the Bahraini law provides for a simple but comprehensive and undifferentiated list of infringing acts, which includes the following:

- counterfeiting or imitating a registered mark in a manner likely to mislead the public;
- using a forged or imitated mark in bad faith;
- using a trademark owned by another party in bad faith;

- knowingly offering for sale or possessing goods bearing a mark which is counterfeited, imitated or unlawfully affixed, or using such mark in connection with services;
- knowingly circulating counterfeit or imitated cards, documents or packaging used or designed to be used in an infringement, even if the infringement occurred;
- using an unregistered trademark or unlawfully indicating on a mark or commercial document that such mark is registered.[71]

Oman adopts an even simpler position, stating that any act that is reserved under the law as the exclusive right of the trademark owner or licensee that is done by a third party without the approval of the owner or licensee is an infringement.[72] Both states view the above infringements with equal gravity and therefore do not differentiate between the levels of sanctions that may be applied.

All Gulf states make provision for the order of precautionary measures in instances of threatened or actual infringements.

4.5 Geographical indications

4.5.1 TRIPS provisions and obligations (Articles 22–24)

TRIPS Section 3 on the protection of geographical indications is different to the rest of TRIPS; it balances the obligations for protection with the exceptions to protection, whereas the rest of TRIPS is weighted heavily in favour of protection of the intellectual property right holder.[73] The geographical indications provisions represent a delicate balance between conflicting European interests seeking high levels of protection, particularly for wines and spirits, and North American interests which are more interested in limiting protection than extending it.

TRIPS Article 22 defines a geographical indication as one which identifies a good as originating in the territory of a member, or a region or locality in that territory, where a given quality, reputation or other characteristic of the good is essentially attributable to its geographical origin. Thus, the quality, reputation or other characteristics of a good can each be a sufficient basis for eligibility as a geographical indication, where they are essentially attributable to the geographical origin of the good. Members are required to provide interested parties with the legal means to prevent use of any designation or presentation which may mislead the public as to the geographical origin of a good, and use which constitutes an act of unfair competition within the meaning of Article 10*bis* of the Paris Convention. Members are also required to refuse or invalidate the registration of a trademark which uses a geographical indication for goods not originating in the territory indicated, if the indication is used in such a manner that it may mislead the public as to the true place of origin of the goods.

TRIPS Article 23 requires members to provide an additional level of protection to wines and spirits, and in particular to provide the legal means for preventing use of a geographical indication identifying wines or spirits not originating in the place indicated by that geographical indication, even where the true origin is indicated, or where the indication is given in a translated form, or where it is qualified. Accordingly, unlike the status in respect of other geographical indications, those for wines and spirits are to be protected even where use by a third party would not mislead the public and unfair competition would not exist. While a multilateral system of notification and registrations of geographical indications, albeit for wines only, is mooted, members are obliged to enter into negotiations on such a system, but are not committed to the outcomes.

Limits are established to obligations for wholesale protection. As described by one commentator, these limits represent the other half of the delicate balancing act of conflicting interests, in favour of those with 'acquired rights' or 'sins of the past', by allowing for a number of exceptions to protection.[74] Members availing themselves of the use of these exceptions are, again, obliged to at least enter into negotiations aimed at increasing the protection for wines and spirits, but are not committed to any outcomes. However, the exceptions cannot be used to diminish the protection of geographical indications that existed prior to TRIPS' entry into force.

4.5.2 Geographical indications protection in the Gulf states

The attention given to geographical indications by the GCC states is slight and mainly as a corollary to trademarks. The prevailing position is to provide only the briefest passing reference to them within the scope of the respective trademark laws, to the limited extent of merely prohibiting the registration as a mark of a geographical name or indication that is liable to mislead or cause confusion as to the origin of the goods or services in respect of which registration is sought. Kuwait, Saudi Arabia, the UAE and Yemen have adopted this simple approach.[75] However, the approach does not give geographical indications *per se* any measure of protection. While it may restrict registration for the offending marks, it does not necessarily prevent the exploitative use or misuse of a geographical indication outside the trademark context, nor provide a form of protection as envisaged by TRIPS Article 23 – that is, where there is no misleading use or unfair competition.

Bahrain and Oman, meanwhile, both make more comprehensive provisions, with Bahrain having a discrete geographical indications law and Oman including a dedicated geographical indications section within its new and comprehensive law on industrial property. Both states also offer some complementary protection under their respective trademark provisions by continuing to recognise the above-mentioned exclusion of geographical indications from trademark registrability.

Table 4.3 includes those intellectual property laws which include some substantive provision for the protection of geographical indications.

4.5.3 Nature and scope of a geographical indication

For those states whose laws define a geographical indication, the definitions generally include the following characteristics (which also closely follow TRIPS Article 22.1):

> 'Any expression or sign indicating the geographical name of a country, region, locality or place which serves to designate a product originating therein, the quality, characteristics and reputation of which are due exclusively or partly to the geographical environment, the natural or human factors of such origin.'[76]

The nature of the protection provided by Bahrain, Oman and, to a lesser degree, Qatar takes three forms, namely, prohibitions on registration of offending marks, systems of registration for geographical indications and legal means for interested parties to oppose registration of a mark or indication.

First, the laws of all three states prohibit the registration as a trademark, and use in designating goods in the course of trade, of a geographical indication presented in a manner which:

- misleadingly suggests or implies that the goods originate in a geographical area other than their true place of origin, even where the geographical indication used is literally correct; or

Table 4.3 Current geographical indications protection in the Gulf states

Bahrain:	Legislative Decree No. 16 of 2004 with respect to Geographical Indications. Legislative Decree No. 10 of 1991 in respect of Trademarks.
Kuwait:	—
Oman:	Royal Decree No. 67/2008, the Law on Industrial Property.
Qatar:	Law No. 9 of 2002 in respect of Trade Marks, Business Names and Data, Industrial Designs and Geographical Indications.
Saudi Arabia:	—
UAE:	—
Yemen:	—

Source: compiled by the author

- by virtue of its use, would constitute an act of unfair competition, including the use of a false geographical indication of the true place of origin, and the use of a geographical indication in translation.[77]

Second, in recognition of the implications of TRIPS Article 24.9, which removes any obligation upon a member to protect a geographical indication which is not or is no longer protected in its own country, Bahrain, Qatar and Oman all make provision for the creation of national registers for the eventual possible registration, protection and recognition by other TRIPS signatories of their own geographical indications. Entitlement to register a geographical indication is limited to natural persons or legal entities carrying on an activity as a producer in the geographical area, or any competent authority.[78] Creation of these national registers is indicative of a small but growing appreciation in these three states of the developing enterprise for geographical indications of local origin, and the necessity to formalise recognition through local registration, if the indications are to obtain recognition internationally.

Third, Bahrain and Oman enable any interested party, whether they are individuals, producers or consumers, to oppose registration or to institute legal proceedings to prevent, in respect of geographical indications:

- the use of any designation or presentation of a good that indicates or suggests the good originates in a geographical area other than the true place of origin in a manner which misleads the public as to the geographical origin of the good;
- any use which constitutes an act of unfair competition within the meaning of Article 10*bis* of the Paris Convention; or
- use of a registered geographical indication identifying goods not originating in the place indicated by the indication, even where the true origin of the goods is indicated or the geographical indication is used in translation or accompanied by expressions such as 'kind', 'type', 'style', 'imitation' or the like.

The Qatari law permits 'persons who reside in a place especially reputed for the production of certain goods to prevent those who trade in similar goods produced in other places from affixing to their goods marks which would mislead the public as to the origin of those similar goods'.[79]

However, limitations apply. Both the Bahraini and Omani laws provide that a geographical indication shall not be registered or protected if the indication is:

- identical to a domestic customary term or common name of a good or service used in good faith;
- also the name of a person or business used in a manner which is not misleading;

- (or may be) confusingly similar to marks currently registered or under application;
- otherwise refused registration as a trademark pursuant to trademarks law;
- not protected or used (or has ceased to be protected or used) in its country of origin; or
- contrary to public order or morality.[80]

The Qatari law defers to implementing regulations to clarify the nature of such protection and the distinctions, if any, between registered and non-registered geographical indications.[81]

4.5.4 Additional protection for wines and spirits

The notion of providing protection, let alone additional protection, for alcohol-related goods or services would be anathema to most Gulf states, notwithstanding their general obligations under TRIPS Article 23.1 to provide protection for geographical indications for wines and spirits. However, the states will exercise their exception prerogatives under Article 23.2, which allows a state to refuse or invalidate a trademark which carries a wine or spirit geographical indication if a state's legislation so permits. And, as already mentioned, each state's trademark law makes provision for a trademark application that is contrary to public order or morality to be refused registration. It is not surprising, therefore, that the states devote little attention to the protection of geographical indications, let alone those relating to wines and spirits.

On the contrary, trademarks related to wines and spirits, irrespective of whether they also contain a geographical indication, are not registrable in most Gulf states. Applications for the protection of marks and/or geographical indications relating to wines and spirits will invariably be rejected on the grounds that the marketing, sale or importation of the goods which they identify constitute a breach of public order and morality and are therefore prohibited. The sale of wines and spirits (and all alcoholic products) is prohibited in Saudi Arabia and some of the UAE Emirates, according to Islamic law.

Oman adopts a slightly more liberal stance to the sale of alcohol products than the other Gulf states, but not necessarily to the protection of geographical indications relating to them. Unlike some of its neighbouring states, Oman permits the sale of alcohol products, as a rather lucrative commercial activity, to non-Muslim resident expatriates under strictly regulated and controlled conditions.[82]

The Omani industrial-property law does not make any specific reference to either a higher level of protection to geographical indications relating to wines and spirits or, indeed, their inclusion or exclusion in respect of protection under the law. Oman has previously advised the WTO that its law grants protection to all geographical indications including those relating to wines and spirits.[83] In practice, as previously indicated, trademarks and geographical indications relating to alcohol products are most likely to be refused registration under the public morality provisions of the industrial property law.

4.6 Industrial designs

4.6.1 TRIPS industrial designs provisions and requirements (Articles 25–26)

In addition to its general standards of protection, TRIPS devotes just two articles to protection of industrial designs, less than the attention given to the additional protection for geographical indications attached to wines and spirits.[84] However, TRIPS requires members to also comply with the Paris Convention's provisions relating to patents generally and to the specific industrial design provisions of Articles 4E, 5B, 5*bis* and 5*quinquies*. Article 5*quinquies* states simply that industrial designs shall be protected. TRIPS Article 25.1, meanwhile, obliges members to provide for the protection of independently created industrial designs that are new or original; a member may deem a design not to be new or original if it does not significantly differ from known designs or combinations of known design features, and may decline to extend protection to designs dictated essentially by technical or functional considerations.

Members are required to grant the owner of a protected industrial design the right to prevent third parties not having the owner's consent from making, selling or importing articles bearing or embodying a design which is a copy, or substantially a copy, of the protected design, when such acts are undertaken for commercial purposes. As with other intellectual property rights, some limited exceptions may be allowed, provided that such exceptions do not unreasonably conflict with the normal exploitation of protected industrial designs, do not unreasonably prejudice the legitimate interests of the owner of the protected design and take account of the legitimate interests of third parties. The period of protection shall amount to at least ten years, the prescription 'amount to' providing some flexibility in respect of initial and renewal terms that might be established.

Textile designs, which come within the scope of industrial designs, receive a special mention. In order to take account of the short life cycle and sheer number of new designs in the textile sector, requirements for securing protection of such designs, in particular in regard to any cost, examination or publication, must not unreasonably impair the opportunity to seek and obtain such protection. Members are free to meet this obligation either through industrial design law or through copyright law.

4.6.2 Regional industrial design laws

The Gulf states address their TRIPS obligations by incorporating some degree of protection for industrial designs either in their patents laws (Kuwait, Saudi Arabia and the UAE), their trademark law (Qatar), a separate chapter in a comprehensive industrial-property law (Oman and Yemen), or by a discrete industrial designs law (Bahrain) – see Table 4.4. Notwithstanding these different approaches, the nature of the protection in each state is quite similar, although the scope of the respective laws varies. Again, Bahrain and Oman offer the most comprehensive provisions, which go beyond addressing the TRIPS minimum standards.

Until the introduction of its discrete industrial designs law in 2006, Bahrain originally provided protection for industrial designs within its 1955 regulation which encompassed patents, designs and trademarks. As part of an overall strategy to adopt discrete laws in each of the main areas of intellectual property, Bahrain removed the trademark provisions into a separate law in 1991 and followed suit with a new patent and utility models law in 2004. As a consequence, any remnant of the original law was rescinded, thereby removing any reference to, and therefore any protection for, industrial designs. The 2006 law has rectified this oversight.

Oman has taken the opposite path to Bahrain and incorporated protection into a separate chapter in its comprehensive industrial-property law. In so doing it has rescinded its discrete industrial designs law of 2000. Yemen has taken a similar approach.

By way of contrast, Kuwait is still reliant upon legislation originally enacted in 1962, but which has been subjected to amendment (rather than total replacement) in 1999 and again in 2001.[85] The only changes of any real substance made to the 1962 law in respect of industrial designs in the amending legislation have related to period of protection, and fees and charges.

Qatar has incorporated industrial design protection in four brief articles within its current trademark law. Because of their brevity and consequent omissions, the industrial designs provisions will likely require further enhancement in the future. Specific reference to industrial designs is limited to acknowledging the right of a person to register a design and to prevent others from exploiting it, to stipulating a period of protection, and a simple statement applying the general provisions of the law to industrial designs, provided that such application 'is without prejudice to its special character'.[86] What is meant by 'its special character' is not explained.

Saudi Arabia and the UAE have, for the first time, incorporated provision for the protection of industrial designs into their patents laws.[87] However, the attention given to designs in the Saudi law is still very slight, namely, just two articles referring to the nature of an industrial design necessary to qualify for protection and the right of the owner of an industrial design to take action against any infringements of those rights. The UAE law goes into a little greater detail, encompassing both industrial designs and models, as well as extending to them the general provisions within the law.

4.6.3 Character and scope of an industrial design

Except for Qatar's law, the various descriptions of an industrial design are very similar in their essential elements and generally encompass most of the elements of the following description as detailed in the Omani law:

Table 4.4 Current industrial designs protection in the Gulf states

Bahrain:	Legislative Decree No. 6 of 2006, in respect of Industrial Designs. Legislative Decree No. 31 of 1996 ratifying Bahrain's accession to the Paris Convention for the Protection of Industrial Property.
Kuwait:	Law No. 4 of 1962 concerning Patents, Designs and Industrial Models, as amended by Law No. 4 of 1999, and Law No. 3 of 2001.
Oman:	Royal Decree No. 67/2008, the Law on Industrial Property. Royal Decree No. 63/1998 promulgating the Sultanate's accession to the Paris Convention for the Protection of Industrial Property.
Qatar:	Law No. 9 of 2002 in respect of Trade Marks, Business Names and Data, Industrial Designs and Geographical Indications. Decree No. 31 of 2001 in respect of Qatar's accession to the Paris Convention for the Protection of Industrial Property.
Saudi Arabia:	Royal Decree No. M/27 of 1425 AH (2004) in respect of Patents, Layout Designs of Integrated Circuits, Plant Varieties, and Industrial Models. Royal Decree No. M/48 of 1424 AH (2003), ratifying Saudi Arabia's accession to the Paris Convention for the Protection of Industrial Property.
UAE:	Federal Law No. 17 of 2002 on the Industrial Regulation and Protection of Patents, Industrial Drawings, and Designs. Federal Decree No. 20 of 1996, concerning the UAE's accession to the Paris Convention for the Protection of Industrial Property.
Yemen:	Law No. 19 of 1994 in respect of Intellectual Property. Law of February 2007 ratifying Yemen's accession to the Paris Convention for the Protection of Industrial Property.

Source: compiled by the author

> '. . . any composition of lines or colours or any three dimensional form, whether or not associated with colours, provided that such composition or form gives a special appearance to a product of industry or handicraft . . . and is judged by the eye.'[88]

The UAE's description goes somewhat further and distinguishes between an industrial design and an industrial model, the former defined as 'any innovative creation of lines or colours, which generates a product that can be used in industry or craft' and the latter as 'any innovative three-dimensional shape that can be used in industry or craft'.[89] Kuwait retains a more conservative definition, omitting reference to any three-dimensional form. An industrial design or model is defined as follows: 'Any arrangement of lines or any type of figure, whether coloured or uncoloured, designed for use in industrial production by a mechanical, manual or chemical process shall be considered as a design or industrial model.'[90] By contrast, and possibly by a drafting oversight, Qatar does not offer any description of an industrial design in its current law, although it offers definitions of the other areas of industrial property covered by the law.

As permitted by TRIPS Article 25.2, none of the states allows protection to extend to designs dictated essentially by technical or functional considerations. An industrial design cannot be registered if it lacks originality or has entered the public domain through publication or use prior to the filing of an application for registration or the priority application date. A common exception to the public domain qualification applies generally in respect of industrial designs which are displayed at international exhibitions or scientific conferences, for which temporary protection may apply.

Commonly excluded from protection are designs which may be contrary to public order or morality, while Saudi Arabia goes one step further by also excluding designs which are contrary to *Shariah* law.[91]

The nature of protection generally accords to the right holder the exclusive right to prevent any third party from using the industrial design in the manufacture of any product, or importing or otherwise possessing any product related to the industrial design or model for the purpose of using or offering for sale. The Bahraini, Omani, Saudi and UAE laws each require an industrial design to be registered to qualify for protection.[92] They enshrine the principle of 'first to register', registration being a presumption of ownership. While some allowance can be made for exceptions to this principle where 'the contrary is established', the absence of implementing regulations or judicial authority in each case does not provide any guidance as to what may constitute 'the contrary'. In the case of the Qatari law, the general application of the trademark provisions may by implication extend some protection to industrial designs, in the absence of any specific reference to an obligation for registration.

Consistent with TRIPS Article 26.3, the period of protection is universally at least ten years from date of application or priority filing, with provision for an extension for an additional five years. Curiously, the Qatari law still provides for only five years' protection, albeit with opportunity for extension for two further similar periods but nonetheless subject to renewal application deadlines and payment of the requisite fees.[93] As the total period of Qatar's possible protection available amounts to more than ten years, it can be argued that Qatar still complies with TRIPS Article 26.3 in outcome if not entirely in spirit.

The laws of Saudi Arabia and the UAE both make particular reference to the protection of textile designs, which are generally acknowledged as being within the scope of industrial designs and therefore are accorded the same degree of protection.[94] They provide no other special protection or treatment for textile designs, other than this acknowledgement, and neither makes reference to the requirements of TRIPS Article 25.2 in respect of the non-impairment of the opportunity for protection.

4.6.4 Infringements

The nature of an infringement against an industrial design right is described very briefly and succinctly. It is described variously as:

- any act of exploitation reserved exclusively for the design right holder undertaken without the prior approval of the right holder (Oman, Saudi Arabia);[95]
- imitating a registered industrial design, knowingly using a registered industrial design with intention to mislead and falsely claiming an industrial design is registered (Qatar and the UAE);[96] or
- knowingly selling, offering for sale, importing or otherwise trading in products or materials on which there appears an imitation of a registered industrial design, or falsely claiming that a design is registered (Bahrain, Kuwait and Yemen).[97]

4.7 Patents

4.7.1 TRIPS provisions and obligations (Articles 27–34)

TRIPS Article 27 requires WTO member states to make patents available for any invention, whether for a product or process, in all fields of technology without discrimination, provided that the invention is new, involves an inventive step and is capable of industrial application. It also requires that patents be available and patent rights be enjoyable without discrimination as to the place of invention, or whether products are imported or locally produced. Three exceptions are permitted to this basic rule on patentability, namely:

- inventions contrary to *ordre public* or morality, including inventions dangerous to human, animal or plant life or health or seriously prejudicial to the environment;
- diagnostic, therapeutic and surgical methods for the treatment of humans or animals;
- plants and animals other than micro-organisms and essentially biological processes for the production of plants or animals other than non-biological and microbiological processes.

However, any member excluding plant varieties from protection under patent provisions must provide an effective *sui generis* system of protection.

The exclusive rights that must be conferred by a product patent are those of making, using, offering for sale, selling and importing for these purposes, while process patent protection must extend rights not only over use of the process but also over products obtained directly by the process.[98] Patent owners shall also have the right to license, assign or transfer the patent. The term of protection available shall extend for a period of 20 years from the date of filing of the application.[99]

Members shall require that an applicant for a patent shall disclose the invention in a manner sufficiently clear and complete for the invention to be carried out by a person skilled in the art and may require the applicant to indicate the best mode for carrying out the invention known to the inventor at the filing date of the application or, where priority is claimed, at the priority date of the application.[100]

Limited exceptions to the exclusive rights conferred by a patent may be allowed, provided that such exceptions do not unreasonably conflict with a normal exploitation of the patent and do not unreasonably prejudice the legitimate interests of the patent owner, and take account of the legitimate interests of third parties. Members may allow compulsory licensing and government use without the authorisation of the right holder, provided the latter's interests are still protected.[101] Compulsory licensing may be permitted only where the right holder has already refused to grant a voluntary licence on reasonable terms and within a reasonable period of time, although this requirement can be dispensed with in times of national or other extreme urgency or in cases of public non-commercial use.[102] Use of a compulsory licence provision should also be limited to the supply of the domestic market, although this requirement and the above condition on use may be waived to remedy anti-competitive practices.

TRIPS Article 34 provides for the reversal of the burden of proof in civil cases involving process patents, whereby the defendant may be required to prove that the process used to obtain an identical product is different from the patented process. Members are obliged to apply this presumption in the following circumstances:

- when the product obtained by the patented process is 'new'; or
- when there is a 'substantial likelihood that an identical product was made by the process and the owner of the patent has been unable through reasonable efforts to determine the process actually used'.

4.7.2 Regional patents laws

As with copyright, the development of formal patent protection regimes within the Gulf states is a fairly recent event (see Table 4.5). Except for Bahrain and Kuwait, which both introduced patent legislation in 1955 and 1961, patent protection laws did not appear until the late 1980s/early 1990s. The concern of the states for a strong patent protection regime has not been particularly strong, simply because the environment to foster local invention and technology transfer has never really been established. Hence there has been neither the generation of patent applications of local origin of any dimension, nor the opportunity for, or the existence of, a thriving patent infringement industry (as exists in the case of copyright). The issue of standards of patent protection performance in the Gulf region has not generated any great concern from the developed countries, except from those governments and industry lobby groups representing the interests of the international pharmaceutical conglomerates.[103] The relatively few patents which have originated from within the Gulf states in recent times have mostly come from the oil and mining industries in Saudi Arabia and Kuwait, have been lodged by expatriate residents rather than nationals, have been invariably owned by a foreign company and have included a claim for priority based on an earlier foreign patent application.[104]

While the principles enshrined in the various laws follow very similar themes and principles, and display a high degree of regional common ground, the laws differ quite significantly in terms of their breadth and attention to detail.

Bahrain was the first Gulf state to introduce a patent law with its pre-independence law of 1955 encompassing patents, trademarks and industrial designs. That law was subsequently upgraded in 1977 and entirely replaced in 2004 with a law that in turn was substantially modified in 2006 to reflect its intellectual property protection obligations under its free trade agreement with the United States. Kuwait issued its original patent law in 1962 and upgraded it in 1999 and again in 2001, but the necessary implementing regulations for this latest amending law have yet to be issued. In essence, Kuwait is still operating under legislation which includes elements of the 1962 law and its associated implementing regulations. Kuwait has declared (but has not yet appeared to have decreed) that the GCC Unified Patent Regulations of 1992 as amended in 2000 are also in force in Kuwait.

Oman issued its first patent legislation in 2000, previously having preferred to adopt and adhere to the GCC Unified Patent Regulations. It has since combined this law and a number of other intellectual property laws issued in that same year into a comprehensive industrial-property law. Notwithstanding the existence of its own patent legislation, Oman continues to recognise the validity of the GCC Unified Patent Regulations.

Qatar did not issue a domestic patents law until 2006, relying previously on the provisions of the GCC Unified Patent Regulations to meet its TRIPS obligations in respect of patent protection. It should be noted, however, that the GCC Unified Patent Regulations is essentially a registration statute and includes very little by way of enforcement provisions, notably in respect of infringements, precautionary measures and sanctions. The GCC regulation defers these matters to each state to establish within their own domestic laws. Although Qatar has now introduced a domestic patent law, it still needs to issue the necessary implementing regulations to bring the law into effect.

Table 4.5 Current patents laws and conventions in the Gulf states

Bahrain:	Legislative Decree No. 1 of 2004 in respect of Patents and Utility Models, as amended by Law No. 14 of 2006. Legislative Decree No. 31 of 1996 ratifying Bahrain's accession to the Paris Convention for the Protection of Industrial Property. Legislative Decree No. 12 of 2004, adopting the GCC Unified Patent Regulations in Bahrain. Legislative Decree No. 19 of 2005 ratifying Bahrain's accession to the Patent Law Treaty Legislative Decree No. 44 of 2005 ratifying Bahrain's accession to the Patent Cooperation Treaty.
Kuwait:	Law No. 4 of 1962 concerning Patents, Designs and Industrial Models, as amended by Law No. 4 of 1999, and Law No. 3 of 2001.
Oman:	Royal Decree No. 67/2008, the Law on Industrial Property Rights. Royal Decree No. 63/1998 ratifying the Sultanate's accession to the Paris Convention for the Protection of Industrial Property. Ministerial Decision No. 14/2000 recognising the GCC Unified Patent Regulations (1992) as the Patent Law of Oman. Royal Decree No. 37/2001 ratifying the Sultanate's accession to the Patent Cooperation Treaty (PCT). Royal Decree No. 37/2007 ratifying the Sultanate's accession to the Budapest Treaty on the International Recognition of the Deposit of Microorganisms for the Purposes of Patent Procedure, and the Patent Law Treaty.
Qatar:	Law No. 30 of 2006 concerning Patents. Ministerial Decree No. 31 of 2001 in respect of Qatar's accession to the Paris Convention for the Protection of Industrial Property. Law No. 12 of 2003, adopting the GCC Unified Patent Regulations as the Patent Law of Qatar.
Saudi Arabia:	Royal Decree No. M/27 of 1425 AH (2004), the Law of Patents, Layout Designs of Integrated Circuits, Plant Varieties and Industrial Models. Royal Decree M/48 of 1424 AH (2003), acceding to the Paris Convention for the Protection of Industrial Property, and the Berne Convention for the Protection of Literary and Artistic works.
UAE:	Federal Law No. 17 of 2002 for the Industrial Regulation and Protection of Patents, Industrial Drawings and Designs. Federal Decree No. 20 of 1996, concerning the UAE's accession to the Paris Convention for the Protection of Industrial Property. Federal Decree No. 84 of 1998, concerning the UAE's accession to the Patent Cooperation Treaty (PCT).
Yemen:	Law No. 19 of 1994 in respect of Intellectual Property. Law of February 2007 ratifying Yemen's accession to the Paris Convention for the Protection of Industrial Property.
GCC:	GCC Unified Patent Regulations of 1992, as amended in 2000.

Source: compiled by the author

Saudi Arabia issued its original patent law in 1989, but replaced it in 2004 with a new law which also encompasses layout designs of integrated circuits, plant varieties and industrial models.

In 2002, the UAE repealed its original 1992 law to both better reflect the changed commercial environment in the UAE since the promulgation of that law and to address the large number of TRIPS obligations in which the original law was deficient. The 1992 law suffered from a number of shortcomings, not least of which was the exclusion of pharmaceutical products from protection, although pharmaceutical processes were still protected. However, the subordinate implementing regulations still need to be issued before the law comes into effective use. The UAE was also the first Gulf state to accede to the Patent Cooperation Treaty (PCT), becoming party to the Treaty in March 1999; Oman and Bahrain followed suit in October 2001 and December 2006 respectively.

By contrast, patent protection in Yemen is still operating under a single intellectual property law dating from 1994, which encompasses both copyright and industrial property and which is very much in a pre-TRIPS state in terms of the standards of protection provided. The implementing regulations for this law have been issued only very recently (July 2007) and reportedly have still to come into effect.

The Supreme Council of the GCC issued its Unified Patent Regulations and statute establishing the GCC Patent Office in Riyadh, Saudi Arabia in December 1992. These were subsequently amended in late 1999 and re-issued in April 2000. The main benefit of the GCC Unified Patent Regulations is that it allows a member state to obtain protection across all GCC states by the lodgement of a single patent application with the GCC Patent Office.[105]

4.7.3 Patentability scope and criteria

In accordance with the requirements of TRIPS Article 27, the laws of all Gulf states and the GCC Unified Patent Regulations generally provide that a patent may be granted for any new invention that is the result of a new idea or an innovative improvement on an invention which may be already patented, in any area of technology. The invention must be scientifically based and useful in industry, whether this entails new industrial products, the development of new industrial techniques, methods or processes, or new ways of applying well-known industrial techniques, methods or processes.[106] An invention can be considered as industrially applicable if it can be used in any kind of industry in the broadest sense of the word – which variously includes agriculture, fishing, handicraft or services. Oman, with the most recent patent statute amongst the states, provides the latest prescription on what may be 'new', 'inventive' and 'industrially applicable':

'3. (1)(b) An invention is new if it is not anticipated by prior art.

Prior art shall consist of everything disclosed to the public, anywhere in the world, by publication in tangible form or by oral disclosure, by use or in any other way, prior to the filing or, where appropriate, the priority date, of the application claiming the invention.

. . .

(2) An invention shall be considered as involving an inventive step if, having regard to the differences and similarities between the claimed invention and the prior art . . . the claimed invention as a whole would not have been obvious to a person skilled in the art at the filing date or, if applicable, at priority date of the claimed invention.

(3) An invention shall be considered industrially applicable if it can be made or used in any kind of industry or if it has specific, substantial and credible utility. The term "industry" shall be understood in its broadest sense, as any human economic activity leading to the production of goods and services; it shall cover, in particular, handicraft, agriculture, fishery and services.'[107]

Bahrain, Kuwait, Oman and the UAE make provision for the registrability and protection of a utility model, provided it is new, involves an inventive step and is industrially applicable. They describe a utility model as an invention which is not sufficiently inventive or creative to obtain a patent but which otherwise meets the requirements of the patent law in terms of being new and of practical application in industry.[108] Qatar and Saudi Arabia do not make any distinction between patents and utility models, omitting from their respective laws any reference to the latter. However, it has been reported locally that the Saudi government is considering the introduction of new industrial designs which may include utility models and that the responsible ministry will therefore be accepting applications for registration in anticipation of the proposed law eventually appearing.[109] It is worth noting that, while TRIPS does not make any reference to utility models, protection afforded to utility models by Articles 1(2), 4 and 5 of the Paris Convention is still binding on WTO members. Article 1(2) of the Convention stipulates that the protection of industrial property includes utility models.

Commonly excluded from patentability is any invention (or the exploitation thereof) which may represent a violation of public order or morality, or which may be harmful to human, animal or plant life, to health, or to the environment. Saudi Arabia and the GCC regulation add a further condition which specifically excludes from patentability any invention which may conflict with the principles of Islamic *Shariah* or which affects national security.[110] The UAE recognises that inventions which may have national security implications may still be protected but directs that they will be dealt with in accordance with special procedures to be stipulated in the implementing regulations.[111] Besides these possible exclusions, the common exclusions from patentability reflect the limitations prescribed by TRIPS Article 27.3, namely:

- diagnostic, therapeutic and surgical methods for the treatment of animals or humans (but not the products used in these methods);
- plants and animals other than micro-organisms, and essentially biological processes for the production of plants or animals (other than non-biological and microbiological processes);
- discoveries, scientific theories and principles, mathematical and business methods, computer programs, pure mental activities and game playing.

In addition to the above, Oman excludes natural substances and known substances for which a new use has been discovered from protection, but extends protection to:

- process inventions which consist of steps performed or directed by a computer program; and
- product inventions consisting of elements of a computer-implemented invention, including in particular machine-readable program code stored on a tangible medium and a general-purpose computer whose novelty arises primarily from its combination with a specific computer program.[112]

Bahrain maintains by far the narrowest range of inventions excluded from possible patentability. Besides the above general *ordre public* and morality exclusion provisions, the only inventions for which patents shall not be granted have been confined to those relating to:

‘1. Animals.

2. Diagnostic, therapeutic and surgical methods necessary for the treatment of humans and animals, with the exception of products used in any of these methods.’[113]

Adequate protection for patented pharmaceutical and agricultural chemical products in the Gulf states has been, and continues to be, a matter for concern for the major multinational pharmaceutical companies and has caused their national governments to scrutinise the states’ patent laws. The pre-TRIPS patent laws of Bahrain, Kuwait, Saudi Arabia and the UAE specifically excluded patent protection for chemical inventions relating to foodstuffs, medicines or pharmaceutical formulae. However, these states would argue that pharmaceutical and agrochemical products now receive full patent protection by virtue of their non-inclusion in the above list of exclusions from patentability. Kuwait, Saudi Arabia and the UAE, for example, each originally excluded from protection:

> 'Chemical inventions relating to foodstuffs, medical drugs or pharmaceuticals unless those products are manufactured in special chemical methods. In this case, the protection shall be for the methods of manufacture not the products themselves'[114]

but have since removed this particular reference in their current laws to bring their lists of patentability exclusions into line with TRIPS Article 27.3.

The Yemeni pre-TRIPS law of 1994 prohibits from patentability any invention which violates the Yemeni social system and the provisions of the Islamic jurisprudence.[115] It further excludes from patentability:

- non-chemical inventions related to foodstuff, medicines or pharmaceuticals (except for any special chemical processes or methods used in their manufacture);
- new methods for the treatment of diseases;
- biological methods for the production of new type of animals or plants.

4.7.4 Rights conferred by a registered patent

The patent laws generally provide that the owner of a patent has the exclusive right to exploit the invention by manufacturing, using such invention and importing what is manufactured thereof, selling and offering it for sale, irrespective of whether the subject of the patent is a product or a process.[116] The owner is also protected against the importation and offering for sale of a patented invention by a third party. Where the patent has been granted for a process, the owner enjoys the right in respect of the process and in respect of any product directly obtained by means of that process. Kuwait's law states in plain and simple fashion that 'the patent owner shall have the exclusive right of utilizing the patent in every way'.[117]

Consistent with the requirements of TRIPS Article 33, all states except Yemen provide for a period of protection of 20 years from the date of filing of the application.[118] Of those states that recognise utility models, namely Bahrain, Kuwait, Oman and the UAE, protection is generally provided for a period of ten years from date of filing; however, Kuwait's 'patents for models of use' may receive protection for only seven years from date of application, with no provision for renewal.[119]

All states, including Yemen, allow for claims of priority under certain conditions in respect of a patent application first lodged in another country. Generally, claims of priority are allowed if the original application is lodged in a country which is a WTO member or is party to an international agreement or treaty to which the state has also acceded. By virtue of their PCT accession, Bahrain, Oman and the UAE further provide for claims of priority on the basis of an application first submitted in any of the other PCT member countries. The period of time for claiming priority is 12 months from date of first filing.

Bahrain and Oman provide for the protection period to be extended for a further period of up to four (Bahrain) or five (Oman) years to allow for delays in granting patent approval where such delays are not attributable to conduct on the part of the patent applicant.[120] They further provide for extension of protection where delays occur in the marketing approval process on product safety and efficacy. Bahrain limits eligibility for such extensions to pharmaceutical products, but sets the maximum possible period as 'sufficient to compensate the patent holder for any justified reduction in actual protection period', while Oman limits such extended period to up to two years, but does not specify any particular products to which the extension provision applies.

By way of contrast, the Yemeni law provides for a limited period of protection of just 15 years from the date of filing of a patent application.[121] At the conclusion of the protection period, ownership of the invention and any residual rights do not enter the public domain but revert to the state.

4.7.5 Process patents: reversal of burden of proof

Oman and Saudi Arabia alone make provision for the reversal of the burden of proof in respect of process patents, to the extent required by TRIPS Article 34; namely, when the product obtained by the patented process is new, or when there is a 'substantial likelihood that the identical product was made by the process and the owner of the patent has been unable through reasonable efforts to determine the process actually used'.[122]

Bahrain acknowledges the need to include such provision, but only in respect of the second of the two conditions stipulated in TRIPS Article 34.1; that is, where there is a substantial likelihood that the identical product was made by the patented process and the patent owner has been unable to reasonably determine the process actually used.[123]

The fact that provision for the reversal of the burden of proof has been considered by some of the other states would seem to indicate that the issue has been put to one side rather than forgotten. The UAE had considered the inclusion of an appropriate clause at a late stage in the drafting process for its 2002 law, but for some unexplained reason did not include any such provision in the final promulgated version.[124] Such omission by the states may not be entirely accidental or unintentional. Retention of the burden of proof upon the complainant, being the right holder of the patent and thus most likely of foreign origin, would work in favour of local industry and against the likelihood of successful 'strategic litigation' by the foreign right holder.[125]

4.7.6 Compulsory licensing

All Gulf states and the GCC itself take advantage of provision for compulsory licensing as permitted by TRIPS Article 31. Generally, the laws provide that a non-inclusive non-transferable compulsory licence may be granted by the responsible minister in circumstances where the patent or utility certificate has not been utilised actively and seriously within two (Qatar) or three years from being awarded, or where the patent holder's refusal to grant a licence to utilise it may impact upon the establishment or development of industrial or commercial activities within the state concerned.[126] The party seeking the award of a compulsory licence must be able to demonstrate that efforts were made to obtain a licence from the patent holder under reasonable commercial terms and conditions, and that the applicant has the means and capacity to sufficiently exploit the invention. Conditions attached to the issuance of a compulsory licence, which largely reflect those stipulated by TRIPS, require that:

- the patent or utility certificate holder is entitled to receive fair compensation;
- the compulsory licence is non-transferable, except where the ownership of the establishment of the licensee or the part thereof utilising the patent has been assigned;
- the issuance of the compulsory licence is intended to satisfy the needs of the local market only (the assumption being that local market means national market); and
- the right holder may still exploit the patent, or license others to do so.

In the case of semi-conductor technology, Bahrain, Oman, Saudi Arabia and the UAE provide that the compulsory licence may be granted only for public, non-commercial use, or to remedy a practice determined after judicial or administrative process to be anti-competitive or an act of unlawful competition.[127]

Notwithstanding the requirements of TRIPS Article 27.1 that 'patents shall be available and patent rights enjoyable without discrimination as to the place of invention . . . and whether products are imported or locally made', Qatar and the UAE stipulate that importation is not deemed to be 'working' a patent and therefore does not constitute justification for precluding the granting of a compulsory licence to another party.[128] This would appear to be in direct contradiction of TRIPS Article 27.1 and the GCC Unified Patent Regulations Articles 12.1 and 12.2, all of which recognise importation as working the patent and thereby a ground for precluding the issuance of a compulsory licence. It would also appear to be discriminating against patents on the grounds of origin, again contrary to TRIPS Article 27.1, but it is a discrimination that works in favour of the states concerned.

Both Oman and the UAE have separately confirmed that import of the product shall not be deemed a legitimate reason to prevent the issue of the obligatory authorisation (compulsory licence).[129] In response to questioning from WTO's Council of TRIPS on this apparent contradiction, Oman has offered the following explanation of its position:

'... it has become clear that Article 27/1 of TRIPS do [sic] not contradict with Article 15/c of the Patent Law as Article 27/1 deals with the Patent Law and the patentable materials in general while the Article 15/c of the Patent Law deals with obtaining the compulsory licence in exploiting the patent and the importation is not considered as legal reason to grant the compulsory licence.'[130]

The Omani response would appear to simply add to the contradiction, or at least to confuse the issue; in any case, the response was not pursued further within the Council of TRIPS. The UAE has similarly confirmed before the Council that importation does not satisfy the requirements of working a patent, but again has also clouded the issue.[131] The WTO developed member states appear to have seen little point in lodging a dispute against (or 'seeking consultations with') any of the three states under the WTO's Dispute Settlement procedures over the states' respective stances on patent working.[132]

Authority for granting and revoking compulsory licences generally rests with the responsible minister (or minister-equivalent in the case of Saudi Arabia).[133] The UAE law, however, requires such decisions to remain within the jurisdiction of the courts, although the responsible minister may grant the compulsory licence where the exploitation of the patent is deemed to be in the national interest.[134] The Kuwaiti law goes to the other extreme and still leaves the authority with government officials – a lingering influence of the law's original 1962 provisions that have not been updated or excised.[135] The Bahraini, Omani and UAE ministerial decisions are still subject to judicial appeal.[136]

While the GCC Unified Patent Regulation prescribes the grounds for issuing compulsory licences, it generally defers to state laws in respect of provision for compulsory licensing. However, the GCC Patent Office may still grant a compulsory licence to a government agency of a member state to exploit a patent, albeit still subject to the conditions that prevail in the state legislation.[137] The GCC Patents Office claims (although it is not specified in the regulations or subordinate bylaws) that the prior consent of all six GCC member states must be given for the Office to issue a compulsory licence, which constitutes an additional assurance against any abuse in the compulsory licensing regime.[138] In practice, however, the granting of compulsory licensing has never been exercised by the GCC Patent Office in order to test this requirement.

4.7.7 Infringements

The patent laws of the Gulf states reveal a fair degree of common ground in their descriptions of the nature of the infringement of patent rights, although the remedies and level of sanctions available can differ markedly. The laws are also rather succinct, perhaps overly so, when compared with the infringement descriptions contained in the corresponding copyright laws. The laws offer only the broadest definition of acts which may constitute an infringement, as generally being 'any act of exploitation of rights provided for in the provisions governing each of the patented subject matters . . . without the written consent of the registered patentee . . .'.[139] Acts of exploitation in essence include the making, importing, offering for sale, or storing for such purposes, in respect of goods the subject of a patent or goods produced directly by a process the subject of a patent. Oman and the UAE, in almost identical terms, both add the act of providing false information or documents to obtain a patent or utility certificate as an infringing act.[140]

The Bahrain and Kuwait laws, again in very similar language, stipulate that a person who knowingly and unlawfully commits any of the following acts infringes the rights of the patent owner:

- imitates an invention or utility model for which a patent was granted pursuant to the law;
- labels products, advertisements, marks, packaging or wrapping materials or the like in a manner indicating that he has obtained a patent or utility model patent;
- produces, sells, displays for sale or distribution, imports, or obtains for trading purposes a product protected by a patent in the state.[141]

As occurs in respect of the other major areas of intellectual property, all GCC states make provision for precautionary measures to be sought in instances of threatened or actual infringements.

4.7.8 Yemen's 'right to a discovery'

The Yemeni intellectual property law retains an interesting feature not seen in the other industrial-property laws of the region. In addition to provisions addressing patent protection, it provides for formal recognition and registration of a 'discovery'. The law defines an act of 'discovery' as 'obtain[ing] knowledge of an existing matter previously unknown in the fields of laws, characteristics and phenomena related to the material world, including the discovery of materials or living things'.[142]

The Act provides that a Yemeni who obtains knowledge of an existing matter previously unknown in the fields of 'laws, characteristics and phenomena related to the material world' may be deemed to have made a discovery and shall be entitled to enjoy certain rights, including the following:

- naming rights over the discovery;
- the grant of an 'incentive remuneration . . . determined by a resolution by the Council of Ministers, and . . . paid to the discoverer as a lump sum'; and
- a certificate attesting to the discovery and granting priority over the discovery.

The law further provides that after the remuneration is paid, the discovery enters the public domain and becomes the right of all citizens. However, where the discovery is within the field of industrial or agricultural development, the discoverer may still enjoy exploitation rights under the patent or industrial designs provisions of the law, as appropriate.

4.8 Layout-designs (topographies) of integrated circuits

4.8.1 TRIPS provisions and obligations (TRIPS Articles 35–38)

TRIPS requires members to provide protection on the basis of certain provisions of the Washington Treaty on Intellectual Property in Respect of Integrated Circuits (Washington, 1989).[143] These provisions deal, *inter alia*, with the definition of an 'integrated circuit' and 'layout-design (topography)' requirements for protection, exclusive rights and limitations, as well as exploitation, registration and disclosure.

TRIPS adds to the Washington Treaty provisions on four points:

- the minimum term of protection shall be ten years, instead of the eight years stipulated in the Washington Treaty (Article 38.1);
- the rights must extend to articles incorporating infringing layout-designs (Article 36);
- unwitting infringers must be allowed to use or sell stock already acquired or ordered at the time of being advised of their infringement (Article 37.1); and
- the conditions of TRIPS Article 31 in respect of compulsory licensing or government use without the authorisation of the right holder apply *mutatis mutandis* to layout-designs, instead of the more generous corresponding provisions of the Washington Treaty (Article 37.2).

In essence, TRIPS excludes provisions of the Treaty (notably those on compulsory licensing) that had been rejected by the US and Japan during the negotiations on the Treaty and supplements the latter with the stricter provisions that those countries had failed to obtain at the Washington Diplomatic Conference.[144]

The TRIPS obligation to protect layout-designs applies to such layout-designs that are original in the sense that they are the result of their creators' intellectual effort and are not commonplace among creators of layout-designs and manufacturers of integrated circuits at the time of their creation.[145] The exclusive rights include the right of reproduction and the right of importation, sale and other distribution for commercial purposes. Members are required to consider unlawful the unauthorised sale, importation or distribution for commercial purposes of a protected layout-design or integrated circuit incorporating such design or an article incorporating such integrated circuit if it contains an unlawfully reproduced layout-design.[146] The minimum period of protection is ten years from date of filing for registration, or from the date of first commercial exploitation where a member does not require registration as a condition for protection; in any case, protection may lapse 15 years after the creation of the layout-design.[147]

4.8.2 Regional layout-design legislation

As is the case with plant varieties, the protection of layout-designs is not an issue generating any great concern or attention with either the Gulf states or developed countries operating, or with interests, in the states. As Correa points out, the semi-conductor industry is highly concentrated in a few industrialised countries, and technological advancement is an interactive, cumulative process in which improvements are directly based on the pre-existing stock of carefully guarded knowledge.[148] Developing countries are most unlikely to have the technological skills and knowledge capacity to manufacture counterfeit products that incorporate chips and chip technology produce; they are net importers of such products. The impact of TRIPS in respect of layout-designs is likely to be felt mainly in respect of the importation of these products, which, in any case, will be slight. While software piracy has been an ongoing problem of some dimension in the states, counterfeit chip technology production or importation involving the states does not appear to have ever arisen as an issue as far as the chip technology industry is concerned. It is not surprising, therefore, that the states have either largely ignored the issue of protection of layout-designs (the UAE and Yemen) or have simply added reference to them in the general provisions of their other intellectual property laws (Kuwait, Oman and Saudi Arabia).

Bahrain and Qatar, however, have discrete laws in place. The Bahraini law in particular is very comprehensive by regional standards. The law includes substantive issues not seen in the other states' laws in respect of creator's rights in the employment context, expiry of rights and grievance procedures.[149] It also contains a fairly comprehensive level of detail relating to registration procedures that would perhaps be normally deferred to implementing regulations.

Kuwait's provision for the protection for layout-designs in its other intellectual property laws is token, to say the least. It has argued that protection has been provided by extending to them the protection already given to industrial designs and models in its patent and industrial designs law.[150] It has achieved this by the simple strategy of inserting the words 'and integrated circuits' after the words 'designs and industrial models' wherever the latter appears throughout the patents and designs law, by amendments in 1999. Accordingly, the period of protection, the nature of infringements and the sanctions and relief that apply in respect of designs and industrial models also apply to layout-designs. For example, a layout-design must therefore be registered to obtain protection and protection is provided for a period of ten years from date of application. However, the Kuwaiti patents and industrial design law as it currently stands does not provide any definition or description of what may constitute a layout-design or integrated circuit (as it does for a design and an industrial model). This strategy has had the effect of creating by implication an inappropriate description of an integrated circuit as being the same as that for a design or industrial model, namely, 'any arrangement of lines or any type of figure, whether coloured or uncoloured, designed for use in industrial production by a mechanical, manual or chemical process . . .'.[151]

Oman introduced discrete legislation for the protection of layout-designs in 2000, the first Gulf state to do so, but has since incorporated such provisions into its comprehensive industrial-property rights law and rescinded the integrated circuits law of 2000.[152]

The Saudi omnibus law on patents, plant varieties, industrial models and layout-designs dedicates just five articles to the protection of layout-designs, but extends its general provisions throughout the law to apply equally to layout-designs.[153]

The nature and authoritative source of any protection for layout-designs within the UAE intellectual property regime are confused and they appear, therefore, to receive protection more by implication than by specific provision. In July 2001, the UAE advised the WTO that layout-designs were protected under its patent law and specifically that the law's provisions relating to industrial designs and models applied equally to integrated circuits – a similar strategy to that adopted by Kuwait, but without the legislative formalisation.[154] The basis for such claim in the patent law was unclear and the relationship between industrial designs or models and layout-designs was equally unclear. In March 2002, the UAE again advised the WTO that topographies were classified among the works protected under its copyright law.[155] The period of protection was the same as that available to other forms of copyrightable material, very much greater than that provided by the corresponding patent legislation. The WTO appeared to have been satisfied with the UAE response since there is no record of the contradictory explanations having been pursued further.

Since the UAE Ministry has not received any applications for registration of layout-designs of integrated circuits at the time of writing, the veracity of the above claims has not yet been tested. Nor have there been cases on infringements of right-holder's rights in respect of layout-designs or integrated circuits to come before the UAE federal or local courts to clarify under which law a prosecution for infringement of the right the owner of a layout-design might proceed. Table 4.6 shows the current layout-designs of integrated circuits protection in the Gulf states.

4.8.3 Nature and scope of a layout-design

The Bahraini and Qatari laws, and the Omani and Saudi layout-designs sections within their comprehensive laws, base their layout-design provisions

Table 4.6 Current layout-designs of integrated circuits protection in the Gulf states

Bahrain:	Legislative Decree No. 5 of 2006, concerning Layout Designs of Integrated Circuits
Kuwait:	Law No. 4 of 1962 concerning Patents, Designs and Industrial Models, as amended by Law No. 4 of 1999 and Law No. 3 of 2001.
Oman:	Royal Decree No. 67/2008, the Law on Industrial Property Rights
Qatar:	Law No. 6 of 2005 on Protection of Layout-Designs of Integrated Circuits
Saudi Arabia:	Royal Decree No. M/27 of 1425 AH (2004), the Law of Patents, Layout Designs of Integrated Circuits, Plant Varieties, and Industrial Models.
UAE:	—
Yemen:	—

Source: compiled by the author

on the corresponding WIPO model law.[156] They borrow directly from Article 1(i) and (ii) of the model law for their definitions of a layout-design and integrated circuit:

- integrated circuit: a product, in its final form or an intermediary form, which consists of interconnections or elements at least one of which is active and which is intended to perform an electronic function;
- layout design: any three dimensional disposition of interconnections or elements of an integrated circuit, at least one of which is active, which is intended for manufacture.[157]

Originality is a fundamental criterion for protection.[158] Hence, excluded from registrability is any layout-design which has already been commercially exploited locally or overseas more than two years ago.

Registration is a prerequisite for protection; at the same time, registration presumes ownership. Unless the contrary is established, the registrant is deemed to be the right holder of the layout-design and thereby its creator. The right holder alone has the right to commercially exploit the layout-design and is entitled to protection against unlawful importation, sale or other commercial exploitation of the layout-design or other articles in which it is incorporated.[159] The emphasis here is on protecting commercialisation; the laws still allow use of a layout-design without authorisation for research or teaching purposes, for personal or non-commercial use, or where the responsible minister deems such use is in the public interest.

In all three instances, protection is provided from the date of filing an application for registration, or from the date of its first local or foreign commercial exploitation, whichever is the earlier. The Bahraini, Qatari and Saudi laws all provide for a period of protection of ten years; the Bahraini and Saudi laws also include the qualification of Article 6(3) of the Washington Treaty and Article 38.3 of TRIPS (but omitted from the WIPO model law), that in all cases the term of protection expires 15 years after the creation of the layout-design (thereby allowing an extension to the original 10-year period).[160] But very strangely, the Omani law, in what can only be a drafting oversight, provides for protection to commence from date of filing or exploitation, but does not stipulate any term for period of protection *per se*.[161]

The Bahraini, Omani and Saudi laws provide for a system of compulsory licensing as included in the Washington Treaty (but for which neither TRIPS nor the WIPO model laws make any provision). In brief, a non-exclusive, non-assignable compulsory licence may be granted by the responsible minister in circumstances where:

- the layout-design is not locally available; or
- the layout-design is available but with unreasonably low quality standards, or in quantities insufficient to meet local demand, or at prices that the appropriate minister deems abusive; or
- other reasons of public interest, including remedying anti-competitive practices, so require.[162]

To preclude compulsory licensing, the Bahraini and Saudi laws require the layout-design to be utilised by the original right holder within four years of the date of application or three years from grant, whichever is the longer period. Oman does not stipulate any such requirement. Conditions attached to the issuance of a compulsory licence, which largely reflect those stipulated by TRIPS, require that:

- exploitation under the licence is limited to satisfying the needs of the local market only (the assumption being that local market means national market);
- exploitation cannot exceed the scope and purpose for which the licence was originally granted;
- the original right holder is entitled to receive fair compensation.

4.8.4 Infringements

The laws provide, in very similar fashion to each other, a simple description of an infringement as being an act without authorisation that includes copying a layout-design in whole or part, or knowingly importing, selling or distributing a layout-design or the integrated circuit of which it may be part.[163] Saudi Arabia adds that falsely claiming or indicating that a layout-design is registered also constitutes an infringement.

4.9 Undisclosed information, trade secrets and anti-competitive practices

4.9.1 TRIPS provisions and obligations (Article 39–40)

TRIPS provides that undisclosed information and trade secrets are deemed to be protectable under the rules of unfair competition. The protection does not confer any exclusive right, but provides the right (and the obligation) to prevent practices contrary to honest commercial practices with respect to both the disclosure and acquisition of undisclosed information. TRIPS Article 39 requires members to ensure effective protection against unfair competition as provided in Article 10*bis* of the Paris Convention by protecting undisclosed information.[164] Persons and legal entities must be able to prevent information lawfully within their control from being acquired by, or disclosed to, others without their consent in a manner contrary to honest commercial practices, provided that such information:

- is secret in that it is not generally known, either as a whole or in its various parts, to persons who would normally deal with that kind of information;
- has commercial value because of its secret state; and
- has been subject to reasonable steps by its owner to keep it secret.[165]

TRIPS Article 39.3 makes a particular requirement to provide protection against unfair commercial use of undisclosed test or other data submitted as a condition for gaining market approval for new pharmaceutical or agricultural chemical products or for products which utilise new chemical entities. It requires members to protect such data against disclosure, except where it is necessary to protect the public or unless steps are taken to ensure that the data are protected against unfair commercial use.

In respect of the control of anti-competitive practices, TRIPS Article 40 requires members to recognise that some licensing practices pertaining to intellectual property rights which restrain competition may have adverse effects on trade and impede the transfer and dissemination of technology. Members may adopt, consistent with other TRIPS provisions, appropriate measures to prevent or control practices in the licensing of intellectual property rights which are abusive and anti-competitive. TRIPS also provides for a mechanism allowing for consultation and exchange of relevant confidential information between members in situations where companies from those members are involved in a dispute over anti-competitive practices.

4.9.2 Current regional undisclosed information and anti-competitive practices provisions

The positions taken by the Gulf states in respect of the provision of protection for undisclosed information and trade secrets within the prescription of TRIPS Article 39 are evenly balanced between either largely ignoring the matter (Kuwait, Saudi Arabia and Yemen), incorporating some provision within the scope of other intellectual property laws (Oman and the UAE) and providing discrete laws for the protection of trade secrets and acts contrary to honest commercial practices (Bahrain and Qatar). However, the UAE has included some provision for 'know-how', as it is thus described, in its patents and industrial designs law of 2002. In respect of anti-competitive practices in contractual licences, as outlined by TRIPS Article 40, only Bahrain and Oman makes specific acknowledgement of the requirement to control such practices, although all states can also refer to, and rely on, the extensive provisions that already exist outside the intellectual property protection regime. All states can justifiably argue that protection of undisclosed information and anti-competitive practices, being essentially commercial matters, are addressed in detail in their respective commercial codes, civil codes and penal codes.

Kuwait and Saudi Arabia would acknowledge that they do not provide any specific legislative protection of undisclosed information or trade secrets in the intellectual property context, but would claim that some levels of protection are already included elsewhere within their legislative frameworks governing commercial conduct, or that the introduction of appropriate legislation is being examined. Kuwait, for example, has argued that its copyright law guarantees protection of undisclosed information in the copyright context since the owner of a copyright has exclusive right to determine publication of his work.[166] Accordingly, anyone who discloses such information without prior consent from the rightful owner commits an infringement under copyright law. However, this line of argument does not take account of the fact that copyright deals with rights of attribution and economic exploitation but does not encompass rights or obligations in respect of disclosure or non-disclosure. It also ignores the freedom-of-use provisions in respect of copyrighted works which can bring a work into the public domain. More importantly it ignores the fact that TRIPS Article 39 and Paris Convention Article 10*bis* address a requirement for the protection of proprietary information that is not otherwise protected by patents, copyrights, or industrial designs and models laws.

Saudi Arabia has claimed that some protection for undisclosed information of a proprietary nature already exists under other laws outside the intellectual property context. It has asserted that rights relating to the protection of undisclosed information are covered by the Islamic *Shariah* and by existing laws such as the commercial code, commercial transactions code and the banks-control regulation.[167] It has also indicated that it is considering the introduction of an unfair competition law, which will encompass provision for trade secrets and undisclosed information. However, the new law has yet to emerge.

Bahrain's law for the protection of trade secrets was originally rather brief. It consisted of just nine clauses, only four of which dealt substantively with trade secrets and dishonest commercial practice (the other five addressing matters relating to enforcement, administration and due process). However, it was expanded rather significantly in 2006 following the completion of Bahrain's free trade agreement with the United States to add fairly extensive clauses on the protection and confidentiality of undisclosed safety and efficacy data relating to the market approval for new pharmaceutical and agrochemical products. The additions also guarantee exclusive market access against new or similar products using test data already used for marketing efficacy in another country.[168] The additions also incorporate and expand upon the requirements of TRIPS Article 39, including protection of test data submitted to government authorities for obtaining marketing approval of pharmaceutical or agricultural products. Oman now provides similar exclusive marketing provisions for pharmaceutical and agrochemical products, but includes them in an expanded section on protection against unfair competition in its new comprehensive law on industrial property.[169]

Qatar's recently introduced trade secrets law (see Table 4.7) of just 14 articles borrows significantly from the Bahraini former law and from a model law prepared by WIPO. In addition to rather brief and general provisions for protection of commercial secrets, the law specifically extends protection in particular to confidential information concerning marketing approval of pharmaceutical and agrochemical products. Penalties for infringements are substantial in comparison with Qatar's other intellectual property laws. Qatar claims that this law is compatible with TRIPS.[170]

Table 4.7 Current trade secrets and anti-competitive practices protection in the Gulf states

Bahrain:	Legislative Decree No. 7 of 2003 in respect of Trade Secrets, as amended by Law No. 12 of 2006.
Kuwait:	—
Oman:	Royal Decree No. 67/2008, the Law on Industrial Property.
Qatar:	Law No. 5 of 2005 concerning Trade Secrets
Saudi Arabia:	—
UAE:	Federal Law No. 17 of 2002 for the Industrial Regulation and Protection of Patents, Industrial Drawings and Designs
Yemen:	—

Source: compiled by the author

4.9.3 Nature of protection of undisclosed information

Bahrain, Oman, Qatar and the UAE, borrowing directly from TRIPS Article 39, all provide that undisclosed information, or 'know-how', must be protected if:

- it is unknown, or not available among, or readily accessible, to persons who normally deal with such kind of information;
- it draws its commercial value from its confidentiality or secrecy;
- the owner or person lawfully in control of the information has taken reasonable steps to keep it secret.[171]

There is no specified period of protection. Rather, the obligation to protect remains in effect as long as the undisclosed information's value is unknown and it remains secret. Know-how acquired through one's own means or through legal means may be used or disclosed or transferred to another party, but that other party may not use, disclose or communicate any element of know-how without consent of its owner. Disclosure without approval of the owner of the know-how constitutes an infringement, provided that the person committing the act was aware of the confidential nature of the know-how or could not have ignored such nature.

4.9.4 Protection of information relating to pharmaceutical products

The Bahraini, Qatari and Omani laws all make some limited provision for the protection of undisclosed test or other data submitted by an applicant for market authorisation of a pharmaceutical or agricultural chemical product which utilises new chemical entities. In language that is virtually identical to the TRIPS Article 39.3 text, the prohibition on disclosure in the laws:

> '. . . shall extend to undisclosed tests or data which were the outcome of considerable effort, and which are submitted to the competent authorities for the purpose of obtaining approval for marketing of pharmaceutical or agricultural chemical products utilising new chemicals entities.'[172]

The laws also provide, as required by TRIPS Articles 70.8 and 70.9, that the government authority in receipt of the tests or data must protect them against disclosure for as long as they remain secret. It must also prohibit their unfair commercial use by preventing any third party using the data without approval in the marketing of similar drugs or products for five years following the date of marketing approval of the drugs or products.

The UAE position on protection of pharmaceutical and agrochemical products realises an equally strong level of protection. It enables inventions dealing with the chemistry of drugs or pharmaceutical compounds to be protected by patents or utility certificates if they meet the conditions required by the law and its implementing regulations as of 1 January 2005.[173] However, some degree of protection has already been in place through Ministerial Decree No. 404 of 2000, which stipulates that no drug or new pharmaceutical compound shall be registered unless it has been granted a patent – thereby extending to the drug or compound the protection and confidentiality applicable to patents. The decree also requires the secrecy of information attached to an application for registration of a drug or pharmaceutical compound to be protected. The issuance of this ministerial decree was a direct response to pressure brought to bear by US pharmaceutical industry groups through the Office of the US Trade Representative.

4.9.5 Control of anti-competitive practices in contractual licences

Oman has recently extensively expanded its provisions for control of anti-competitive practices and protection against unfair competition. An act or practice that is contrary to 'honest practices' now includes, but is not limited to, the following:

- breach of contract, breach of confidence and inducement to breach;
- acquisition of undisclosed information by third parties who knew, or were grossly negligent in failing to know, that such practices were involved in the acquisition;
- breach of legal duties in general when their purpose or consequence is to obtain illicit advantages over competitors, such as the breach of environmental or labour law;
- any act or practice, in the course of industrial or commercial activities, that may cause confusion or mislead with respect to another's enterprise or its activities, in particular, its products or services;
- any similar act or practice that may damage the goodwill or reputation of another's enterprise, regardless of whether such act or practice causes confusion;
- any false or unjustifiable allegation that may be likely to discredit another's enterprise or its activities, in particular its products or services;
- any act or practice that results in the disclosure, acquisition or use by others of undisclosed information without the consent of the person lawfully in control of that information and in a manner contrary to honest commercial practices.[174]

Bahrain's law provides that the following constitute acts which are contrary to honest commercial practices:

- disclosure of secret information acquired by a party to a 'confidentiality agreement';
- disclosure of, or inducement to disclose, secret information in breach of a duty of trust;
- misappropriation of information by unlawful means including fraud, espionage, theft or other improper means;
- acquiring trade secrets from another person while knowing, or being capable of knowing, that such other person has acquired the trade secrets unlawfully.[175]

As a rather curious and awkward inclusion for a law of this nature – which indicates that the law was largely and loosely constructed by borrowings from Bahrain's other intellectual property laws – provision is included for a person whose rights have, or appear to have, been infringed to seek provisional relief. Such relief includes the cessation of the infringement, the provisional seizure of articles and goods including imported goods on arrival, and the seizure of infringing machinery and tools and related evidence.[176]

4.10 New plant varieties

4.10.1 TRIPS provisions and obligations

Protection of new plant varieties as a distinct and separate intellectual property right falls outside the scope of TRIPS, which confines the treatment of their protection to being a patent matter. TRIPS Article 27.3(b), in addressing patentable subject matter, provides that inventions which include plants and essentially biological processes for the production of plants, other than non-biological and microbiological processes, may be excluded from patentability. However, it still requires members to provide for the protection of plant varieties either by patents or by an effective *sui generis* system or by a combination of both.

It has been suggested that this flexibility reflects the lack of consensus on the form that protection of plant varieties should take – that is, whether they should be protectable under the European approach of breeder's rights, or the US and Japanese approach of protection under a patents regime.[177] These different approaches lead to a different scope and extent of protection. While the breeder's rights regime permits protection of a plant variety as determined by a specific combination of genes, it does not allow for the protection of particular genes, a possibility instead allowed under patent law.

Outside of the TRIPS patent-protection approach, the international standard of protection is that established by the Convention of the International Union for the Protection of New Plant Varieties (1999) (UPOV Convention).[178] The Convention grants protection of a new plant variety to the breeder – the breeder being defined as the person who breeds, or discovers and develops, and registers, a new plant variety. The bounds or characteristics of 'discovers and develops' are the subject of intense international debate. However, 'breeding' may include the isolation and propagation of a naturally occurring mutation or variation. To be deemed protectable, a plant variety must meet the conditions of being:

- new, by virtue of not being the subject of prior commercial acts;
- distinct, by being clearly distinguishable from any other variety;
- uniform or homogeneous in its relevant characteristics;
- stable, after a cycle of propagation or repeated propagation;
- variety denominated, having a denomination under which it may be commercialised.[179]

The breeder's basic right in respect of a particular plant variety encompasses the production, reproduction and conditioning for propagation, together with the selling, marketing, importing or exporting and stocking of the new variety. The scope of the right includes not only the plant variety or propagated material itself but also the harvested material and may extend to products made directly from the harvested material.[180] The breeder's rights do not prohibit use by others of protected propagation material for non-commercial or private purposes, for experimental purposes or for the purpose of breeding other varieties. But this is a limited use, in effect confined to research and experimental uses. The use by others provision does not automatically extend to include farmers or recognise their rights to use farm-saved or own-harvested propagating material or seed for replanting. The existence and possible application of a farmer's right, if any, is left to the Convention signatories to decide, depending on their own circumstances or interests, or to the bargaining outcomes of multilateral or bilateral agreements.

4.10.2 Current regional new-plant-varieties provisions

As is the case with layout-designs of integrated circuits, statutory protection of new plant varieties or plant breeder's rights has received little attention or action from the Gulf states, and there is little indication of external pressure upon them within the context of the WTO to comply with their TRIPS obligations at this stage. The states either largely ignore the issue of protection of new plant varieties (Bahrain, Kuwait, Qatar, the UAE and Yemen) or add specific provisions on the protection of new plant varieties to the general provisions of their patent laws (Oman and Saudi Arabia).

Bahrain, Kuwait, Qatar, the UAE and Yemen do not make any substantive provision, either in their respective patent laws or other intellectual property laws, for the protection of new plant varieties, although Bahrain has recently removed plants from the types of inventions excluded from patent protection. Kuwait, the UAE and Yemen have stipulated in their patent laws that patent protection shall not be extended to plant varieties and essentially biological ways for producing them (excluding microbiological processes or the products thereof), but have not developed any alternative protecting legislation.[181] The GCC Unified Patent Regulations also excludes plant species and varieties from patent protection in the same manner as these individual states.[182] Bahrain for some years has had in local circulation a draft new plant variety protection law along similar lines to Oman's law. Both Bahrain and Oman have acceded to the UPOV Convention as part of their respective free trade agreements with the United States; Bahrain's draft *sui generis* law will now need to be enacted, or its patent law updated, to enable local implementation of the Convention's provisions.[183]

Saudi Arabia, meanwhile, has adopted a hybrid approach that borrows both from the patent-protection approach and the *sui generis* option. It dedicates five articles within its patent law specifically to the protection of new plant varieties, but also provides for the general patent provisions to apply equally to new plant varieties.

Oman originally followed the *sui generis* alternative offered by TRIPS Article 27.3(b) by enacting specific legislation for the protection of new plant varieties in 2000. The law follows the plant breeders' regime for the protection of new plant varieties enshrined in the UPOV Convention and draws upon some (but not all) elements of the UPOV Model Law on the Protection of New Plant Varieties, from which it draws much of its text. However, in 2008 it issued a comprehensive industrial-property law which extended the scope of patent protection to include new plant varieties, in similar fashion to the Saudi approach (see Table 4.8).

Table 4.8 Current new-plant-varieties protection in the Gulf states

Bahrain:	Legislative Decree No. 12 of 2005 ratifying Bahrain's accession to the International Convention for the Protection of New Plant Varieties (UPOV Convention)
Kuwait:	—
Oman:	Royal Decree No. 67/2008, the Law on Industrial Property Royal Decree No. 37/2007, ratifying Oman's accession to the International Convention for the Protection of New Plant Varieties (UPOV Convention) Royal Decree No. 92/2000, the Law on the Protection of New Plant Varieties
Qatar:	—
Saudi Arabia:	Royal Decree No. M/27 1425 AH (2004) in respect of Patents, Layout Designs of Integrated Circuits, Plant Varieties, and Industrial Models.
UAE:	—
Yemen:	—

Source: compiled by the author

Oman is now in the curious position of providing protection for new plant varieties under its industrial-property law of 2008 as well as under its *sui generis* law of 2000. It has also acceded to the UPOV Convention. However, provisions between the two laws and UPOV differ somewhat – not least being the periods of protection, with patent provisions stipulating a period of protection of 20 years, while UPOV provides for 20 years for plants and 25 years for vines and trees. This situation appears to have arisen because a different ministry is responsible for the original plant-varieties law and the plant-varieties law was omitted – by accident or by design – from the 2000 suite of other intellectual property laws that was specifically rescinded by issuance of the new comprehensive industrial-property law in 2008.[184]

4.10.3 Scope of protection for new plant varieties

Both the Omani and Saudi laws provide that to qualify for protection, a plant variety, or its propagation types or elements, must be new or novel, distinct, homogeneous, and constant or stable.[185] A variety is new or novel if it (or its propagating material) has not been marketed within the country for more than one year or marketed elsewhere for more than six years in the case of trees or vines or four years in the case of all other plant varieties. A variety is deemed to be distinct if it is distinguishable from other known varieties by at least one characteristic, is uniform if the differences between its elements are within generally accepted limits, and is stable if its main characteristics remain unchanged after repeated propagation.

The right of protection by registration is granted to the breeder of the plant variety or his successors in title, the breeder being commonly defined as the person who breeds, discovers or develops a plant variety. Registration grants to the breeder, being the right owner, the right of:

- sole utilisation of propagating types and elements for the commercial plant production;
- transfer of all or part of the utilisation right, with or without financial consideration;
- preventing third parties from utilising the right and to seek precautionary relief;
- legal compensation against infringements;
- requiring any person offering for sale or marketing the plant variety or its propagating elements to use the registered designation or name for that plant variety.[186]

However, exceptions to this right permit use of the protected plant variety for experimental or research activities and personal non-commercial use.

Neither the Omani *sui generis* law nor the Saudi law formally recognise or even acknowledge the right of the farmer to further propagate and use plant material which is the product of a harvest on his own holding, but which may otherwise be patent-protected plant material. In fact, the Saudi law in effect excludes any provision for farmer's rights by stipulating that such acts as producing or propagating patented plant material, adapting it for the purposes of propagation, or storing it for such purposes, constitutes an infringement of the rights of the plant patentee.[187] Such rights extend to harvested material in whole or in part.

The Omani industrial-property law, meanwhile, rather succinctly provides that patent rights relating to new plant varieties shall not extend to any acts by farmers to propagate a patented variety or an essentially derived variety which is the product of a harvest from their own holdings, provided that such acts are within reasonable limits and the legitimate interests of the patent owner are still safeguarded.[188]

Both Omani laws and the Saudi law also provide for a system of compulsory licensing to be available for plant varieties, as is permitted under the TRIPS patent provisions, but for which no provision is made in the UPOV and the WIPO model law.[189] The responsible minister may grant a non-exclusive compulsory licence where the owner of the plant variety has not made sufficient use of the plant variety within three years from registration and has not otherwise agreed to grant a licence on reasonable terms to the applicant, or where the award of the compulsory licence is necessary to protect the public interest. The issuance of a compulsory licence does not prejudice the right of the right holder to reasonable compensation.

Neither of Oman's laws have received any real scrutiny from the WTO. During the WTO Council of TRIPS review of Oman's intellectual property protection regime in June 2001, Oman escaped any questioning by members on its plant variety protection law.[190] Up to December 2007, the Omani responsible ministry, being the Ministry of Agriculture, had not received any applications for the registration of plant breeding rights, so the efficacy of either the new-plant-varieties law or the comprehensive industrial property law, and the extent to which they are in conflict, has yet to be tested.

4.11 Concluding remarks

The picture that emerges from the foregoing examination of the Gulf states' intellectual property legislative regimes is that, at the global level, the regimes have a thread of common purpose and generally a broad strategic direction. However, at the lower level of individual laws, there exist instances of both considerable similarity and significant deviation in their content and structure. In some instances, laws share common material, and it is apparent that there has been wholesale borrowing in a number of cases – to the extent that their texts (in the English-language translations at least) are virtually identical. However, some laws also retain their own peculiar idiosyncrasies in other instances; they reveal glaring omissions and are notable for their brevity and lack of sophistication when compared with the corresponding statutes of their sister states. This is particularly the case in respect of some of the region's copyright laws.

What also emerges from a scrutiny of the states' performance in respect of their adoption of the latest international standards on intellectual property protection is that those states which currently lead the vanguard in this regard – namely Bahrain and Oman – have done so outside the multilateral context. Instead, their latest suites of laws since 2006 have developed out of the context of their free trade agreements with the United States. While these agreements have often incorporated a requirement for adherence to multilateral conventions sponsored by the WTO or WIPO, they have also incorporated higher standards of intellectual property protection, but only in areas of particular concern to the United States. Developed in a bilateral context, they are then utilised in subsequent bilateral agreements as the new international standards.

It should be no surprise that the intellectual property laws which are the most comprehensive and sophisticated are those relating to copyright and neighbouring rights and trademarks, since these are the two areas which have most concerned the developed countries in ensuring that their own rights and investments in the Gulf region are protected. Patents rights and the remaining rights enshrined in TRIPS, in which there is not the same imperative for preservation of interests and investments, either have gained some degree of protection by laws noticeable for their brevity or by association, or have been largely passed over.

From mid 2000, the WTO's Council of TRIPS initiated a review programme of national implementing legislation of member states which had taken advantage of WTO's five-year transitional period from the date of introduction of TRIPS and states that had joined after January 2000. Bahrain, Kuwait, Oman, Qatar and the UAE all participated in the review at different times. The review is illuminating because it would appear to indicate that, at least as far as the Council of TRIPS and the states were concerned, the process was more important than the outcome. Kuwait was the first of the Gulf states to undergo the review process, with the review of its laws initiated at the Council's November 2000 meeting. At its subsequent meeting a year later, the Council Chair informed members that Kuwait had now provided answers to all follow-up questions, which had been circulated.[191] The Council agreed that the item concerning the review of Kuwait's intellectual property laws be deleted from the agenda, it being understood that any delegation was free to revert to any matter stemming from them at any time. No further debate or analysis of Kuwait's responses to individual questions, the adequacy or otherwise of those responses, or the general efficacy of its intellectual property laws appears to have taken place.

A similar scenario existed in respect of the reviews of the intellectual property laws of Bahrain, Oman and the UAE, all of which were initiated in June 2001. By November that year, it was reported that the initial answers provided by Bahrain and Oman were still being analysed by some members, and responses from Oman and the UAE to some follow-up questions posed by members were still outstanding.[192] The meeting agreed that the review of Bahrain's laws be deleted from the agenda, while Oman and the UAE were urged to provide outstanding responses without delay. The UAE reported in June 2002 that it was due to soon introduce patents, trademarks and copyright laws which were TRIPS-compliant. Although the UAE still had some responses to questions outstanding, the Council agreed to delete its review from the agenda.[193] Similarly, Oman's review was deleted at the September 2002 meeting when the Council learned that it had provided answers to outstanding questions.[194]

Qatar's review, scheduled for November 2001, was postponed to the second half of 2002 because Qatar was still finishing the process of bringing its intellectual property laws into TRIPS compliance. At the June 2002 meeting of the Council, members were informed that Qatar had responded to most of the questions submitted by members. Qatar provided a brief introductory overview of the structure of its legislation in the areas covered by TRIPS and proposed changes to make its legislation TRIPS compatible.[195] However, the review remained incomplete. Thereafter, references to Qatar's incomplete review of its legislation appear spasmodically between the November 2002 and June 2005 meetings, without any further input from Qatar or resolution of the review. And there the matter appears to have rested.

The form of the responses provided by these states in their respective reviews consisted substantially of repeating extracts and quotes from the laws themselves, with little in the way of commentary, analysis or explanation of any great substance. It should be remembered that the states construct their responses with the guidance of WIPO; perhaps more accurately, the answers were prepared for them. One could be forgiven for assuming that the reviews were simply going through the motions, except in areas of genuine concern to the major players. Perhaps one reason for this role-play and the nature of the responses is that the real action of the developed countries to preserve their hold on the areas of intellectual property rights of concern and commercial interest was already moving into other fora outside the TRIPS context, such as the environment of the TRIPS-plus treaties and the forum of bilateral relationships. If the outcome of the Council of TRIPS reviews is, in essence, a 'signing off' on the compliance level of the states' intellectual property laws, then the states might feel entitled to argue that, by the end of 2002, they had established legislative regimes for the protection of intellectual property which generally comply with the international standards as laid down by TRIPS. However, as the foregoing review of the states' intellectual property laws has pointed out, and which the states themselves would freely acknowledge, the legislative regimes still contain many shortcomings and omissions.

The intellectual property laws of the Gulf states are ripe for, and would be significantly enhanced by, a process of review leading towards a greater degree of regional harmonisation. Such review should focus upon the elimination of some of those idiosyncrasies and the mutual adoption of the positive and comprehensive elements of the more recent and robust laws.

The existence of intellectual property laws which enjoy a greater degree of regionally common substantive provisions would make a useful contribution to state initiatives towards effective implementation. Given the importance of effective border controls as a crucial element in any enforcement strategy, common provisions relating to movement and control of goods across state borders would make a significant contribution to the campaigns to combat the increasing problem of regional intellectual property piracy and counterfeiting. Harmonised laws would also complement other GCC and Gulf regional trade initiatives – such as those directed towards regional free trade areas, common customs union, regional power grids, financial structures and the proposed common currency. The GCC member states as a regional group have already embraced a regional patents protection law to complement their national patents laws and are now deciding whether to similarly embrace a regional trademark law – again, to complement national laws.

At a more pragmatic level, a greater degree of harmonisation of the region's intellectual property laws may well lead to an enhanced understanding of the laws themselves at the operational level and facilitate the collectivisation of locally nurtured talent and expertise that is emerging in the states' various ministries, judiciaries and enforcement agencies. A negative side of regional harmonisation is that the most recent laws would likely be the drivers in such an exercise – these being the Bahraini and Omani laws driven by the higher protection standards across a broad spectrum of intellectual property arising from their recent free trade agreements with the United States. But the paucity of strategic regional direction also leaves the individual states susceptible to the external unilateral pressures to conform to the intellectual property laws of the industrialised countries rather than local laws which more appropriately address national and regional needs.

However, having the requisite laws, irrespective of whether they have TRIPS-related shortcomings, are TRIPS-compliant or include TRIPS-plus provisions, is one thing; being able to effectively enforce them and achieve the desired national objectives is another matter – as Chapter 5 explores.

5 Post-TRIPS and the enforcement dichotomy

5.1 Introduction

Having the requisite intellectual property laws, even if they are not fully TRIPS-compliant, is one thing; being able to effectively enforce them and achieve the desired outcomes is another matter. The most challenging element of the post-TRIPS period, as perceived by both the Gulf states themselves and the developed industrial countries, is the regional enforcement of the states' intellectual property protection obligations consistent with the standards enshrined in TRIPS, the TRIPS-plus treaties and bilateral agreements to which the states have acceded. Notwithstanding the presence of comprehensive sets of laws and treaty commitments, there exists a dichotomy between the principle of intellectual property protection as enshrined in the various legislative regimes and its practical application as exemplified by the degree of effective enforcement action. On the one hand, the states now enjoy comprehensive statutory regimes and are progressively initiating the consequential structural, judicial and institutional reforms to give the regimes full and proper effect; on the other hand, the effectiveness of enforcement actions against infringing activities, particularly in respect of piracy and counterfeit goods, the nature and frequency of judicial actions and the severity of penalties available, has yet to reach the standards required by the developed nations which constitute the major global exporters of intellectual property.

The barriers to the elimination of intellectual property infringements, which lie at the heart of this dichotomy, do not rest solely in the domain of the administering and enforcement authorities or the judiciary; entrenched local societal, cultural and commercial attitudes and practices are also major contributing factors.

The TRIPS enforcement regime is addressed in Part III of the Agreement and applies equally to all intellectual property rights covered in Part II. The regime is primarily self-contained, but is also based in part on the Paris and Berne Conventions. The Berne Convention provides reference in respect of the right to enforce protected works (art. 15), seizure of infringing copies (art. 16) and application of the convention (art. 36), while the Paris Convention includes articles in respect of seizures (arts 9 and 10) and appropriate remedies (art. 10*ter*). Neither the Rome Convention nor the Washington

Treaty contain any enforcement or sanction provisions. The principal features of Part III are the existence of adequate norms and minimum standards for the protection of intellectual property, the effective enforcement of those norms and standards, both domestically and at state borders, and an effective dispute-resolution settlement mechanism to ensure that member states comply with their obligations to provide those adequate norms and standards for their effective enforcement.

TRIPS Part III requires WTO members to provide under their domestic laws a comprehensive regime that ensures that the intellectual property rights established in TRIPS Part II can be effectively enforced, both by their own nationals and by foreign right holders. As part of that regime, members are required to make provision for:

- fair and equitable civil and administrative procedures;
- independent judicial review of final administrative decisions on appeal;
- provisional measures;
- border-control measures on application and *ex officio*;
- damages and indemnification;
- criminal procedures and remedies.

The Gulf states have achieved only partial success in meeting the TRIPS Part III requirements. They have generally succeeded in establishing the necessary legislative regimes and judicial frameworks that address the above TRIPS requirements (although not exclusively within intellectual property frameworks). However, they have not been as successful in creating and bringing to a state of operational effectiveness the essential infrastructural and administrative strategies and processes. All states now allow for matters relating to intellectual property rights to be pursued in civil and criminal jurisdictions. They also enable aggrieved right holders to seek provisional measures against actual or potential infringements. In some states and in some laws, enforcement provisions have been strengthened by increases in the nature and scale of sanctions and by the introduction of sanctions which provide for seizure of infringing goods and material, closures of infringing premises, compensation and increased penalties for repeat offences. In respect of the issue of independent judicial review, the post-2000 laws have moved to reduce such discretion by transferring much of the officials' discretionary powers and functions to the civil courts or by requiring administrative decision-making to be subject to at least semi-independent, quasi-judicial appeal, or final judicial review.

The majority of the states' intellectual property laws have benefited from an extensive input into their creative development and legislative drafting by WIPO through its International Bureau. They have also been subject to frequent exchanges of views and borrowings from within the states themselves. It is not surprising, therefore, that in most cases the laws generally conform with the thrust of the TRIPS enforcement obligations, the main exception in this regard being Yemen's pre-TRIPS law. However, they still fall well short of the TRIPS-plus standards in respect of deterrent levels of sanctions being increasingly demanded by the developed nations through bilateral trade agreements. This has caused them to continue to attract critical attention from the developed countries and particularly the international watchdog organisations and lobby groups representing the major global producers and exporters of the main forms of intellectual property.

5.2 TRIPS enforcement obligations[1] and the response of the Gulf states

5.2.1 General obligations and civil and administrative procedures (TRIPS Articles 41–49)

TRIPS Article 41 requires members to have in place enforcement procedures which permit effective action against infringements and remedies that constitute an effective deterrent to further infringing activity. The enforcement procedures must be equitable and fair; they must not be unnecessarily complicated or costly or involve unreasonable time limits or unwarranted delays. Nor must their application create a barrier to legitimate trade. However, a member is not obliged to put in place a special judicial system for intellectual property rights enforcement distinct from that for the enforcement of law in general; nor is a member required to make a preferential allocation of resources to intellectual property enforcement at the expense of the law in general. Members are required to make provision for parties to a proceeding to have opportunity for judicial review of final administrative decisions, and subject to jurisdictional provisions in a member's law concerning the importance of a case, of at least the legal aspects of initial judicial decisions.

Members are required to make civil judicial procedures available to right holders to enforce their intellectual property rights established by TRIPS, including procedures that will provide:

- timely and detailed written notice of the basis of any claims;
- representation by independent legal counsel;
- the right to present evidence and to substantiate their claims;
- protection from 'overly burdensome requirements concerning mandatory personal appearances';
- protection of confidential information, unless contrary to constitutional requirements.[2]

Judicial authorities must be given the authority to order parties in control of evidence which may substantiate another party's claim to produce such evidence.[3] Where a party refuses or otherwise does not do so, judicial authorities must be empowered to make any preliminary and final determinations, affirmative or negative, on the basis of the information presented to them, provided that all parties have had the opportunity to be heard on the allegations and the evidence. Discretion is granted to members to authorise judicial authorities to order the infringer to inform the right holder of the identity of third persons involved in the production and distribution of the infringing goods or services and of their channels of distribution. The exercise of such authority must not be 'out of proportion to the seriousness of the infringement', although no guidance is provided as to the benchmarks for 'proportion' or 'seriousness'. To militate against the frivolous or abusive use of enforcement provisions, judicial authorities are to have the authority to order a party who has abused enforcement procedures to provide adequate compensation for the injury suffered because of such abuse to a party wrongfully enjoined or restrained. This provision extends to government officials, whose exemption from liability to appropriate remedial measures exists only to the extent that their actions are taken or intended in good faith in the course of administration of a particular law.

The provisions within the states for civil and administrative processes in relation to the enforcement of intellectual property rights as required by TRIPS tend to be prescribed in statutes other than the states' intellectual property laws. All states possess longstanding statutes relating to civil and commercial procedures, the judiciary and judicial procedures, and penal codes which include extensive provisions on the conduct of criminal investigation, evidence and prosecution.[4] The longstanding existence of Islamic jurisprudence with a complexity and sophistication that compares favourably with western legal systems, together with a comprehensive codification of civil and commercial regimes, ensured that the states enjoyed well-established civil and administrative review procedures in judicial proceedings prior to TRIPS-related intellectual property laws coming into effect. However, one conspicuous element which has been given some attention in the TRIPS-related intellectual property laws is the degree of discretionary administrative final decision-making. This has been progressively curtailed by the emergence of provisions for judicial authority to have the powers to review such decision-making, although such inclusions are still not uniform across the states' intellectual property laws.

Where the exceptions arise because of the absence or inadequacy of such judicial provision, they generally appear as curious variations to the norm. It would seem that their occurrences are more likely to be due to continuing adherence to the conservative position or oversight, rather than a deliberate stratagem to avoid independent review. Some of the more recent laws, such as the various industrial-property laws of Bahrain and the comprehensive industrial-property law of Oman, introduce into the appeal process an additional level of administrative authority through the creation of quasi-judicial appeals committees.[5] While the committees generally enjoy a degree of independence, they are still appointed by the minister responsible for that particular area of intellectual property. This additional process has two benefits – first, it acts somewhat as a facilitator, providing a filter for a judicial system already overburdened with largely trivial or procedural matters; second, it retains the decision-making in the area in which the main expertise in the practical issues relating to intellectual property rights is likely to reside. Where the appeals committee strategy falls short of the standard required by TRIPS is that the effective source of higher authority still rests with the minister concerned. While the committee may in certain instances contain external or independent members, it still falls largely within the gift of the minister concerned to make or recommend the appointment of its members. However, it must be stressed that, notwithstanding the role of the minister and the appeals committee, further provision still exists in most laws in most states for final appeal to rest with an independent judicial authority through the civil courts.

Like Bahrain and Oman, Kuwait, Qatar and the UAE provide for the ministerial appeals committee process. The UAE goes to some lengths to emphasise the committee's independence. In respect of patent and industrial designs and models, the committee is 'headed by a judge nominated by the Minister of Justice and Islamic Affairs and Awqaf and two persons with experience in relation to industrial property rights regulated by this Law from outside the Department. . .'.[6] The corresponding trademark law provides for a committee, again appointed by the Minister of Economy and Commerce but which comprises the Ministry Under-Secretary as chairman, two representatives of the Ministry and one representative of each Emirate chosen by the competent authority. Even so, decisions of both committees may still subsequently be appealed to the civil court in accordance with the Civil Procedures Code.

Saudi Arabia's industrial-property laws provide that appeals against administrative decisions may be made to the quasi-judicial Board of Grievances.[7] In the case of trademark matters, the Board serves as the first and only forum for appeal against administrative decisions, whereas in the case of patents and industrial models, a standing committee of five members plays an intermediate role. The committee is vested with the power to initially hear all disputes and contests of administrative decisions, with appeals against decisions of the committee being heard by the Board of Grievances.

The GCC Unified Patent Regulations, which have been recognised *de jure* or at least *de facto* by all GCC member states, as constituting or complementing their domestic patent laws, provide for the establishment by the GCC Ministerial Council of a 'Grievance Committee' to consider appeals against decisions of the GCC Patents Office.[8] However, the GCC also acknowledges that the final authority in respect of appeals must still rest with the respective GCC member states themselves, by stipulating that such final appeal shall be made in accordance with the laws of the state concerned.

Although the copyright laws do not provide the same scope as the industrial property laws for discretionary administrative decision-making, some provision still exists in limited instances – notably in respect of the granting of local licences for the translation into Arabic of foreign works. The Kuwaiti and Saudi laws allow appeals against administrative decision-making to be made directly to the courts of first instance (Kuwait) or the equivalent Board of Grievances (Saudi Arabia).[9] No specific provision exists in the copyright law of Qatar and, rather unusually, in the recent copyright laws of Bahrain and Oman for appeal to independent judicial authority against decisions of administrative bodies or the responsible minister, although the extent of discretionary authority available to administrative bodies is considerably less than that available under the industrial-property laws.

Again, even the pre-TRIPS intellectual property law of Yemen includes provision for the civil courts to adjudicate on administrative decision-making in matters relating to patents, trademarks and industrial designs, but does not make similar allowance in respect of copyright matters.[10] Right of appeal exists directly from the administrative decisions without the need for intermediate internal review processes, as apply in some of the GCC member states.

5.2.2 Provisional relief (TRIPS Article 50)

TRIPS Article 50 requires WTO members to provide their judicial authorities with authority to prevent an infringement of an intellectual property right from occurring or to stop an infringement in progress, preserve relevant evidence in regard to an alleged infringement, and in particular prevent goods, including imported goods, from entering the commercial market, by the ordering of injunctive relief. The measures may be adopted *inaudita altera parte*, particularly where any delay is likely to cause irreparable harm to the right holder or poses a demonstrable risk of evidence being destroyed. The judicial authorities can require an applicant for *ex parte* orders to provide any reasonable evidence in order to establish that an infringement has occurred or is imminent, and to supply other information necessary for the identification of the goods concerned to assist the authority which will enforce the provisional measure. The judicial authorities must also be authorised to require, at their discretion, that the applicant provide a security or equivalent assurance sufficient to protect the defendant and to counter abuse of provisional measures. If proceedings have not been initiated within a reasonable period, the defendant may request that the provisional measures be revoked or cease to have effect. Where provisional measures are revoked or lapse, or where no infringement is subsequently found, the judicial authorities may order the applicant upon request of the defendant to compensate the defendant for any injury caused by the provisional measures.

Common to the intellectual property laws of all Gulf states are provisions for a range of precautionary measures and provisional relief against threatened or actual infringements of intellectual property rights. There are some instances, as mentioned below, where the precautionary measures in individual laws fall somewhat short of the standard required by TRIPS Article 50.

Again, where these deficient laws are disparate from the provisions enshrined in other domestic intellectual property laws, it would appear that the deficiency lies more with drafting or translation issues than a deliberate stratagem on the part of the legislators. Notwithstanding these few instances, the intentions at least of the prescribed measures are generally very similar across all states and across all areas of intellectual property law. Perhaps again not surprisingly, arguably the most comprehensive statements of precautionary measures are to be found in the recent Bahraini and Omani copyright and industrial-property laws. They both stipulate that a court may generally order the following measures:

- direction that the alleged infringement cease or not take place;
- appointment of an expert to prepare a detailed description of the alleged infringing activity, work, goods or material, together with the materials, equipment and devices suspected of being used in the infringement;
- orders for the preservation of related evidence;
- attachment on the alleged infringing versions or copies of the work, goods or material and the materials, equipment, implements and devices suspected of being used in the infringement together with the proceeds generated from the suspected infringement;
- prevention of the entry into the channels of commerce of suspected infringing goods, including imported goods immediately after customs clearance.[11]

By contrast, Oman's now anachronistic, but still in force, law on the protection of new plant varieties lacks any authority for the award of provisional measures, or prescription of what such measures may or may not constitute. Instead, it merely stipulates rather incongruously that 'anyone requesting precautionary measures should deposit a bond, as estimated by the court, prior to pronouncing the order, and raise the relevant case . . .'.[12]

In similar fashion, the other states do not see an imperative to be so comprehensive. Saudi Arabia, for example, makes provision in its patents, industrial models, layout-designs and new-plant-varieties law for the Board of Grievances to take such emergency action as it deems appropriate in respect of an actual or threatened infringement. However, the law does not provide any prescription or make any specific mention of provisional measures *per se* or the consequent warranty and succeeding substantive action, deferring such detail to the subordinate implementing regulations. The law provides simply that '. . . the Committee may take the necessary prompt measures it deems necessary to prevent the damages resulting from the infringement'.[13] In like terms, the Saudi copyright law simply stipulates: 'It [the committee] may take any temporary measure it finds necessary to protect the copyright till a final decision is reached regarding the complaint or grievance.'[14]

The measures for the preservation of related evidence are in essence the local equivalent of the UK Anton Piller orders, in that they may be taken as conservatory measures where delay may prejudice the right holder beyond compensation or where there is an established risk that material which constitutes evidence related to the infringement will be lost. The measures may be taken without prior notification to the defendant, although the defendant must be notified of the measures as soon as they are implemented. The defendant may appeal the orders within a prescribed period of time after notification or implementation, and the court may confirm, amend or withdraw the measures at its discretion.

As a countermeasure against abuse of the availability of provisional measures, or frivolous complaints of alleged infringement, most laws require applications for relief to be accompanied by a surety as determined by the court and which must be lodged with the court. The issuance of any orders must be followed within a stipulated and limited period of time – ranging from 8 days (the UAE) to 30 days (Oman, copyright) – by a substantive action brought before the court. Failure to do so causes the orders to cease to have effect and leaves the complainant liable to claims for compensation by the party against whom the orders were sought. The Saudi (except for its trademark law) and the Kuwaiti laws do not require lodgement of sureties.

5.2.3 Special requirements relating to border measures (TRIPS Articles 51–60)

The special requirements relating to border measures constitute a significant proportion of the TRIPS enforcement obligations. They establish a scheme for suspension of the release into circulation of suspected counterfeit trademark or pirated copyright goods, either on application by a right holder or by *ex-officio* action by border authorities.[15]

The strategy of utilising border seizure to control the trade in infringing goods is foreshadowed in the Paris Convention, which provides that 'all goods unlawfully bearing a trademark or trade name shall be seized on importation into those countries of the Union where such mark or trade name is entitled to protection'.[16] Members are required to make provision for the holder of an intellectual property right to make application to administrative or judicial authorities for customs authorities to suspend the release of goods into free circulation where grounds exist for suspecting that the importation of counterfeit trademark or pirated goods may occur.[17] Such provision need not apply in respect of goods in transit, or where a particular border is subject to a customs union between two members. Members may permit the competent authorities to act upon their own initiative in suspending the release of goods where *prima facie* evidence exists that an intellectual property right is being infringed. Members may order the destruction or disposal of infringing goods outside the channels of commerce, but shall not allow the re-exportation of counterfeit goods in an unaltered state or subject them to a different custom procedure, other than in exceptional circumstances.[18]

The right holder may be required to lodge a bond or surety in order to protect the defendant and the competent authorities, and to prevent abuse.[19] Payment of such surety shall not prejudice any other remedy available to the right holder. The surety shall be released if the right holder fails to pursue the right of action within the prescribed period of time.

Suspended goods must be released if customs authorities are not informed within a prescribed period that provisional measures have been ordered prolonging the suspension or that judicial proceedings have been initiated.[20] Where suspension of the release of goods is carried out or continued in accordance with a provisional measure, the suspension shall be revoked or cease to have effect if proceedings are not initiated. Where an importer has suffered injury because of the wrongful detention of goods, or where the goods are released because the right holder does not initiate an action within the prescribed period, authorities shall be empowered to order the right holder to pay compensation to the importer, consignee and owner of the detained goods for any injury suffered.

The attention given by most Gulf states in their intellectual property laws to the special border-control requirements of TRIPS is slight to say the least. This might in part be attributable to the eventual establishment of the customs union between the GCC member states in January 2003, after a very long gestation period. A footnote to TRIPS Part III, Section 4 allows that a member shall not be required to apply the provisions of Section 4 at borders with other members with which it has formed a custom union and amongst which all controls over movement of goods across these borders have been substantially dismantled. However, reliance on this provision ignores the fact that the amount of intra-GCC trade represents a small percentage of the total trade of each state. In any case, the states might well argue, as Oman has done before the Council of TRIPS, that the provisions relating to infringements of an intellectual property right and to the remedies and provisional relief apply equally to infringing imported and export goods.[21] They would also argue that a right holder can obtain orders on the suspension of customs clearance of allegedly counterfeit goods as part of the provisional measures and relief generally available, and that these provisions by and large correspond to TRIPS Articles 51–60. Customs have the legal authority to act *ex officio* to detain and/or seize suspected goods at ports of entry, to confiscate and destroy infringing goods and to suspend the release of imported counterfeit and pirated goods, as required by TRIPS.[22] Nevertheless, few intellectual property laws include any substantive provision for border measures. At one end of the spectrum is Kuwait, whereby none of its intellectual property laws makes any reference to border measures. The UAE copyright law provides a brief substantive provision for border-control authorities to act to suspend the release of suspected infringing goods, but only on application from a right holder, and not *ex officio* or on their own cognisance.[23]

Saudi Arabia was the first Gulf state to make provision for measures that arguably come close to addressing the border-measure obligations enshrined in TRIPS Articles 51–60. No doubt driven by the external scrutiny of its intellectual property regimes arising from its campaign WTO membership, Saudi Arabia has enshrined these provisions in a ministerial order on border measures in respect of trademarks and copyright.[24] Bahrain and Oman have followed suit in respect of including similar provisions. Bahrain, however, has limited such provisions to its copyright law, but has not extended them to any areas of industrial property. Oman provides the most comprehensive prescription of border-control measures, including very similar principles and processes in both its intellectual property law and its general industrial-property law. Hence Oman's border-control provisions apply equally across the broad spectrum of intellectual property with equal force.

All three states provide that customs authorities, acting either *ex officio* or on complaint from the right holder, may suspend the clearance of suspected infringing goods upon obtaining *prima facie* evidence of infringement. Alternatively, the courts, or the Board of Grievances in the case of Saudi Arabia, may issue *ex parte* orders suspending clearance on application of the right holder. When acting on the application of the right holder, the courts or the customs authorities may require lodgement of a security bond before issuing the order or seizing the goods. Orders for suspension on application must be followed with the initiation of civil or criminal proceedings within a specified period of time; failing such proceedings, the goods shall be released. Seized infringing goods may be disposed of through non-commercial channels, but they are not allowed to be re-exported or allowed to enter the local market under another customs procedure. While the Saudi regulation permits the parties concerned to challenge the decisions of the customs authority before the Board of Grievances, there is no indication in the Ministerial Order whether a decision of the Ministry or the Board can be similarly challenged.

5.2.4 Damages, indemnification and other remedies (TRIPS Articles 45–46)

TRIPS Articles 45 and 46 require members to accord to their judicial authorities the capacity to award damages adequate to compensate for any injury suffered because of the infringement, as well as expenses and legal costs. Recovery of profits and/or payment of pre-established damages may be ordered, even where the infringer did not knowingly engage in the infringing activity. Judicial authorities must have the capacity to order infringing goods to be destroyed or otherwise disposed outside the channels of commerce without any compensation to the infringer and in such manner as to avoid any harm to the right holder. To ensure that the risk of further acts of infringement is minimised, the authority extends to orders for the disposal in similar fashion of materials and implements that have been used predominantly in the creation of the infringing goods, again without compensation to the infringer. However, account must be taken of proper proportion between the seriousness of the infringement and the remedies ordered, as well as the interests of third parties. In the case of counterfeit trademarks, the simple removal of the unlawfully affixed trademark will not normally be sufficient to enable them to be released back into channels of commerce.

As is the case with the availability of provisional measures, the statutory provision for judicial authority in respect of the award of damages and the application of other remedies is likewise inconsistent – both across the states and within the respective intellectual property laws of each state. In particular, since the common convention throughout the region in respect of civil cases is for either party to bear its own legal costs, the states' legislation is singularly quiet on the issue of authority to award costs. Kuwait, for example, makes allowance for the award of damages in its copyright and patents laws, but not in its trademarks law; all three laws are quiet on the question of costs. The UAE, in contrast, makes allowance for award of damages in its trademarks law but not in its copyright or patents laws. Qatar allows for damages in its earlier copyright, trademarks and geographical-indications laws, but not in its later patents and layout-designs laws. Oman makes provision in its later copyright and industrial-property laws, but not in its earlier, now anachronistic plant-varieties law. Yemen does not make any provision for damages in its longstanding single intellectual property law.

All states make some provision across virtually all intellectual property laws for offending goods, and any tools, machinery and equipment used in the commission of the infringement, to be confiscated, destroyed or otherwise disposed of in such other way as a court or administrative authority may deem appropriate. Kuwait's copyright, trademark and patent laws all authorise the court upon the request of the right holder to order the destruction of the infringing work or goods and the materials and equipment used.[25] However, the copyright law allows for an exception to this requirement where the author's economic rights expire within two years from the date of issue of the judgment.[26] Instead, the court may rule for confirmation of the precautionary attachment to fulfil any compensation awarded in favour of the right holder. This exception necessarily includes the case of a work unlawfully translated into Arabic, on the basis that this violation is not so serious as to warrant a judgment for destruction.

Oman shows the benefit of rationalisation by demonstrating consistency across its recent major intellectual property laws. Both laws, in virtually identical terms, contain seizure and destruction provisions and make allowance for the award of damages.[27] Neither law allows for closures, even in the case of recidivism. The older new-plant-varieties law allows for the destruction of any offending propagation and/or elements, but does not provide for destruction of tools or equipment used in the infringement.[28]

The UAE courts may also order offending goods to be confiscated, destroyed or otherwise disposed of in such other way as they deem appropriate, as well as the tools, machinery and equipment used as part of the infringing activity.[29] Infringing premises may be closed for a period of up to six months in respect of copyright and trademark infringements, but not in the case of patents and industrial-design infringements. Neither the copyright law nor patents law make provision for compensation, while the trademark law retains such provision from its predecessor law of 1992.[30]

Most of the laws do not allow for closure of the infringing establishment except as one of the options available in respect of repeat offences. The few inconsistent exceptions are the earlier copyright laws of Qatar, Saudi Arabia and the UAE, and Qatar's trademarks law.

5.2.5 Criminal procedures and sanctions (TRIPS Article 61)

TRIPS Article 61 requires WTO members to make provision for criminal procedures and penalties to be applied at least in cases of wilful trademark counterfeiting or copyright piracy on a commercial scale. Remedies, which include imprisonment and/or fines, must be sufficient to provide a deterrent and must be consistent with penalties applied for crimes of corresponding gravity. Remedies may also include seizure, forfeiture and destruction of the offending goods and any materials, tools or equipment predominantly used in the commission of the infringement. Since these are minimum requirements, members may provide criminal procedures and penalties for other cases of intellectual property right infringement.

Notwithstanding the existence of a fair degree of common ground between the various types of national intellectual property laws in respect of the nature of infringements, the penalties that infringements attract still vary markedly between the states and even between the intellectual property laws in each state. The one exception is Oman, which has applied the same sanctions and scale of penalties across its new intellectual property laws. The marked differences have left certain states open to accusation from some developed countries that the perceived inadequate levels of sanctions still engender an environment which is tantamount to fostering unchecked piracy and counterfeiting and which is providing safe haven for illegal importers, traders and manufacturers. However, as one senior government official from the region wryly described life in a local prison: 'There are no single cells, weekly linen changes, basketball games, movies or even regular meals in a local prison.' A similar statement could be made about prison conditions in the other Gulf states.

Bahrain has recently taken some steps to increase the severity of sanctions which were formerly the most lenient in the region, but with limited success. In 2003 and 2004 it issued new geographical indications and trade secret laws which carried penalties for infringements of up to BD3,000 and two years' imprisonment.[31] However, laws issued in 2006 for patents, trademarks, designs and integrated circuits actually carry reduced sanctions of up to BD2,000 and one year's imprisonment.[32] The copyright law of 2006 fares a little better, with a maximum BD4,000 and one-year imprisonment provision.[33] It is uncertain what impact the intellectual property provisions of Bahrain's recently completed free trade agreement with the United States may have on further increasing the level of sanctions across all of Bahrain's intellectual property laws. What is certain is that the Bahraini sanctions are still very lenient even by regional standards, but the free trade agreement requires Bahrain to provide strong deterrence against piracy and counterfeiting.

Kuwait's longstanding copyright law of 1999 provides for a maximum fine of only KD500 – the lowest financial penalty of any regional copyright law (except that of Yemen) by a wide margin – and/or imprisonment for up to one year.[34] Its trademark law penalties are only marginally higher, retaining from its much earlier law of 1980 a very simple scale of an unspecified term of imprisonment and/or a fine of up to KD600 for counterfeiting or improper use of a registered mark, but it does not impose a penalty for use of a sign or mark excluded from registrability.[35] In contrast, its patent law carries penalties of up to KD5000 and one year's imprisonment, essentially a tenfold increase over the penalties provided by the trademark and copyright laws, even though patent infringements are not a major area of concern.[36]

Qatar's penalties, at least in respect of copyright infringements, are reasonably substantial by regional standards, even though they are largely unchanged from earlier legislation. However, they remain at the lower end of the regional spectrum in industrial-property areas. Penalties range up to QR100,000 and imprisonment for up to 12 months for copyright infringement acts, but are as low as QR10,000 and two years for patents infringements.[37] However, rather curiously, acts relating to manufacture or import of electronic deactivation or satellite-decoding devices, or their illegal modification or removal, do not have a monetary penalty specified and carry a maximum term of imprisonment of only one year.[38] While a logical presumption may be that the financial sanctions relating to other copyright offences shall apply, the fact that different types of offences carry differing minimum and maximum financial penalties would militate against this presumption. Also noteworthy is the fact that the most recent of the laws, namely the patents law of 2006, carries the most lenient penalties, while the longest-standing current law, namely the copyright law, carries the most stringent.

The UAE's laws are also internally inconsistent, but at least fairly high standards have been set in some cases. The patents and industrial-designs laws now carry maximum penalties of up to AED100,000 and two years' imprisonment for patents and design infringements, but the copyright law has provision for penalties up to an impressive AED500,000 and an unspecified maximum period of imprisonment.[39] Penalties for manufacturing or importing means to commit a technological fraud, to delay or discredit technological anti-fraud or anti-copy software, or to load or store computer programs and databases without authorisation – for which no provision existed in the earlier copyright law – are now recognised as the most serious of copyright violations and accordingly may attract above maximum penalties. But in stark contrast, and at the other end of the spectrum, penalties for trademark infringements, such as use of a counterfeit trademark or improper use of a registered trademark, may attract a penalty of up to 12 months' imprisonment and/or a fine of between AED5,000 and AED10,000.[40] However, the fine for fraudulent use has in effect been lessened in impact by being altered from a previously uncapped minimum amount to a capped maximum amount.

Saudi Arabia has established the new regional benchmark in terms of the deterrence value of its sanctions by increasing them dramatically from their previous levels and by applying them across all intellectual property laws. In particular, harsher penalties for infringements in respect of information-technology-based intellectual property and for repeat offences are introduced. These penalties stand in stark contrast to those extant in neighbours Bahrain, Kuwait and Yemen. But the penalties also illustrate the impact of the greater degree of critical scrutiny and pressure that Saudi Arabia is receiving from the United States and from international business and intellectual property watchdog organisations as part of its drive for WTO membership and the consequent necessity to demonstrate its commitment to TRIPS minimum standards. Accordingly, any unlawful act of exploitation of a patented subject matter carries a financial penalty of up to SR100,000, while violation of any provision of the copyright law may be subject to a fine of up to SR250,000, a dramatic increase on the maximum fine of SR10,000 (without any imprisonment provision) available under its 1989 law.[41] Fraudulent use of a registered trademark has attracted the most dramatic increases in financial penalty, with the fine having increased from a maximum of SR50,000 under the 1984 equivalent law to one of between SR50,000 and SR1 million.[42] The maximum term of imprisonment remains unchanged at 12 months in respect of patents and trademark violations, but has been reduced from 12 months to 6 months in respect of copyright and neighbouring rights infringements.

Oman has taken an entirely different approach to the other states. It initially achieved consistency by adopting a common scale of penalties across the full suite of seven intellectual property laws introduced during the year 2000, providing for imprisonment for up to two years and/or a fine of up to OR2,000 or both. Hence the maximum allowable penalties for counterfeiting or a trademark infringement are the same as those for trade secret or new-plant-variety infringements. The general severity of the sanctions has recently been increased fivefold in respect of the financial penalties, with maximum fines of OR10,000 now available.[43] The Omani strategy has attracted criticism from some quarters, notably the United States, on the grounds that its sanctions are too lenient and are not in accordance with the TRIPS Article 61 requirement that sanctions should be sufficiently effective to act as a deterrent.[44] Indeed, the United States, on more than one occasion, has accused Oman of being a haven for copyright piracy in the region because of the apparent laxity and softness of the sanctions in its copyright law.[45] Oman's response has been that the sanctions are sufficiently severe to meet the deterrence objective of TRIPS Article 61, particularly the term of imprisonment.

Yemen is in an entirely different class to the other states in the region. Its single intellectual property law provides for sanctions of up to 10,000 Yemeni rials and up to six months' imprisonment for intellectual property infringements.[46] However, the financial sanction equates to just US$50 on current exchange rates. And on the basis of the largely anecdotal information available on levels of penalties imposed by Yemeni courts for intellectual property infringements, maximum fines are not imposed. Yemen will no doubt be required to drastically increase its level of sanctions to at least mid range for the region as part of its drive for WTO membership.

National attitudes towards recidivism also vary amongst the Gulf states and are reflected in their respective laws. Bahrain generally provides for the maximum penalties for a first offence to be mandatory if re-offending occurs within a period of three years from the first offence, but this would appear to presuppose that the maximum penalties would not have been imposed in respect of the first offence, if this provision is to have any effect. It would also seem to presume that further offences will not occur within the three year time frame. Kuwait generally allows for a 50 per cent increase in the maximum penalties to be imposed if the recurrence occurs within five years of the first offence, while Qatar and Saudi Arabia generally allow for a doubling of penalties for repeat offences without time limitations from the initial offence. The UAE generally does not make any provision for increasing penalties for repeat offences, except in the case of copyright infringements where a repeat offence attracts a minimum fine of between AED30,000 and AED200,000 and imprisonment for at least nine months, the level of penalty depending on the nature of the repeated offence.[47] Yemen does not make any provision for increased sanctions for repeat offences.

Table 5.1 summarises the provisional measures, damages, remedies and sanctions that are available under the respective intellectual property laws of the Gulf states. To place them into a meaningful perspective, and to facilitate comparison between the states and between their respective laws, the monetary penalties have been listed in both the local currencies and in US dollars in brackets. The table highlights the differences between the states in respect of the range and nature of the various elements of their available sanctions. It also illustrates the concerted effort by Bahrain and Oman in particular to standardise their enforcement provisions across all their respective intellectual property laws that are largely reactions to external pressures, in contrast to the other states. Where anomalies do appear, for example in respect of the different seizure provisions between Bahrain's laws, it is suggested that the difference could be explained by accidents of drafting design by different initiating bodies rather than by deliberate intent. The anomaly in sanctions in Oman's laws that is created by the law on the protection of new plant varieties, as the remaining remnant of the 2000 suite of laws, will be removed when that law is excised from the statute books – as is likely to occur in the near future.

However, what stands out most markedly is the significant spread in the range of financial penalties now extant across the Gulf states, ranging from the equivalent of a pitiful US$2,059 (Kuwait), or an even more pitiful $50 if Yemen's financial penalties are taken into account. At the other end of the spectrum there exists an impressive US$268,096 (Saudi Arabia) in respect of trademark infringements, and an equally pitiful US$1,716 (Kuwait, copyright) to an almost equally impressive US$136,836 (UAE, copyright). In the latter cases, recidivism provisions can significantly increase these penalties – doubling them in the case of the Saudi laws. Of the Gulf states, Saudi Arabia and the UAE have been under the greatest pressure from developed countries, and especially the United States, to introduce sanctions that will serve as effective deterrents, and Table 5.1 illustrates the success of that concerted pressure. Saudi Arabia across all intellectual property laws, and the UAE and Qatar in some instances, now provide for financial penalties which are severe by local economic standards and which are arguably well within the scope of being effective deterrents. What is surprising is that Qatar and the UAE have managed to emerge relatively unscathed from US pressure in respect of their very lowly penalties for trademark infringements. But this clearly illustrates that copyright infringements through counterfeiting and piracy, and patent infringements, particularly in respect of pharmaceutical products, are the key concerns for the United States in terms of intellectual property rights protection in the UAE. The other states – Kuwait and Yemen – will no doubt continue to attract criticism for the perceived inadequacy of their financial penalties. Kuwait has consistently been placed on the USTR's Annual Special 301 Watch List for egregious conduct in respect of the perceived inadequacy of its intellectual property protection. Kuwait has reportedly initiated steps to double the maximum fines and jail sentences for copyright infringements, but the increases have yet to be put into effect and the maximum fines would still be only the equivalent of US$3,430 – hardly at a level to satisfy the US government.[48]

5.3 The enforcement dichotomy

5.3.1 The challenges for effective enforcement

The most challenging element of TRIPS, as perceived by both the Gulf states themselves and the developed countries with established commercial interests in the region, has been that of the enforcement of the states' intellectual property protection obligations consistent with the standards enshrined in TRIPS Parts II and III. Notwithstanding the fact that most states have taken significant strides in recent years in setting in place comprehensive legislative regimes for the protection of intellectual property rights, and most already

Table 5.1 Comparison of sanctions for intellectual property infringements in the Gulf states

	Statute	Provisional relief	Maximum sanctions		Seizures etc	Closures (maximum)	Damages	Recidivism sanctions	Border measures
			Fine	Jail					
Bahrain	Copyright 22/06	yes	4,000 ($10,610)	1 year	yes	no	yes	both doubled & up to 6 months closure	yes
	Trademarks 11/06								limited
	Patents 14/06		2,000 ($5,305)		no				nil
	Integrated circuits 5/06				yes		no		
	Designs 6/06								
	GIs 16/04		3000 ($7,957)					Up to 6 months closure	
	Secrets 7/03								
Kuwait	Copyright 64/99	yes	500 ($1,880)	I year	yes	no	yes	50% increase 6 months closure	nil
	Trademarks & G.I.'s 1/01		600 ($2,256)	unspecified			unspecified	nil	
	Patents etc 3/01		5000 ($18,800)	I year			yes		
Oman	Copyright 65/08	yes	10,000 ($25,983)	2 years	yes	no	yes	both doubled	yes
	Industrial Property Rights 67/08								
	Plant Varieties 92/00		2,000 ($5,196)						nil
Qatar	Copyright 7/02	yes	100,000 ($27,480)	1 year	yes	3 years	yes	both doubled	nil
	Trademarks, GIs Designs, 9/02		20,000 ($5,486)	2 years		6 months			
	Patents 30/06		10,000 ($2,748)			no	no	nil	
	Integrated circuits 6/05		50,000 ($13,738)	1 year				both doubled	
	Trade Secrets 5/05						yes		
Saudi Arabia	Copyright 41/03	yes	250,000 ($66,650)	6 months	yes	2 months	yes	both doubled	Implementing regulations
	Trademarks 21/02		1,000,000 ($266,666)	I year		no		both doubled 6 months closure	nil
	Patents, Designs, Circuits, Plant Varieties 27/04		100,000 ($26,666)	unspecified			no	fine only doubled	nil
UAE	Copyright 7/02	yes	500,000 ($136,800)	unspecified	yes	6 months	no	min 9 months min 200,000	limited
	Trademarks 8/02		10,000 ($2,733)	1 year			yes	nil	nil
	Patents, Designs 17/02		100,000 ($27,326)	unspecified		no	no		
Yemen	Intellectual Property Rights 19/94	yes	10,000 ($50)	6 months	yes	no	no	nil	nil

Source: compiled by the author

have laws that are largely TRIPS-compliant, there nevertheless exists a dichotomy between the principle of enforcement as enshrined in the various legislative regimes and the practice as exemplified by the degree of effective action. In all states, the practical application of compliance obligations through effective enforcement has been, and continues to be, the most difficult area with which to contend.

According to a WIPO survey conducted in 2002 on counterfeiting and piracy, the ineffectiveness of enforcement systems can be attributed, in many cases, to:

- legislation not being drafted effectively or extensively;
- lack of human resources, funding and practical experience in the enforcement of intellectual property rights;
- insufficient knowledge on the part of right holders and the general public, concerning their rights and remedies;
- a general lack of training of enforcement officials, including the judiciary; and
- systemic problems resulting from insufficient national and international coordination, including a lack of transparency.[49]

These shortcomings are not necessarily the exclusive confine of the Gulf states, or even of other developing countries only. But they do apply to, and are a succinct exposition of, the challenges facing the states with respect to their enforcement obligations.[50] To the above list, however, should be added the challenges posed by the clash of alien cultural and economic mores with entrenched local societal attitudes.

With most of the states, the principal barriers to the elimination of infringement of intellectual property rights do not subsist so much in the substantive law as in the practical application of the remedies and sanctions available (or not available, as the case may be) to deter counterfeiting and piracy and other infringements. In those states which still have pre-TRIPS laws in force, the negative impact of the barriers is exacerbated by the presence of sanctions which are both inadequate and incomplete in scope and scale. But irrespective of these inadequacies of scope and scale in a few older laws, the sanctions available to the authorities across the broad spectrum of the region's intellectual property laws are not being fully exploited. The reasons do not rest solely with the enforcement authorities or the judiciary; entrenched local societal, cultural and commercial attitudes also contribute to the development of this enforcement dichotomy.

5.3.2 Societal attitudes – 'an honest trade?'

The leaderships of the Gulf states generally recognise that being part of the world trading community through membership of the WTO and adherence to its terms of membership through the adoption and implementation of its multilateral agreements, such as TRIPS, is crucial for their respective economic growth and health.[51] Accordingly, they also recognise that the obligations that accompany such membership must be enforced domestically. By contrast, there still exists throughout the states a widespread lack of public awareness of the western concept of intellectual property rights – what they mean, what constitutes an infringement and the wider implications of infringing activity. This lack of public awareness is particularly prevalent within the older generations, amongst whom the everyday use of the English language with its subtle complexities is still not widespread; the lack of public awareness is shared by local merchants, as well as some small-scale infringers and end-users of potentially infringing material.[52]

Even where an awareness or understanding of intellectual property rights does exist, there nevertheless also still prevails a conservatism that questions the desirability and necessity to comply with international and national intellectual property protection obligations, which may seem so removed and irrelevant, at the local community level or in the local *souk* (marketplace). Commonplace is a deep-rooted societal attitude that holds that ownership of a good confers an unlimited right of use and disposal, including copying and resale, while imitation is deemed to be legitimate practice.[53] No harm is held to have been done to the owner of the original good if the resale is on a reasonable scale and if it is conducted in a different – in either a geographic or economic sense – market. The sale of counterfeit versions of luxury western goods in the local *souk* at a fraction of the genuine products' retail price is not perceived as disadvantaging the owner of the luxury goods, since the buyer would not purchase the genuine product if the counterfeit versions were no longer available. The claim of 'genuine imitation', frequently offered in the *souks* and on the street stalls as an unwritten assurance as to the quality and value of the counterfeit and pirated goods on offer, is still asserted with candour and with a certain degree of conviction that such claim is a positive marketing ploy. Hence external attempts to fetter this *laissez faire* and perceived non-competing micro-economy are neither welcome nor fully comprehended in the local environment. This common sentiment, as expressed by an illegal trader in response to a raid on his shop by government officials, is that anti-piracy measures are 'not fair'. 'We pay money for these [disks] and we sell them. This is an honest trade,' the trader protested.[54]

Also widespread is the perception that the protection of intellectual property rights, particularly in respect of software and audiovisual copyrights, foreign trademarked consumer goods and pharmaceutical patents, represents a protection of western (and particularly US and European) commercial interests at the expense of technology transfer and industrial development for the benefit of the local markets and communities.[55] This perception is reinforced by the cynical view that western countries, formerly imperial overlords in living memory, are now continuing their exploitation as political and commercial bullies. Trade with western countries is desired, but the perceived imposition of a new western-style commercial colonialism, bolstered by western intellectual property protection regimes, may well be an unpalatable consequence.[56] It is not surprising, then, that attitudes develop to justify the use of infringing, counterfeit or pirated material or goods. This justification can be seen in the following reasons offered by locals in response to a local media survey on using pirated software:

- the software is priced too high;
- the company that has created the software is already very rich, so stealing the software doesn't really matter;
- the morality or business practices of the company that has created the software are questionable, so it is acceptable to steal their software;
- the people using the pirated software are poor, so it is acceptable for them to steal from the rich company;
- the software is defective so paying full price is silly;
- the software is only for personal private use;
- the software has poor local support so the company shouldn't expect people to pay for it;
- buying one copy of an application (and then sharing) is good enough.[57]

Hence, attempts by western companies to wean locals away from counterfeit or pirated products by a positive reinforcement strategy can sometimes produce an unexpected and negative result. For example, an offer by a leading global operating systems and software manufacturer to educational institutions and students of discounts of up to 90 per cent off the normal retail price of some of its leading products, in an attempt to steer consumers and end-users away from pirated versions of its leading software, was not received with wholesale enthusiasm. In some quarters, the reaction to the offer was a cynical one – along the lines that the normal pricing structure of the software to members of the public must be exorbitant to allow such a generous discount to educational institutions and students. Acceptance of the discount offer was legitimising the original pricing structure and endorsing the commercial practices of a major foreign yet global company that was still over-exploiting the local markets.[58]

Further contributing to an environment of enforcement less rigorous than that sought by western countries is a perception by the more conservative sections of the populations of the states that the Middle East is being subject to an ongoing cultural penetration by western countries that contributes to an erosion of Islamic beliefs, values and local culture at every turn. Western culture is seen as often immoral and corrupt, and so the enforcement of intellectual property rights for goods and services that are largely western in origin constitutes governmental and religious sanction of these immoral and corrupting influences.[59] Enforcement of intellectual property protection by the governments of the Gulf states on behalf of predominantly western right holders not only reinforces these corrupting influences but also provides the governments with powerful tools for controlling cultural content and eliminating the 'informal' but commonplace and socially acceptable cultural distribution mechanisms that have long been in place (in other words, the uncontrolled copying and duplication that the west would describe as counterfeiting and piracy).[60] This cynicism and resentment toward the west in respect of the latter's protected goods is reinforced by some local attitudes towards the western expatriate populations, who in most states represent a significant proportion of the population and who lead a very visible, comfortable and often culturally insensitive lifestyle.

There also prevails a cultural dilemma in the local populations of some states insofar as the necessity to resort to public judicial processes for the resolution of a dispute, as distinct from the utilisation of informal and private mediation, is perceived by many as a negative reflection on both parties. One characteristic of an Arab community is the confidential treatment of local disputes. Public disclosure of those disputes through court proceedings, particularly those relating to family companies, is liable to prejudice the personal and professional standing of the family, the family company and the traditions of the immediate community of which the family is a part.[61] Accordingly, there appears to be a widespread disinclination to pursue a dispute or infringement through the judicial system, other than as a last resort. The paramount consideration for all parties is to achieve a mutually satisfactory resolution in which the acknowledged direct commercial losses of the aggrieved party are compensated, while still allowing for some saving of 'face' by both sides. Punishment of the infringing party by the imposition of the financial or custodial sanctions available in legislation may stop the infringing act, but does not necessarily benefit the aggrieved party; in fact, imprisonment of a family breadwinner may simply create a burden for the local community. Hence, where a local complaint concerning infringement of intellectual property rights is formally raised with the local authorities or the responsible ministry, common practice throughout the states is for local officials or ministry officials to act as mediator between complainant and infringing party in order to attempt to engineer a solution satisfactory to both parties. The solution may include an 'appropriate gesture' to the complainant. The nature of the 'appropriate gesture' depends on the circumstances and extent of the alleged offence, but may consist of a financial payment by way of compensation and cessation of the offending activities. Hence what may appear to western eyes as inaction in the face of infringing activity actually constitutes an alternative dispute resolution that locals would argue is more effective in achieving a better possible outcome than that which might be achieved by following the slow and tortuous path of civil and/or criminal litigation.[62]

The issue of transparency arises in this context. Many of the leading business organisations in every state in the region are close-knit, family-run enterprises whose principals, by virtue of being members of either the extended royal families or the societal and commercial elite, also hold considerable political and economic influence. There can exist a reluctance to comply either with public disclosure of commercial and financial information customarily required under western laws, or with laws of western origin which counteract the profit-making imperative of past, *laissez-faire* practices. The continued lack of transparency springs from some political and government practices that are still beyond successful attempts at legal reform.[63]

To offset these conservative values, a pro-western youth culture fuelled by a domestic population that is predominately under the age of 25 is growing in numbers and influence in each state. A further offsetting factor is that the native-born nationals constitute the minority of the domestic population in all but two states. Accordingly, the rate of regional internet connectivity and growth in computer hardware and software market penetration is dramatic, and the regional market for pirated western goods and particularly western music, Hollywood and Bollywood movies, and computer software, continues to grow apace.[64]

Complicating, or rather reinforcing, the growing societal attitude towards non-compliance with enhanced standards of intellectual property protection is the existence of a large and dynamic expatriate population, which in most states can contribute to an environment of evasion rather than compliance.[65] The combination of government enforcement strategies which still target end-sellers rather than consumers, and the existence in all states of lengthy court lists that can result in delays of years for both civil and criminal cases, means that the likelihood of expatriates who knowingly and willingly participate in illegal activities being caught and prosecuted is remote. Hence participation in counterfeiting or piracy activities and possible prosecution are worth the risk when weighed against the financial savings that counterfeit or pirated goods or services can provide over their genuine counterparts. Government officials in some states complain that the expatriate participation in infringing activity is particularly prevalent in respect of computer software and illegal reception of TV cable and satellite transmission.[66]

5.3.3 Regional piracy and the enforcement response

The challenges for the effective enforcement of intellectual property rights throughout the region are exacerbated by the fact that counterfeiting and piracy, particularly of software, video and music, are still widespread and lucrative businesses. All states experience a ready supply of illegal vendors, mainly low-paid expatriate workers from the Indian subcontinent and East Asia, for whom the chance of quick reward far outweighs the risks of seizure and possible deportation. There is also a constant demand for access to pirated goods which are much cheaper, more easily available and often more up to date than their legitimate equivalents.

The nature and *modus operandi* of an end-selling operation at the grass-roots level are well described in the following report from the Kuwaiti News Agency (KUNA) on the operation of a prevalent activity involving the sale of counterfeit DVDs and videos on the streets of Kuwait City.[67] While the KUNA Report focuses on a typical small-scale street vendor activity, it also makes pointed reference to what would appear to be a well-organised infrastructure for producing the counterfeit goods and organising distribution networks, with links that would appear to reach high into Kuwaiti society. It also helps to illustrate the dimension of the problem in combating counterfeit material and the concern and response of manufacturers and distributors to the problem. The report comes after years of reports in KUNA of action by government officials in conducting raids, confiscating infringing material and closing infringing establishments for violations of Kuwait's intellectual property laws. While the report is confined to the situation in Kuwait, the picture that it paints is similar to scenes that can be found on the streets, outside the shopping malls and in the *souks* of cities in the other states:[68]

> 'Nowadays, one Kuwaiti dinar buys the latest bootlegged Hollywood movie, pirated software, or even ripped music albums from street vendors who transform entrances to shopping malls and supermarkets into mobile stores. Albeit responsible authorities maintain that they are committed to protecting intellectual property rights and the Ministries of Interior and Information and Kuwait's municipality persistence in seeking out violators, infringements did not abate, in fact they may have augmented ... copyrights violations dominate, and range from the illegal extensions of satellite TV subscriptions to non-subscribers, illegal publishing and selling of copyrighted books – especially children's books, sale of ripped music, sale of pirated software, and the revenue generating sale of bootlegged movies, TV shows, and taped local theatre shows. Vendors selling bootlegged merchandise can be seen on the corners of many shopping malls.'
>
> 'A young man lays his rug on the pavement in front of a shopping mall ... and lays out more than 50 video tapes of movies on the rug ... several of the movies are still in theatres while others are not released yet. He says he constantly worries about authorities confiscating his merchandise. The ... stock he carries belongs to his ambiguous "boss", who pays [the young man] 100 fils for each item he sells.[69] He ... has no information pertaining to the center of operations or who supplies him, he meets his boss in a public place, settles accounts and leaves, and the next delivery is scheduled over the phone.'
>
> 'Selling bootlegged (video) tapes in Kuwait is a business that generates incredible revenues for its owners; four or five individuals in all of Kuwait ... the "business" is, in essence, an oligopoly operated by several individuals through an ambiguous yet intricate network of production, warehousing, and distribution .... all one needs to pull off a similar operation is 12 video recorders and one video player, costing no more than 450 Kuwaiti Dinars all together ... the cost of video tapes range from 100 to 120 fils per tape, mounting the total production cost for a single video tape of the latest Hollywood movie to around 250 fils which

> then sells for one Kuwaiti Dinar. The utilities are stored in a secure secret place, known only to one person, trusted by the owner, and most of the persons who work at the copy-production centers are women. Once the women copy the tapes, the owner transports them to the head distributor, who on his part transports the merchandise to several other distributors who then supply the vendors.'

Some three years after the above media report appeared, the local media was continuing to report that Kuwait still carried a proliferation of pirated material which was available from street vendors, within the souks, and from merchants within the numerous shopping malls.[70] Hence, it is not surprising that Kuwait's performance in curbing copyright piracy continues to come under particular attack from the USTR and the industry lobby organisations which have input into the USTR reporting process. Although the USTR reports need to be read with some reservation because of their obvious bias in favour of promoting the self-interest of US business, they still illustrate why the USTR argues that it has good reason to continue to be concerned over the Kuwaiti lack of apparent success with its enforcement effort. In 2005, the International Intellectual Property Alliance (IIPA), an intellectual property watchdog and lobby consortium representing US copyright-based industries, was complaining to the USTR that:

> 'Piracy continues to thrive in Kuwait, as hundreds of thousands of pirate optical disks (DVDs, VCDs, CDs, CD-ROMs, "burned" CD-Rs, and, increasingly, DVD-Rs) of movies, music, business software, and entertainment software are openly sold in retail stores, on the streets, and in the *souqs* each month . . . Distributors operate with impunity, supplying retail stores and street vendors alike. Increasingly, domestic piracy ventures are "burning-to-order" at storefronts, or "burning" content onto recordable disks and distributing those to street vendors. Retail stores continue to maintain large stocks of pirate product . . . large numbers of street vendors openly display and sell pirate disks ("burned" CD-Rs and, increasingly, burned DVD-Rs) . . .'[71]

By its corresponding report to the USTR in 2008, however, the IIPA was able to comment to the USTR on what it saw as some improvement in Kuwait's enforcement efforts, noting that 'the impressive efforts of the Ministry of Information (MOI) against optical disk piracy have had a net impact on piracy for some industries'.[72] But on the negative side, the same report still notes that, notwithstanding the MOI's efforts, optical disk piracy, both imported and home grown, remains the chief form of piracy in the markets in Kuwait. Locally duplicated pirate CD-Rs with foreign music remain widely available, and in many retail outlets the burning of such CD-Rs is on demand, exacerbating enforcement issues since such practice keeps merchant-retained levels of piracy stock to a minimum.

Regional media abound with frequent reports of raids and confiscations, with pirated software, video and audio material, printed material, brand-name sportswear, cigarettes and cosmetic lines being the more common targets. The raids are generally targeted at small-scale participants towards the end of the distribution line – wholesalers, resellers, street and *souk* traders, and end-user businesses (although reports occasionally appear of raids in the UAE in particular on importers and distributors involving large-scale confiscations). The raids are often conducted on a regular basis and often with prior public warning, when they are also meant to serve as part of a public awareness campaign on intellectual property rights. According to Omani government officials, and generally confirmed by their Bahraini counterparts, the following strategy is commonplace in respect of raids and inspections and can also be observed in the other states:[73]

- pre-raid: businesses in a certain shopping district or area are given warning of the impending raid and are warned to dispose of or surrender any possible infringing product;
- first infringement: usually confiscation of the offending goods and a formal warning against re-offending; a future inspection is listed to check against any re-offending. Notice is generally given of an impending follow-up inspection;
- second infringement: further confiscation and fine imposed by the Ministry; premises may be closed for at least a few days, or until the fine is paid, or even longer;
- third infringement: further confiscation, fines and longer closure of the premises;
- fourth infringement: formal criminal prosecution is launched; possible permanent closure of the premises.

More often than not, raids serve as both an enforcement action and as part of a public awareness/education strategy. Hence local press and electronic media frequently form an integral part of a police/ministry raiding party, and the detail and success of the raid are reported at length. Presence of the media is also useful for displaying to regional watchdog bodies and to the key authorities in western countries, such as the USTR, that the local authorities are sincere and active in their attempts to stamp out piracy and counterfeiting. Also present on appropriate occasions are representatives of the right holder or the regional watchdog body. Hence the nexus between enforcement authorities and media is a deliberate one; it is noticeable, for example, that the intensity of the reporting in the local press of enforcement activities increases immediately prior to or after the introduction of a new intellectual property law, only to ease soon thereafter.

Nevertheless, the raids can, and do, occur without warning, particularly when a large-scale operation, such as a major international company or the regional office of an influential industry watchdog organisation, such as the

IIPA or the Business Software Alliance (BSA), is the right holder or initiator of the formal complaint. The infringements are then likely to be referred to the public prosecutor's office for initiation of a criminal action. However, since the court lists in most Gulf states are very full, it may be a matter of years before the case is listed and then heard.

A commonly repeated accusation from government officials in the states is that counterfeiting, piracy and the associated smuggling of counterfeit goods are not conducted by locals but instead mainly by expatriates, notably from the Asian and Indian subcontinents, in collaboration with foreign importers who are their fellow countrymen.[74] And this subtle ethnic distinction is often highlighted in the media reports of raids.[75] A report in the Saudi press on the seizure of over 200,000 imported pirate optical disks asserted that the vast majority of the disks originated from Indonesia and that more than 75 per cent, or over 150,000, were 'hand carried' by couriers.[76] As part of the public awareness promotion for Qatar's new trademarks and copyright laws in mid 2002, the Qatari Chamber of Commerce blamed foreign merchants for the existence of imported counterfeit products circulating in Qatar and claimed that such acts as importation of pirated goods 'are new and peculiar to the Qatari business community'.[77] In view of the fact that all states still require foreign merchants to have a local partner or commercial agent, and in light of the general commercial astuteness of local businessmen and traders, the accusations do not stand up to scrutiny. This is borne out by the above-quoted Kuwaiti media report which clearly points to local involvement at the highest levels, and by the following reports on enforcement activity which indicate counterfeiting and piracy on a scale of such magnitude that would not seem feasible without active local involvement:

- Seizures by Saudi Ministry of Commerce officials of more than 1.7 million fake watches in Jeddah, in June 2004. The watches, which had come by road from Dubai, had already been allocated for distribution to 37 regional retail outlets.[78]
- Seizure by Dubai police in January 2002 of more than 120 million counterfeit cigarettes, including 90 million counterfeit Marlboro cigarettes, having a reported street value of 27 million dirham (US$7.5 million) and representing one of the largest seizures of its kind anywhere in the world at the time.[79]
- Raids on three warehouses in Jeddah, Saudi Arabia, in January and February 2003 resulting in the seizure and confiscation of more than 1.2 million pirated Playstation CDs, reportedly worth more than 26 million Saudi riyals, one of the biggest hauls of pirated games in a single operation.[80]
- Seizure and destruction by Yemeni authorities on 29 August 2007 of more than 1 million counterfeit Panadol tablets, constituting one of the largest destruction exercises of fake pharmaceuticals in the region.[81] The tablets came in packages carrying the mark 'Panadole' that was nearly indistinguishable from the genuine product.

The above reports illustrate that the counterfeiting and piracy operations which surface in the states are becoming increasingly international in character, are growing in their level of sophistication and are occurring on a much greater scale. As some states already acknowledge, it would appear that organised crime is becoming increasingly involved in the production, distribution and marketing of counterfeit and pirated goods.[82] As one regional response to this emerging trend, the Saudi Ministry of Commerce and Industry recently moved to establish a national investigation group responsible for large-scale piracy, the role of which will include research into the nature of organised crime activities and intelligence gathering, as well as specialised enforcement.[83]

5.3.4 Judicial processes

In its 2002 Report, the UK Commission on Intellectual Property Rights and Development Policy argued that the 'private' nature of intellectual property rights suggests the importance of disputes between parties being resolved either out of court or under civil law, rather than through the criminal justice system.[84] It further argued that, since state enforcement of intellectual property rights was a resource-intensive activity, there was a strong case for developing countries to adopt intellectual property legislation that emphasised enforcement through a civil rather than a criminal justice system. This would reduce the enforcement burden on the government in the case of counterfeiting on a large scale, although the state enforcement agencies would still be required to intervene. The Commission noted that developing countries had come under pressure from industry which advocated enforcement regimes based on state initiatives for the prosecution of infringements.[85] It suggested that such pressures should be resisted and that right holders should assume the initiative and costs of enforcing their rights. Intellectual property rights were essentially private rights and, as with any other kind of private right, the enforcement of those rights was primarily a matter for the individual owners of those rights.

However, Blakeney and others have rightly argued that enforcement of intellectual property rights often cannot be done in any meaningful or effective way in developing states without the support of governmental authorities[86] and this is particularly the case in the Gulf states. Where there is significant intellectual property infringement at street level, as occurs in the states, the government must take the initiative through the public prosecutor to bring criminal cases and thereby commit its authority to the elimination of widespread infringement. Without such support, it is difficult for private right holders, using civil remedies alone, to bring the situation under control. More will be gained for right holders by well-publicised raids on suspected premises, convictions of individuals and their punishment with meaningful levels of fines or imprisonment, destruction of infringing goods and the equipment used to produce them, and the closure of premises, than would be gained by proceedings with the object of obtaining for the right holders compensation for the loss and expense suffered by them as a result of the infringement.[87] It is only when street-level piracy has been largely eliminated and intellectual property has become widely recognised as a permanent feature of the state's legal order that civil litigation, as opposed to criminal prosecutions, can become the norm in intellectual property matters.[88]

The UK Commission and the Blakeney approaches are not necessarily mutually exclusive, and the Gulf states have tended to follow elements of both approaches in their judicial aspects of intellectual property enforcement. Hence one can find instances of the resolution of disputes between parties being achieved outside the court system, of civil and criminal actions proceeding both jointly and separately, and of numerous reports of well-publicised raids accompanied by seizure and destruction of infringing goods and business closures. However, while reports of raids against infringing individuals and establishments for copyright piracy or trademark infringements are numerous, it is very difficult to assess the extent to which the outcomes of these raids are being pursued within the judicial system. It is this perceived lack of connectivity and continuity between policing actions and judicial proceedings that generates much of the criticism from developed countries on the intellectual property enforcement climate in the GCC states. It may also create the impression to the casual observer (or, indeed, the not-so-casual observer such as the IIPA) that states' courts are doing little to enforce intellectual property rights. The IIPA has argued, in respect of Saudi Arabia's recent performance in this regard:

> 'Due to lack of transparency (or we fear, lack of action), no case information has been provided and there is no way to track cases brought, including sentencing. In the rare cases in which industry was able to learn about the results of cases, fines imposed were non-deterrent, and there were no sentences of imprisonment, to IIPA's knowledge, meted out in 2004.'[89]

The IIPA has been even more critical of what it holds as Kuwait's ineffectual efforts to mete out justice against intellectual property infringers. In respect of Kuwait's reaction to copyright piracy, IIPA has complained:

> 'The rare cases that have been brought to court have not gone particularly well . . . [there was] one conviction for copyright piracy in 2002, but the fine was a paltry 500 Kuwait Dinars, and no imprisonment was imposed . . . The Kuwaiti courts did not sentence any violator to prison nor close any shop or company dealing with illicit software in 2003.'[90]

Some states, notably Oman, Qatar and the UAE, have drastically overhauled and restructured their judicial systems in recent years as part and parcel of their constitutional, political and administrative reforms.[91] These overhauls, while crucial to the establishment of effective and modern judicial systems, may also have a negative impact on the enforcement of the intellectual property regime in the medium term. The necessary changes and the rate of change have largely outstripped the capacity of the system to integrate them, and the community's capacity and willingness to understand, adopt and respond properly to them.

Contributing to the negative impact of the legislative changes and judicial reforms is the unfamiliar nature in a jurisprudential sense of some of the legal concepts enshrined in the new laws. According to Hirst, some of the TRIPS enforcement-procedure concepts and mechanisms, for example, have no natural place in a civil law system and their terminology has no natural counterpart in the lexicon of modern legal Arabic.[92] For example, the new enforcement standards provide judicial authorities with the power to make provisional orders so as to prevent the occurrence of infringement even when it is merely threatened and to preserve relevant evidence in regard to the alleged infringement. It has been suggested that judges are usually unwilling to make such an order so early in a case.[93] The evidence would need to be very compelling to convince them that the damages threatened by infringement could not be made good by monetary compensation. Also unfamiliar to local judges and officials is the nature of intellectual property itself, as may be the nature of the adversarial legal process as envisaged in TRIPS. Hence it is not uncommon to find that prosecutions of actions that constitute an infringement against a right of an intellectual property nature may proceed under other laws, such as the commercial agency or criminal/penal codes, with which the judiciary is more familiar. For example, the Omani media in 2005 reported that charges currently pending against a number of Asian nationals arrested for counterfeiting 'classified arts' and pornographic CDs would be laid under Royal Decree No. 65/1987, the much older law governing the printing and distribution of published works, rather than Royal Decree No. 37/2000, the then current copyright law.[94]

The common law principle of *stare decisis* is not recognised in Islamic states. As discussed earlier, the guiding source for legal judgment can be either the *Shariah* or statute law, depending on the particular jurisdiction. Insertion of an opinion from a secular judge as a legal precedent would be to deny or usurp the authority of the *Shariah* and to place the opinion of a judge above Islamic law. The extent to which previous judicial decisions might at least be taken into account or even consulted varies from state to state and will in part depend on the degree of Islamic conservatism within that state. Hence in Saudi Arabia, adherence will be strictly to the *Shariah*, whereas in the UAE, decisions of a superior court, while not binding on the lower courts, might at least be persuasive.[95] However, a consequence of the absence of the principle of *stare decisis* in the judicial system is that one imperative for the explanation and careful recording of legal argument and explanation of the basis for judicial decision-making is absent. The quality of records of judicial proceedings and judgments across the states varies markedly, but in any case does not approach the standard assumed in western countries. Legal practitioners complain that court records are often incomplete, or even missing.[96] Judgments often record the decision without reference to any reasoning or argument, are not always publicly available and are at best published haphazardly. In Bahrain, for example, only judgments made by the Court of Cassation are publicly available and then only in the Official Gazette and, of course, only in Arabic, while *Shariah* court judgments are not (officially, at least) publicly available.[97] In Kuwait, court proceedings and judgments may be made publicly available, but then only at the discretion of the courts.[98] However, it must be remembered that almost all intellectual property laws (with the exception of those of the UAE) provide for the court's judgment to be published in a local Arabic daily paper, at the expense of the guilty party, and this publication, albeit incomplete and non-authoritative, forms a public record of sorts. This practice, which is often followed, can also serve as a form of public awareness-raising of the nature of the offence and public admonition of the guilty party.

Because of the very full court lists which all states currently face, alternative dispute-resolution procedures take on increasing importance and play a greater role than they would otherwise in resolving disputes. Accordingly, government officials of a number of Gulf states would argue that on-the-spot confiscation of infringing goods and equipment, financial penalties which are realistic in light of the economic circumstances of the infringing parties and closure of the infringing premises are very effective, and even arguably more effective than the threat of possible prison sentence after a lengthy process of litigation.[99] If, however, organised crime continues to encroach on the territory of the petty infringer, as suggested earlier, then the customary methods of control and enforcement which target the tail of the supply chain and the end-seller will become totally ineffective.

All Gulf states make extensive use of alternative dispute-resolution strategies, both within and outside the judicial structure, and all have in place formal processes for the utilisation of alternative dispute-resolution and mediation processes and reconciliation committees.[100] The purpose of the committees is to encourage and facilitate the amicable settlement of commercial and civil disputes of whatever value, and if possible to obviate the necessity for the matter to proceed to formal litigation. A party to a dispute is not obliged to defer to the alternative dispute-resolution process, but the courts generally may not hear a case unless the matter has been before the relevant reconciliation committee or a party has been given the opportunity to utilise the process but has expressed its prerogative not to so proceed. The reconciliation committees do not have authority over summary matters or matters at which the attendance of the public prosecutor may be required, that is, in respect of criminal cases. These alternative dispute-resolution processes, which occur within the context of legislative authority and an extra-judicial framework, reinforce the informal mediation processes undertaken proactively by local authority and ministry officials.

Omani government officials freely acknowledge that very few cases involving the infringement of intellectual property rights ever reach the courts, notwithstanding the legislative provisions and the number of raids that are undertaken, particularly in respect of copyright and trademark infringements.[101] But this scenario is as much due to the widespread practice of alternative dispute-resolution options as to any shortcomings in judicial structures and processes. In the opinion of the officials, the notion that the law and its penalties should be used as a first resort to punish the wrongdoer is inconsistent with Omani (and Muslim) values and commercial practices. Accordingly, the officials would assert that the fact that only a few civil cases, and no criminal cases, on intellectual property rights infringements have come before the Omani courts is not necessarily a negative reflection on the judicial system; instead it is an indicator that the alternative dispute-resolution processes are working effectively.[102] Where a case, mainly involving a foreign right holder, goes to court, the court tends to play a similar role as the government officials, namely, that of a mediator in reaching a settlement acceptable to all parties, albeit within the parameters of the legislation under which the dispute is proceeding. On occasion, the ministry official who may have attempted (unsuccessfully) to resolve the dispute that has become the subject of the court hearing will appear before the court as an expert in the case.[103]

A combination of weak measures of criminal and civil damages and the inability to recover the costs of enforcement can actually serve to encourage infringement and discourage civil enforcement by right holders.[104] These weak measures, often based on a formulation of lost profit to the right holder, encourage infringers to anticipate that the sanctions imposed through a criminal action together with damages recoverable through civil litigation would amount to only a fraction of the wholesale price for resale, and an even smaller fraction of the retail price for commercial or personal use, particularly if amortised over a number of infringing operations. Under such circumstances, infringement becomes a calculated business risk that can still leave an infringer with a handsome profit from the proceeds of his infringing activity, even if caught and punished.[105] This is best illustrated by the deterrent capability of the Yemeni intellectual property law and the Kuwaiti copyright law. The Yemeni law, with no specified minimum sanctions and maximum sanctions of a YER10,000 (US$50) financial penalty and a term of imprisonment of up to six months, is the most lenient of all Gulf states. The Kuwaiti law, which has a statutory maximum fine of KD500 (US$1,716) and imprisonment for up to one year, has the most lenient sanctions of all the GCC member states. The application of the law by the courts is apparently even more lenient, with the courts reportedly imposing fines of only KD100 (US$343), a token financial penalty even by local and regional standards.[106] The aforementioned seizure by Dubai authorities of 90 million counterfeit cigarettes worth some US$7.5 million in January 2002 reportedly eventually resulted in the imposition of fines of up to US$2,750 upon each of the accused in the criminal case, and $56,000 in compensation to the cigarette manufacturer in the civil proceedings.[107]

A 'fear factor' survey conducted by the Arabian Anti-Piracy Alliance has produced some striking results in respect of local attitudes towards the deterrence impact amongst traders and members of the public of sanctions within Saudi intellectual property laws. Conducted in 2005–6, the survey results indicate that the deterrence impact of the sanctions in the current Saudi copyright law would appear to be insignificant – notwithstanding the fact that the law provides for the imposition of fines of up to SR250,000 (US$66,650) and up to six months' imprisonment, both of which may be doubled for repeat offences. The survey found that:

- 79 per cent of respondents believed that an employee convicted of selling non-original software, games or movies/music would not be imprisoned;
- 89 per cent felt that the owner of the establishment would not be imprisoned;
- 70 per cent considered that the establishment would not be closed;
- 85 per cent felt that a non-national infringer would not be deported;
- 72 per cent believed that financial penalties would be imposed, but 54 per cent of those believed that the penalty would be less than SR10,000.[108]

Interestingly, though, financial penalties rather than imprisonment were considered to be the most effective deterrent by a margin of some significance – 87 per cent as against 67 per cent. The survey results demonstrate that there is little fear that infringers would be punished to any great degree if caught and convicted. But it could also be argued that the survey indicates that, in light of the perceived already substantial levels of financial sanctions, education and awareness-raising is likely to be a more effective strategy in reducing infringing activity rather than further increases in local penal sanctions.

Those Gulf states that are perceived as being committed to reducing the incidence of intellectual property infringements to internationally accepted levels – and Bahrain and the UAE are arguably the leading states in this respect – place a greater reliance on, and utilisation of, the criminal justice system. As the most active and vigorous of the states in enforcing intellectual property rights by this strategy, the UAE has experienced the most dramatic decreases in copyright piracy and trademark violations for the region, and has also established a number of precedents for the region in terms of judicial determinations.[109] But even this level of commitment does not ensure that maximum or even severe sanctions are fully, comprehensively and consistently utilised. Even where courts of first instance may have imposed sentences perceived locally as being severe, there appears to be a fairly common tendency for appellate courts to act in the defendant's favour in ameliorating the severity of the sentence by reducing or dismissing one or more of their elements.

In a recent case, for example, the Dubai Court of First Instance convicted a dealer for illegally copying satellite pay-television smart cards, which permitted access without subscription payment to encrypted pay-television. The Court fined the dealer AED50,000, sentenced him to one month's imprisonment and ordered that he be subsequently deported. The court further ordered that the offending material and equipment used in its manufacture be confiscated. This particular case has been heralded as a landmark case in the UAE in respect of its subject matter and the perceived severity of penalty imposed, thereby illustrating the seriousness with which the UAE regards intellectual property infringement matters – notwithstanding the fact that the financial penalty imposed was the minimum specified under the Emirati copyright law.[110] It is interesting to note that the convicted dealer, by virtue of the deportation order, was not an Emirati national. However, to illustrate the inconsistency that can still exist across the UAE in the application of enforcement action against intellectual property infringements, a local court in Ajman, the neighbouring Emirate, subsequently considered a similar case against the owner of a local satellite receiver and electronics shop, but merely fined the owner and his salesman AED10,000 each and ordered confiscation of the infringing material.[111] No reference was made in the court's judgment to any closure of the premises or to any other sanctions being imposed.

But even the UAE, which the BSA describes as 'the touchstone for the other countries in the region to aim for . . . with one of the best regulatory structures as well as the enforcement record',[112] still errs too much on the side of leniency, according to some local legal practitioners. It is claimed that, as a general rule, financial penalties commonly tend to be towards the bottom rather than the top of the statutory range, and the imposition of prison terms is infrequent – notwithstanding the substantial penalties available under its main intellectual property laws and the very occasional and heralded court case in which the maximum available penalties are applied.[113]

The following case in Abu Dhabi, in which the Court of Appeal (Criminal Division) reduced the sentences imposed by the primary court upon a local merchant for the unauthorised copying and installation of computer software on a number of computers being offered for sale, illustrates the nature of judicial leniency.[114] A software company and the Abu Dhabi Public Prosecutor had separately brought actions against the merchant for illegally copying the company's software and installing it on a number of computers. The merchant admitted the offence and entered into a restitution settlement with the software company, which withdrew its complaint as a consequence. However, the Public Prosecutor continued with the criminal charges. On the basis of the admission, the primary court sentenced the merchant to three months' imprisonment and imposed a fine of AED50,000 on one charge and AED10,000 in respect of a second charge. The court also ordered that the infringing software and the computers on which it had been loaded be confiscated, that the merchant's establishment be closed for one month and that the court's decision be published in a local daily newspaper at the merchant's expense. The court also ordered a stay of execution for three years on the jail sentence subject to successful execution of the restitution settlement.

The merchant appealed the primary court's judgment, seeking annulment of the lesser fine and all other orders. The appellate court held that the primary court had erred in imposing two separate penalties when the charges originated from one and the same act. The charges were indivisibly linked such that, if proven, they would attract the penalty prescribed for the more serious offence. Accordingly, the appellate court cancelled the lesser fine of AED10,000. It also confirmed the primary court's order regarding the stay of execution but extended it to include both the prison sentence and the greater fine of AED50,000, in accordance with the provisions of Article 83 of the Penal Code in light of the restitution settlement.[115] The court further held that the primary court's orders directing the confiscation of the computers carrying the infringing software were without basis, since Article 40 of the UAE copyright law stipulated that confiscation may only be directed against machinery specifically designed and used for the purpose of infringement. This description did not apply to the seized computers even when they carried infringing software since the computers could be used for legitimate purposes after the software was removed. In respect of the merchant's request for cancellation of the primary court's order for closure of the business, the court held that closure was a mandatory provision under the copyright law, for which execution could not be stayed. However, it reduced the period of closure to one week from the original one month imposed by the primary court. In the final analysis, the convicted merchant was merely required to close his business establishment for just one week.

However, one should not assume that, although the states may appear to have been reluctant to act forcefully in respect of criminal prosecutions, they have been on more solid ground and correspondingly more active in respect of their role in civil proceedings and in judicial review of decisions by administrative bodies. One can find numerous instances of longstanding practice amongst the states (albeit with lesser or greater degrees of activity), but particularly in the UAE in establishing some judicial parameters in respect of the interpretation of statutes. This has occurred particularly in such areas of trademark law as the protection of well-known marks, deceptively misleading marks, passing off, and more recently the registrability requirements of non-conventional marks, such as colour marks.

The *Brylcream v Berylcream* case in the UAE in 1977 and the *Dettol v Bettol* case in Saudi Arabia in 1984 have been discussed already in Chapter 3. In both cases the courts established clear positions in respect of misleading and fraudulent marks and found in favour of the appellants as the owners of marks that were well known both internationally and locally. Further, the UAE case was not dependent upon the existence of a *sui generis* trademark law for the court to find in favour of the appellant.

In a fairly recent case in Saudi Arabia, the Saudi Board of Grievances was required to adjudicate on a case involving deceptively similar marks in the same class but in different languages. Intel Corporation appealed to the Board against the decision of the Registrar of Trademarks to allow the registration by a local company of the mark 'INTELTEC' in Arabic and Latin, in class 42.[116] Intel had already locally registered its INTEL mark in class 42 and in other classes. The Board held that, notwithstanding the registrations were in different languages, the respondent's marks were confusingly similar to the INTEL mark contrary to Article 2(j) of the Saudi Trademarks law, notwithstanding the fact that registration was sought only in Latin and Arabic. The fact that registration of the marks was for goods and services in the same class would, in the Board's view, reinforce the likelihood of public confusion as to an association between the appellant's products and those of the respondent. The Board ordered that the registration of the respondent's marks be cancelled.

In Qatar, the courts have recently affirmed established principles in respect of the protection of well-known marks, including well-known marks that are not registered locally. The Court of First Instance ruled in favour of Escada Ag, owner of the trademark ESCADA, in an action brought by the company against a local chain of barber shops trading under the name ESCADA.[117] The court held that Escada Ag had established an international reputation and the services denoted by the mark were recognised regionally and locally. The court found that the use of the identical trade name by the local company would cause the public to reasonably assume an association between the two marks and contravened the provisions of articles 8(8), 36 and 37 of the Trademarks Law No. 9 of 2002. The court ordered that the registration of the local mark be cancelled and that the local company cease all usage of the infringing mark.

In a rather different trademarks matter, the UAE Trademarks Office established a precedent in trademark registrability when it accepted and registered a single-colour trademark. Mars Inc. succeeded in registering the colour orange in class 30 for its Uncle Ben range of rice products.[118] Mars was able to demonstrate that its use of the colour in its packaging of the rice products had established distinctiveness through use and a clear association in the marketplace between its products and the colour orange. It should be noted that Mars had been successful securing registration in other jurisdictions for the colour orange and did not face any opposition to its application for local registration of the colour mark.

In Yemen, the Court of First Instance considered an appeal by the French tyre company Michelin against a decision of the Registrar of Trademarks to allow registration of the local mark 'M-MICHELIN INTERNATIONAL' and to disallow Michelin's opposition to the registration.[119] The court noted that Michelin is a well-known trademark with an established international reputation and had been registered in Yemen since 1983 in classes 9 and 12 for tyres and car parts. Registration was sought for the local mark in class 4. The court held that the local mark was deceptively similar to the appellant's mark to the extent that the public would be misled and thereby contravened the provisions of Yemen's intellectual property law article 89(g) and the Commercial Law article 63. The court ordered that the decision of the Registrar be set aside and that registration of the M-MICHELIN INTERNATIONAL be cancelled.

In a case before the Dubai Court of First Instance, the petitioner, a foreign company, sought an order to overturn the action of the Dubai customs to seize goods owned by the company on the grounds that they were both counterfeit goods and that they bore trademarks registered in the UAE by a UAE company.[120] The petitioner did not dispute the claim relating to the goods being counterfeit. However, it argued that the trademarks were not infringing since the marks were registered in its own jurisdiction, and that Dubai customs did not have the right of seizure since the goods were only in transit through a trade free zone. The court found that, notwithstanding the foreign registration, the marks infringed the local registration. It held that the customs' right of seizure existed both in respect of the counterfeit nature of the goods and the infringing trademarks.

5.3.5 Structural and legislative processes

When described in layman's terms, the fundamental elements of the various areas of intellectual property protection encompassed by TRIPS may appear relatively easy to comprehend. But the translation of the layman's description into national legislation is a different matter, since TRIPS itself and its related international conventions set requirements and standards which are very complex and sophisticated. The reality, as asserted by the UK Commission on Intellectual Property, is that in developing countries, intellectual property is a relatively new and specialist area of public policy.[121] Accordingly, the developing countries lack experienced and well-qualified officials to provide the necessary expertise, requiring them to have an inordinate dependence on technical assistance provided by WIPO and other bodies – including developed countries with their own agendas. The problem can be particularly acute in the case of intellectual property since there are few people who possess both the specialised technical skills of legislative drafting and expertise in intellectual property law. Hirst adds another dimension to the problem. He suggests that from a technical perspective, it can be difficult to incorporate into the national laws the very specific requirements of TRIPS Part III relating to enforcement.[122] As mentioned above, some of the procedural concepts and mechanisms provided for in TRIPS Part III are of Anglo-American common law origin: they have no natural place in a civil law system and their terminology has no natural counterpart in the lexicon of modern legal Arabic.[123]

The legislative drafting, therefore, requires expertise, skill and care in law, language and technical translation. In some respects, the Gulf states have endeavoured to address the difficulties identified by the UK Commission and Hirst by virtue of the technical assistance they have sought and received from

WIPO in the form of legislative advice, drafting assistance and expert commentary in the creation of their intellectual property laws. These endeavours have not been entirely successful, since a number of incongruities and structural inconsistencies still exist in the laws (and upon which comment has earlier been made). However, the challenge re-emerges at the domestic secondary level, as the states tackle the task of drafting procedural statutes and regulations which create the necessary implementation mechanisms and processes and yet are still comprehensible to both the local administrators and the general public.

An inherent weakness in the legal structures of the Gulf states is the inadequacy and at times absence of procedural laws and subordinate regulations to give practical effect to a substantive law. This is particularly the case in respect of the timeliness of the production of enabling regulations following the enactment of a substantive intellectual property law. The substantive law generally comes into effect either on its publication in the Official Gazette or at a specified period of time thereafter (commonly 30 or 90 days) or upon issuance of the subordinate implementing regulations.

Almost all intellectual property laws require the drafting, approval and introduction of the corresponding subordinate implementing regulations before they can come into practical effect. Implementing regulations address a broad range of issues, not least amongst them being scales of registration fees and other charges, administrative structures, registration requirements, composition of review committees, authorisations and delegations – without which any implementation of the substantive laws in question cannot proceed. While some intellectual property laws establish the authority for ministry officials to carry out enforcement activities, the implementing regulations generally define the bounds of that authority.[124] An inordinate period of time, measured in years, can, and often does, exist between gazettal of the substantive law and issuance of the necessary implementing regulations to bring the laws into effect, thereby creating an imponderable impediment to effective enforcement. This may not be a matter of great import in areas of little or no local activity, such as protection of new plant varieties or integrated circuits, but it can have significant ramifications in respect of the daily administration of copyrights, trademarks and patents. Oman, for example, issued a new suite of intellectual property laws between May and October 2000, but five years later only some of the corresponding implementing regulations had just started to emerge.[125] The reasons offered for the delay in issuing the other implementing regulations included delays by WIPO in its preparation of the regulations, delays by the other GCC states which Oman felt obliged to consult on the nature and content of the regulations as part of its GCC membership, or obstacles thrown up by other government departments which were a necessary part of the regulation issuance process. Oman has just issued a new copyright law and industrial property law; the implementing regulations for the industrial-property law at least, being close to final draft form, should be released by mid 2009 –

which, it is suggested, may well become somewhat of a record for speedy action for the region.

Similarly, Kuwait's original 1962 patents law, as amended in 1995 and 1999, is still current, pending the issuance of implementing regulations to give effect to its new law enacted in 2001. At the time of writing, Qatar is still awaiting implementing regulations for its trademarks and copyright laws enacted in 2002. Article 53 of Qatar's trademark law of 2002 requires the implementing regulations to be issued within three months of the law coming into effect (which occurs on publication in the Official Gazette), but some five years later the implementing regulations have yet to appear. The common practice in such circumstances is to continue to use the implementing regulations for the now repealed prior law, thus exacerbating the confusion and uncertainty in the minds of the administrators and the public as to which law is in force. Some GCC states in recent times have been in the situation of having repealed an intellectual property law without it ever having been brought into effect.[126]

At the other end of the spectrum for timeliness is the case of the introduction of the implementing regulations for Yemen's patent-protection provisions. The provisions were issued as part of a comprehensive copyright, trademarks and patents law in 1994; the implementing regulations for the patents provisions eventually appeared in July 2007. According to the new regulations, patent applications will be examined as to form, novelty and industrial applicability, and that protection shall apply as from filing date.

Consequently, uncertainty can and does exist as to the extant validity of a particular law and the extent to which it should or can be enforced. In such circumstances, the common reaction is to do nothing, or at best act conservatively. In May 2004, for example, the Directorate of Industrial Property at the Bahrain Ministry of Commerce publicly announced that it would cease accepting patent applications for filing because the implementing regulations for its new patent law enacted in January 2004 had not yet been issued.[127] The announcement advised that the cessation would stay in place until such time as the implementing regulations, which were to stipulate the required lodgement processes and fees structure, were issued. The implementing regulations were eventually issued in May 2006.[128] In July 2006 the Directorate announced that it would begin accepting the filing of patent and utility model applications, consequent upon the recent issuance of the implementing regulations.[129] However, the filing exercise was not for the purpose of conducting examination but for recordal purposes and for noting priority dates only. A saving grace in this confusion is the fact that, up to mid 2006, the Directorate had not received any patent applications of local origin for filing or examination.[130]

By contrast, its sister government agency responsible for copyright protection, the Directorate of Publications and Press in the Ministry of Information, was reportedly already conducting raids, seizing alleged counterfeit or pirated material, instituting fines, ordering closures and initiating prosecutions for infringements in accordance with the provisions of the proposed new copyright law, even though the law had not yet been enacted.[131] This Directorate believed that retrospective application of the new law, which it anticipated would be in force by the time the prosecutions came to court, should not be a major issue for either the public prosecutor or the judiciary and should not therefore prejudice the conduct of the case under the old or new rules as appropriate at the time.

However, sometimes the issuance of the implementing regulation can have a different effect to that intended. Qatar's recently issued ministerial regulation, substantially increasing the scale of fees for trademark registrations, is an example at hand. The regulation increased the fees by at least 100 per cent, and even 12-fold for the registration of a licensing agreement, leading to a reported 'scandalous upheaval in the IP community' and a downturn in registration activity.[132]

5.3.6 Administrative structures

In terms of the institutional structures and frameworks in place in the Gulf states for the administration and enforcement of intellectual property rights, a number of common elements can be seen, although each state retains its own distinctive individual organisational features to best suit its particular needs. The more common model is for responsibility to be vested across two ministries (or three ministries if one includes police and security forces involved in conducting raids), although in some states their administration and enforcement may require the involvement of agencies across five discrete government ministries. Typically, responsibility for the administration of industrial property rights encompassing trademarks and patents (and notionally other areas such as geographical indications, trade secrets, unfair competition and new plant varieties) resides within a ministry whose terms of reference may include some or all of commerce, finance, industry or trade. Copyright and neighbouring rights often reside within a ministry whose description and terms of reference may encompass some of cabinet affairs, national heritage and culture, and information – the latter in some respects being a logical extension of the earlier censorship function and control of publications and publishing houses. Customs and border control matters relating to the movement of goods generally lie within the purview of a ministry for trade, while internal enforcement involving police-force actions requires the authority of the ministry of internal affairs or internal security.

Table 5.2 illustrates the organisational structures and division of primary responsibilities for industrial-property protection and copyright protection across the Gulf states.

Qatar and the UAE offer the simplest and most integrated organisational structure. They both incorporate all responsibility for the implementation and administration of intellectual property within the portfolio of a single Ministry. Within the Ministry, subordinate departments administer trademarks,

Table 5.2 Government organisation structures for intellectual property administration in the Gulf states

	Trademarks	Patents & designs	Plant varieties	Copyright and neighbouring rights	Border control
Bahrain	Ministry of Industry & Commerce – Industrial Property Directorate – Commercial & Company Affairs Directorate – Registry of Patents, Designs and Trade Marks – Industrial Property Tribunal			Ministry of Cabinet Affairs & Information – Directorate of Press & Publications – Copyright Protection Office	Ministry of Trade
Kuwait	Ministry of Commerce & Industry – Patents & Trademarks Office			Ministry of Information – Intellectual Property Directorate – Censorship Department	Finance Ministry – General Administration of Customs
Oman	Ministry of Commerce and Industry – Commerce Directorate – Intellectual Property Department – Copyright Section		Ministry of Agriculture & Fisheries	Ministry of Heritage & Culture – Organisations & Cultural Heritage Ministry of Information	Royal Oman Police – Inspectorate General of Police and Customs
Qatar	Ministry of Economy and Commerce – Commercial Affairs Directorate – Trademarks Office – Patents Office – Copyright Protection Office				Ministry of the Interior – IP Enforcement Office
Saudi Arabia	Ministry of Commerce – Trademarks Office – Commercial Anti-Fraud Department	King AbdulAziz City of Science and Technology – General Directorate of Patents		Ministry of Culture & Information – General Directorate of Copyright Protection	Finance Ministry – Public Directorate for Customs
UAE	Ministry of Economy – Industrial Property Directorate – Trademarks Office – Patents Office – Copyright Department				Federal Customs Authority Customs Directorates of each Emirate
Yemen	Ministry of Industry & Trade –General Administration of Industrial Property			Ministry of Culture – Copyright Office	
GCC	GCC General Secretariat		n/a	n/a	n/a

Source: compiled by the author

patents and copyright affairs. Oman is moving to a similar model, having recently enhanced the responsibilities of its Ministry of Commerce and Industry in administration and enforcement in both industrial property and copyright issues. However, its Ministry of Culture still plays a role in respect of copyright infringements, notably counterfeit software and piracy. Oman also complicates the administration of its intellectual property protection regime by vesting in the Ministry of Agriculture responsibility for new plant varieties and maintenance of registers on new plant varieties. The division is a legacy of the former protection model with discrete laws for each major intellectual property activity, rationalised in mid 2008 with their replacement by the comprehensive industrial-property law. It is quite likely, according to local speculation, that the intellectual property protection elements of new plant varieties will be similarly rationalised in the foreseeable future, with responsibility moving to the main supervising ministry.

Bahrain, Kuwait and Yemen share very similar structures. In each case, responsibility for intellectual property enforcement has evolved across three ministries, namely a commerce ministry for industrial-property matters, an information ministry for copyright and related rights, and a further trade-related ministry for customs, police and border controls. The Kuwaiti Ministry of Information, in which responsibility for copyright and neigbouring rights is vested, also monitors the government press and the radio and television broadcasting stations. All literature, audio, video and any other media material coming into Kuwait from abroad must still pass through the Censorship Department of the Ministry of Information for approval.

Saudi Arabia has a 'four-ministry' model for the administration of intellectual property rights, in structures that are both undergoing change and development, namely in each case:

- a commerce ministry, primarily responsible for implementing the trademarks law, but also responsible for ensuring compliance with national standards in respect of products and goods that come within the purview of the trademark, patent and copyright laws;
- an information and culture ministry, which is primarily responsible for implementing the copyright law, but which also administers the printing and publications laws;
- a finance and economy ministry, which supervises the respective customs authority which is charged with implementing the customs laws;
- a quasi-ministry, the King Abdul Aziz City for Science and Technology (KACST), which is primarily responsible for implementing the patents law, and the proposed industrial-designs law.[133]

Perhaps 'dynamic' is the most apt description of the organisational infrastructures responsible for intellectual property governance and administration amongst the states, particularly as the structure of government is constantly changing and developing. As can be seen in the case of the Omani and UAE recent experiences, the assignment of ministerial responsibilities for intellectual property rights is shifting away from being based on traditional notions of control towards an economic rationalism and exploitation. Consequently, organisational structures at the operational levels are still evolving. By the states' own admissions, effective enforcement of intellectual property rights is hampered by a shortage in the ministries, enforcement agencies and the judicial system of personnel expert in the interpretation and understanding of intellectual property legislation and trained in enforcement strategies and practice. Oman, for example, indicated to the WTO just prior to its accession in 2000 that it would take a full transitional period of five years to effectively implement the minimum standards of TRIPS, and particularly its enforcement provisions, because the country did not have appropriate and effective enforcement laws, procedural laws, the institutional machinery for enforcement, or the trained and experienced personnel to implement them.[134]

The divisions of authorities and responsibilities for the national management of intellectual property, as outlined in Table 5.2, are viewed with some dissatisfaction by those developed countries with commercial interests or ambitions in the Gulf states. The involvement of multiple ministries in the management and enforcement structures is perceived as a fundamental cause for inadequate enforcement performances by the states. Developed states have been prompted to pressure some of the states to legislate for a single comprehensive intellectual property rights enforcement law and to establish a single administration, monitoring and enforcement agency under the supervision of one government ministry.[135] The pressure has been resisted to date by all states, although some states have established inter-ministry coordination agencies – not always with complete success, it appears. According to the IIPA, the story of Kuwait's recent copyright enforcement performance is a tale of three ministries (or more).[136] Industry continues to receive good cooperation from the Ministry of Finance's Department of Customs intercepting pirated shipments at the borders, while the Ministry of Commerce and Industry stepped up efforts in late November/early December 2004 with some impressive raids. Yet the Ministry of Information enforcement unit remains sorely lacking in its ability and perhaps its will to stamp out piracy, taking only sparse enforcement actions in 2004. The Ministry of Interior, which is responsible for the Kuwaiti police force, and even customs remain unable to take *ex-officio* action necessary to defeat piracy in Kuwait. The IIPA argues that Kuwait should establish a specialised IPR unit within the police force in order to have a permanently operational law-enforcement body with trained officers that can carry out immediate raids as and when information about piracy becomes available.[137] It has also been very critical of the performance of a much vaunted Kuwaiti inter-ministry task force established in 2000 between the ministries of commerce, the interior, customs and the public prosecutor, suggesting that the task force was 'mired in red tape and bureaucracy and may in fact be hindering enforcement in Kuwait'.[138]

While the governmental structures that have been adopted, or have been allowed to evolve, have contributed to some of the coordination and performance problems that they experienced, they are not the only key issues. In each case, one ministry at least appears to be gaining a leading, even dominant role in the administration of the laws and the enforcement of intellectual property rights. As with the judicial system, the key problem confronting the respective ministerial departments involved in intellectual property management and enforcement has been the lack of expert human resources and institutional capacity. While processes for the registration and administration of trademarks are generally well established, having been in operation for a number of years, the same cannot be said of patents. While all states maintain patent offices, they generally serve as filing offices only, with none of the states (or the GCC Patent Office) carrying out searches and substantive and technical examinations. By the same token, the registration of works of copyright has been well established under the former publication and printing control legislations, but the allocation of primary responsibility for monitoring of and enforcement of neighbouring rights and rights in the digital environment is also still evolving.

5.4 Concluding remarks

It is rather challenging to obtain reliable longitudinal data from authoritative sources within and between the Gulf states on the states' and region's performances in enforcing their intellectual property laws and protecting individual rights. It is also difficult to obtain reliable data on the success of raids and judicial activity in controlling the prevalence of counterfeiting and piracy and other forms of illegal intellectual property activity in the Gulf. There are four fundamental reasons for this situation, namely:

- the absence of reliable and independent data-collection structures and processes in and across the Gulf states, and the absence of public access to such data if and where they are collected;
- laxity or uncertainty in procedures and practices in the secure control, monitoring and destruction of infringing goods and equipment, thereby allowing confiscated illegal and counterfeit goods to remain in or return to the marketplace (and in a sense be subject to double-counting by being on occasion the subject of subsequent seizures);
- where raids are publicly reported, they are invariably linked to another political agenda or strategic objective process and are thus often presented in a manner best suited for that particular agenda or initiative; an example of such an agenda might be the issuance of a new intellectual property law and a consequent public-awareness campaign;
- competition between ministries for resources and status; governmental departmental reports, which are often on restricted circulation, concentrate on the positives and do not always portray the global picture.

Where information does appear, it is often second-hand, anecdotal and lacking any consistency or format that easily allows comparative analysis across sectors or years. Hence such reports that do appear still should be read in the context of the political environment in which they appear. This is not to say that they should be discarded; rather that recognition should on occasion be given to a symbiotic association between local colour and hard facts. It has also been suggested that there is another, more sinister, explanation for the inherent difficulty in obtaining reliable statistics, namely the 'clandestine and mobile nature of the facilities used to manufacture pirate and counterfeit goods, and of the persons involved in producing and distributing such goods', the apparent implication being that such persons are likely to be 'well connected'.[139]

However, it should not be assumed that, in the absence of authoritative and verifiable reports and statistical data, the states are not making progress in their fights against counterfeiting, piracy and other intellectual property rights enforcement. Saudi Arabia and Bahrain, being the largest and the smallest respectively of the Gulf states in terms of population and area, are the states with the largest and smallest intellectual property infringement problem and enforcement activity. Hence they provide both contrast and comparison. The following are extracts from a local Saudi legal profession newsletter of enforcement activity by the Saudi authorities during the first half of 2005:

April: the Saudi Ministry of Commerce and Industry seized 1,000 tons of counterfeit products, and destroyed 8 million items in 2004. 1600 cases, mainly related to food products and auto parts, were currently being investigated.

April: the Commercial Anti-Fraud Department of the Ministry of Commerce and Industry reported that it had imposed fines totalling SR4 million (US$1.07 million) during February 2005 on businesses for marketing 'fraudulent' and counterfeit consumer goods. At the same time the department stated that 371 cases of counterfeiting were reported during 2003 and 2004, resulting in fines of SR12 million being imposed.

May: the Arab Federation of Software Producers advised that the national software piracy rate in Saudi Arabia had dropped from 73 per cent in 2000 to 25 per cent in 2004 (although the following BSA Global Study on Software Piracy figures for Saudi Arabia for the same period are 59 per cent to 52 per cent).

June: the Ministry of Culture and Information recently destroyed over 3 million counterfeit copyright items, including CD and video tapes, computer software and Playstations.

June: during 2004, the Ministry of Culture and Information's Ministerial Committee responsible for dealing with copyright infringements considered 400 cases, made final determinations on 353 of the cases and handed down the following penalties:

- closed down 31 businesses and revoked their trading licences;
- made orders for compensation totalling SR118,000 (US$-31,000) to various right holders;
- forced 900 out of 1,500 companies identified as using counterfeit software to replace their illegal software with licensed software.[140]

July: over 600,000 pirated CDs seized at King Abdul Aziz International Airport, Riyadh were recently destroyed by the Ministry of Culture and Information.

The *Bahrain Tribune* reported over a four-month period between August and November 2005 on the following enforcement activities undertaken by the Directorate of Press and Publications in the Ministry of Information:

4 August: over the last six months the Directorate carried out 493 inspections of business establishments, during which 62,000 pirated and illegally copied audio, video, print and electronic products were found and confiscated.

7 September: the Directorate recently destroyed 9,385 pirated movies confiscated over the last three months. It also reported an 85 per cent drop in the rate of pirate movies in Bahrain, bringing it down to 10–15 per cent of the total movie market in Bahrain.

9 November: the Directorate reported that software piracy in the Kingdom is now 30–35 per cent, and less than 20 per cent for movies.

The Gulf states have attracted praise from some sectors for the progress made to date, in what has been a remarkably short period of time by international standards. If the USTR's Annual Special 301 Report is any measure, then the Gulf states have made commendable progress, although Yemen, not surprisingly, lags well behind the GCC member states. In 1995, when the GCC member states were first examined by the USTR and included in its Annual Report, the USTR placed all states on either its Priority Watch List or its Watch List. By contrast, in its latest report, the USTR has retained only Kuwait and Saudi Arabia on its Watch List. The retention of Kuwait on the Watch List may be justifiable in light of its outmoded intellectual property laws, which are still in essence of a pre-TRIPS standard, and its less than committed enforcement performance. However, the retention of Saudi Arabia and the USTR's planned out-of-cycle review in late 2005/early 2006 of its intellectual property regime was more part of a US strategy to maintain pressure upon the Saudi government to extract the maximum trade and commercial concessions in the final round of political negotiations prior to formalisation of Saudi Arabia's WTO membership in November 2005.

The latest benchmarking BSA Global Study on software piracy, conducted in May 2008 for the previous year, reveals that local enforcement strategies have led to an ongoing decline amongst the Gulf states in software piracy.[141] BSA, which is also a member of IIPA, claims to be the leading global computer software protection lobby organisation and asserts that its Annual Global Study is the premier survey on international software piracy. The 2008 Study reports that, in 2007, piracy rates decreased in 67 countries, remained unchanged in 33 countries and decreased in only 8 countries.[142] The average world piracy rate increased by three percentage points to 38 per cent; in more than half the countries studied, the piracy rate exceeded

75 per cent. Only a third of the countries studied had a piracy rate below 50 per cent.

The Gulf region has improved from 89 per cent in 1994 to 53 per cent in 2007, mainly due to the performance of the UAE, which achieved a greater than 50-point decrease, from an 86 per cent piracy rate in 1994 to 35 per cent for 2007. This achievement places the UAE on a par with Japan, South Africa and Western Europe overall, and according to the Gulf regional office of BSA explains why the UAE has become the IT hub of the region.[143] This result retains the UAE in the top 20 countries in terms of lowest global piracy rates. Not far behind the UAE is Saudi Arabia, which has managed to reduce its piracy rate to 51 per cent, a result which still has not been of sufficient significance to enable it to be removed from the USTR 2008 Special 301 Listing. None of the GCC member states is included in the BSA's list of the 20 top countries with the worst piracy rates (Qatar and Bahrain appeared on the list in 2003). According to the Study commentary, the UAE's achievement is attributable to deliberate attempts by the UAE government to adopt stronger intellectual property protections during the 1990s, when a new generation of policymakers came into power and began luring foreign investments.[144]

Kuwait has shown the least improvement amongst the GCC member states, but has still managed to reduce its piracy rate by 29 percentage points from 91 per cent to 62 per cent since the Report's inception. Yemen, included for the first time in the BSA study, shows a piracy rate of 89 per cent, a figure which has a fairly significant negative distortion on the region's performance. When Yemen's data are excluded, the piracy rate of the remaining Gulf states comes down to 53 per cent – placing them all well within the top half of well-performing states, with two states – Saudi Arabia and the UAE – being well within or close to the top third of all states reviewed in the study.

Table 5.3 looks at the piracy rate in the Gulf region between 1995 and 2007.

The revenue losses arising from piracy have experienced a similar decline for the Gulf states, notwithstanding the dramatic growth in the regional and domestic technology markets and the consequent significant increase in computer hardware and software usage. Despite annual fluctuations, revenue losses more than halved between 1994 and 2002, declining from US$78.4 million to US$35.9 million. Saudi Arabia has shown the most dramatic improvement, with a two-thirds reduction in revenue losses. However, in the last two surveys, all Gulf countries except Saudi Arabia and the UAE have experienced actual slight increases in revenue losses despite continuing marginal piracy-rate reductions, a situation which is more a reflection on rapidly expanding software markets and the dramatic increases in market penetration that has been experienced right across the Gulf region rather than absolute increases in levels of piracy.

This is in contrast to the situation in the United States and the United Kingdom. Although the United States has the lowest global piracy rate, its

Table 5.3 1995–2007 BSA piracy study results – Gulf region piracy rate (%)

	1995	*1996*	*1998*	*2000*	*2002*	*2004*	*2006*	*2007*
Bahrain	92	90	89	80	76	62	60	57
Kuwait	91	89	88	80	73	68	64	62
Oman	96	95	93	78	70	64	62	61
Qatar	91	89	87	81	76	62	58	54
Saudi Arabia	77	79	73	59	50	52	52	51
UAE	86	50	49	44	36	34	35	35
Yemen	–	–	–	–	–	–	–	89
Gulf Total	89	81	80	71	64	57	54	58
Middle East Total	83	79	69	57	50	–	–	–
ME/Africa Total	–	–	–	–	–	58	60	60
North America Total	27	28	26	25	24	22	22	21
Central Europe Total	83	80	76	63	71	61	68	68
W Europe Total	49	43	36	34	35	35	34	33
North America Total	27	28	26	25	24	24	22	21

Source: compiled by the author from the BSA and BSA & IDC Annual Global Piracy Studies 2001–2008

revenue loss remains the highest due to the volume of computer sales. Similarly, piracy in the United Kingdom has declined by 16 per cent since 2003, but revenue loss due to piracy has almost doubled.

There is no doubt that the Gulf states have yet more work to do in the construction of their intellectual property protection regimes. Enforcement and infrastructure issues will continue to require attention in the mainstream areas of trademarks, copyright and patents as mainly external forces continue to pressure the Gulf states to conform to the emerging international 'norm' of TRIPS-plus standards. The UAE and Saudi Arabia constitute the largest of the Gulf economies and the states with the greatest profile in terms of intellectual property activity and need for effective enforcement strategies and performance. However, they are arguably the two states which have been the most successful in curbing infringing activity. Bahrain, Oman and Qatar represent the middle position, in respect of both activity and performance. Kuwait, meanwhile, is the least compliant of the GCC member states and will continue to attract critical attention and pressure to improve on its performance. Yemen trails the other Gulf states; as it seeks WTO membership, it will experience a similar degree of scrutiny of its intellectual property protection regime as did Saudi Arabia, and will no doubt be required to introduce a regime that is consistent with the current best international standards of protection and thereby exceeds current TRIPS standards.

But instead of coming from within the TRIPS context, the pressures have been generated by the developed countries for the states to move to TRIPS-plus levels of intellectual property protection. The strategy operates through adherence to a web of international conventions and commitment to bilateral trade agreements which contain a comprehensive compendium of requirements for enhanced levels of intellectual property protection that far exceed the TRIPS-required standards – as the next chapter discusses.

6 TRIPS-plus and 'raising the bar'

6.1 Introduction

With the arguable exception of Kuwait and Yemen, which still have in place some pre-TRIPS laws or laws with pre-TRIPS origins, the Gulf states now have intellectual property regimes which are generally TRIPS-compliant, even if they still show shortcomings in some matters of detail. The states have also demonstrated a general willingness to address the contentious issue of the enforcement of their intellectual property protection obligations – albeit still with mixed success. Yet, in common with other developing and least developed countries, they now face additional pressures from the major developed countries, and from the United States in particular, to adopt more comprehensive and higher standards of intellectual property protection that go well beyond those required by TRIPS – in other words, TRIPS-plus standards. The term 'TRIPS-plus' lacks precise definition, but has come into increasingly common usage in the debate on post-TRIPS intellectual property rights. It has been described, in a general sense, as 'commitments which go beyond what is already included or consolidated in the TRIPS Agreement', and more specifically as 'both those activities aimed at increasing the level of protection for right holders beyond that which is given in the TRIPS Agreement and those measures aimed at reducing the scope or effectiveness of limitations on rights and exceptions under the TRIPS Agreement'.[1]

This pressure to adopt TRIPS-plus standards of intellectual property protection is being applied in two ways:

- directly, through bilateral trade and investment agreements which include extensive and detailed intellectual property protection frameworks, and which require accession to or compliance with a number of TRIPS-plus international intellectual property protection conventions;[2]
- indirectly, through the coercive use of a threatened or actual withdrawal of preferential trade provisions or imposition of trade-related sanctions or retaliation to 'persuade' trading partners to adopt TRIPS-plus intellectual property protection standards.

Bilateral trade and investment agreements, particularly free trade agreements (FTAs), are the most common medium for imposing TRIPS-plus provisions. They typically contain extensive intellectual property protection provisions, which the major industrialised countries use to establish standards which exceed those enshrined in TRIPS, or to remove or reduce the flexibilities provided by or permitted in TRIPS, or to even establish protection in new areas of intellectual property rights which go beyond the parameters of TRIPS.[3]

The process of utilising bilateral trade and investment agreements to impose TRIPS-plus intellectual property protection has been described as a process which constitutes 'raising the bar' or a 'global ratcheting' of intellectual property protection benchmarks.[4] This process, which is seeing certain national intellectual property norms globalise upwards to those higher standards at a remarkable rate, is dependent upon the following key elements:

- forum shifting, in which the standard-setting agenda is moved from one forum in which difficulties are encountered in imposing TRIPS-plus standards (such as the WTO) to another forum in which success is more likely to be achieved (such as bilateral and regional agreements);
- coordinated bilateral and multilateral intellectual property protection strategies; and
- entrenchment in bilateral agreements of the principle of ever-increasing minimum protection standards.

The two major protagonists in this process of global integration are the United States and the European Union, although the United States has been the lead player in respect of the Middle East region. Utilised as key elements of the US bilateral strategy is the tactic of reward and coercion – the former illustrated by the application of its Generalised System of Preferences (GSP) and the promise of preferential access and tariff treatment to US markets, and the latter by the use of its Annual Special 301 Listing and the threat of trade retaliation.

The intellectual property provisions of the FTAs that the United States has recently concluded with Bahrain (Bahrain FTA) and Oman (Oman FTA) dramatically illustrate how it continually strives to raise protection standards and mostly (but not always) succeeds. While the United States has stated that it is pleased with the strengthened protection of intellectual property rights in its recent FTAs (including those with Morocco, Australia, Bahrain and Oman), it also stated at the commencement of subsequent negotiations and discussions, including those in the Gulf with the UAE, Kuwait and Qatar, that it would be seeking even higher levels of protection and enforcement.[5] However, negotiations on these particular FTAs have largely ground to a halt or slowed considerably.

6.2 Bilateralism – 'multilateralism by the backdoor'

Bilateral trade and investment agreements are promoted by their advocates as being stepping stones towards full integration of their participants into a global free-market economy by ensuring that governments implement the liberalisation, privatisation and deregulation measures of the globalisation agenda.[6] They argue that the introduction of free trade and the removal of regulations on investment that the bilateral agreements generate will lead to economic growth, the reduction of poverty, increased living standards and employment opportunities. The critics of bilateral agreements, however, argue that there is ample evidence to show that, on the contrary, the agreements merely allow transnational corporations more freedom to exploit workers and to shape the national and global economies of the junior partners to suit the corporations' interests.[7] They further posit that these binding international agreements severely constrain future governments in their policy options and help lock in existing economic reforms which may have been imposed by the International Monetary Fund, the World Bank or the Asian Development Bank, or are pursued by national governments of their own volition. Some commentators have argued at length that the self-interest mechanisms which are particular to the US-sponsored bilateral agreements, such as the conditions relating to the protection of intellectual property rights, their enforcement, and the control or check mechanisms for managing the agreements, are tantamount to an intrusion into domestic lawmaking.[8]

Bilateral agreements have been critically painted as part of an insidious fast-expanding and bewildering web, popping up like a hydra's heads throughout the world, and constructing in patchwork fashion what the developed nations have not been able to impose through such international forums as the WTO, or through multilateral negotiations.[9] They are also seen as insidious because they are invariably conducted in unequal contest in closed session between unequal partners – mainly a developed country and a developing or least developed country. With the stronger partner having an established objective to protect its own economic and trade interests, and having little or no interest in making allowance for the divergent or conflicting national and developmental interests of the weaker partner, the resultant agreement is both inevitable and predictable. As two commentators on bilateralism so colourfully, yet accurately, describe the outcome of such a scenario, 'bilateralism is like cooking an elephant and rabbit stew: however you mix the ingredients, it ends up tasting like elephant stew'.[10]

It has been suggested that, on intellectual property issues that really matter to it, the United States has been able to utilise webs of coercion.[11] One of those webs of coercion is its strategy of establishing bilateral agreements which include the introduction of TRIPS-plus standards of intellectual property protection. Developing countries operate within an intellectual property paradigm dominated by the United States and the European Union, and by international business. TRIPS sets minimum standards, while bilateral arrangements raise them. Developing countries can expect very few concessions on intellectual property issues, but are prepared to sign the bilateral agreements containing TRIPS-plus provisions in intellectual property rights in order to gain access to US and EU markets or to avoid losing access to them.

However, critics of bilateralism tend to concentrate on the policies and practices of the United States and the European Union, and appear to overlook the fact that many developing countries also enter into bilateral trade and investment treaties with each other and with least developed countries. These 'south–south' bilateral agreements tend to include the same essential features as the north–south agreements, particularly in respect of a broad definition of investments which encompass intellectual property rights, restrictions on and compensation for expropriation, and dispute resolution, although not to the same degree of complexity as the US- or EU-sponsored agreements.[12] Where US bilateral agreements in particular differ from the majority is in respect of four crucial elements, which constitute the agendas for control and self–interest, namely:

- the creation in each case of a joint committee of the two parties to manage and monitor the particular agreement;
- the imposition of strict limitations on performance requirements as a condition of investing in the host country;
- the wholesale attachment, in effect, of TRIPS-plus protection obligations and international conventions to the agreement; and
- most importantly, the gross imbalance in the political power, industrial might and negotiating expertise of two unequal parties.

The United States develops its bilateral strategy to expand and deepen control over its economic ties with countries in the Middle East through a series of graduated steps which encompass a range of bilateral agreements which either creates a protection framework for intellectual property rights or contains specific protection provisions.[13] They include:

- establishing Trade and Investment Framework Agreements (TIFAs), to initiate trade liberalisation within the target state and to 'promote the establishment of legal protections for [US] investors, improvements in intellectual property protection, more transparent and efficient customs procedures and greater transparency in government and commercial regulations';[14]
- establishing Bilateral Investment Treaties (BITs) to introduce common rules for investment in each state, by incorporating international (that is, US) business rules and norms into the domestic laws;
- establishing the more comprehensive FTAs, as the principal process by which US intellectual property rights industries are able to ensure that their required and sought-after standards of protection keep pace with new developments;[15]

- expanding these FTAs by bringing other regional or neighbouring states into them, and eventually weaving these 'subregional FTAs' into a greater US–Middle East Free Trade Area;
- supporting applications for WTO membership for those 'peaceful countries in the region that seek it';[16]
- providing financial and technical assistance and training to assist states develop the capacity to take part in negotiations, implement trade agreements, and build legal and entrepreneurial infrastructures;[17]
- using the US GSP programme and the USTR's Special 301 provisions as positive and negative reinforcement to control trade ties with eligible and/or recalcitrant states.

TIFAs are promoted by the United States as precursors or stepping stones to FTAs and/or BITs. They establish a political and legal commitment between two governments to cooperate on promoting mutual trade and investment under a certain number of conditions. One of those conditions commonly includes the establishment of a joint council or committee to oversee the cooperation of the two parties and the operation of the agreement. Historically, TIFAs pave the way to full-fledged bilateral agreements on trade and investment at a later date.

In contrast to its public rhetoric to its signatory partners in respect of equal mutual protection, the United States promotes BITs to US investors as designed to ensure that the investors receive national or MFN treatment (whichever is the more favourable) in the other signatory state and to ensure that their investments are protected against performance requirements, restrictions on transfers and arbitrary expropriation. In both BITs and TIFAs intellectual property rights are deemed to be investments: the Bahrain BIT, for example, defines 'investment' as encompassing every kind of investment owned or controlled, directly or indirectly, by a national or company, including:

> 'intellectual property, including, but not limited to:
> copyrights and related rights,
> patents,
> rights in plant varieties,
> industrial designs,
> rights in semiconductor layout designs,
> trade secrets, including, but not limited to, know-how and confidential business information,
> trade and service marks, and
> trade names.'[18]

BIT standard conditions, which represent potential obstacles and barriers to local development in the other country, include the following restrictions imposed upon the host government in respect of its capacity to direct and control the conduct of foreign investments in its own country:

- expropriation of an investment by the host government can be made only for a public purpose, must be carried out in a non-discriminatory manner consistent with international law and must be accompanied by prompt, adequate and effective compensation;
- investors are guaranteed the right of immediate transfer into and out of the host state of all funds related to an investment – including (but not limited to) interest, profits, dividends, capital gains, sale of all or part of the investment, royalties, management and technical fees, liquidation proceeds and compensation from dispute settlements;
- a host government may not impose mandatory local content or local purchase requirements, the 'balancing' of imports or sales in relation to exports or foreign exchange earnings, requirements to export products or services, technology transfer requirements, or requirements to conduct research and development in the host state, as a condition for establishing or maintaining an investment;
- an investor enjoys the right to submit a related dispute with the host government to binding international arbitration and cannot be required to use the state's domestic courts or obtain the consent of the host government to submit the dispute to arbitration.[19]

These obligations severely restrict the capacity of the host government to introduce measures to ensure that the host country can also share the technological advances and other benefits generated within the country from the foreign investment. This imposed restriction would appear to run contrary to the fundamental spirit and objectives of TRIPS Article 7, which states in its general provisions and basic principles that:

> 'The protection and enforcement of intellectual property rights should contribute to the promotion of technological innovation and to the transfer and dissemination of technology, to the mutual advantage of producers and users of technological knowledge and in a manner conducive to social and economic welfare, and to a balance of rights and obligations.'

The Bahrain BIT 'lowers the bar' in respect of the moral obligation of developed countries to commit to technology transfer and promotion for mutual benefit as enshrined in TRIPS. Article 31 of the BIT enhances the level of protection for the foreign investor by stipulating that 'neither party shall expropriate or nationalize a covered investment either directly or indirectly through measures tantamount to expropriation or nationalization . . .'.

The United States considers 'tantamount to' as being 'creeping expropriation' – a series of measures that effectively amounts to expropriation without taking actual title.[20] 'Tantamount' may encompass the slow and incremental encroachment on one or more of the ownership rights of a foreign investor that diminishes the value of the investment, even though the property remains vested in the investor. This situation has been often considered creeping expropriation by the United Nations Commission for Trade and Development (UNCTAD).[21] The breadth of the definition of investment and the coverage of action 'tantamount to expropriation' in a BIT may well be utilised by foreign investors as a device to dissuade a state from invoking the compulsory licensing provisions of its intellectual property laws, or to challenge the state's action on the grounds that it constitutes an indirect measure tantamount to expropriation. Some bilateral agreements include specific provision to preserve a host country's rights to grant compulsory licences by stipulating their exclusion from the bounds of expropriation and compensation, but this stipulation is not included in any of the TIFAs or BITs of the Gulf states.

BITs and TIFAs do not lay down specific standards of intellectual property protection *per se*. Rather, they require signatories to formally acknowledge 'the importance of providing adequate and effective protection and enforcement of intellectual property rights and the importance of adhering to international intellectual property rights standards'.[22] To give practical effect to this commitment, they provide for the establishment of joint committees, the declared purpose of which is to serve as the forum for permanent dialogue between the USTR and the partner state. A joint committee's tasks include a consideration of whether further agreements relating to intellectual property, amongst other trade issues, are desirable. However, the authority vested in the joint committee gives it considerable capacity and opportunity to introduce, unnoticed, a range of TRIPS-plus standards or to take the evolution of intellectual property rights beyond TRIPS and other multilateral standards. Drahos, using the example of the US–Jordan FTA, suggests that the joint committee created thereby 'to supervise the proper implementation' of a particular Agreement comes close to exercising a law-creating function, since its proper activity includes the consideration and adoption of amendments to the Agreement and the development of guidelines and rules for its proper implementation.[23] The fact that this joint committee shall also act as the dispute-resolution mechanism in the first instance, instead of the WTO or other international arbitration avenues, would reinforce this argument. Even if the joint committee does not go as far as suggested by Drahos, it would certainly be a very powerful lobby, with the full force of the USTR and the persuasive re-invocation of a Special 301 Listing behind it, to reinforce its demands for change, including change in a particular direction.

6.3 The role of the USTR and the Annual Special 301 Report

The US trade and investment policy, which encompasses intellectual property standards, is the responsibility of the Office of the USTR. Created by the US Congress in the 1962 Trade Expansion Act, the Office is authorised to set and administer overall trade policy, including all matters in respect of the

WTO, bilateral and multilateral trade and investment issues, trade-related intellectual property protection issues and administrative responsibility for the GSP and Section 301 (including Special 301) complaints against foreign trade practices which the USTR considers to be unfair to its own interests.

As a key part of its international monitoring of the activities of the nation's trading partners, the USTR reports annually on the conduct of different countries in respect of their treatment of intellectual property rights which are owned by US business or citizens, or in which they have an interest. The Annual Special 301 Report on intellectual property rights represents the coercive element in the US bilateral strategy. The Report is conducted annually pursuant to S.182 of the Trade Act of 1974, as amended by the Omnibus Trade and Competitiveness Act of 1988 and the Uruguay Round Agreement Act (URAA) of 1994. Under the Special 301 provisions of S.182, the USTR identifies those countries that it considers deny adequate and effective protection for intellectual property rights, or deny fair and equitable market access for US businesses that rely on intellectual property protection. The Special 301 provision was amended in the URAA to clarify that a country could be found to deny adequate and effective intellectual property protection even if it was in compliance with its obligations under TRIPS.[24] This clarification meant in effect that the USTR could take unilateral trade action against a trading partner which it deemed to have inadequate (by US standards) national intellectual property laws, even where the WTO Dispute Settlement Body had absolved the trading partner of any liability under international trade law.[25]

Under the Special 301 provisions, the USTR has created three levels of 'egregious activity', in respect of US intellectual property rights, namely the Priority Foreign Country, Priority Watch List and Watch List. Countries that are deemed to have the most onerous or egregious acts, policies or practices, resulting in the greatest adverse impact (actual or potential) on US products, are designated as a Priority Foreign Country and could potentially be faced with a unilateral withdrawal of US trade benefits or the lodgement of a complaint by the United States for resolution through the formal WTO Dispute Settlement process. Placement on the Priority Watch List or Watch List indicates that the USTR considers that particular problems exist with respect to the protection or enforcement of US intellectual property rights or market access for US interests. Countries placed on the Priority Watch List also become the focus of increased bilateral attention in respect of the areas of US concern. The Watch List indicates that countries have practices that meet some of the US requirements but still need close monitoring in implementing their commitments with regard to intellectual property protection and market access for US products and interests.

A Special 301 listing may not necessarily lead directly to some form of retaliatory action, but the coercive influence and impact of a listing, particularly when associated with an out-of-cycle country review, can be such that it may still lead to a TRIPS-plus consequence without the necessity for the threatened action to take place. Drahos (using the example of the US–Nicaragua BIT) suggests that there can be a causal relationship, or at least a very influential interaction, between BIT and other bilateral agreement negotiations, the Special 301 process and TRIPS-plus in the US context.[26] He provides the following remark by a senior USTR official as an illustration of the effectiveness of the Special 301 process:

> 'One fascinating aspect of the Special 301 process occurs just before we make our annual determinations, when there is a flurry of activity in those countries desiring not to be listed or to be moved to a lower list. IP laws are suddenly passed or amended, and enforcement activities increase significantly.'[27]

However, a certain degree of caution should be observed in trying to establish too close a causal association between these events above, since other factors – not least of which are those arising from international strategic alliances and rewards for 'friends' in the war against international terrorism – can also impact on the appearance, reappearance or disappearance of a state from the Special 301 Listings. While it may be easy to establish an obvious causal association between a Special 301 listing and the subsequent commitment to a bilateral agreement, promulgation of a national intellectual property law, or accession to a post-TRIPS convention, a Special 301 listing can still play a role in achieving a less obvious but desirable outcome in the greater political context.[28]

The undue influence of the US intellectual property industry lobby groups upon the USTR and upon the direction of US trade policy and intellectual property protection strategy has been extensively documented and debated.[29] They are intimately involved in the Special 301 assessment process (as well as the bilateral agreement and FTA process) and exert considerable influence on the nature and direction of the Report and their recommendations – their views are often reflected in the final decisions on Special 301 listings. They actively lobby the USTR and Congress. Some are also particularly influential in the Gulf states and maintain an active regional presence, operating local infringement 'hotlines', initiating prosecutions and participating in local enforcement and business re-education activities. Foremost amongst these lobby groups are the aforementioned Business Software Alliance (BSA), International Intellectual Property Alliance (IIPA) and particularly the Pharmaceutical Researchers and Manufacturers of America (PhRMA), all of which interact directly with the Gulf national governments at the most senior levels.[30] At times they appear to assume pseudo-state authority in their dealings with the states, making representations direct to state rulers, ministers and authorities.

The USTR started to review the GCC member states in 1989, with Saudi Arabia appearing in the Priority Watch List in that year, followed by the UAE on the Watch List in 1993 and the other states making their first appearances in 1995. Yemen has not yet been reviewed by the USTR so does not appear on any listing – had it been so reviewed, it is very likely that it would have appeared at least on the Priority Watch List.

The extent of influence of the intellectual property industry lobby groups is illustrated by the following situation in respect of Saudi Arabia's new copyright law. Saudi Arabia introduced extensive changes to the law in 2003, bringing it largely into TRIPS compliance. The law was constructed with the technical and drafting assistance of WIPO's International Bureau and included deterrent penalties of up to SR500,000 (for repeat offences). Even so, IIPA, which criticised the 1993 law, argued to the USTR that the new 2003 law still 'fails to meet the basic minimum standards of [TRIPS] and fails to fully meet the standards set by the two WIPO "digital" treaties'.[31] IIPA went on to state that 'Saudi Arabia must live up to commitments to bring its copyright system up to adequate standards – both substantive and enforcement – before they should be rewarded with favourable trade treatment and WTO accession'. In similar vein, PhRMA roundly criticised Saudi Arabia's patent enforcement practices as 'having become impossible' and 'Alice in Wonderland' and urged the US Administration to seek comprehensive patent reforms as a condition of Saudi WTO accession.[32] As a consequence, whether directly or indirectly attributable to the pressures brought to bear by IIPA and PhRMA on the US Administration, Saudi Arabia for the time being remained unfulfilled in respect of its aspirations for WTO membership and continued to be listed on the Special 301 Report Watch List.

The 2008 Special 301 Report is a statement of the US Administration's 'commit[ment] to using all available methods to resolve IPR-related issues and ensure that market access is fair and equitable for U.S. products of IPR-intensive industries'.[33] The Report focuses upon 'the need for significantly improved enforcement against counterfeiting and piracy, Internet piracy, counterfeit pharmaceuticals, transshipment of pirated and counterfeit goods, requirements for authorized use of legal software by government ministries, and full and proper implementation of TRIPS by WTO members, and TRIPS standards by new members at the time of their accession'. The Report adds that, in regions such as the Middle East, the United States uses an increasing number of TIFA negotiations to enhance intellectual property protection and enforcement, and then works closely with its trading partners to ensure proper implementation of FTA obligations under domestic law. Amongst the Gulf states, the Report retains Kuwait and Saudi Arabia on its Watch List.

Table 6.1 shows the record of the Gulf states in being included, or otherwise, in the Special 301 Annual Report over the last decade or so.

Bahrain was first placed on the USTR Special 301 Watch List in 1995 and was retained there until 1998 because the USTR considered that its intellectual property laws were not consistent with its international obligations under TRIPS, and because high piracy levels continued while enforcement was weak. However, because of what it considered to be concerted enforcement actions throughout 1998 and into 1999, the USTR

Table 6.1 US Special 301 Listings of the Gulf states 1996–2008

	1996	*1997*	*1998*	*1999*	*2000*	*2001*	*2002*	*2003*	*2004*	*2005*	*2006*	*2007*	*2008*
Bahrain	Watch	Watch	Watch	–	–	–	–	–	–	–	–	–	–
Kuwait	Watch	Watch	Priority# Watch	Priority Watch	Watch	Watch	Watch	Watch	Priority Watch	Priority Watch	Watch	Watch	Watch
Oman	Watch	Watch	Watch	Watch	Watch	–	–	–	–	–	–	–	–
Qatar	Oo	Oo	Watch	Watch	Watch	–	Watch	–	–	–	–	–	–
Saudi Arabia	Watch#	Watch	Watch	Watch	Watch	Watch	Watch	Watch	Watch	Watch	Watch#	Watch	Watch
UAE	Watch	Watch	Watch	Watch	–#	Watch	–	–	–	–	–	–	–
Yemen	Not assessed by USTR under Special 301												

Source: compiled by the author from USTR Annual Special 301 Reports, 1996–2008
– indicates a state has not been listed
# indicates the state was also listed for an out-of-cycle review during that year
'oo' – other observation. Generally used for initial entries, as an informal listing, where the 'egregious activity' is not quite to the Watch level

removed Bahrain in 1999. Bahrain was the first of the Gulf states to succeed in being removed, and has not reappeared on any list.

At first glance, Bahrain's removal and non-reappearance is hard to fathom and difficult to justify, if viewed in the narrow context of domestic standards of intellectual property protection and when compared with the performance of the other Gulf states. When the USTR last included Bahrain in its Special 301 Listing in 1998, Bahrain's copyright and trademark laws still dated from the early 1990s and had not been brought into TRIPS compliance, and patent protection for pharmaceutical products was only available in practice through re-registration of patents filed in the UK (a legacy of its 1955 pre-independence law). Furthermore, end-user business software piracy was still almost 90 per cent according to US industry estimates, giving Bahrain the second worst piracy rate of any Gulf state after Oman.[34] Even in 2003 its software piracy rate was still only marginally better than then worst-performing Kuwait. Nevertheless, its removal coincided with the commencement and successful conclusion of negotiations with the United States for a BIT, the first Gulf state to enter into such an agreement. Its removal further coincided with the emergence, albeit only in draft form, of a comprehensive suite of individual intellectual property laws, which had been prepared with the assistance of WIPO and some of which were largely based on the WIPO model laws.[35] Yet it took another six to seven years before the new copyright and trademarks laws in particular appeared – while the respective pre-TRIPS (and thereby TRIPS non-compliant) 1991 and 1993 laws remained in force.

Since its first appearance in the Special 301 Listings in 1995, Kuwait has moved regularly between the Priority Watch List and the Watch List, mainly because of ongoing USTR concerns about the lack of proper copyright legislation and software piracy. Kuwait was elevated from the Watch List to the Priority Watch List in 1998 and remained there in 1999. The 1999 Report described Kuwait as the worst pirate market in the Gulf region and the only WTO country without a copyright law, and threatened to elevate it to Priority Foreign Country status – the highest status of egregious activity.[36] Kuwait's performance the following year improved sufficiently for it to be removed to the Watch List, where it remained until 2004, when it was again elevated to the Priority Watch List. Kuwait was retained on the Priority Watch List in 2005, because of its continuing high rates of copyright piracy, lack of progress in amending its copyright law to meet international obligations and failure to fully implement the 2002 work plan it had agreed with the United States to increase intellectual property rights enforcement. The 2005 Report noted that Kuwait 'continues to have high levels of retail optical disc piracy, as well as problems with corporate end-user software piracy, cable piracy and internet piracy'.[37] In what the aforementioned critics of the US bilateral strategy would no doubt consider as intrusion into or interference with internal administration of domestic policy, the Report urged Kuwait to make public declarations that piracy would not be tolerated, increase the frequency of raids on suspected infringers, prosecute offenders and impose deterrent sentences, publish the outcomes of raids to deter others and amend its copyright law in the near future to correct its deficiencies. The USTR emphasised that it would continue to address the above issues under the US–Kuwait TIFA of February 2004, a repeat of the warning it made in its corresponding Report a year earlier.

In the latest USTR Report for 2008, Kuwait is retained on the Watch List due to its failure to make progress on amending its outdated intellectual property laws.[38] The USTR acknowledges that Kuwait customs, police and Ministry of Interior officials continued to make progress on enforcement in 2007. However, the USTR has expressed concern that Kuwait has failed to make satisfactory progress on amending its outdated IPR laws and that several key pieces of intellectual property legislation have been pending for many years, including legislation regarding copyrights, data protection, geographical indications, trademarks, patents and customs. The USTR urges Kuwait to enact and implement this legislation in the near term. The USTR again reinforces the coercive interaction between the Special 301 Report and its bilateral agreement strategy by emphasising that it will continue to work with Kuwait on the passage of this legislation and on improved enforcement through the US–Kuwait TIFA of February 2004, in order to ensure that Kuwait meets its international IPR commitments.

Oman was examined by the USTR for the first time in 1995 and raised to the Watch List in 1996, the USTR describing the country's intellectual property protection regime as 'minimal and stagnant'.[39] The USTR retained Oman on the Watch List for the following three years after accusations from US copyright industry lobby groups that Oman's market was 'dominated by piracy' and was 'a haven for pirates fleeing less hospitable neighbouring states'.[40] But within just a few years, and in a remarkable turn-around, Oman progressed from being the worst Gulf state in terms of intellectual property protection to becoming the best performing. It reduced its software piracy rate as measured by the BSA from 96 per cent in 1996 to 78 per cent in just five years.[41] During 2000 it promulgated a suite of intellectual property laws which, at that time, was the most comprehensive, modern and TRIPS-compliant amongst all Gulf states, achieved membership of the WTO and acceded to TRIPS in September of that year. It also acceded to the Patent Cooperation Treaty in February 2001. Accordingly, Oman was removed from the Special 301 List in 2001 and subsequently has not reappeared on any listing.

The USTR first reported on Qatar in 1995 and accorded it a 'Special Mention', a listing repeated in 1996 and 1997, because of the perceived shortcomings in its intellectual property regime. The USTR raised Qatar to the Watch List in 1998, because of US industry concerns that Qatar was becoming a potential 'haven of piracy', and called upon it to legalise the software used in government offices, improve copyright enforcement and implement its TRIPS obligations.[42] Qatar remained on the Watch List for the next two years because of its failure to enact TRIPS-consistent legislation and perceived serious enforcement problems. Despite US copyright industry concerns, the USTR removed Qatar from all lists in 2001, but returned it to the Watch List in 2002 for failure to sign and implement a new copyright law. Qatar's removal from any listing in 2003 coincided with the issuance of new copyright and trademark laws during 2002, and the USTR's view that it had instituted improved, sustained enforcement actions against copyright infringement. According to the BSA, Qatar's software piracy rate fell dramatically between 2002 and 2003, from 76 per cent to 63 per cent, arguably the best improvement in performance of any Gulf state for these years.[43]

Saudi Arabia was first reviewed by the USTR in 1989 and was immediately placed on the Priority Watch List. It moved regularly between the Priority Watch List and the Watch List between 1989 and 1995 and has remained on the Watch List since 1995. The USTR kept Saudi Arabia on the Watch List for several years in the late 1990s, despite recommendations from the US copyright industry that it be elevated to the Priority Watch List for continued piracy, lack of effective and deterrent enforcement actions and a TRIPS-incompatible copyright law. In its report for 2003, the USTR repeated concerns initially expressed the previous year about the continued piracy and trademark infringement substantially affecting US industries, and the lack of deterrent penalties and transparency in the Saudi enforcement, prosecutorial and judicial processes.[44] It also expressed concern over reports that a Saudi company in 2002 had attempted to register unauthorised copies of patented US pharmaceutical products with the Saudi Ministry of Health.

The USTR retained Saudi Arabia on the Watch List for 2005 because it considered that its 2003 copyright law lacked some basic minimum standards that were required not only by TRIPS but also by the WIPO Internet Treaties, including provision for destruction of seized goods, materials and machinery, and failure to provide for recovery of litigation costs.[45] It asserted that the US copyright industry reported that piracy rates remained high due to the absence of deterrent penalties and lack of transparency in the enforcement system. The Report also noted that Saudi Arabia's patent registration system was seriously deficient, with a backlog of thousands of applications, a comment it also made in the previous year's report. However, the Report did acknowledge that Saudi Arabia had been protecting intellectual property rights relating to pharmaceutical products and that there had been no major instances of patent infringement over the last year.[46] As it did with Kuwait, the USTR maintained the pressure on Saudi Arabia to comply with its demands by warning that it would continue to work on these issues through the TIFA Agreement. It compounded this pressure by adding that it would also work on these issues through the WTO accession process, the clear implication being that Saudi Arabia would need to accede to US demands in respect of intellectual property protection standards if it wished its accession to the WTO to be approved. Saudi Arabia eventually achieved WTO membership in December 2005.

In its 2008 report, the USTR acknowledges that Saudi Arabia has made some progress in the enforcement of intellectual property rights, partly by an increased number of raids and the reported disposal of a number of cases by the recently created copyright enforcement Violations Review Committee.[47] It recognises that Saudi Arabia is pursuing improvements, especially with regard to its improving cooperation with private right holders and increasing transparency of its copyright enforcement administrative processes within the Ministry of Culture and Information. However, the USTR considers that Saudi Arabia needs to improve further by continuing sustained raids and inspections to combat piracy and counterfeiting, encouraging courts to impose deterrent-level sentences, including jail sentences for serious offences, and improving border enforcement. The USTR has welcomed the Saudi agreement to establish a US–Saudi IPR Working Group and asserts that it will work closely with Saudi Arabia to address outstanding intellectual property issues through this Working Group and the TIFA of July 2003. Saudi Arabia remains on the Watch List for 2008.

Saudi Arabia's retention on the Watch List is in spite of achieving WTO membership and compliance with TRIPS, a new patents, industrial models, integrated circuits and new-plant-varieties law in 2004, a long-awaited new copyright law and accession to the Berne and Paris Conventions towards the end of 2003, and a success rate for combating software piracy that is second only to that of the UAE amongst the Gulf states according to the BSA.

6.3.1 The UAE's experience with the Special 301 Annual Report

The UAE's experience with the Special 301 Listings not only strikingly illustrates the nature of the USTR's strategy and operation in respect of individual countries but also is a prime example of the undue influence that certain industry lobby groups exert in contributing each year to the direction of the USTR Report. Throughout the UAE's period of inclusion in the Special 301 Listing, it has experienced ongoing pressures to comply with US requirements, first in respect of copyright protection and then for patent protection and marketing exclusivity for pharmaceutical products, which at times has more than offset progress or performance that it has made in other areas of intellectual property protection. Despite being generally considered to have had the best performance in the Middle East over the last decade for tackling copyright piracy, the UAE was on the Special 301 Watch List almost continuously since its first review in 1991 until 2001.

In 1997, the BSA recommended that the UAE be removed from any Special 301 Listing because of the UAE's record of reducing software piracy, according to the BSA's benchmark annual piracy review, from 86 per cent to 50 per cent over the preceding triennium. The USTR acknowledged that piracy of motion pictures and sound recordings had been largely eliminated in the UAE and efforts to reduce software piracy had increased with considerable success.[48] However, it retained the UAE on the Watch List on the recommendation of PhRMA because its patent law exempted medicines and pharmaceutical compounds from protection and contained compulsory licensing provisions which the USTR deemed to be onerous, notwithstanding the fact that these exemptions and provisions were consistent with TRIPS.

Between 1998 and 2001, despite the US copyright industry and IIPA recommendations that it be removed, the USTR kept the UAE on its Watch List. The USTR noted that efforts to reduce software piracy had 'not been sufficient to reduce the level of illegal activity' (1998) or because of deficiencies in the area of patents, particularly in respect of protection for pharmaceutical products subject to patent protection, and because of little progress toward enactment of a new patent law.[49]

In early 2000, PhRMA urged that the UAE be placed on the Priority Watch List because of its continued failure to protect patented pharmaceutical products and commercially valuable confidential data as required by TRIPS.[50] PhRMA subsequently withdrew its request following assurances that the UAE would provide adequate and effective protection for patented pharmaceutical products and requested that it even be taken off the Watch List. The UAE was finally removed from the Watch List following a written commitment to take specific measures to assure adequate and effective protection of patented products, including specific commitments on the implementation of TRIPS, data protection and the withholding of marketing approval for unauthorised copies of patented products.[51] In December of that year, PhRMA accused the UAE of express violations of bilateral and multilateral commitments to protect intellectual property rights for patented pharmaceutical products and confidential data, and failure to live up to written commitments and its WTO obligations, and sought an immediate USTR out-of-cycle review of the UAE for these alleged violations and its designation as a Priority Foreign Country.[52] It also urged the UAE government to de-register all unauthorised copies submitted for marketing approvals, on the grounds that they were derived from patented pharmaceutical products of PhRMA-member companies and other pharmaceutical multinationals, or directly or indirectly relied on, referred to or used, original protected clinical and laboratory data of PhRMA Gulf members.

The UAE Ministry of Health dismissed the PhRMA claims that it had abrogated its WTO obligations. It argued that it respected patented pharmaceutical products and commercially valuable confidential data as required by TRIPS, and that all medicines registered in the country complied with UAE federal laws, including a ministerial decree banning the registration of any drug or pharmaceutical compound which was not already the subject of patent protection in its country of origin.[53] The impact of the ministerial order was to effectively counter the inflow into the UAE and thereby the other Gulf states of generic drugs, a matter of considerable concern to PhRMA and its members. The Ministry also correctly countered that it was still within the WTO's grace period for developing countries in respect of patented pharmaceutical products (the grace period not expiring until 1 January 2005).

The USTR accordingly re-listed the UAE for 2001, despite the fact that its efforts in reducing copyright piracy had been widely praised, even by the USTR. According to the USTR, 'the UAE was removed from the Watch List last year [2000] in recognition of its commitment to not provide marketing approval to unauthorised copies of patented pharmaceutical products . . . however, the UAE subsequently granted marketing approval for a number of unauthorised copies of patented pharmaceuticals'.[54]

The USTR finally removed the UAE from the Watch List in 2002, mainly as a result of specific provision in its new patent law of 2002 for immediate transitional protection and marketing exclusivity for patented pharmaceutical and agrochemical products – the only Gulf state to have done so.[55] The UAE also had agreed to allow the United States to review and have input into a draft of its new patent law, in order to ensure compliance with TRIPS. The UAE's success in finally being removed from a Special 301 Listing also coincided with its introduction during 2002 of updated TRIPS-compliant laws in respect of copyright and neighbouring rights, trademarks and industrial designs, and the signing of a TIFA with the United States early the following year. However, the pressure continues: even though the UAE has not since returned to the Special 301 Listings, it has been receiving mention in the subsequent Reports, including the 2008 Report, to the effect that measures above the minimum standard laid out by TRIPS, that is, TRIPS-plus measures, need to be implemented to ensure effective enforcement at the national and local levels, particularly in respect of commercial activity in the UAE's burgeoning free trade zones.[56]

6.4 Bilateralism and the TRIPS-plus treaties

Accession to the TRIPS-plus multilateral treaties and conventions has been highlighted by some critics of the US bilateral strategy as a prime example of the way in which developing countries are being further drawn into a web of intellectual property treaties designed not for their own development but for the preservation of the commercial and investment interests of the United States and its transnational business corporations.[57] The United States is forthright in asserting that it seeks to heighten standards of intellectual property protection by incorporating as substantive obligations into all bilateral agreements it negotiates a number of multilateral treaties that have yet to gain universal acceptance, and in particular the WIPO Internet Treaties – the WIPO Copyright Treaty (WCT) and the WIPO Performances and Phonograms Treaty (WPPT). However, its FTA negotiations do not rely solely on TRIPS and the WIPO Internet Treaties to establish benchmarks but will continue to incorporate its own latest copyright and enforcement requirements as well as those requirements that it anticipates may exist at the time that a particular round of negotiations might be concluded.[58]

The WCT and WPPT were approved by WIPO members in 1996. Their primary objective is to establish and raise the level of international protection for copyright and related rights which had been established before the development and widespread use of personal computers and the internet. The WCT supplements the Berne Convention and introduces new and far-reaching norms to protect the rights of authors of literary and artistic works within the digital environment. Similarly, the WPPT builds upon the Rome Convention and serves to safeguard the interests of producers of phonograms and performers whose performances are fixed in phonograms. In particular, both treaties raise the minimum standards of global intellectual property protection with respect to internet-based delivery of copyrighted works.

Both treaties require countries to provide a framework of basic rights to enable creators of protectable work to commercially exploit their creations and to control the way they are used by others. Most importantly, the treaties ensure that the owners of those rights will continue to be protected when their works are disseminated through new technologies and communications systems such as the internet. The treaties thus clarify that existing rights continue to apply in the digital environment and create new online rights.

Signatories are required to provide not only the rights themselves but also technological adjuncts to those rights. These are intended to ensure that right holders can effectively use technology to protect their rights and to license their works online. The 'anti-circumvention' provisions require countries to provide adequate legal protection and effective remedies against the circumvention of technological measures (such as encryption) used by right holders to protect their rights. The second type of technological adjuncts safeguards the reliability and integrity of the online marketplace by requiring countries to prohibit the deliberate alteration or deletion of electronic rights management information, that is, accompanying information which identifies the work, its creators, performer or owner, and the terms and conditions for its use.

These two treaties are of considerable interest and importance to US copyright-based industries. They were actively endorsed by the United States during their negotiations on TRIPS and subsequently have continued to be vigorously promoted by the USTR.[59] Since its 2002 Special 301 Report, the USTR has regularly described both treaties as representing the consensus view of the world community that the vital framework of protection under existing treaties, including the TRIPS Agreement, should be supplemented to eliminate any remaining gaps in copyright protection on the internet that could impede the development of electronic commerce. The 2002 Report also declared that the USTR's strategy was to incorporate the highest standards of protection for intellectual property, of which the two WIPO Internet Treaties are key elements, into any bilateral and regional trade agreements that it negotiated, and acknowledged that its success in doing so with the Jordan FTA laid the foundation for it to repeat the strategy.[60] However, elements of the treaties are still the subject of ongoing and sometimes contentious debate within WIPO.

WIPO treaties require a minimum number of ratifications by WIPO member states before they enter into force; the effect of the US bilateral agreements is that they will require more countries, mainly least developed and developing countries, to accede to these WIPO treaties with the result that they will come into force on the back of these bilateral agreements. The WIPO treaties will then become the catalyst for further pressure on other developing and least developed countries to accede to them, on the grounds that they represent the latest international standards. Although the WCT and the WPPT were both agreed upon by WIPO members in 1996, the treaties did not attract the necessary minimum 30 accessions to enable them to come into force until early 2002 – conveniently, just prior to the publication of the above-mentioned USTR 2002 Special 301 Report. By May 2004 and the successful conclusion of the Bahrain FTA negotiations, only 47 countries had acceded to the WCT and only 43 had acceded to the WPPT, in each case a very small proportion of WIPO's then 148 members. The great majority of the accessions were by least developed countries, while the United States and Japan were the only major developed countries to have ratified either treaty. By July 2008, 65 countries had acceded to the WCT and 64 had acceded to the WPPT, amongst the signatories in both cases being China, Japan and the United States.[61] However, the great majority of accessions are still drawn from least developed and developing countries – which would constitute wholesale importers rather than importers of intellectual property protected under a TRIPS-plus regime. Conspicuous by their absence are the EU members and other European states.

The USTR 2008 Special 301 Report continues to herald that the WIPO Internet Treaties are now part of the international IPR legal regime and represent the consensus view of the world community that the framework of protection under existing agreements, including the TRIPS Agreement, should be supplemented to eliminate any remaining gaps in copyright protection on the internet that could impede the development of electronic commerce.[62] At the time of publication of the Report, there were 65 accessions to the WCT and 62 accessions to the WPPT. However, these numbers still represent just over a third of the WIPO membership and well under half of the WTO membership, which would appear to be somewhat short by any measure of being able to justifiably claim that such numbers constitute a 'consensus view of the world community'. However, the US claim of a world community consensus in respect of these two treaties, irrespective of their merit as effective tools of intellectual property protection, cannot be justified or sustained in light of the significant proportion of members of the global forums who have *not* embraced the treaties.

The same criticism can also be extended to some of the other WIPO-administered TRIPS-plus treaties which the United States includes in its bilateral negotiating agenda. For example, as of May 2004 and the completion of the Bahrain FTA, the Trademark Law Treaty (TLT) had attracted the bare minimum 31 accessions, while the Patent Law Treaty (PLT) had not yet come into force, and the Brussels Convention, the Hague Agreement and the UPOV Convention had attracted only 26, 37 and 54 accessions respectively – again, the majority of which were by least developed or developing countries. By July 2008 the membership of the main WIPO-administered treaties generally incorporated in the FTAs stood at PLT (18 states), TLT (40 states), Brussels (32 states), PCT (139 states), Madrid Protocol (76 states), Budapest (69 states), Hague (51 states), UPOV (65 states), with the majority still being drawn from the groups of least developed and developing countries.

In respect of the Gulf states, Bahrain and Oman are required to accede to the WCT and WPPT, as well as the UPOV Convention and a number of other international treaties, as a condition of their FTAs. However, adoption of the internet treaties does not constitute a matter of any great concern for any of the states. On the contrary, it constitutes a preferred option if it serves as an alternative to opening up their respective intellectual property laws to incorporate changes appropriate for the digital environment, since such course of action leaves the laws open to demands from developed countries for a range of other changes – such as significantly increasing the deterrent values of the enforcement provisions or removing some of the remaining exception provisions permitted by TRIPS. Accordingly, some of the states have already initiated moves to join the internet treaties before being required to do so as part of a bilateral agreement. Bahrain lodged its instruments of accession to the WCT, the WPPT, the PLT and the Madrid Protocol in September 2005 and to the UPOV Convention in June 2005 after concluding its FTA with the United States. However, it was already favourably considering the idea of joining all five treaties, including UPOV, some years prior to the commencement of its FTA negotiations.[63] Likewise, Oman and the UAE joined the WCT and WPPT ahead of their FTA negotiations (the UAE had already acceded to the WCT, in July 2004). Qatar has also joined the WCT and the WPPT. At this stage, only Bahrain and Oman have acceded to the UPOV Convention.

6.5 Bilateral agreements between the United States and the Gulf states

6.5.1 The Middle East Free Trade Area (MEFTA)

The United States leads the European Union in the installation of its bilateral agreements in the Middle East region, and in the Gulf in particular, with its bilateral agreement strategy a small part of a much bigger picture. As part of its Middle East Peace Initiative, a key element in its war against international terrorism, the United States envisages the creation of a US–Middle East Free Trade Area by 2013, to complement and extend its already significant economic and military involvement in the region.[64] Accordingly, US trade and investment relations with the countries of the Middle East have considerable potential importance and urgency in terms of both US political and economic interests.

The United States has repeatedly declined to negotiate collectively with the Gulf states as a regional or GCC bloc, insisting instead on separate individual negotiations and agreements with each of the six GCC member states. It justifies this state-by-state approach on the grounds that it recognises the differing levels of development across the Gulf region and it is thereby pursuing a step-by-step approach tailored to individual states' particular needs.[65] However, this argument cannot be sustained in view of the fact that the bilateral agreements which the United States has entered into with the states, and other developing countries, are all based on model agreements whose objective is to achieve standardisation with minimal deviation. Change is permitted to the extent that such change constitutes refinement of the model. Hence the intellectual property chapters of the US–Oman FTA are almost identical with those of the US–Bahrain FTA, which in turn are closely aligned with those of the Jordanian, the Moroccan and even the Australian agreements. Similarly, the TIFAs of all Gulf states are identical in substance and virtually identical in text. Critics would argue that this 'step-by-step' approach enables the United States to implement a divide-and-conquer strategy and to prevent the creation of opposition alliances of the kind that it has encountered in the multilateral forums of the WTO and WIPO.[66] It also allows the United States to maximise its immense political and economic bargaining power to extract the most favourable trading terms and intellectual property protection regimes terms from its agreement partners, and this tactic is being used in its implementation strategy for the MEFTA.

In contrast, the European Union has consistently refused to enter into separate bilateral discussions with the individual states and has chosen instead to negotiate its proposed FTA with the GCC as a bloc. The European Union has pushed for a greater degree of economic integration between the GCC member states as a key issue in the continuation of negotiations, and the establishment of a GCC Customs Union was an EU precondition for eventually signing an FTA. The European Union also views GCC integration as a step toward greater regional stability and mutual prosperity. Yet, negotiations with the European Union have taken a considerable time, and in mid 2008 had yet to be concluded. Negotiations have recently stalled again after the European Union presented conditions and tried to introduce issues, such as those relating to terrorism and human rights, which appeared to the GCC to stray away from the economic agenda and into the political arena. However, since the United States has now moved to strive to reach bilateral agreements with all GCC member states, and is well advanced in the implementation of its MEFTA policy, the European Union appears to have felt the urge to fast-track its own FTA with the GCC. It recognises the imperative to protect its position as the Gulf's largest trading partner and to counter the US ambition to establish a US-dominated free trade region in the Middle East by 2013.[67]

However, as recently as July 2008, the GCC were threatening to withdraw from the protracted negotiations with the EU if the outstanding issues were not resolved quickly.[68] Dispute still exists over EU insistence upon including in negotiations such issues as human rights, national government systems and GCC member states' restrictions on foreign ownership – issues which the states see as being irrelevant to the FTA, but which are also central to the US negotiations with the individual states. The states view the EU insistence on including these issues in negotiations as interference in their domestic affairs and criticisms of their systems of government.

Because of the stalled nature of EU–GCC negotiations over an extended period of time, the European Union impact on intellectual property protection regimes of the Gulf states in the context of a bilateral strategy has been negligible and has been put to one side for the purposes of this work.

Bahrain was the first Gulf state to enter into a bilateral agreement with the United States which incorporated provisions relating to the protection of intellectual property rights, when it signed a BIT in September 1999. The treaty was promoted by the United States at the time of its completion as an open investment policy that would contribute to economic growth and would assist Bahrain in its efforts to develop its economy by creating conditions more favourable for US private investment and thereby strengthening the development of Bahrain's private sector.[69] However, in reality, the Bahrain BIT establishes a secure, predictable and unduly favourable legal framework for US investors operating in Bahrain.[70] All forms of investment are protected under the Treaty, with intellectual property in its broadest sense deemed to be another form of investment. While the Treaty itself stipulates that each party shall accord to investments covered by the Treaty fair and equitable treatment and full protection and security no less favourable than that required by international law,[71] it is also promoted as being fully consistent with US policy towards international and domestic investment.[72] The BIT imposes substantial restrictions on the capacity of Bahrain to impose any conditions relating to expropriation, transfers, local performance or dispute settlement, irrespective of whether they are aimed at developing technology transfer or local capacity.

The Bahrain BIT was complemented by a TIFA in June 2002. The TIFA also provides for the establishment of a joint committee of both countries to pursue issues such as inadequate levels of intellectual property rights protection or less than desired enforcement performance. These pre-existing bilateral agreements, which remain in force, provide a firm foundation upon which the Bahrain FTA has been developed.

While Bahrain is the first Gulf state to complete the above graduated steps with the signing of its FTA, other states are in various stages of progression towards possible eventual FTAs. All states, including Yemen, have now completed TIFAs, Oman has also concluded an FTA and some of the other states have commenced preliminary discussions or negotiations on FTAs. The main exception is Saudi Arabia; neither Saudi Arabia nor the United States has given any indication of when negotiations on a possible FTA will commence, and it is quite likely that the United States will strive to secure the other five agreements before it expresses a willingness to commence negotiations with Saudi Arabia. The triple-agreement approach appears to have been rationalised, with the other GCC states moving from an initial TIFA directly into an FTA round. The significant elements of the Bahrain BIT have either been included in the other states' TIFAs (such as the joint committee provision) or will be included in the FTAs (namely, expropriation and dispute resolution). By the same token, neither Yemen nor the United States has given any indications of entering into discussions together towards a possible future FTA.

The current status of bilateral agreements between the United States and the Gulf states is shown in Table 6.2.

Table 6.2 Bilateral agreements between the United States and the Gulf states (at January 2008)

	Bilateral Investment Treaty (BIT)	*Trade Investment Framework Agreement(TIFA)*	*Free Trade Agreement (FTA)*
Bahrain	September 1999	June 2002	completed May 2004
Kuwait	–	February 2004	discussions stalled
Oman	–	July 2004	completed October 2005
Qatar	–	March 2004	discussions stalled
Saudi Arabia	–	July 2003	–
UAE	–	March 2003	negotiations commenced March 2005–now stalled
Yemen	–	February 2004	–

Source: Compiled by the author

6.5.2 The US–Bahrain Free Trade Agreement objectives

On 29 May 2004, the United States and Bahrain announced the signing of an FTA between their two countries. The Agreement, which was greeted with general positive enthusiasm on both sides, was concluded in less than five months of negotiations, a remarkably short period of time in the context of free trade agreement negotiations.[73]

The Bahraini Prime Minister, Shaikh Khalifa bin Salman Al Khalifa, described the FTA as a reflection of the respect and appreciation the Kingdom had gained as a consequence of its constant development, which in turn had boosted the safety and success of the country's political, economic and social policies.[74] He suggested that the Agreement was certain to open new horizons for investors within the Kingdom and abroad, and investors would be encouraged to make Bahrain the hub of their activities to access the US market. The status of the FTA as being much more than just a simple trade-based agreement is illustrated by the response to its completion by the Bahraini Minister of Finance and National Economy, Abdullah Hassan Saif, who led the Bahraini negotiating team. He described the Agreement as providing 'the essential tools that will fortify our two nations' political, economic, cultural and strategic relationships'.[75]

With somewhat different emphasis, the USTR's Robert Zoellick declared that the FTA:

> 'is a high quality, comprehensive agreement that will provide American workers, consumers and businesses unprecedented economic opportunity in Bahrain. Bahrain will substantially open its services market, streamline digital trade, protect intellectual property. . .'[76]

The Bahrain FTA is based on a model agreement that the United States has been developing in recent years over the course of negotiations on a number of FTAs, including those of Jordan and Morocco. In its detail it derives much from the Jordan FTA signed in 2000 and therefore includes and extends many of the Jordan FTA characteristics and provisions. Being the first of a number of FTAs that the United States was originally determined to negotiate with the Gulf states in order to establish its MEFTA, the Bahrain FTA is therefore the most crucial. The standards achieved and concessions gained in this agreement establish a precedent and the new enhanced benchmark for future agreements in the Gulf region, just as Jordan's did in the Middle East and Morocco's is likely to do in North Africa.

Prior to commencement of the Bahrain FTA negotiations, the United States declared that its objectives for the negotiations in respect of the intellectual property rights provisions were to:[77]

- establish standards to be applied in Bahrain that build on the foundations established by TRIPS and other international intellectual property agreements, such as the WIPO Copyright Treaty, Performances and Phonograms Treaty and Patent Cooperation Treaty;
- ensure that Bahrain applies levels of protection and practices in line with US law and practices, including appropriate flexibility, in respect of patent protection and protection of undisclosed information;
- strengthen Bahrain's procedures to enforce intellectual property rights;
- strengthen measures in Bahrain that provide for compensation of right holders for infringements of intellectual property rights and to provide for criminal penalties under Bahraini laws that are sufficient to have a deterrent effect on piracy and counterfeiting.

The United States can justifiably claim to have been very successful in achieving its negotiation objectives. According to the USTR's Industry Trade Advisory Committee tasked with providing expert comment and advice to the US President and the USTR on the intellectual property provisions of the Agreement, the Bahrain FTA meets most of the negotiating goals and objectives contained in the US Trade Act of 2002 and the goals of the US intellectual property-based industries, creators and innovators.[78] The Committee, commonly known by the acronym 'ITAC-15', asserts that the intellectual property chapter of the FTA requires Bahrain to make a number of significant concessions and commitments which go considerably beyond the level of protection already provided by its national legislation and which markedly exceed TRIPS standards. They encompass issues relating to Bahrain's international treaty requirements as well as new domestic requirements in respect of copyright and neighbouring rights, trademarks and geographical indications, patents including the special status of pharmaceuticals, trade secrets and enforcement of intellectual property rights generally.

The intellectual property chapter of the Bahrain FTA does not constitute a comprehensive agreement encompassing all areas of intellectual property protection. Instead, it addresses only those particular areas of concern to the USTR and US business in terms of their own intellectual property investments and their keenness to ensure that intellectual property rights involving the new technologies in the digital environment are fully protected while that environment is still in the fledgling stage.

6.5.3 The Bahrain FTA outcomes

According to the USTR, the following outcomes in respect of the protection of intellectual property rights were achieved with the successful completion of the FTA:

'<u>International Treaties and Conventions</u>

Each Party shall ratify or accede to the following agreements:

- Patent Cooperation Treaty, as revised and amended (1970) [PCT];
- Convention Relating to the Distribution of Programme-Carrying Signals Transmitted by Satellite (1974) [Brussels Convention];
- Protocol relating to the Madrid Agreement Concerning the International Registration of Marks (1989);
- Budapest Treaty on the International Recognition of the Deposit of Microorganisms for the Purposes of Patent Procedure (1980);
- International Convention for the Protection of New Varieties of Plants (1991) (UPOV Convention);
- Trademark Law Treaty (1994) [TLT];
- WIPO Copyright Treaty (1996); and
- WIPO Performances and Phonograms Treaty (1996).

and make best efforts to ratify or accede to the Patent Law Treaty (2000) [PLT], and the Hague Agreement Concerning the International Registration of Industrial Designs (1999).

Trademarks

- Each government shall maintain a system to resolve disputes involving trademarks used in Internet domain names.

Copyrights

- Authors, composers and other copyright owners have the exclusive right to make their works available online. Copyright owners have rights to temporary copies of their works on computers and the Internet;
- Each government commits to protect copyrighted works, including phonograms, for extended terms, namely the life of the author plus seventy years, consistent with U.S. standards;
- Each government is required to prohibit tampering with technologies (such as embedded codes on discs) that are designed to prevent piracy and unauthorized distribution over the Internet;
- Each government commits to using only legitimate computer software;
- Protection shall be provided for encrypted program-carrying satellite signals (including the signal itself and the programming), to prevent piracy of satellite television programming;
- The Agreement sets out obligations concerning the liability of Internet service providers, reflecting the balance struck in the U.S. Digital Millennium Copyright Act between legitimate ISP activity and the infringement of copyrights.

Patents & Trade Secrets

- Patent terms may be adjusted to compensate for unreasonable delays in granting the original patent, consistent with U.S. practice;
- Grounds for revoking a patent are limited to the same grounds required to originally refuse a patent;
- Protection shall be provided for newly developed plant varieties.

Pharmaceuticals

- Test data and trade secrets submitted to a government for the purpose of product approval will be protected against unfair commercial use for a period of 5 years for pharmaceuticals and 10 years for agricultural chemicals;
- Government marketing-approval agencies will not grant approval to patent-infringing pharmaceuticals.

Intellectual Property Rights Enforcement

- Each government will criminalize end-user piracy, providing strong deterrence against piracy and counterfeiting;
- Both statutory and actual damages will be mandated under Bahraini law for intellectual property rights violations, which will deter piracy. Monetary damages can be awarded even if actual economic harm (retail value, profits made by violators) cannot be determined.'[79]

A. *International treaty and convention obligations*

Accession to the above group of treaties, and particularly the WIPO Internet Treaties, is a key condition incorporated into the US model FTA and was included in the Jordan and Morocco FTAs, as well as the Free Trade Area of the Americas (FTAA), and the Chile and Singapore and Australia FTAs. The obligation to ratify or adopt the above treaties applies equally to both parties and therefore might appear to be a balanced obligation. In fact, the United States has already adopted most of the treaties and so the treaty adoption obligations in reality represent a somewhat uneven imposition upon Bahrain of the US status quo.[80]

B. *Trademarks and geographical indications*

The trademarks and geographical indications provisions attract succinct but significant attention. Both parties are required to accede to the TLT, but since the TLT applies only to visually perceptible signs, the FTA again broadens the scope of available protection by stipulating that a trademark need not be visually perceptible to be registrable and that registration shall not be denied on the grounds that a mark or sign is composed of a sound or includes a scent.[81] Certification marks are recognised as trademarks and thereby receive protection. The FTA extends the protection of well-known marks provided by Paris Article 6*bis* and TRIPS Article 16 by extending protection against dissimilar goods and services irrespective of whether or not they are registered.

The precedence of trademarks over geographical indications is clearly established, enabling the owner of a registered trademark to prevent the use by third parties of confusingly similar signs, including geographical indications, where they are likely to cause confusion with the registered trademark.[82] It goes further by including specific provision to prohibit the protection or recognition of a geographical indication that is confusingly similar to a prior mark, thereby unequivocally protecting prior marks against later geographical indications. This stance is consistent with US law and policy in the relationship between trademarks and geographical indications, and in direct opposition to the European position.

C. *Domain names on the internet*

Domain names on the internet also receive only brief but important mention. Provision is included for the introduction of uniform domain name dispute-resolution procedures for each country's top-level domains (TLDs), and for public access to a reliable and accurate database of contact information for domain-name registrants.[83] However, these provisions relate only to trademark cyber piracy.

D. *Copyright and related rights*

The copyright and related rights protection provisions constitute the predominant part of Chapter 14, reflecting the concern held by the USTR and the US copyright industry with the extent of global copyright piracy in general and the Gulf region in particular, and their determination to ensure that such piracy in the digital environment is eliminated before it can become too entrenched. The copyright and related rights protection provisions go well beyond TRIPS and provide substance and detail to the general provisions of WIPO Internet Treaties. They focus upon enhanced protection, extended control and effective exclusion mechanisms.

While the WCT and WPPT already provide authors, performers and producers with the exclusive right to make their works available by transmission or online, the FTA draws a significant distinction between authorisation and prohibition, and adds the exclusive right to right holders to prohibit the availability of their works. The right to authorise or to prohibit applies to all reproductions of their works in any manner or form, whether it be permanent or temporary (including temporary digital storage form).[84] The exclusive right to prohibit, which also applies equally to performances, recordings, broadcasts and the retransmission of broadcast signals,[85] effectively prevents the works or signals from being subject to the imposition of any form of compulsory licensing.

In particular, the FTA provides for an extension in the minimum period of protection for a copyright work, performance or recording of the life of the author, or date of performance or recording plus 70 years, significantly exceeding both the TRIPS and Berne Convention provision of life of author or date of performance or fixation plus 50 years.[86] The United States for some years has been using its bilateral agreements as an alternative route outside the WTO/WIPO forum to achieve this higher standard (which is nevertheless still less than the 95 years which the US copyright industry sought to have included in the FTA).[87] Photographic works (and by reasonable inference, works of applied art), which TRIPS and the Berne Convention deferred to national legislation to determine any period of protection in excess of their stipulated minimum period of 25 years, will also enjoy this new extended protection.[88]

The FTA reinforces the control aspects of the WCT and the WPPT by placing severe limitations on the general provision afforded in those treaties and TRIPS for countries to mandate within their national laws certain limitations or exceptions to protection, by incorporating the limits and exceptions into the FTA, along very similar lines to the provisions in the US Digital Millennium Copyright Act 1998.[89] In respect of the circumvention of technological measures controlling access to protected works, a very limited and circumscribed list of circumstances is permitted. Technological control measures are given a very broad description, encompassing any technology, device or component that, in the normal course of operation, controls access to a protected work, performance or recording, notwithstanding any other purposes, functions or applications.[90] Even more embracing and draconian is the prohibition placed upon the manufacture, sale, import or export, or general dealing of any product or service that could be used for circumvention but which has only a limited commercially significant purpose, irrespective of whether such limited use may be entirely legitimate or due to unrelated factors, such as a high degree of specialisation.

The FTA requires the implementation of measures contained in the WCT and WPPT prohibiting the removal or alteration of electronic rights-management information systems. Both criminal and civil remedies apply in respect of their removal or alteration, as well as in respect of importing, distributing, transmitting, broadcasting or generally dealing in material from which rights-management information has been removed.[91] The nature of an infringement of intellectual property rights enshrined in TRIPS generally requires the existence of elements of wilful activity and commercial gain. The FTA language broadens the scope of possible infringing activity by replacing the wilfulness and commercial gain standards for liability with the lesser standards of knowing or having reason to know, and private financial gain. The latter may be interpreted as any activity which bypasses the payment of copyright fees to a collection agency and thus may include the download of a transmission or electronic recording or performance, irrespective of whether such download is for commercial use or for private use.

In respect of the protection of encrypted programme-carrying satellite signals, the FTA draws a distinction between the contents of a transmission or signal and the transmission or the signal itself, establishing that each owner has separate rights of equal standing and is therefore entitled to compensation where those rights are infringed.[92] It makes a criminal offence the manufacture, sale, import or export or otherwise possession of any device that could be primarily of assistance in decoding an encrypted signal, irrespective of whether the device has legitimate applications or is being legitimately used. The FTA also restricts local retransmission by similarly criminalising the further distribution or receipt of a transmission knowing that it has been decoded without the authorisation of the lawful distributor of the signal. At the same time it again reduces the wilfulness requirement.[93]

According to ITAC-15, except for a few shortcomings, the substantive copyright text achieves all that the US copyright industry sought in the FTA negotiations.[94]

E. Patent and trade secrets

The FTA provisions extend and strengthen the patent protection standards of TRIPS and at the same time severely reduce the TRIPS flexibilities, to the extent that protection, once granted, becomes virtually unassailable. Bahrain's discretion to refuse or limit patentability, challenge a patent application or revoke a patent is severely limited. Revocation may only be made on the grounds that would have justified a refusal to grant the patent in the first place.

The FTA makes the clear and uncompromising statement that 'each party shall make patents available for plant inventions',[95] thereby removing the national discretion permitted by TRIPS Article 27.3(b). However, the discretion in respect of the patentability or exclusion therefrom of animals remains with Bahrain. Protection is extended to any new uses or methods of using a known product, including products to be used for particular medical conditions, thereby encouraging the practice Fof 'evergreening' or allowing defensive patents to essentially extend the life span of the original patent.

The requirement for Bahrain to ratify the UPOV Convention removes the discretion afforded by TRIPS Article 27.3(b) for a state to provide for the protection of plant varieties either by a patents system or by an effective *sui generis* system of its own construction or by any combination thereof. Further, the UPOV Convention poses a threat to traditional farming and agricultural practice of re-using, exchanging and local trading in surplus and propagation seed stock practices by limiting the exceptions to the comprehensive nature of a registered plant breeder's rights to private, non-commercial and experimental activity.[96] Removal of the *sui generis* option also prevents a state, such as Bahrain, from developing laws appropriate to the peculiar state of development and nature of its own agricultural industries in light of the strength and significance of its traditional farming practices.[97]

Pre-grant opposition, or provision to challenge a patent application, is removed, any opposition permitted only after the patent has been granted.[98] To impose further limitation on the chances for a successful challenge, the FTA stipulates that revocation may be permitted only on grounds that would have justified refusal to grant the patent – that is, because of its patentability or because of fraud, misrepresentation or inequitable conduct in respect of the patent application.

The FTA acknowledges the right of either party to provide limited exceptions to the exclusive rights conferred by a patent, provided that such imposition does not unreasonably conflict with a normal exploitation of the patent or does not unreasonably prejudice the legitimate interests of the patent owner – a restatement of TRIPS Article 30.[99] However, the FTA neither specifically prohibits nor acknowledges Bahrain's right to impose compulsory licensing requirements, as permitted by TRIPS Article 31, and enshrined in the patent laws of the Gulf states and the GCC. This has prompted ITAC-15 to express its disappointment that the FTA did not confine the possibility of compulsory licensing to explicit situations that are needed to remedy anti-trust violations, national emergencies or other circumstances of extreme urgency, and to govern situations of public non-commercial use[100] – confining it to the limited circumstances of TRIPS Article 31(b) only. This creates some uncertainty as to whether an application for or granting of a compulsory licence may be challengeable on the grounds that it is an action tantamount to investment expropriation. References to compulsory licensing present in other US-sponsored bilateral agreements, such as the model BIT (Article 6.5), and the US–Chile and NAFTA agreements stipulate that expropriation and compensation provisions do not apply to the issuance of compulsory licences granted in relation to intellectual property rights in accordance with the TRIPS Agreement.[101] However, this protection of the right of compulsory licensing is not included in the Bahrain FTA.

F. Pharmaceutical products

Further provisions apply to the protection of pharmaceutical products in addition to those addressed under the general patent provisions. The FTA reinforces the provisions of TRIPS Article 39.3 in respect of the data exclusivity and marketing approvals for pharmaceutical products subject to a patent, and extends the level of protection even further by imposing an obligation of non-reliance on either the pioneer approval or the pioneer data package itself for a period of at least five years from the date of approval for a pharmaceutical product and ten years for an agricultural product.[102] As with the Jordan FTA, and reinforcing the same provision introduced in respect of patents generally, the same level of protection provided for new pharmaceutical products is extended to new products incorporating a previously approved chemical entity or new uses for current protected products.

The FTA imposes measures that explicitly restrict Bahrain from terminating the data-protection period with the expiration of the underlying patent and prohibits generic drug approvals during the term of the patent covering a pharmaceutical product.[103] These measures go a considerable way to preventing parallel importing or local production of cheaper generic pharmaceutical or agricultural products, by excluding market access to products with the same or similar applications. Approval of generic pharmaceutical products is further effectively blocked by the requirement that the state shall implement approval processes that prevent third parties from marketing a product covered by the patent or its approved method of use, and by the requirement that the owner of a patent shall be notified of the identity of any other person seeking market approval to enter the market during the term of the patent.

G. Enforcement

The FTA significantly strengthens the principle of adhering to a standard in both civil and criminal procedures and remedies sufficient to act as a deterrent to further infringements – perceived by the United States as a key element of any effective enforcement system.[104] Introduced into the FTA is the long-established US regime of statutory or pre-established damages, thereby obviating the inherent difficulties in establishing actual damages in a piracy or counterfeiting case. At the same time, some elements of judicial discretion are also removed.[105] For example, the FTA includes provision for the aggrieved right holder to enjoy the prerogative to decide whether to elect between relying on statutory damages and proving actual damages. It requires the courts to use the suggested retail price of the legitimate product being infringed upon as a measure of the loss to the right holder, rather than merely allowing the court to consider using this measure on request. Except in exceptional circumstances, the destruction of pirated or counterfeit goods must be carried out on request of the right holder, rather than left to judicial authority to decide.[106]

In recognition that piracy and counterfeiting 'industries' are becoming increasingly complex and organised, the FTA mandates that courts have the authority to order an infringer to identify other persons or parties involved in any aspect of the infringement, including distribution, and to provide this information to the right holder.[107] Failure to comply renders the infringer liable to a fine or imprisonment. Provision for the award of monetary damages, again of sufficient severity to deter piracy even where actual economic harm cannot be determined, significantly extends TRIPS discretionary provisions for the award of damages adequate to compensate for injury suffered. Judicial authorities may order the seizure of all suspected counterfeit or pirated goods, any related materials and equipment used in the commission of the offence, as well as any traceable assets and any documentary evidence which may be relevant to the offence. The items subject to seizure need not be individually identified as long as they may fall within general categories specified in the seizure order.

Both parties are required to establish policies and guidelines (including sentencing guidelines) to encourage the imposition of deterrent penalties, in an effort to address the perceived problem of judges or other enforcement authorities not actually imposing penalties that deter further infringements.[108] Criminal procedures and penalties are to be applied in respect of trademark or copyright or related rights piracy on a commercial scale, with the definition of 'commercial scale' encompassing both wilful infringements for commercial advantage or private financial gain and wilful infringements that may have no direct or indirect motivation of financial gain. Importation or exportation of counterfeit or pirated goods is to be treated as criminal activities to the same extent as if the goods were for trade in the domestic market.

While TRIPS requires that penalties must be of sufficient severity to act as a deterrent, it leaves it to individual countries to determine and give expression according to their own circumstances as to what may constitute sufficient deterrence. It also places some qualification on the level of severity of sanctions that may be imposed by requiring that they be consistent with the level of penalties applied to crimes of a corresponding gravity. However, matters of detail which would normally fall within the competence and authority of local legislators or judicial authorities to address or determine, taking account of domestic legislation, judicial precedent or societal norms and standards, could be overridden by FTA supplementary or consequential provisions which may dictate the new level of penalties within Bahrain's intellectual property laws.

While the enforcement provisions are generally viewed favourably by ITAC-15, it is nonetheless advocating stronger language in the FTA in respect of the deterrent effect of sentencing guidelines and broader discretionary powers in respect of search and seizures.[109]

H. Internet service providers

The FTA introduces provision for the liability of internet service providers (ISPs), but also includes limitations on the extent of that liability. It establishes the basic functional equivalent of the concepts and provisions embodied in US law as found in S.512 of the US Digital Millennium Copyright Act 1998. The provision encourages ISP's to cooperate with copyright holders and government and judicial authorities in deterring the unauthorised storage and transmission of copyrighted material. Where ISPs do so cooperate, particularly in respect of removal of allegedly infringing material and provision of information on sources of the material, the FTA limits the remedies available against ISPs for copyright infringements that they do not control, initiate or direct but which occur through their systems or networks.[110]

I. Transitional and implementation provisions

With two exceptions, all obligations in respect of intellectual property protection, including adherence to international conventions and treaties, must be implemented upon entry into force of the FTA.[111] The FTA overall, and the intellectual property protection provisions specifically, will place an undue and unrealistic burden upon Bahrain; considering that Bahrain had yet to fully implement TRIPS some four years after the deadline for developing countries, the enforcement deadline may well prove to be somewhat academic.

The implementation arrangements applying generally to the FTA as a whole provide that the United States will give targeted assistance to Bahrain in implementing the high level of commitments achieved in areas such as 'modifying its current laws and regulations to meet its FTA obligations'.[112] Thus the United States can ensure that its requirements and standards for the maximum protection of its own interests can be incorporated where necessary, and in the most suitable form, into amendments or additions to Bahraini intellectual property legislation. The first impression is that US participation with Bahrain in revising its current laws or introducing new laws to meet its obligations under the FTA seems reasonable and sensible, since Bahrain readily acknowledges that it is severely lacking in the legislative, administrative and judicial expertise necessary to fast-track its intellectual property protection regimes to a standard comparable with developed countries. However, this US strategy also guarantees that the United States can ensure that the current Bahraini laws will be amended or written according to the US formula. The United States, through the USTR and its system of trade-specific advisory committees, can and will draw upon a complex and sophisticated infrastructure with numerous levels of legal and technical expertise, which Bahrain cannot hope to come anywhere near to matching in the defence and protection of its own interests. There is the possibility that the FTA text, constructed with the protection of US interests at its core, may create an environment of future disputation and counter-disputation, as US and Bahraini expectations and perceptions diverge.

6.5.4 The US–Oman FTA

Following completion of the Bahrain FTA, the USTR quickly notified Congress (in November 2004) of its intention to negotiate with Oman and the UAE on their respective FTAs. The USTR subsequently announced that negotiations were due to commence in March 2005. The USTR announcement advised that:

> 'These FTAs [with Bahrain and Oman] will build on those that we already have with Jordan and Morocco, as well as the FTA that we have recently signed with Bahrain . . . these FTAs will directly benefit the United States . . . a comprehensive FTA with Oman and the UAE will generate job opportunities for US companies, farmers and ranchers, help create jobs in the United States, and help American consumers save money while offering them more consumer choices.'[113]

Because of the negative reaction amongst some of the GCC states to the way that the Bahrain FTA was conducted and presented as a *fait accompli* to the GCC, a degree of reluctance initially appeared to develop in Oman and the UAE about entering into an FTA as willingly as did Bahrain. In December 2004, after the differences emerged within the GCC member states over Bahrain's FTA, the Omani Minister for Economy was reported in the local press as saying that it was too soon to say whether it would seek a free trade agreement with the United States.[114]

However, these early misgivings and expressions of cynicism did not stand in the way of the negotiations, which commenced in March 2005 and proceeded apace. The FTA took just seven months to negotiate and conclude, marginally longer than the Bahrain FTA.[115] The Omani Minister of Commerce and Industry, H E Maqbool bin Ali Sultan, described the agreement on the conclusion of negotiations as 'a balanced and mutually advantageous agreement'.[116] However, he continued that the agreement 'will consolidate, slowly define and further strengthen the existing economic and trade relations between our two countries'. His use of the qualifier 'slowly' in respect of redefining the relationship between Oman and the US expresses, it is suggested, a note of caution and reservation about the FTA and its overall benefits to Oman.

The US Trade Commissioner, Rob Portman, described the agreement as one which would help to 'advance economic growth and democracy in the region'.[117]

The intellectual property chapter (Chapter 15) of the Oman FTA builds on its Bahraini predecessor, to the extent that, with the exception of a few key provisions which are discussed below, it replicates the Bahrain text. Oman's Chapter 15 reproduces virtually word for word the text of the intellectual property chapter in the Bahraini Agreement, to the extent that, of the 88 clauses in the Oman chapter, 76 are identical to the corresponding Bahrain FTA chapter. Of the remaining 12 clauses, only 7 include changes of any substance, namely those dealing with:

- public availability of information on trademark applications (art. 15.2.12);
- precedence of trademarks over similar geographical indications (art. 15.2.13);
- protection for well-known marks against other trademarks and geographical indications (art. 15.2.14);
- copyright periods of protection (art. 15.4.4);
- exclusion of animals from patentability (art. 15.8.20);
- omission of explicit provision for patentability of plants (art. 15.8);
- maintenance of inventories of seized infringing goods and materials (art. 15.10.27).

As with the Bahrain FTA, the Oman FTA requires both parties to accede to a number of international protection treaties that represent TRIPS-plus standards, namely the:

- Patent Cooperation Treaty (1970), as amended in 1979;
- Convention Relating to the Distribution of Programme-Carrying Signals Transmitted by Satellite (1974) [the Brussels Convention];
- Protocol relating to the Madrid Agreement Concerning the International Registration of Marks (1989);
- Budapest Treaty on the International Recognition of the Deposit of Microorganisms for the Purposes of Patent Procedure (1977), as amended 1980;
- International Convention for the Protection of New Varieties of Plants (1991) (the UPOV Convention);

- Trademark Law Treaty (1994) (TLT);
- WIPO Copyright Treaty (1996); and
- WIPO Performances and Phonograms Treaty (1996).

Both parties are also required to make all reasonable efforts to ratify or accede to the Patent Law Treaty (2000) and the Hague Agreement Concerning the International Registration of Industrial Designs (1999). However, the United States had already acceded to the above treaties, except for the Hague Agreement; Oman had already acceded to the PCT, WCT and WPPT, and its new-plant-varieties protection regime loosely adheres to the UPOV Convention.

However, there are a few crucial areas where the two FTAs are not identical – where, on the one hand, the Oman FTA has not adopted further enhanced standards as enshrined in the Bahrain FTA and, on the other hand, its provisions go beyond those achieved by the Bahrain FTA, as follows.

Trademarks and geographical indications

ITAC-15 considered that, at the time of its completion, the Oman FTA provided the greatest degree of protection for well-known marks yet provided in a FTA.[118] It includes provision for owners of well-known marks to prohibit or cancel registrations of marks that are identical or similar to the well-known mark. This protection extends not only to the registration of conflicting marks but also to the use of such marks. It also extends protection for well-known marks so as to prevent infringement by geographical indications as well as other trademarks, a provision that is not included in the Bahrain FTA. The Oman FTA reinforces the US position on trademarks and geographical indications and squarely subordinates the latter in relation to the former. Article 15.2.2 provides that geographical indications are eligible for protection as trademarks and thus strongly implies that they should be treated as trademarks in all respects. According to ITAC-15 the language of this clause lends itself to a system of protection for geographical indications similar to the preferred US system where geographical indications are 'eligible for protection' through the trademark system of protection. However, in so doing it removes the special status or provision for a preferential system of protection, as advocated vigorously by the European Union collectively and most European states individually and enshrined in TRIPS Articles 22 and 23, but which has been opposed by the United States.

While the Morocco and Bahrain FTAs both include provision for improving the protection of trademarks at the expense of geographical indications, the Oman FTA takes this protection even further by introducing additional provisions in favour of trademarks. The Agreement introduces an obligation to refuse to protect or recognise a geographical indication where it is likely to cause confusion with a trademark which is already registered or under application for registration, or which is already in use in good faith, or which has already become well known.[119] Further, the Oman FTA extends the definition of a geographical indication, for the purposes of the FTA, to include signs which apply to marks generally and geographical indicia in addition to the actual names of geographical places.[120] In so doing, it increases the scope of geographically related names or terms susceptible to non-protection or trademark precedence, and thereby even further protects the priority status of trademarks over geographical indications. In some respects, Oman, Bahrain and the other Gulf states (assuming that these limiting provisions on geographical indications will also be included in their FTAs) are becoming pawns in the ongoing differences of opinion between the United States and the European Union over the nature of protection for geographical indications. It is most likely that the US will argue, as it is now doing with other areas of intellectual property protection, that these provisions as enshrined in its FTAs with a number of countries represent the modern international standard in respect of geographical indications and their relationship to trademarks and their consequent restricted degree of protection.

Copyright

The Oman FTA extends the term of protection of a work (including a photographic work), performance or phonogram for a period of the life of the author plus 70 years, when calculated on the basis of the life of a natural person, the same provision as exists in the Bahrain FTA. However, where the term of protection is calculated on a basis other than the life of a natural person, the Oman FTA extends beyond the Bahrain FTA provisions by providing for a term:

(a) not less than 95 years from the end of the calendar year of the first authorised publication of the work, performance or phonogram; or
(b) failing such authorised publication within 25 years from creation of the work, not less than 120 years from the end of the calendar year of the creation of the work, performance or phonogram.[121]

Both these terms far exceed the term of protection of life of author, or date of performance or recording, plus 50 years as provided in TRIPS, and also exceed the 70-year term included in the Bahrain FTA. The terms also exceed the standard sought by the US copyright and recording industry and actively promoted to the USTR by the IIPA, the copyright industry's main lobby organisation. The IIPA argued in its submission to the USTR prior to the start of the FTA negotiations that, given developments in communications media which were making cross-border transmissions the norm, it was essential that all countries further harmonise the term of protection on a global basis; accordingly it sought the same terms of protection that it had sought for the Bahrain FTA, namely, not less than 70 years and 95 years respectively.[122] The USTR clearly took heed of the IIPA's arguments, including the latter's position into its negotiating agenda and successfully incorporating them into the FTA.

Patents

ITAC-15 comments that the Oman FTA generally provides strong patent protection. However, Oman has not retained the express provision in the Bahraini and Moroccan Agreements to the effect that each party shall make patents available for plant inventions, much to the marked disappointment of ITAC-15. Instead, Oman has simply reaffirmed the general statement of TRIPS Article 27.1 – that is, that patents shall be available for all inventions in any field of technology which are new, inventive and industrially applicable.[123] It also confirms that patents will be available for new uses of or methods of using known products.

While this strategy may give Oman some discretionary provision in respect of future patents on plant varieties or form, or plant-derived inventions, it still tends to continue a shift of emphasis on patentable inventions from an exclusive focus to an inclusive focus – that is, an invention may be presumably deemed patentable unless there is express provision to the contrary. Nevertheless, extending the parameters of patentability to be as inclusive as possible by providing both general statement and express provision was an important issue for the United States in the FTA negotiations. Oman's stand caused ITAC-15 to express its serious concerns, describing the stand as 'a disappointing trend'.[124] To minimise further damage to the US position, it urged the US government to pressure Oman to reform its patents system to meet its commitments under the FTA as soon as possible (ITAC-15).

The removal of the express provision in respect of plants either from patentability or from patentability exclusion also maintains the status quo of providing protection within a *sui generis* framework of its discrete UPOV-based law, as permitted by TRIPS.

In the case of animals, Oman has affirmed the Bahraini position that animals other than micro-organisms, and essentially biological process for their production, are excluded from patentability.

Enforcement

In respect of patent infringements, the Oman FTA requires the parties to provide its judicial authorities with the power to award damages of up to three times the actual damages, unless in exceptional circumstances. This provision, which appeared in the Morocco FTA but was omitted from the Bahrain FTA, meets with the approval of ITAC-15[125] in that it both increases the range of options available to the judicial authorities and increases the deterrent value of the sanction options available.[126]

The Oman FTA adds a new (and welcome, in the view of ITAC-15) provision which does not appear in the Bahraini and other earlier FTAs. It requires each party to maintain an inventory of goods and equipment proposed to be destroyed, and to permit the delay of the destruction of these goods and equipment so that they may be used as evidence in civil and administrative cases.[127] Hence the provision, constituting the preservation of evidence, adds another element of deterrence to the enforcement system.

Transitional arrangements

The intellectual property chapter of the Oman FTA does not include any transitional arrangements. Hence the FTA is due to come into immediate effect after it has been approved by both governments.

The Advisory Committee for Trade Policy and Negotiations (ACTPN), the US government's most senior trade advisory committee, greeted the Oman FTA with enthusiasm. It unanimously endorsed the Agreement, describing it as strongly promoting the economic interests of the United States and fully achieving the overall and principal negotiating objectives set forth in the US Trade Act 2002.[128] It added that the Agreement will advance not only the US President's programme for a MEFTA but overall US objectives 'in this important and volatile area of the world'. As a signal of what the UAE, Kuwait and Qatar can expect in respect of pressures to increase protection standards even further, ACTPN suggests that the Agreement sets a new high standard for future FTAs with other GCC member states and other countries in the region. In respect of the FTA's intellectual property provisions, the ACTPN endorsed what it considered to be the high level of protection in the Agreement. In its view, the Agreement includes state-of-the-art protection for trademarks and digital copyrights and expands protection of patents and trade secrets. It commended negotiators from both sides, but Oman in particular, for their willingness to adopt such high protection standards.

With only minor exceptions, the Oman FTA now represents the highest standards of protection in the areas of copyright, trademarks, geographical indications and enforcement, and will no doubt be held up as the new international standards for future FTAs. It is not surprising, therefore, that the ACTPN urged the US Administration to ensure that the Oman FTA was signed into law as quickly as possible so that American farms, factories, services providers and consumers could begin to receive the benefits of the Agreement at the earliest possible time.[129]

6.5.5 The US FTA negotiations with the UAE and Qatar

Negotiations on a US–UAE FTA commenced in March 2005 – at around the same time as the Oman negotiations. As the Oman FTA negotiations were being concluded, significant differences were emerging between the negotiating teams, with the UAE indicating that US insistence on a range of labour, intellectual property and human rights issues, even at so early a stage in the negotiations, warranted a call for a cautious approach.[130] A former UAE Cabinet Minister suggested that the UAE would not benefit from a bilateral free trade agreement with the United States and that the UAE should resist US pressure to amend its domestic legislation as part of the conditions of signing a free trade agreement. The former minister criticised the United States for demanding changes to the UAE law in a number of areas including investment and sponsorship laws.[131] However, these early misgivings and expressions of cynicism did not stand in the way of the two sets of negotiations proceeding apace. However, by early 2006, the UAE negotiations had stalled.

While neither negotiating team would admit as much, a significant factor in the stalled UAE negotiations has been the furore over the acquisition by a UAE company, Dubai Ports World, of the British Company P&O Ports, which brought with it infrastructure ownership of six US ports. The acquisition, which was consistent with Dubai Ports World's global development and acquisition activity, generated an intense degree of hysteria in some sectors of US government and business that the UAE's ownership of these US ports would constitute a grave risk to US security.

More than three years later and after five major rounds of talks, both sides were still unable to reach agreement on an FTA. Prior to the latest round, the UAE has declared in the local Arab press that it would resist the latest pressure by the United States to immediately open its telecommunications sector to foreign investors. The UAE Minister for Public Sector Development, Sultan bin Said Al Mansuri, has been quoted in the Arab-language daily, *Al Hayat*, as stating that 'the entry of foreign companies to the sector is one of the main stumbling points in the negotiations'.[132] In remarks published in the Dubai-based Arab-language paper *Emarat Al Yom*, the Minister has said in respect of the US telecommunications demand that 'this is rejected, we will not give up one of our rights. We must give the current operators the chance to develop before we allow new ones in'.[133]

The UAE FTA negotiations continue to be marred by several contentious issues, including US demands for UAE labour market reforms, the opening of the services sector and provision for 100 per cent foreign ownership across the whole of the UAE business sector. At the time of writing, no date has been set for a future round of talks, and the United States and the UAE have since announced that they are unable to complete FTA negotiations under the existing time frame for the US Administration's fast-track trade promotion authority. Nevertheless, in a display of diplomatic cordiality, the United States has announced that both sides agree that they remain committed to completing FTA negotiations at some later date.[134]

In similar vein to the UAE reluctance to concede to unacceptable US demands, Qatar has taken a firm stance in respect of its negotiations. The Qatari local press has reported that Qatar has frozen bilateral free trade talks with the US on the grounds that Washington was imposing preconditions that were not in Qatar's interests. In particular, the Qatari FTA negotiators have raised objections to US demands for full access for US investors to Qatar's services and energy industries and 100 per cent foreign ownership of Qatari companies. The Qatari Ambassador to the United States, Nasser bin Hamad al Khalifa, was quoted in the daily *Al Sharq* newspaper as saying:

> 'The talks were not proceeding in the right direction. They were going nowhere. It was like two deaf people talking to each other. There was no sense continuing with the dialogue . . . Sometimes powerful countries put preconditions that are not in the best interests of smaller countries.'[135]

Questioning the need for a free trade agreement in the first place, the Qatari Ambassador has suggested that the WTO agreements are sufficient for mutual trade and investment between any two member countries. Qatar was already a major destination of investment for US companies because of the country's very favourable investment laws and liberal trade regime. The Ambassador has also suggested that Qatar 'does not need a free trade agreement with the US'.

The Qatari government's current stance is that, with one of the strongest global economies and one of the highest per capita income rates in the world, it does not need either US financial support or preferential treatment for entry into US markets to enable its economy to continue to grow. It can therefore take a strong bargaining position in respect of US negotiating points, to the extent of walking away from the negotiating table if it is not satisfied – a situation which the United States may well feel unused to in recent times.

6.6 Concluding remarks

Where TRIPS and the Berne and Paris Conventions establish general levels of intellectual property protection, the Bahrain and Oman FTAs significantly raise those levels and establish new parameters; and where the international conventions allow limitations or exceptions to that protection, the FTAs reduce or confine those limitations and exceptions. Further, the FTAs introduce into the national and regional environments the protection of copyrights and neighbouring rights in the digital context, particularly in respect of the internet and satellite transmission where TRIPS has been overtaken by the march of technological progress. They also greatly enhance and widen patent protection, particularly for pharmaceuticals and plant varieties, where the United States has deemed TRIPS to be sorely inadequate.

For Bahrain, this may not be a real issue as it pursues its objective to establish itself, with US support, as the pre-eminent financial centre in the Gulf and a regional hub for service- and knowledge-based industries.[136] Bahrain's ongoing commercial objective is to become a major gateway for US trade in the region and a service-based economy, emulating the example of Singapore.[137] Of major concern to Bahrain is that it is the least endowed of all the Gulf states in terms of oil and gas and other natural resources.

The fact that the Bahrain FTA negotiations were concluded in less than five months is a clear indication of both US determination to adopt an aggressive bargaining stance and obvious Bahraini keenness to reach an agreement. The rapid progression and conclusion of negotiations took even the USTR by surprise.[138] However, notwithstanding the speedy conclusion, it may be some time before the FTA is given full practical effect and the benefits or otherwise to both parties are realised and can be assessed. A time-lag between agreement and implementation of the FTA in itself may not be a particular issue for either side, insofar as the United States has achieved its new enhanced benchmark standard on intellectual property protection for projected FTA negotiations with the other Gulf states, while Bahrain would have achieved US endorsement and support for a local business environment deemed facilitative and protective of US investment. However, ITAC-15 warns that the updated protections afforded by the Bahrain FTA will be of little value to the US investors without the capability and willingness of the Bahraini government to enforce those new standards against piracy, counterfeiting and other infringements.[139] The real measure of success will lie in the administration of the new standards on the ground by the local police, judicial and administrative agencies responsible for enforcement and implementation of the enhanced protection regime of the FTA.

Although the Bahrain FTA sets a precedent for the Gulf region by allowing national interests and bilateral agreements to override collective interests and multilateral talks, Bahrain's desire to raise its economic profile internationally, expand its economic base and attract increasing levels of foreign investment is undoubtedly the main reason behind the deal. It has long sought to strengthen its economic ties with the United States; with the lowest oil and gas reserves of all the Gulf states, it has been forced to diversify its economic base more urgently than its neighbours. While there are ample reasons to justify the Bahrain FTA at the economic level, politics appears to have played its role as well. Local commentators have also suggested that the FTA can be viewed as a political reward for the close support that Bahrain has consistently provided the United States in the region.[140]

The real significance of the intellectual property provisions of the Bahrain and Oman FTAs lies not so much in the conditions and requirements that they impose on both states. Rather, the precedents which they have established will impact significantly on the other Gulf and Middle East states by establishing the new regional benchmark for intellectual property protection to which the other states will be pressured to accede. The other states can expect to receive US demands for even higher standards of protection as they enter into their own FTA negotiations. Because of the precedents already established, they may find it extremely challenging to avoid or modify these benchmarks to suit their particular national developmental or societal requirements, although the Oman FTA shows that it can be done. Oman's disinclination to extend specific protection to plants within the patent regime and to retain the UPOV-based protection regime would have disappointed the US pharmaceutical and biotechnology industries, but may well constitute a far-sighted and wise decision as its own technologies in these fields develop in the future. While the United States uses its immense bargaining power in bilateral discussions to extract conditions from individual states that arguably it would not otherwise be able to achieve in collective negotiations with the GCC as a regional entity, the capacity of the remaining states to extract concessions may not be completely nullified after all.

The national treatment and MFN obligations enshrined in the Bahrain and Oman FTAs ensure that, notwithstanding any otherwise limiting provisions in their national laws, Bahrain and Oman will be required to extend to US potential and actual investors conditions no less favourable than those already extended to all of its regional partners. This situation may well be to the detriment of the particular regional and economic benefits that the states have so far developed amongst themselves for their mutual regional benefit and advancement, but to the United States' advantage. In so doing, the erosion of particular preferential regional provisions may undermine the very foundation of unity of the GCC itself. Some of the GCC member states, chiefly Saudi Arabia, raised strong objection to the Bahrain FTA on the grounds that it violated the basic tenets of the economic agreement signed by the GCC Supreme Council in 2001, which stipulates that 'no member state may grant to a non-member state any preferential treatment exceeding that granted herein to member states, nor conclude any agreement that violates provisions of this agreement'.[141]

Saudi Arabia's initial strong opposition to independent bilateral deals by GCC member states eventually softened – one likely reason being its own (then still impending) WTO membership. During a visit by Crown Prince Abdullah bin Abdul Aziz to the United States in April 2005, during which Saudi Arabia's membership of the WTO was a major item of discussion, it was announced that 'the issue of free trade (agreements) with the United States . . . is no longer a bone of contention between the GCC states'.[142] However, Saudi Arabia will no doubt insist on restoring customs barriers for non-GCC members (except for the United States) once the regional FTAs with the United States have been applied. And in an extraordinary face-saving display of solidarity, a special meeting of GCC finance ministers held in Bahrain in early May 2005 agreed to accord the United States special treatment and to exempt it from GCC resolutions restricting external (to the GCC) bilateral agreements.[143] The ministers agreed to this course of action in an attempt to patch over conflicting GCC opinions on bilateral agreements and to restore some degree of cohesion to the regional body. The ministers also reportedly agreed that the exemption would not adversely affect the proposed EU–GCC free trade agreement; indeed, under WTO rules on most-favoured-nation treatment, it may very well cause the same exemption, and the same FTA concessions, to be extended to the EU.

As events have come to pass, the Bahrain and Oman FTAs have been concluded, FTA negotiations have commenced but stalled with the UAE, and discussions have been initiated but also stalled with Qatar and Kuwait. External forces, spearheaded by the United States, will continue to pressure the remaining Gulf states to adopt the TRIPS-plus bilateral standards instead of the lesser multilateral standards of TRIPS and international conventions on which it is based. The United States will continue to strive to establish an intellectual property regime of its own creation as a key part of its trade and trade-related interests in the region – which is one element in a greater design for political and diplomatic hegemony in the region. If the driving up of intellectual property standards continues, Saudi Arabia, the largest of the states and the last to enter into FTA negotiations with the United States, is likely to face the highest of standards.

However, the furore over the Dubai Ports World controversy during FTA negotiations between the United States and the UAE, and the consequent difficult passage through Congress of the Oman FTA, has also given clear notice to Middle East states that the United States will seek to impose what those states will view as double standards when it suits US interests. While the United States seeks to hold a veto over foreign investment in certain US enterprises in the name of national security, it continues to demand full access, including 100 per cent foreign ownership of local companies in its UAE and Qatar negotiations. The collapse of the Dubai Ports World US ports deal has been described in the local UAE press as a shattering episode that has damaged the US–UAE relationship.

> 'The 9/11 paranoia, relentless Arab and UAE bashing, in addition to a weak president and a hysterical Congress, have all pulled together to abort a sound business transaction by the Dubai Ports World that would have been a key element in building a stronger US–UAE relationship.'[144]

The hardening line by the UAE and Qatar in their respective stalled FTA negotiations should be a signal to the United States that there has been a diametric shift in the balance of negotiating power, dynamics and willingness.

The United States' bilateral approach to global harmonisation of international intellectual property protection gives reason for the continuing relevance of the multilateral forums, such as the WTO and WIPO, and the international conventions such as TRIPS to be called into question.

7 TRIPS-minus and protection still pending

7.1 Introduction

The multilateral intellectual property protection framework, as exemplified by TRIPS, has been constructed to best deliver the protection on those intellectual property rights that the major players – the developed countries – have sought to have protected. The multilateral framework is given further substance by the network of TRIPS-plus treaties and bilateral agreements, in which the same developed countries figure prominently. The dominant characteristic of this framework is that, to be protectable as intellectual property, a right must be private in nature, identifiable, ascribable and commercially exploitable. Issues or rights which do not fit within this framework – notably traditional knowledge and cultural heritage in the broadest sense – enjoy little, if any, of the protection offered by TRIPS, the TRIPS-plus treaties and the bilateral agreements. The absence of protection on an international mutually agreed scale for these issues has witnessed them subject to potential and actual encroachment by the multilateral protection framework on terms dictated by that framework. In essence, they suffer a TRIPS-minus protection environment.

Whilst a number of descriptions for traditional knowledge and cultural heritage have been in widespread circulation, as yet there is no universal agreement on the terminology or the definitions or even agreed parameters in the major multilateral forums as to what might or should be included in their deliberations. Although traditional knowledge seems to be the most commonly used term, others frequently arise – such as cultural heritage, folklore, traditional cultural expressions, indigenous knowledge. This is as much a reflection of the broad scope of what may be encompassed within their bounds as uncertainty on what might constitute 'traditional' or 'knowledge', or even 'protection' and its purpose. It has been suggested, for example, that the term 'folklore' is quite inappropriate in this context since it presumes matter of a historical nature only and suggests that 'expressions of culture', being current self-expressions of living functional traditions, should be used instead.[1] What seems a common consensus is that 'protection' in the narrow and conventional intellectual property sense does not address the needs or scope of these concepts, even allowing for differences in their possible definitions.

WIPO currently prefers to mainly use in a fairly generic way the terms 'traditional knowledge' (TK) and 'traditional cultural expressions' (TCE), with 'folklore' being used less widely. WIPO draws a distinction between these two major terms. It uses 'traditional knowledge' to refer to tradition-based literary, artistic or scientific works, performances, inventions, scientific discoveries, designs, marks, names and symbols, undisclosed information, and all other tradition-based innovations and creations resulting from intellectual activity in the industrial, scientific, literary or artistic fields.[2] 'Traditional cultural expressions' encompass productions consisting of characteristic elements of the traditional artistic heritage developed and maintained by a community or by individuals reflecting the traditional artistic expectations of such a community, in particular:

- verbal expressions, such as folk tales, folk poetry and riddles, signs, words, symbols and indications;
- musical expressions, such as folk songs and instrumental music;
- expressions by actions, such as folk dances, plays and artistic forms or rituals, whether or not reduced to a material form; and,
- tangible expressions, such as productions of folk art (in particular, drawings, paintings, carvings, sculptures, pottery, terracotta, mosaic, woodwork, metalware, jewellery, basket weaving, needlework, textiles, carpets, costumes), crafts, musical instruments and architectural forms.[3]

'Tradition-based' refers to knowledge systems, creations, innovations and cultural expressions which have generally been transmitted from generation to generation, are generally regarded as pertaining to a particular people or its territory, and are constantly evolving in response to a changing environment.[4]

Whatever precise terminology might be used, many developing countries, holders of traditional knowledge, expressions of culture and cultural heritage, and non-governmental and civil society organisations are advocating for greater protection to be made available. Within both the WTO and WIPO, extended debate has taken place on the nature of the appropriate system to protect traditional knowledge and expressions of culture and cultural heritage within the international sphere. Central to the debate is the question of whether they can be protected under the current multilateral intellectual property protection system and, if not, what *sui generis* system might be adopted.

Proponents of the current system would argue that the system has adequate flexibility to provide a reasonable degree of balance between the holders of non-conventional intellectual property rights within the established framework, the entitlement of society to enjoy the benefits of exploitation of those rights and the imperative of those with the capacity to commercially exploit those rights. In instances where the nature of those rights is not contemplated within the conventional framework, voluntary contractual arrangements between right holder and exploiter should be adequate to compensate and address the inadequacies of the framework.

Some commentators argue that the very attributes of traditional knowledge prevent it from being included into the conventional IP system.[5] Traditional knowledge-seeking protection under conventional copyright provisions runs afoul of the requirement for identification and attribution. In the area of patent protection, traditional knowledge does not meet the patentability requirements of novelty, inventive step and industrial application. Some countries have decided that the existing intellectual property framework is inadequate to protect traditional knowledge and are pursuing their own *sui generis* systems of protection.[6] However, the calls for the creation of an international *sui generis* system are increasing.

Early multilateral attempts at creating a protection regime to encompass these areas have met with only limited success. In 1981, WIPO and UNESCO adopted a model law on folklore. In 1989 the concept of Farmers' Rights was introduced by the FAO into its International Undertaking on Plant Genetic Resources and in 1992 the Convention on Biological Diversity highlighted the need to promote and preserve traditional knowledge. The protection of traditional knowledge and folklore has also been discussed for a number of years within the framework of UNESCO and other international organisations such as UNCTAD and WHO. In spite of these efforts, a comprehensive and universally acceptable legislative framework for the protection and promotion of traditional knowledge, folklore and genetic resources has yet to emerge.

In 1998 and 1999, WIPO undertook a number of global fact-finding missions 'to identify and explore the intellectual property needs and expectations of new beneficiaries, including the holders of indigenous knowledge and innovations, in order to promote the contribution of the intellectual property system to their social, cultural and economic development'.[7] These missions were intended to enable the 'study of current approaches to, and future possibilities for, the protection of intellectual property rights of holders of indigenous knowledge, innovations and culture'. During the subsequent WIPO-sponsored conferences to discuss the missions' findings in respect of the linkages between intellectual property and traditional knowledge and their implications, three primary issues which were of universal concern to the countries involved in the studies emerged, namely:

- the protection of traditional knowledge, innovations and creativity, whether or not associated with those resources;
- the protection of expressions of folklore, including handicrafts; and
- access to genetic resources and benefit-sharing.[8]

The missions and the subsequent forums made a number of observations and recommendations to the member states themselves, to the international community and to the international organisations with an interest in the protection of traditional knowledge. The recommendations included that WIPO, UNESCO and the other international organisations should work towards the creation of a *sui generis* international convention for the protection of expressions of folklore. Most of the forums also commented on the WIPO–UNESCO model law for the national protection of expressions of folklore from illegal exploitation of 1982 as a relevant basis for national laws.

The missions also included an examination of traditional knowledge in Arab countries. The subsequent consultative forums made a number of pertinent observations and recommendations. They observed that:[9]

- Arab countries are rich with one of the most precious cultural and civilisational heritages in the world, which constitutes an important pillar for human civilisation and an integral part of the world patrimony;
- Arab folklore (Arab popular heritage) is a strong means of bringing together the Arab peoples. However, this common aspect does not exclude or diminish the importance of the local variations specific to each people;
- Arab folklore (Arab popular heritage) and traditional knowledge are subject to various dangers, including negligence, disappearance, piracy, mutilation and illegal exploitation; therefore, there is a need for the provision of legal protection at national, regional and international levels;
- currently, there is no legal framework available for the protection of expressions of Arab folklore at either national or international levels.

The missions and forums recommended to the Arab countries that they should:

- create specialised institutions or centres as a national and cultural necessity for the collection, classification, conservation, documentation and dissemination of folklore (Arab popular heritage) and develop a specialised environment;
- work together on their national legislation for the provision of measures aiming at the protection of expressions of folklore;
- (each) prepare an open list of expressions of folklore and traditional knowledge the preservation and protection of which is considered necessary;
- rely, when reviewing and amending their legislation, on the WIPO model provisions set, as adapted to recent developments in the field.

At the same time, they recommended to international organisations that WIPO, UNESCO and the specialised international organisations intensify their efforts in order to provide greater assistance to Arab countries in particular and developing countries in general by:

- providing training and technical and legal cooperation to Arab countries;
- elaborating an international convention on the protection of expressions of folklore;
- establishing a standing committee on expressions of folklore and traditional knowledge in both WIPO and UNESCO.

But since the WIPO missions, little progress has been achieved in respect of the key issue of the creation and universal acceptance of a *sui generis* international protection convention. However, WIPO has established a senior committee, as recommended above, and the Gulf states have taken some steps towards the creation of national protection schemes and the identification, documentation and preservation of their cultural heritages.

While WIPO now has a committee, being the Intergovernmental Committee on Intellectual Property and Genetic Resources, Traditional Knowledge and Folklore, charged with the responsibility of examining the feasibility of establishing *sui generis* or other systems of protection for expressions of traditional knowledge, the work of the committee to date has largely revolved around establishing the parameters and meanings of key terms, such as what is meant by tradition, knowledge, culture and heritage. Its major undertaking so far has been to try to establish agreed meanings for terms in use and to undertake a knowledge 'gap analysis' in order to:

(a) describe what obligations, provisions and possibilities already exist at the international level to provide protection for traditional cultural expressions/expressions of folklore;
(b) describe what gaps exist at the international level, illustrating those gaps, to the extent possible, with specific examples;
(c) set out considerations relevant to determining whether those gaps need to be addressed;
(d) describe what options exist or might be developed to address any identified gaps, including legal and other options, whether at the international, regional or national level.

The work of the WIPO committee has two major areas of focus, namely traditional knowledge/folklore and genetic resources. To these two areas can be added another of potential and actual importance to the Gulf states, namely, geographical indications as expressions of traditional knowledge and cultural heritage.

7.2 Copyright and traditional knowledge, folklore and cultural heritage

Again, whatever terminology is used, traditional knowledge, folklore and cultural heritage are characterised by the fact that, generally, they are not produced systematically but in accordance with the individual or collective creators' responses to and interaction with their cultural environment. Being representative of cultural values, they may constitute elements that integrate a vast and mostly coherent complex of beliefs and knowledge. More than likely they will be held collectively, being vested in the community rather than in individuals (although individuals as leaders or elders may hold them in trust). Furthermore, most traditional knowledge, folklore and cultural heritage are transmitted orally from generation to generation and thus remain largely undocumented. They are also dynamic in the sense that they are current, possess everyday relevance and are subject to processes of constant evolution. Accordingly, existing intellectual property mechanisms, which are intended to function in a trade-related, private protectionist context and are governed by a predetermined and static time frame, do not fully respond to the essential nature of traditional knowledge, folklore and cultural heritage.

A major problem with the effective and just protection of indigenous knowledge is that the creative work or knowledge must still fit in with western ideas of intellectual property in general and copyright in particular, and the legislative structure which develops from it, that is, an intangible personal property right expressed in a tangible way. But conventional mechanisms based on western ideas which are intended to function in a trade-related, private protectionist context do not adequately respond to the essential nature of traditional knowledge and cultural heritage. The international treaties, such as TRIPS and the Berne and Paris Conventions, and the domestic intellectual property laws based upon them, still require a copyrighted work, a trademark or a patentable invention to be in material or reproducible form, to belong to an identifiable individual, group of individuals or legal entity, to be original and to be independently created rather than derived or copied. Even though the Berne Convention, for example, actually makes reference to traditional knowledge, it still requires a work to meet certain criteria if it is to gain copyright protection. These requirements mean that some important forms of traditional knowledge have not gained intellectual property protection. For example, the traditional custodians of areas in which cave or rock art occurs cannot assert copyright over the art because they cannot and should not identify an individual creator or artist; because the art was created so long ago, it no longer fits within copyright protection time frames. By the same token, orally transmitted folklore or heritage passed down over generations find it difficult to gain copyright protection because they have not been reduced to fixed, material or reproducible form. Other issues arise where the process of reducing the traditional knowledge to material form was done by a third party. The operation of copyright law may provide some protection for traditional knowledge custodians where they are also owners of copyright in the work, but it can also operate to create difficulties over ownership of traditional knowledge. The act of recording in written form or fixation of an oral tradition may create for the recorder a legally enforceable right to the copyright of that recording as a producer or publisher, but it may well create further problems where such a fixation or transmission may be contrary to tradition and practice or where the producer has no traditional right of access to such tradition.

Nevertheless, the use of recordings, databases and registers for creating a permanent record or digital repository of expressions of traditional knowledge is gaining increasing attention. The documentation or fixation of traditional knowledge is also crucial to protecting it. Conversely, there are some negative aspects to recording and documenting traditional knowledge. First, because traditional knowledge is oral, performative, expressive and multidimensional, the documentation or fixation causes it to lose those distinct elements. Second, once in fixed form, the knowledge becomes vulnerable to exploitation and unlawful use.

In addition to the development of a suite of *sui generis* laws, other protection proposals have included amending current copyright laws to allow for:

- extending copyright protection to oral works and non-assigned community works;
- protecting traditional knowledge material through original and non-original database protection;
- extending the moral rights provisions in copyright to traditional knowledge;
- making greater use of international conventions on the protection of the rights of performers (e.g. 1961 Rome Convention for performers, producers, broadcasters, TRIPS and the 1996 WIPO Internet Treaties);
- using a *domain public payant* system, under which royalties continue to be paid for the use of literary and musical works in the public domain; and
- using the *droite de suite,* a resale royalty under which an artist receives a share of the price paid for his or her original work from all sales subsequent to the first sale of the work by the artist.

Some of the Gulf states have moved to include, to a lesser or greater degree, formal recognition of expressions of culture and traditional knowledge in their respective copyright laws. Although this inclusion provides some form of legal standing for traditional knowledge, they still do not fully address the dilemmas of protection in a conventional intellectual property context. On occasion, it appears that the references may be more of a token gesture than a conscious and determined effort to provide or enhance protection.

The Yemeni general intellectual property law does not make any formal provision for the protection of any particular forms of traditional knowledge. In fact, it specifically excludes from protection works which are 'not fit to be the subject of the right of an author, such as works which contain anthologies from the tradition or folklore whose author is unknown . . .', but does not give any further guidance as to what those works may constitute.[10] However, it does provide that ownership of works in which copyright has expired reverts to the state, which may determine how those works may be used or exploited.[11]

Similarly, Kuwait does not make any substantive reference to the protection of traditional knowledge or expressions of cultural heritage in its laws. Folklore or similar is not included in its statement of works to which protection is extended, but added at the very end of its copyright law is a declaration of a moral position without any accompanying practical means of affording any form of protection. It provides that 'the national heritage of Kuwait society is a public property of the state. And the state, acting through the Ministry of Information, has the right to exercise the author's literary and financial rights for him'.[12] It still requires attribution to an individual for protection to be able to have effect, or for the state to act on the individual's behalf to protect that individual's private rights.

The UAE copyright law contains a definition of folklore as 'every expression of people's heritage, oral, musical, dynamic, or tangible in distinct elements which reflects the artistic traditional inheritance, developed or endured in the State and which cannot be attributed to an author'.[13] The law also acknowledges derived work as being any expression of a people's heritage, whether oral, musical, dynamic or tangible (in distinct elements that reflect the artistic traditional inheritance), which has developed or survived in the state and which cannot be attributed to an author. Folklore is not included amongst the range of works or activities entitled to protection, but provision does exist for moral rights to revert to the state once the economic rights expire, although there is no guidance as to the nature of the protection that the law might provide other than by implication.[14]

Saudi Arabia goes a little further than Yemen, Kuwait and the UAE. Its copyright law adopts a slightly stronger position on the protection of folklore, which is acknowledged as including:

> 'all literary, artistic or scientific works which are assumed to have been created on Saudi territory and transmitted from one generation to the next and constitute part of the traditional Saudi cultural and artistic tradition.'[15]

Compilations of expressions of folklore enjoy protection of the law as derived works. The law also provides that the national folklore shall be considered the public property of the state, the relevant copyrights for which are exercised by the Ministry of Information as the responsible ministry.[16] Arguably as an initiative to preserve the internal integrity of, and to maintain some control over, works deemed to be Saudi folklore, the importation or distribution of copies of classified works of folklore or copies of translations or reproductions of folklore produced outside the Kingdom is prohibited, except with the permission of the Ministry.

Oman makes a stronger statement of intent on protection. The copyright law recognises expressions of folklore and includes them in those works to which the protection of the law extends. It defines expressions of national folklore as:

> 'any expression or production of distinguishable elements reflecting the traditional popular heritage that was originated, developed and maintained in the Sultanate of Oman to express the traditional cultural identity which is communicated through generations, including particularly the following expressions:
>
> - Oral expressions such as popular stories, anecdotes, sayings, mysteries, poems and other folklores.
> - Musical expressions such as folk songs accompanied by musical instruments.
> - Movement performances such as dances, popular artistic presentations and traditional popular rituals.
> - Concrete expressions such as drawings or paintings, sculptures, pottery, porcelain, carving, sculpture, mud, engraving on wood and metals, jewelry, needlework, textiles, clothing, carpets, traditional musical instruments, architectural forms and all products of plastic folk art.'[17]

It also includes in its definition of works of applied arts any artistic creation of useful functions or integrated into a tool for use concerning a work for producing traditional or industrial crafts.[18] Performers include persons who 'act, sing, orate, recite, play, dance or otherwise perform other works and national folklore expressions'.[19] Protection of the law extends to expressions of these cultural forms in general, whether they come within the parameters of oral, musical or concrete expressions, or performances. While the notion of private ownership is still a central theme, provision exists for the state to assume ownership of the moral rights, but only where no natural right of succession occurs.[20]

Bahrain and Qatar go even further than Oman insofar as their copyright laws make particular detailed references to the position of national folklore and give the broadest illustration of the range of folkloric expressions which may be protected. As such, they adopt the strongest positions on the protection of traditional knowledge and folklore amongst the Gulf states.

The Bahraini copyright law extends its protection to all creative works, including those of a cultural nature irrespective of the nature of such works and their form of expression. It includes in the scope of expressions of folklore all productions of a community heritage, whether verbal, musical, expressed by movement, or tangible as represented by distinctive elements reflecting traditional heritage that originated or were developed and preserved in a particular geographic area and which cannot be attributed to a known author.[21] They include the following expressions in particular:

- folk tales, proverbs, puzzles and popular poetry;
- folk songs with musical accompaniment;
- folk dances and performances;
- traditional products such as line or colour drawings; sculptures, pottery and ceramics; engravings on wood, metal or ornaments; needlework, textiles, carpets and clothes; musical instruments; and architectural shapes.

'Performers' include actors, singers, musicians, dancers and other persons who act, sing, deliver, declaim or perform in any way works that are protected or unprotected pursuant to the provisions of this law, or that have fallen into the public domain after their protection period has expired, as well as expressions of folklore. Performances to a wider public audience outside the immediate community context receive specific attention, public performance being any activity 'in a place where persons other than family members and friends may be present'.

Recognised amongst the infringements listed in the law is the use of expressions of folklore in a manner that violates certain other provisions in the act, namely a requirement that the use must be in an appropriate manner that respects the integrity of the expressions and acknowledges their source.[22] In many respects this requirement is a restatement for expressions of folklore of the general moral rights of attribution and integrity. While they may be used, such use must be in an appropriate manner and must not mutilate the expressions and their source mentioned. As is the case in the other states, the copyright act stipulates that expressions of folklore which reflect the traditional popular heritage of the state, originated and were developed and consistently preserved in the Kingdom shall be the property of the state.[23] The copyright law also provides for rights management, requiring that associations or organisations managing rights of authors and neighbouring rights be licensed by the responsible ministry and subject to the supervision and control of the ministry.[24]

The Qatari copyright law defines national folklore as:

> 'Any expression which consists of distinctive elements of the traditional artistic heritage, originating or developed in the State of Qatar and reflects its artistic heritage, shall be considered as national folklore, including in particular the following expressions:
>
> (1) oral expressions such as tales, popular poetry and riddles;
> (2) musical expressions such as popular songs accompanied by music;
> (3) motion expressions such as popular dances, plays, artistic forms and rituals, whether or not incorporated into material form;
> (4) tangible expressions such as:
>
> (a) products or popular art particularly drawings with lines and colors, engravings, sculptures, ceramics, pottery, woodwork, mosaic, metal, jewelry, hand-woven bags, knitting, carpets, textiles, (b) musical instruments; and (c) architectural forms.'[25]

'Performers' include those who perform expressions of folklore, while collections of works and expressions of folklore are protected as derived works – although, again, this protection does not necessarily extend to the folklore itself. Collective works where individual authorship cannot be distinguished can also be protected.

As is provided in the laws of the other states, the Qatari copyright law declares that national folklore is the public property of the state and the state is charged with the responsibility of protecting the national folklore by all legal means and methods. It is empowered to exercise the author's rights – in fact, to act as the author of works of folklore with respect to any acts of distortion, alteration or commercial utilisation.[26]

The problem with all the above laws, to the extent that they provide differing degrees of protection for traditional knowledge and expressions of culture, is that they still operate with the paradigm of the global convention of copyright as a private economic right. Notwithstanding any recognition of the particular character of traditional knowledge or expressions of culture, the laws are still based on the premise that ownership can be attributed to a person, a discrete group or a legal entity. They extend protection to an author, performer, publisher or broadcaster rather than to an item, work or performance itself; hence works which cannot be clearly attributed to an owner or defined group of owners may not be protectable. The laws also still assume a limited period of protection, for example the life of the author plus a specific number of years.

Furthermore, the bilateral agreements which Bahrain and Oman have settled tend to militate against the provision that exists in the national copyright laws to extend protection to traditional knowledge. Both FTAs include in their definitions of performers 'actors, singers, musicians, dancers, and other persons who act, sing, deliver, declaim, play in, interpret, or otherwise perform literary or artistic works *or expressions of folklore*'[emphasis added].[27] But, at the same time, the FTAs create two problems: first, in the context of their provisions on copyright, 'performance' means a performance fixed in a phonogram unless otherwise specified.[28] The specific rights granted to performers are limited to the authorisation or prohibition of the broadcast or fixation of their unfixed performances – they do not extend to protection of the cultural heritage enshrined in the performance. The rights, being private rights, must belong to the individual and do not cover the situation where individual ownership cannot be attributed. Second, both FTAs restate the position of TRIPS Article 70.3, to the effect that neither party shall be required to restore protection to subject matter that has fallen into the public domain in its territory on the date that the FTA comes into force. This exclusion applies equally to all traditional knowledge, including knowledge relating to genetic material and the pharmacological properties of plants and their medicinal applications.

Outside the conventional intellectual property protection regime all states have laws to protect various elements of traditional knowledge. In fact in many instances these laws pre-date intellectual property laws, an indication in itself of the better understanding on the part of the states and the higher priority that they place on the protection of their national heritages. All Gulf states are very sensitive to and very proud of their respective rich cultural heritages, and are mindful of the need, particularly in recent years, to protect them. The states have in place laws for the protection of artifacts and historical sites but these relate to the physical protection of these objects, their preservation and the prevention of their illicit export, as distinct from protection from copying or similar expropriation or unfair commercial exploitation by third parties.[29]

Oman has been pre-eminent amongst the Gulf states in its efforts to protect and preserve its cultural heritage. Oman's primary law for the protection of its cultural heritage, the National Heritage Protection Law, was promulgated in 1976.[30] The law's principal objectives are the physical preservation of the integrity of cultural property of the state and the prohibition or restriction of export of any property or object of historical significance. It encompasses all kinds of monuments as well as 'chattels of cultural properties'.[31] Oman has also taken steps to document and preserve some aspect of its traditional knowledge and cultural heritage, as illustrated by these few examples:

- The Public Authority for Craft Industries, established in 2003 and responsible for preserving every aspect of Oman's traditional craft industries, is undertaking a census of all Omani crafts, including geographical sources and spread, tools and machinery used, social, cultural status of the craftsman and the product, significance and traditional Arabic names.
- The Oman Center for Traditional Music, established in 1983 to document, conserve and promote traditional Omani music, has documented and digitised since its inception more than 80 per cent of Oman's musical traditions including photographs and audiovisual and sound recordings.
- At the Omani Traditional Medicine Clinics, established in 1988 with the aim of conserving Omani national heritage in the field of traditional medicine, traditional healers from different regions of Oman provide to the public free-of-cost medical treatment based on plant medicines. Each healer keeps his specialised medicinal knowledge secret.

The states also participate in the international forums for protection of elements of traditional knowledge, all having ratified the UNESCO Convention on the Protection of the World Cultural and Natural Heritage (1972). Oman (2005), Qatar (2008), Saudi Arabia (2008), the UAE (2005) and Yemen (2007) have further ratified the UNESCO Convention on the Safeguarding of the Intangible Cultural Heritage (2003). Kuwait (2007) and Oman (2007) have acceded to the UNESCO Convention on Protection of Cultural Expressions. Oman and Yemen have gone a step further and each has listed a number of sites on the World Heritage List, while Bahrain and Saudi Arabia have tentatively identified sites for potential listing.[32]

7.3 Patents, biodiversity and access to genetic resources

The issue of protection of traditional knowledge also arises in the context of the TRIPS-mandated provisions concerning patentable products and processes, particularly in respect of genetic resources, biodiversity and inventions derived from native flora and fauna. The issue arose in the WTO in 1999 during the review of Article 27(3)(b) of TRIPS, which requires WTO members to protect new plant varieties either by a patents or by an effective *sui generis* system, or any combination thereof.

Developing countries have been seeking clarification of the exclusion provisions of TRIPS Article 27(3)(b). At the same time, they have expressed concern at the ongoing shrinkage in matters protected from patentability and therefore open to exploitation by multinational business. They have long argued that life forms in the broadest sense should be excluded from patentability, that information relating to the origins of a biological invention should be enshrined in the patent application process, and that the principle of prior informed consent should be incorporated into TRIPS.[33] In particular, they have expressed concern over the granting of patents and other intellectual property rights over traditional knowledge to parties other than the indigenous peoples/communities who own and control it. They are further concerned that their traditional knowledge is being exploited without their prior knowledge or authorisation and without a sharing of the benefits that accrue from such exploitation and use. In some instances, the commercial harvesting of the indigenous flora, as in the case of the Hoodia cactus plant of southern Africa to extract the valuable patented material, has threatened the very survival of the plant.

The strong position taken by the developing countries on the protection of traditional knowledge led to its inclusion in the Doha Ministerial Declaration in November 2001. Paragraph 19 of the Declaration instructed the Council for TRIPS – as part of its review of TRIPS Articles 27.3(b) and 71.1 – to consider the relationship between the TRIPS Agreement and the Convention on Biological Diversity, and the protection of traditional knowledge and folklore. The Declaration instructed the Council to be guided by the objectives and principles set out in TRIPS Articles 7 and 8 and to take fully into account the development dimension.[34]

The Convention on Biological Diversity, which was agreed in 1992, seeks to promote the conservation of biodiversity and the equitable sharing of benefits arising out of the utilisation of genetic resources.[35] It asserts the sovereign rights of nations over their national resources and their right to determine access according to national legislation with the aim of facilitating the sustainable use of these resources, promoting access and their common use. It notes that access to genetic resources should be on the basis of prior informed consent and on mutually agreed terms that provide fair and equitable sharing of the results of R&D and the benefits of commercialisation and utilisation.[36] The Convention calls for the fair and equitable sharing of the benefits derived from the use of traditional knowledge and states that access and transfer of genetic resources should be consistent with the 'adequate and effective protection of intellectual property rights'.[37]

The countries which endorse the formalisation of a linkage between TRIPS and the Convention are generally countries which enjoy many of the genetic resources and associated traditional knowledge which have raised concerns over the misappropriation of biopiracy of genetic resources and knowledge, for use in patented inventions. These countries, led by India, Peru and Brazil, are overwhelmingly developing country WTO members. They point to high-profile cases, such as the neem tree, basmati rice and ayahuasca juice, as evidence for the need for an internationally binding, enforceable disclosure requirement that would oblige patent applicants to disclose the source of the genetic materials and associated traditional knowledge used in the invention claimed, evidence of prior informed consent with the original holders of the resource or knowledge, and evidence of a benefit-sharing agreement with the original holders.

The developing countries also argue that the present intellectual property regime is inadequate to address their concerns on the protection of traditional knowledge. They propose that TRIPS be suitably amended or provide a mechanism to require an applicant for a patent on biological material or traditional knowledge to disclose the source and country of origin of the biological resources and traditional knowledge used in the invention as a condition for the granting of a patent.[38] They further propose that, at the same time, the applicant should be required to provide evidence of prior informed consent and fair and equitable benefit sharing under the relevant national regime.

The major users of genetic resources in patent inventions, which are overwhelmingly developed countries with significant research and development interests, have argued that a disclosure requirement could place unnecessary burdens on industry that could harm development. They have also argued that the WTO is not the right place to negotiate a full-fledged system of protection for a complex, and as yet undefined, subject matter such as traditional knowledge or folklore.[39] They suggest that WIPO, rather than the WTO, should first clarify conceptual issues of traditional knowledge, address the issue of legal protection of traditional knowledge, examine the possible options and prepare model national legislation. Only at that point should the WTO take responsibility for the matter.

The debates in international forums such as WIPO show just how polarised and entrenched are the opposing views on the need, scope and nature of legal protection of traditional knowledge and its format. The developed countries are of the view that any legally binding international *sui generis* system at this stage is premature and unnecessary and that attempts should first be made at the national level to determine its feasibility.[40] Developing countries, meanwhile, are seeking to expedite work to be undertaken on a possible new system. Despite their strong, polarised positions on these issues, the countries have agreed that WIPO should produce the elements for a model *sui generis* system of protection for traditional knowledge.

While some developed countries have shown a degree of willingness to address these issues either in the WTO or in WIPO, others including the United States and Japan remain firmly opposed. They do not see any conflict between the Convention on Biological Diversity and TRIPS, and argue that patent-disclosure requirements would be ineffective with respect to prior informed consent and access to benefit-sharing goals, as well as adding a burden to the patent system.

In view of the fundamental differences in the international forums over the issue of protection of traditional knowledge and genetic resources and the form that the protection, if any, should take, and in light of the low level of patent activity in the Gulf region, it is perhaps not surprising that the Gulf states have not taken legislative steps to protect their biodiversity and genetic resources in the intellectual property context. Also contributing to this status is the fact that domestic patent activity amongst the states involving indigenous genetic resources is very low, most patent activity originating in the Gulf region having arisen from the oil and gas industry. Accordingly, the patent laws or plant protection laws of the states generally follow a conventional format and show a common WIPO-sourced heritage.

However, the Saudi patent law, which incorporates specific reference to protection for new plant varieties, either by design or good fortune, provides some exemptions for farmers against the exploitation of crop-genetic resources under the guise of breeder's rights. Under the good faith usage provisions of the patent law, a third party who exploits a plant variety or makes serious arrangements to do so prior to the filing of a plant-variety patent, or the related priority date, shall be entitled – despite the issuance of a patent – to continue to perform those acts without expanding them.[41]

A Bahraini proposed plant-varieties protection law, which has been in local circulation in draft form for a few years, proposes to exempt from the scope of protection propagating material which is the product of the harvest obtained by farmers from their own holdings.[42] The Omani new-plant-variety protection law restricts breeder's rights to Omani nationals and expatriates residing in Oman, and subjects of countries that provide in their respective legislation the same level of protection for Omani citizens, provided that such subjects have a legally resident agent in Oman.[43] But the Omani status is confused by the existence at the same time of a patents-style protection environment with conflicting provisions within its new industrial-property law.

However, these fledgling efforts are again being undermined by external pressures aimed at reinforcing their TRIPS-plus protective environment. The Bahrain and Oman FTAs limit the grounds on which a patent may be revoked to those that would have justified a refusal to grant a patent, that is, the application does not satisfy the tests of being new (or a new use), involving an inventive step and being capable of industrial application.[44] The FTAs also provide that only fraud, misrepresentation or inequitable conduct may be the basis for revoking a patent or holding it unenforceable, and opposition to the grant of a patent may not proceed until after the patent has been granted. Since disclosure of any genetic material in respect of the patent is not a condition for granting the patent, its non-disclosure would not come under the classification of either fraud or misrepresentation and would not be grounds for revoking a patent.

However, this is not to say that the Gulf states have not made any moves in the area of protection of genetic resources. As initial steps, some states have already begun to register their traditional-knowledge heritage across a number of areas. In the area of plant varieties, the UAE is the host country for the UN-backed Date Palm Global Network, the general objective of which is to increase technical and strategic co-operation among all (new and traditional) date-producing countries in the development and improvement of the global date-palm industry.[45] It has also set up the Gulf region's first genetic plant bank to identify plants which can resist salinity. The aim of the bank is to expand cultivated areas in the country and other Gulf and Islamic states. The bank has more than 6,500 kinds of such plants that can resist salinity, gathered from all around the world. All states contribute to this database.[46]

Similarly, Oman is developing a database of all indigenous plant varieties and has started work on a special botanical reserve to complement the database.[47] The primary objective of the database is to lay foundations for future research, environmental protection, access and intellectual property protection. It has already completed the database for Omani date varieties and at the time of writing is working on native shrubs and plants. The new-plant-varieties protection law provides for governmental discretion to accommodate some local knowledge, conventions and practices. However, in the absence of any registrations of new plant varieties on the register to be established under the law, the efficacy of these provisions has yet to be tested.

Indigenous plants are still in common usage for therapeutic and medicinal purposes throughout the Gulf states. The following are just a few examples of plant varieties used for medicinal purposes in the Gulf region and which are currently the subject of scientific research in the UAE:[48]

- seeds of the senna plant, *Cassia italica*, used as a laxative and for stomach pains;
- seeds of the desert squash, *Citrullus colocynthi*, highly acclaimed as a cure for diabetes;
- the bitter sap of the milkweed *Calotropis procera,* dried and used to treat toothache; poultices made from the leaves are applied to joints to heal rheumatism;

- *Salsola imbricata* and several *Suaeda* species, dried and powdered, used as snuff to clear the sinuses;
- poultices of the henna plant used to soothe headaches; henna is also extensively used as a hair dye and particularly to decorate hands and feet in intricate designs for special occasions such as weddings and *Eid* celebrations;
- the poisonous plant, *Rhazya stricta,* used in small quantities to settle gastric upsets;
- the fragrant herb, *Teucrium stocksianum*, a member of the sage family, used for combating fevers;
- the seeds of garat, *Acacia nilotica*, ground to a powder and used to dry out second-degree burns.

7.4 Geographical indications

The nature of the protection currently afforded to geographical indications under TRIPS, and the form and extent of future protection, is another matter of considerable ongoing contention within the WTO and other international forums. The original negotiations on the geographical indications provisions of TRIPS were among the most difficult to resolve, because of the fundamental differences between the two main protagonists of the Agreement, namely the United States and the European Union. Accordingly, in recognition of the compromises that had to be made to finalise the negotiations, TRIPS has created an artificial distinction by providing a basic standard of protection for all geographical indications and a higher standard specifically for those relating to wines and spirits.

Two issues have been debated in the TRIPS Council under the Doha mandate, namely the extension of the higher level of protection of TRIPS Article 23 beyond wines and spirits, and the creation of a multilateral register for wines and spirits. In respect of the issue of extending the levels of protection beyond wines and spirits, some WTO members have been seeking to initiate negotiations to amend TRIPS, while other members oppose the move.[49]

Those advocating extension argue that the higher level of protection enables them to improve marketing their products by differentiating them more effectively from their competitors. A proposal by the European Union calls for TRIPS to be amended so that all products would be eligible for the higher level of protection of Article 23 and for inclusion on the multilateral registration system currently being negotiated for wines and spirits. Those opposing extension argue that the existing level of protection, under TRIPS Article 22, is adequate. They posit that extending the additional protection to other products would impose extra financial and administrative burdens on all WTO members, and most heavily on developing countries, and that these burdens would outweigh any trade benefit. WTO members remain deeply divided on the issue, with no agreement in sight.

The issue of the introduction of a multilateral system of notification and registration of a wines and spirits register is being treated separately from the question of extending the higher level of protection – although some countries consider the two to be intimately linked. The debate on the multilateral registration system began in 1997 under TRIPS Article 23.4 and continues under the mandate provided by the Doha Agenda (paragraph 18 of the Doha Declaration). Three main proposals have been under consideration – two opposing proposals from the European Union and from the US-led group of countries, and a compromise proposal from Hong Kong.[50]

The European Union's proposal calls for TRIPS to be amended by the addition of an annexure to TRIPS Article 23.4. It advocates the establishment of a registration system that would be mandatory upon all WTO members, irrespective of whether they have any geographical indications listed on the register. Registration would require a geographical indication to be protected in other WTO members – except in a country that has lodged a reservation within a specified period. A reservation would be limited to the grounds that the term has become generic or that it does not fit the definition of a geographical indication. If it does not make a reservation, a country would not be able to refuse protection on these grounds after the term has been registered.

A contrary joint proposal has been offered by a group of countries led by the United States and including Australia. This proposal advocates the creation of a voluntary system where notified geographical indications would be registered in a database. Those governments choosing to participate in the system would be required to consult the database when taking decisions on protection in their own countries. Non-participating members would be 'encouraged' but not 'obliged' to consult the database.

The Hong Kong proposal is a compromise solution, whereby participation in the system would be voluntary. Members would be free to participate and notify geographical indications protected in their territories, and the obligation to give legal effect to registrations under the system would only be binding upon those members choosing to participate in the system.

Protection of geographical indications in the context of the above-mentioned debates on an extension of protection and a multilateral register creates somewhat of a conundrum for the Gulf states. While they may well give limited support to a proposal for a multilateral register, they would have considerable difficulty in endorsing a proposal which advocated an extension of protection beyond wines and spirits if such proposal presupposed any degree of commitment to also protecting wines and spirits. The states are also unlikely to be supportive of the proposal for a register which includes wine and spirits because of the religious, legal and bureaucratic issues domestically. Yet the issue of broadening the scope of geographical indications may be attractive since the states realise that they themselves have products which are generic to their own territories and to the Gulf region and which may be worthy of protection. These products include certain blends and brews of coffee, traditional Arabic clothing, ceremonial weapons, woven products and methods, sweets, perfumes and fragrant oils, to mention just a few. It could also be argued that domestically the states inadvertently provide a form of protection to geographical indications for wines and spirits and pork-derivative products by not allowing any trademarks directly related to these products to be registered and/or protected – irrespective of whether those marks originate from the original owners or from foreign or domestic competitors or counterfeiters.

The states would perceive that the need for a formalised system of protection does not arise as much domestically as it does abroad. Domestic protection can call upon a combination of custom and cultural traditions, as well as provisions of domestic-trademark laws and commercial-conduct codes. However, adequate protection overseas for domestic geographical indications will require protection at home as well as local protection for the other country's geographical indications.

As mentioned earlier, only two states, namely Bahrain and Oman, have specific geographical indications laws or substantive provisions in force, while the other states incorporate some notional reference or slightly stronger provision within their trademark laws. The Bahraini geographical indications law requires a geographical indication to be protected in its country of origin to obtain local protection.[51] To enable local protection to occur, it requires the Ministry [of Commerce and Industry] to maintain a register of geographical indications. The Omani geographical indications provisions and the geographical indications provisions of Qatar's trademark law do not require registration as a precondition for local protection, notwithstanding the fact that they both also provide for the existence of a register.[52] The Omani law also restricts protection to those geographical indications that remain protected or which are still used in their country of origin. According to recent local advice, these three states are in the early stages of preparing such registers and receiving any applications for registration of a geographical indication, but there are a number of local products which they consider could qualify for protection and which they consider should be protected under local laws.[53] The unresolved question is which particular laws might most appropriately and effectively provide protection, that is, whether they should be protected under trademark laws or geographical indications laws. Just a few of the products that have been suggested as suitable for some form of protection include:

- 'Masafi' mineral water from the UAE, as well as a number of mineral/spring waters from the different states;
- Mocha coffee from western Yemen;
- *karwa* and other local and regional blends of Arabic coffee and cardamom;
- perfumes, particularly those which utilise frankincense, myrrh and other indigenous plant derivatives;

- Omani *halwa*, a date-based sweet traditionally and still customarily served with *karwa* to visitors and as a mark of Gulf hospitality;
- other date-based food and handicraft/artisan products;
- 'Doan' honey from the Hadramout region of eastern Yemen;
- Sukary al-Qasim – special types of dates from the Qasim area of mid Saudi Arabia;
- Qatari pearls and pearl-shell products.

These products do not yet enjoy an international market warranting a high degree of protection of their geographical indications elements. What is still unclear to the Gulf states is whether commitment to any of the three major proposals expounded will lead to protection of local geographical indications in foreign markets, or whether it will be primarily geared to protecting foreign geographical indications in domestic markets. A number of foreign geographical indications are already excluded from protection in the Gulf on moral or religious grounds and would continue to be so.

The recent movement by some Gulf states towards closer trade relationships with the United States through bilateral agreements may also militate against the generation of benefits by their adoption of an enhanced protection regime for geographical indications. In the absence of any clear and identifiable benefit, it is most unlikely that the states would commit to an enhanced protection regime that extends beyond the current status quo. But the states would also hold that a more compelling reason for them to maintain the status quo is the inability of the major players in the WTO to agree amongst themselves as to the nature that an enhanced level of protection, if any, should take. The states would see little need or point to travel any further in respect of protection for geographical indications in an intellectual property protection context.

7.5 Concluding remarks

Despite the involvement of several inter-governmental bodies working on the protection of traditional knowledge and an impressive body of literature and documents produced by international, national and non-governmental bodies, the progress achieved in this respect is not very impressive so far. In fact, the major achievement to date has been the provision of a sustained and active debate over a number of years, which has enabled the developing countries to ensure that the issues surrounding the appropriate protection of traditional knowledge, biodiversity and access to genetic resources continue to maintain a high profile and undergo intense public scrutiny.

As they have done previously with other areas of intellectual property, the Gulf states are likely to stand back and to observe the negotiating and positioning of the major representatives from both the developed nations and the other developing countries. Since the major players cannot yet resolve their diametrically opposed positions on protection of traditional knowledge in an intellectual property context, the states would no doubt consider that refraining from becoming too heavily involved would be the appropriate course of action. In the meantime, the states will continue with their own national initiatives to identify, record, register and protect the abundant elements of their national cultures and heritages, until the appropriate mode for the protection of the intellectual property aspects of those cultures and heritages is clarified in the multinational forums. They will no doubt become involved if the benefits, potential and actual, to them are abundantly clear, or if their obligations in the international context require them to support a particular position of commitment.

8 TRIPS anew – Insha'allah

8.1 Introduction

The primary objective of this work has been to examine the endeavours of the GCC member states and Yemen in establishing national intellectual property protection regimes which both meet their international treaty obligations and are congruent with their domestic policy objectives and needs. The benchmark for this examination has been the TRIPS Agreement, with the study encompassing the status of protection prior to the introduction of the WTO and TRIPS (the 'pre-TRIPS stage'), the states' response to their obligations to meet TRIPS requirements ('TRIPS stage'), the impact of external influences through bilateral trade agreements ('TRIPS-plus stage') and areas which fall outside the TRIPS protection spectrum ('TRIPS-minus stage').

The work argues that, since the late 1960s/early 1970s when they either gained their independence or emerged from sustained periods of international isolationism, the Gulf states have undergone a transformation of their intellectual property legislative regimes at a very rapid rate – virtually in the time frame of a single generation. This period of transformation has been marked by three major, but very different, phases of development of the regimes. Each phase has been characterised by significant degrees of foreign intervention which have directed or strongly influenced the construction of the states' intellectual property laws. But this foreign intervention has not necessarily caused the creation of laws which have been congruent with the states' needs or have achieved their objectives in terms of enforcement effectiveness.

The first of these phases, namely the pre-TRIPS period that continued through to the mid 1990s, is notable for the dearth of *sui generis* intellectual property laws in existence; the laws that were in force were few in number and existed mainly in the fields of trademarks and patents. But even these laws were subject to foreign design; Bahrain's 1955 law on patents, industrial designs and trademarks was almost entirely and directly subordinate to the corresponding UK laws and processes. The Kuwaiti trademark and patent laws of 1961 and 1962 respectively were based on Egyptian models which in turn derived much from corresponding continental laws. However, this dearth of *sui generis* laws does not mean that protection for certain types of intellectual property rights was not available; it existed in an overarching perspective in the divine laws of social and moral conduct laid down in the *Qur'an* and the *Sunna* of the Prophet. In a more corporeal and secular sense, and in the absence of any mainstream intellectual property framework, it also existed in the form of laws governing commercial activity and conduct. However, even these commercial laws were generally subject to foreign influence and secular codification. In addition, the national frameworks for the control of publishing and public dissemination of printed material, which all Gulf states possessed and actively enforced, also provided some limited protection for certain types of copyrightable material.

The second developmental phase is marked by the establishment of the WTO, the consequential introduction of TRIPS and a post-TRIPS flurry of legislative activity by the GCC member states as they attempt to meet their statutory obligations to make their intellectual property laws TRIPS-compliant and their enforcement effective. Yemen, still to achieve both GCC and WTO membership, had in place a pre-TRIPS law enacted in 1994. TRIPS heralded a major shift in the perception and treatment of intellectual property rights by establishing unprecedented levels of protection for global implementation. However, the shift took shape by reference largely to the needs of the leading industrialised nations (and, to a lesser extent, those of the other developed countries). WIPO, which had already been a significant influence on the states' pre-TRIPS intellectual property laws, continued to play a crucial role in guiding the states in their compilation of their TRIPS-compliant laws and the judicial, structural and administrative capacity-building so crucial for their enforcement. With fluctuating degrees of commitment, the states embarked on reshaping their intellectual property protection regimes. At one end of the spectrum, Oman, which possessed few intellectual property laws in the pre-TRIPS phase, introduced in 2000 in a single swoop a full suite of laws which addressed the TRIPS areas of intellectual property rights, plus protection for new plant varieties. Bahrain and Kuwait, meanwhile, both of which had been the early pace-setters in regional intellectual property protection, still relied on copyright, trademark and patent laws which were either pre-TRIPS or were derived from earlier pre-TRIPS laws.

Hardly have the GCC member states come to terms with the enormity of the dimension of the transformation required to their respective intellectual property protection regimes as necessitated by the TRIPS and post-TRIPS phase than they are faced with a new round of emerging changes as they enter the TRIPS-plus phase. The dominant driving factor shaping the character of their laws during this phase is the bilateral strategy pursued by the United States. This new round commenced with a series of bilateral trade and investment agreements from the late 1990s; more recently, the United States has concluded FTAs with Bahrain and Oman, both agreements incorporating extensive provisions on intellectual property. These intellectual property provisions constitute much higher standards of protection than those set by TRIPS, and further restrict or remove the limited degree of manoeuvrabililty that TRIPS permitted developing and least developed countries to enjoy by reducing or eliminating the Agreement's exception or discretionary provisions. The bilateral agreements are reinforced by demands that the signatory states not only adopt higher standards enshrined in the FTAs themselves but also adopt and adhere to a range of multilateral treaties which reconstitutes TRIPS-plus standards. The multilateral treaties also reduce and restrict the discretion that TRIPS grants to signatory states to craft their laws so that they may include some allowances sympathetic to their respective national needs and objectives. As a consequence, both Bahrain and Oman have again recently upgraded their intellectual property laws with enhanced protection standards and committed themselves to a further number of multilateral intellectual property conventions.

The most challenging element of the TRIPS and TRIPS-plus phases, as perceived by both the states themselves and the industrialised nations, is the regional enforcement of the states' intellectual property protection obligations consistent with the standards enshrined in TRIPS, the TRIPS-plus treaties and the bilateral agreements to which the states have made commitment. Notwithstanding the presence of comprehensive sets of laws and treaty commitments, there nevertheless exists a dichotomy between the principle of enforcement as enshrined in the various legislative regimes and the practice as exemplified by the degree of effective policing and judicial action. In all states, the practical application of compliance through effective enforcement has been, and continues to be, the most difficult area with which they have had to contend. The ineffectiveness of enforcement systems can be attributed, in many cases, to:

- inadequacy and inappropriateness of the legislation by not being drafted effectively or extensively;
- lack of human resources, funding and practical experience in the enforcement of intellectual property rights;
- insufficient knowledge on the part of right holders and the general public concerning their rights and remedies;
- a general lack of training of enforcement officials, including the judiciary; and
- systemic problems resulting from insufficient national and international coordination, including a lack of transparency;
- challenges posed by the clash of alien cultural and economic mores with entrenched local societal attitudes.

For most of the Gulf states, the principal barriers to successfully dealing with intellectual property infringements do not subsist so much in the substantive law as in the practical application of the available remedies and sanctions. In a number of states, and not only those which still have pre-TRIPS laws in force, the negative impact of the barriers is exacerbated by the presence of sanctions which are deemed both inadequate and incomplete in scope and scale. But, irrespective of inadequacies in a few older laws, the sanctions available to the authorities across the broad spectrum of the region's intellectual property laws are not being fully exploited. The reasons do not rest solely with the enforcement authorities or the judiciary; entrenched local societal, cultural and commercial attitudes also contribute to the development of this enforcement dichotomy.

8.2 The current status of intellectual property protection in the Gulf states

By early 2008, all GCC member states had established comprehensive legislative regimes for the protection of intellectual property. Most, but by no means all, of their intellectual property laws generally reveal a willingness to comply with the international standards as enshrined in TRIPS, even if at times they fall a little short in respect of the detail. And some, notably the Bahraini and Omani laws, now exceed those standards with room to spare. The comprehensive fabric of intellectual property protection that has now been constructed through a network of domestic laws and international conventions stands in stark contrast to the status at the beginning of the pre-TRIPS and TRIPS stages. With only a few exceptions, notably the Yemeni general law, the states' current laws post-date TRIPS and together encompass the major areas of intellectual property addressed in TRIPS. Membership of the WTO has also had an impact on the nature and timing of the implementation of these laws. Hence, both Oman and Saudi Arabia received closer and more rigorous examination of their legislative regimes by the other WTO members through the avenue of the Council of TRIPS than did the other GCC member states. They progressively upgraded their major laws from 2000 as part of their efforts to achieve WTO membership. Yemen, currently a generational stage behind the other Gulf states and still at the pre-TRIPS stage, will need to comprehensively upgrade its current intellectual property law, most likely introduce new laws and accede to a number of WIPO and other international conventions if it is to succeed in its WTO membership campaign.

The status in respect of membership of the international bodies and adherence to the major international conventions and treaties encompassing intellectual property protection has also advanced apace. All states except Yemen are now members of both WIPO and the WTO, and all except Kuwait and Yemen have acceded to the Berne and Paris Conventions. A majority of states have also acceded to the WIPO internet treaties – the WCT and WPPT – and most states refer to, use or have formally adopted the Madrid Protocol on the international registration of trademarks.

Table 8.1 summarises the current situation in respect of domestic laws and international commitments in intellectual property in the Gulf states. The years listed in respect of national laws represent the year of introduction of the current law or most recent amendment of any significance, and the year in which an international convention came into force domestically.

In any case, the benchmark for the quality of an intellectual property rights protection regime cannot be measured solely by the number of laws on the statute books or the number of international bodies joined or conventions adopted. 'Any nation, industrialized or not, can choose virtually overnight to introduce any amount of intellectual property law it chooses but that would not necessarily change its backwardness.'[1] 'Shorn of the economic and cultural roots that it is, or supposed to be, based on and evolve around, intellectual property is a set of indeterminate value except to those that the rules happen to serve because they codify the latter's national needs.'[2]

Outside the conventional intellectual property paradigm, the states have also been active in attempting to identify, preserve and protect elements of their own cultures and societies – areas in which there has been much debate in the international forums but little effective progress in establishing global standards of protection, notably traditional knowledge and cultural heritage, genetic resources, biodiversity, traditional medicines and indigenous plant species. The states themselves have for some years held a particular interest in these areas and have taken the initiative in introducing some protection standards. They have introduced laws to protect both their tangible and intangible cultural heritage; the exposure to the international norms of intellectual property rights has engendered an appreciation that these subjects are also forms of intellectual property entitled to protection within a domestic and international context. Oman in particular has taken a lead in this endeavour with the construction of a national database to register a number of forms of cultural heritage that encompass song and dance, traditional arts and crafts and traditional medicines. It has also commenced work on the registration of native plant species and their applications in traditional and folk medicines.

8.3 A climate of domestic change

The efforts of the Gulf states to protect mainstream intellectual property rights in a remarkably short period of time are impressive. But the achievement has been largely ignored by the major developed countries in their drive to impose upon the international community in general, and the states specifically, even higher standards constructed upon a western-developed template, under the guise of global harmonisation.

However, the picture is still one of dynamic change. Attention has largely focused on the major areas of activity and concern, namely copyright, patents and trademarks; the intellectual property rights which have received a lesser degree of attention, such as industrial designs, integrated circuits, new plant varieties and trade secrets, have not attracted the same imperative for preservation of interests and investment. Hence they have received only brief attention by most states, or have gained some degree of protection by association, or have been largely passed over. They will attract attention as the major areas become settled and established.

The rapid rate of progress has meant that, on occasion, laws and enforcement initiatives have been superseded almost before they have had time to come into practical effect. Delays amounting to years on the passage of a necessary implementing regulation or enforcement strategy for a particular law have meant that the regulation gets overtaken by amending or repealing legislation. But the administrative processes to rectify this conundrum and remove the invalidated regulation are themselves not always in place or operationally effective. The next major phase unfolding in this ongoing and fascinating story will undoubtedly be the development of human resource and infrastructural development in the administration of the intellectual property regimes – aided by training programmes and technical expertise from external sources. Another major phase will then be the introduction of strategies and initiatives more attuned to national interests and needs, such as a stronger protective regime for traditional knowledge and cultural heritage. Associated with this initiative will be a fine-tuning of the more conventional intellectual property laws to also better reflect national interests. However, in this latter case, the opportunities for such refinements will be confined by, and will need to take place in the context of, the multilateral conventions and bilateral agreements into which the states have already entered.

Domestically, some current intellectual property laws still require further refinement to remove the idiosyncratic remnants of former laws, to bring them up to at least TRIPS standards in those few cases of the older laws, and to introduce sanctions that are generally seen to be effective deterrents. Furthermore, some will also need to re-examine and upgrade their laws and enforcement strategies to now take account of the TRIPS-plus obligations to which they have agreed under their respective bilateral agreements, and the TRIPS-plus treaties to which they have recently acceded. Bahrain's former statutory shortcomings have been largely addressed by giving effect to the provisions included in its FTA – which generated extensive changes and a subsequent suite of new laws from 2004 to 2006.

Kuwait in particular still has on its statute books intellectual property laws which not only fall well short of the current 'highest international standard' but are also perceived to be TRIPS-deficient. Kuwait remains on the USTR Special 301 Priority Watch Listing, in part for the perceived deficiency in respect of the deterrence factor in general and because of lack of progress in amending its outdated laws.[3] Authorities in Kuwait have for some time been under intense pressure from the United States to add tough new measures to its existing legislation, including at least a doubling of the financial penalties and terms of imprisonment for infringements.[4] The United

Table 8.1 Current intellectual property laws and international conventions in the Gulf states

		Bahrain	*Kuwait*	*Oman*	*Qatar*	*Saudi Arabia*	*UAE*	*Yemen*
National IP laws	Copyright	2006	1999	2008	2002	2003	2006	
	Trademarks	2006	2001		2002	2002	2002	
	Patents	2006	2001		2006	2004	2002	1994
	Industrial designs	2006	2001	2008	2002			
	Geographical indications	2006	–		2002	2002	2002	–
	Integrated circuits	2006	2001		2005	2004	2002	–
	Trade secrets	2006	–		2005	2002	2002	–
	New plant varieties	–	–	2000/08	–	2004	–	–
	GCC patent reg'n	2004	?	2000	2003	?	2000	–
	GCC trademark reg'n	–	–	–	2007	pending	2007	–
	Arab Agreement on Author's Rights	–	1986	–	1986	1985	–	?
Bodies	GCC	1981	1981	1981	1981	1981	1981	–
	Arab League	1971	1961	1971	1971	1945	1971	1945
	WTO (and TRIPS)	1995	1995	2000	1996	2005	1996	–
	WIPO	1995	1998	1997	1976	1982	1974	1979
	IP protection treaties							
	Berne, literary works	1997	–	1999	2000	2004	2004	2008
	Brussels, satellite signals	fta	–	2007	–	–	–	–
	Geneva, phonograms	–	–	–	–	–	–	–
	Madrid, false indications	–	–	–	–	–	–	–
	Nairobi, Olympic symbol	–	–	1986	1983	–	–	–

		Bahrain	*Kuwait*	*Oman*	*Qatar*	*Saudi Arabia*	*UAE*	*Yemen*
WIPO Administered Treaties	Paris, industrial property	1997	–	1999	2000	2004	1996	2007
	PLT	2005	–	2007	–	–	–	–
	Rome, performers, etc	–	–	–	–	–	2005	–
	TLT	2007	–	2007	–	–	–	–
	WCT	2005	–	2005	2005	–	2004	–
	WPPT	2005	–	2005	2005	–	2005	–
	Classification treaties							
	Locarno, designs	–	–	–	–	–	–	–
	Nice, marks	2005	(use)	(use)	(use)	(use)	(use)	–
	Strasbourg, patents	–	–	–	–	–	–	–
	Vienna, marks elements	–	–	–	–	–	–	–
	Global protection treaties							
	Budapest, microorganism	fta	–	2007	–	–	–	–
	Hague, industrial designs	fta	–	fta	–	–	–	–
	Lisbon, appellations	–	–	–	–	–	–	–
	Madrid Protocol, marks	2005	–	2007	–	–	–	–
	PCT	2007	–	2001	–	–	1999	–
	UPOV, plant varieties	2005	–	2007	–	–	–	–
	UCC, copyright (1971)	–	–	–	–	1994	–	–

Source: compiled by the author

Notes: While all GCC states have endorsed the GCC Unified Patent Regulations, and at various times have declared that they recognise their validity, Kuwait and Saudi Arabia do not appear to have enacted statutes formally adopting the Regulations.

The 'fta' notation indicates commitments made by Bahrain and Oman under their respective FTAs, but yet to be implemented.

Bahrain has formally acceded to Nice, but the other states have declared they subscribe to its classifications.

States will also expect Kuwait to enact and implement several key pieces of intellectual property legislation regarding copyright, data protection, geographical indications, trademarks, patents and customs that have been pending for a number of years, as well as greater coverage of technology-based issues within the scope of the implementing regulations. The implication here is that, amongst other measures, the United States will continue to apply pressure for compliance through its Annual Special 301 Report process. Kuwait is remarkable as the only Gulf state that has yet to accede to either the Berne or Paris Conventions and is thus the most conservative of states on its international memberships, being surpassed even by Yemen.

Saudi Arabia will continue to face criticism from US quarters that its copyright law still lacks some basic minimum standards that are required by the WIPO Internet Treaties and TRIPS. Saudi Arabia is accused of still failing to adequately protect sound recordings, to provide for *ex parte* civil search orders and adequate remedies, to initiate criminal prosecutions against intellectual property infringements and to take action at its borders to confiscate pirated and counterfeit goods.[5] Saudi Arabia has also been criticised for its failure to ensure transparency in the Saudi enforcement system generally, particularly in respect of timely information on policing and judicial action to aggrieved right holders.

In the international context, the future of the US MEFTA strategy in its present guise must be considered to be very uncertain. With a new President and a Congress at odds with the former Administration on its bilateral trade strategy, it is likely that any future bilateral trade agreements and their key intellectual property chapters will receive close and painful scrutiny. The MEFTA strategy had already encountered further problems with the shift in the balance of power in Congress from the Republicans to the Democrats. The growing opposition in Congress to the Bush Administration's Middle East policies had caused the non-renewal of the Administration's Trade Promotion Authority (TPA), which provided the framework for fast-track ('all-or-nothing') Congressional approval process for the Administration's bilateral trade agreements, but which expired on 1 July 2007. The UAE FTA negotiation, which was mooted originally to be completed at roughly the same time as the Oman FTA, has stalled, as have the Qatar and Kuwait discussions, and it may be some months or even years before they recommence. The final state to complete an FTA with the United States may well be Saudi Arabia, but this may be academic, since many intellectual property issues have already been addressed as part of its market access agreement on goods and services which it entered into with the United States as part of its WTO membership requirements. In fact, the local Saudi press was incorrectly, but understandably, already calling this bilateral market access agreement a free trade agreement.[6]

The admission of Saudi Arabia to the WTO in November 2005 and its accession to TRIPS is unlikely to have any obvious impact of great significance on its intellectual property protection regimes in the near future. Saudi Arabia has already been required to undertake a major overhaul of its intellectual property legislation as part of the accession process – hence the impact has already occurred. In any case, the US stance of a hard line on endorsing Saudi membership of the WTO was not directly related to intellectual protection but to matters of international politics, trade and investment, notably US access to all aspects of the Saudi financial, banking and services sectors. However, the pressure upon Saudi Arabia to conform to US demands as a condition of membership should not presuppose that the way for TRIPS-plus standards to be introduced as part of any FTA will be a straightforward process. During its final accession acceptance Saudi Arabia still raised notice of prohibitions in respect of a number of imports and services, as allowed by Article 20 of the WTO Charter, in order to protect Islamic values and traditions. The reservations included a total ban on the import of satellite internet receivers, pork, alcohol and narcotics, as well as bans on foreign investment, and travel, tourism and transport services in Makkah and Madinah, being the sites of Islam's two holy mosques.[7]

Likewise, Yemen's accession to membership of the WTO and of the GCC will, in all likelihood, pass largely unnoticed outside the Gulf. Yemen has been seeking WTO membership since 2000 and GCC membership since 1996. While its intellectual property laws and enforcement systems as a whole are the most TRIPS non-compliant of all the Gulf states, it is also arguably the least important strategically and the least problematic in terms of the dimension of regional intellectual property piracy and other violations. However, its membership of the WTO will complete the memberships from within the Gulf region and may well coincide with full membership of the GCC.

As the paradigm in international intellectual property protection moves from the traditional and well-established trade-related forms of protection – centring on trademarks, copyright and neighbouring rights and patents – to encompass the new emerging areas of traditional knowledge and cultural heritage, biodiversity, global geographical indications (as distinct from a European context) and public health policy, so there will be a shift in the balance of the powers in the major international forums of the WTO and WIPO. The Gulf states, which to date have largely forsaken the international forums, may possibly assume in them a more vocal role as they develop domestically a growing understanding of intellectual property in the international context and an expertise and appreciation of the benefits of effective enforcement.

The establishment of the national and regional intellectual property infrastructures, and the skills development of the human resources to give effect to these national needs and aspirations, will continue to be significant but surmountable challenges. The states readily acknowledge that their infrastructures and human-resource expertise are such that they face considerable challenges in the medium to long term to enforce their intellectual property laws to the standards they would seek and the standard expected of them by the developed countries and intellectual property right holders.

But there will be other factors remaining in play as the systemic and structural challenges are resolved. It has been suggested that piracy is not necessarily simply a manifestation of the lack of intellectual property protection or enforcement, but rather characterisation of the incongruity of the laws to the degree of industrial development in the state.[8] It may also be a manifestation of the denial of the sovereign right of a state to engage in law-making as it sees fit, which pushes it to adopt a position of indifference at best, or active resentment at worst, as regards the enforcement of foreign intellectual property rights.[9] The perceived lack of legitimacy and fairness in forcing developing countries to subscribe to laws that significantly ignore their plight, and in particular to set up legal forms that are not congruent to the state of their economy and technology, will make the enforcement of foreign intellectual property in these countries an uphill struggle.[10] Societies in developing countries will continue to resist changes to their intellectual property laws and when they do make changes, they will be slow to enforce them in favour of foreign corporations at the expense of local merchants. To the extent that TRIPS-plus rules may adversely affect the economic interests of developing countries, passive resistance may be the most likely counter mechanism. The enforcement dichotomy shall remain for the time being, even though some of the states will continue to achieve major successes against the virtually uncontrolled counterfeiting and piracy that existed in the past. But as the imperative for change becomes more internally driven, the successes against piracy will accelerate.

8.4 The Gulf states and the international arenas – new agendas?

Developing countries have been described as 'observers' in the intellectual property protection process, the implication being that they are unable in terms of expertise and capacity to match it with the developed countries.[11] To use a sporting analogy, it might be more accurate to describe them as reluctant reserves from the second grades – content to watch the main game from the bench, but occasionally required or cajoled to enter the field of play. And in some sense the Gulf states have been willing to play an observer or reserve role because it suits them at this point in time. They are only too aware of their limitations – in terms of legislation, infrastructure, judicial capacity and expertise in strategic intellectual property policy development and implementation. However, in this approach there is an altruistic pragmatism at play that can be too easily overlooked. Since adoption of TRIPS required laws encompassing particular and complex requirements, it made eminent sense to turn to the administrators of this multilateral benchmark, namely WIPO, to obtain such laws. By the same token, enforcement needs to be a visible action, which may be addressed by raids that are well publicised but ultimately resolved with quietude. Yet, just as there exists a cynicism on the part of the United States in respect of these attitudes, being perceived as a lack of commitment to intellectual property protection, there is also a cynicism about the US publicly orated objectives in the region. The states are not taken in by what some see as double standards on the part of the major developed countries. They see the global trade community, of which the United States and the European Union are the driving forces, establishing a particular set of standards, albeit minimum ones, and are then confronted by the US government acting as agent for US-based multinational corporations striving to drive up those standards through bilateral agreements.

Arab countries have been exhorted to play a more active role in the international arena by joining forces with like-minded countries.[12] However, they are unlikely to be inclined to do so by their own volition unless there arises a particular need to develop a regional agenda that pays attention and care to their development needs and priorities. Nevertheless, the GCC member states already have in existence a regional structure that could serve as the logical springboard for launching a greater presence in international forums, namely the GCC itself. Yet the GCC Council has its own internal dysfunctionality at present that militates against acting as a springboard for the creation of a regional voice on behalf of the Gulf states, the Middle East, the greater Arab world or another consortium of developing and least developed nations. The GCC member states, either collectively as a regional bloc or individually, have not attempted to make their presence felt in the affairs of the WTO or WIPO councils and committees, even with long-standing Saudi membership of the latter. The lack of active participation to date reinforces the view expressed earlier that membership of these two bodies, although necessary, was not always positively viewed and embraced with active participation by the states.

Where Saudi Arabia's WTO membership may have some regional impact is in repairing to some extent its uneasy and strained dominating influence in the GCC and thereby giving greater credence and influence to a GCC bloc within the WTO and WIPO in the ongoing debate on the role and future directions of both forums. There could also emerge a regional bloc which, if it joins forces with other League of Arab States members and with other regional blocs such as ARIPO,[13] and the 'Group of the Friends of Development' bloc,[14] may make a significant contribution to a shift in the balance between the developed and developing/ least developed countries in the major intellectual property and development forums. With Saudi Arabia and Yemen achieving WTO membership, and Yemen securing membership of the GCC, there also arises the opportunity for these seven states to form their own Gulf regional influence within a greater Middle East or even wider Arab forum. This, in turn, could possibly make a change to the negotiating dynamics in the WTO.

In some respects, TRIPS has been somewhat superseded by the emergence of the new round of intellectual property law-making in the post-TRIPS world through the web of bilateral trade agreements. At the same time, the WTO has stumbled at its recent ministerial meetings on efforts to liberalise global trade generally and to also inject a greater degree of equity and access into TRIPS. WIPO has been confronted with internal issues requiring self-examination and active debate amongst members over proposals and counter-proposals which have the potential to significantly change its role in the global intellectual property arena. The 'new international standard' of intellectual property protection in practical terms is fast becoming that which is defined by the terms enshrined in the latest round of bilateral agreements together with the prescriptions of the TRIPS-plus treaties, such as the WIPO Internet Treaties and TRIPS-plus conventions. The 'highest international standard' has become very much a moving target.

Subsequent to the 2001 Doha Development Round, WIPO has been exhorted to shift its focus away from the promotion of intellectual property as a tool for economic development and instead place a greater emphasis on a development agenda. A proposal for a development agenda for WIPO was first launched by Argentina and Brazil and supported by a further 12 developing countries (the 'Group of Friends of Development') at the 2004 WIPO General Assembly.[15] Over the next 12 months a further eight proposals were presented by WIPO member states on this issue, not all of which supported the development agenda. The Group of Friends of Development submission included proposals to:

- amend the WIPO Convention to include explicit language on the development dimension;
- establish a WIPO Standing Committee on Intellectual Property and Technology Transfer;
- consider the elaboration of a treaty on access to knowledge and;
- formulate and adopt principles and guidelines for the development and implementation of technical assistance.

The United States countered with a proposal which advocated a partnership programme between members to match specific needs with available resources and to build on the current WIPO development programme. While the programme would operate under the WIPO banner, the role envisaged for WIPO would be mainly confined to administration, maintenance and matching needs and resources. In other words, WIPO would no longer continue to play its current active, autonomous and influential role in carrying out its development activities.

The US proposal would appear to be a targeted campaign to transfer WIPO's influential role in the development agenda to those few developed countries that have both the economic and political will to promote their own national agendas on international intellectual property protection. The partnership strategy is essentially a bilateral approach to international intellectual property development. It largely bypasses the WIPO inherent system of equality amongst members and forums for checks and balances. It also enhances the legitimacy of the current US bilateral strategy, which has attracted considerable and sustained criticism from quarters of the civil society by placing the strategy squarely into the context of an apparent UN specialised agency. However, in the US proposal there is no reference to audit or monitoring of the nature or direction of the assistance given – this being simply a matter between the developing country seeking assistance and the developed country providing it. The unequal partnerships without effective moderation or independent audit, as envisaged by the US proposal, would have significant implications for developing and least developed countries. It would effectively establish investment and trade protection regimes of the type that the United States and the EU in particular have been attempting to achieve through the international forums, but on which they have been largely frustrated.

In a surprise move, Bahrain, in June 2005, injected its own proposal into the development debate.[16] Its proposal, co-sponsored by the other GCC member states as well as Yemen and Jordan, Lebanon, Libyan Arab Jamahiriya, focuses on the importance of intellectual property in the social and economic development of developing countries, and their national development programmes. The proposal advocates:

- expanding WIPO's advice and technical assistance provided to small and medium-sized enterprises (SMEs) and sectors dealing with scientific research and cultural industries;
- WIPO assisting member states in setting up national strategies in the field of intellectual property;
- WIPO undertaking studies to demonstrate the economic, social and cultural impact of the use of intellectual property systems in Member States;
- increasing financial resources for technical assistance for promoting an IP culture with an emphasis on introducing intellectual property at different academic levels;
- establishing a voluntary contribution fund to promote the legal, commercial and economic exploitation of intellectual property rights in developing countries and LDCs;
- requesting developed countries to encourage their research and scientific institutions to enhance cooperation and exchange with research and development institutions in developing countries and least developed countries;
- while considering the Development Agenda process, adopting guidelines that address the financial implications for each proposition, means to avoid conflict between the role of WIPO and the international obligations of members, means to avoid confusion between the role of WIPO in facilitating negotiations on international treaties that it administers and the sovereign decision of members on whether to adhere or not to a specific treaty.

The Bahrain proposal is a conservative alternative, in essence maintaining the status quo while increasing the level of WIPO funding available to developing and least developed countries for development assistance. It sits somewhere between the US and Group of Friends of Development proposals, and in practical terms is not that dissimilar to the US proposal. The carriage of the proposal by Bahrain is a clever move – presented by a non-aligned member from a group that has not had a strong presence in the past in the major issues before WIPO. Bahrain's conservative proposal also represents an alternative to the US retrograde proposal and has received public support within WIPO from the United States.

But the significance of the proposal by Bahrain and its co-sponsors in the context of this work is that it also constitutes a precedent for any of the Gulf states in leading a major proposal to a WIPO General Assembly on a hotly debated subject of importance to the future direction of WIPO. Although not yet on the winning side, the Bahrain delegation has cleverly maintained sufficient distance between itself and the other major camps in order to keep its perceived non-aligned position. It is also logical that Bahrain, arguably now having a closer diplomatic relationship with the United States than the other Gulf states following the completion of its FTA some months earlier, should be the main sponsor of its compromise proposal. Bahrain has also been the most diligent of the states in attending meetings of WIPO and its standing committees. The question arises, which only time can answer, whether this initiative may constitute the beginning of a higher profile for any of the states in particular and the other Middle East countries in the affairs and politics of WIPO and the WTO. Cynics would argue in the negative, since all GCC states have been represented on WIPO for some years, without developing a vocal presence in its diplomatic and political arenas.

8.5 The Gulf–United States relationship

The push by the leading developed nations, led by the United States and the European Union, to establish a network of regional controlled trade and political blocs as part of a global policy network-building exercise – which is what the US is striving to achieve with the Middle East Free Trade Area (MEFTA) – will not be without its eventual costs. There are few illusions in the minds of the senior members of the Gulf states that the United States, despite its public rhetoric to the contrary, will continue to place its own interests to the fore, irrespective of whether those interests may be contrary to international norms on intellectual property or whether they disregard the best interests of the protagonist states. Omani officials, for example, well remember that the United States, in a move that was tantamount to coercion, tried to pressure Oman into adopting a 25-year period of protection for patents at the very last minute before Oman's accession to the WTO was approved – a move which Oman successfully resisted, but which nevertheless generated some Omani resentment.[17]

At a Gulf major regional workshop on future GCC–US relations held after the 2004 US Presidential elections, the view was oft expressed that the US approach to the democratisation of the GCC states constituted outright interference in their domestic affairs.[18] The 'messianic fervour' with which the United States pursues its democracy US-style agenda while ignoring the local character of the societies it is aiming to reform was seen as particularly problematic.[19] Although the US Administration is a fervent driver of the 'democratisation' initiative in the Middle East, contradictory American regional interests will ensure that the initiative remains largely cosmetic in nature. The states in particular accuse the United States of not listening to the needs of the countries in the region or understanding the realities of the situation on the ground.[20] Regardless of the prevalence of such views, there is no doubt that pressure from the United States on the individual Gulf states to continue to move towards the 'highest international standard' will be ongoing.

Statements by US policy-makers continue to reinforce a message of imposed change without consultation or consideration of local cultural values. When those statements include remarks that are critical of the states' efforts at modernisation and reform and are derogatory to the region's rulers, particularly when made while a guest in an Arab country, they are also unlikely to be forgotten or quickly forgiven. The following remarks of the USTR, which were made in the context of the launch of the US Administration's MEFTA strategy, would not have endeared the US Administration to Gulf state leaders:

> 'There is a vast wealth of human capital in the Middle East, waiting to be empowered. Now, the United States is making a long-term commitment to help those who will strive to reclaim a splendid past and create a new future: one of peace, hope, and opportunity.
>
> The United States aims to brighten the Middle East with as many success stories as stars in the desert sky. To do so, we are charting a new constellation: shining lights of trade and investment that offer a clear course for countries in the region wishing to embark on a journey of economic openness and reform.'[21]

The following remarks, aimed at the ruling elites of the Gulf states, would also have created considerable pique and caused some disquiet:

> 'The U.S.–Middle East trade initiative complements and extends America's already significant economic engagement with this region. Yet our efforts have been limited by old hatreds, political instability, corruption, bureaucracies and the privileged few who resist the competition of economic reforms, a search for enemies to blame instead of partners to build with, and price uncertainties for oil-dependent economies. To move forward, we need a unified regional strategy and a commitment to work together.'[22]

The reactions of local policy-makers and businesses to the US attitude to the Gulf region surfaced during a recent Arab Business Council Conference in Bahrain on the Bahrain FTA. A number of participants reacted negatively to what they termed the 'Big Brother' attitude of the United States in respect of its bilateral trade agreements, perceiving them to be political devices to serve US interests in the region rather than tools to enhance the region's economic prosperity.[23] The claim by one US speaker at the Conference that 'if Arab countries can integrate with the US through FTAs, it will be easier for them to integrate with each other' was both resented and ridiculed by some subsequent speakers. The Jordanian Ministry of Industry and Trade responded:

> 'I really fail to see the logic that if you want to achieve Arab integration, you have to go to the United States.'[24]

Another local speaker argued that 'FTAs are creating a negative environment. It is a waste of time to think that we will achieve economic integration through the United States. The United States will not be the gateway for our economic integration'.[25]

The heated debates in the US Congress during the approval process for the Oman FTA and the major negotiating points during the UAE FTA negotiations allowed the public airing of hostility in some US quarters to any concession to Gulf interests that might be counter to the maximisation of US business opportunities abroad and US jobs at home, or even to any substantive association with these states on grounds of national security. These domestic attitudes stand in contrast to the above rhetoric of the President and USTR Zoellick and his successors.

The furore over the Dubai Ports World controversy and the consequent difficult passage through Congress of the Oman FTA has further clearly demonstrated to Middle East states that the United States seeks to impose what those states view as double standards when it suits US interests. While the United States demands a veto over foreign investment in its domestic enterprises in its FTA negotiations, it continues to demand full access, including 100 per cent foreign ownership, in their negotiating protagonists. The collapse of the Dubai Ports World US ports deal has been described in the local UAE press as a shattering episode that has damaged the US–UAE relationship:

> 'The people in the UAE will never forget America's handling of the Ports deal, and the treatment given to it in the US Congress are turning points in the US–UAE relationship. The ports controversy has left a huge dent in the usually friendly relationship between the two countries.'[26]

According to the Gulf Research Centre, an influential regional think tank and research centre, the United States under the Bush Administration had lost much credibility with the leadership of the Gulf states, not to the point where the overall usefulness of the relationship has come into question but at least to the point where individual leaders are beginning to think about and contemplate alternatives.[27] The underlying dilemma, within the existing complexities of regional and international politics, is that the United States has so far failed to come to terms with the states defining their own interests outside of the context of the need for US military protection. The Centre suggests that there are a number of areas in which the differences between US and Gulf states' positions are increasing – such as the Arab–Israeli conflict, the Iran nuclear programme and, above all, the US position in Iraq. While the states may have willingly, albeit grudgingly, gone along with much of US policy in the past, US policies are increasingly being seen more as part of the problem of regional instability than as part of the solution. Instead, the Gulf states have begun to define their own national priorities and interests.

These general sentiments can be equally and validly applied to the specific area of intellectual property protection. The Gulf states may accede to demands from the US and other developed countries in respect of providing the legislative framework according to the demands of the developed countries, but may not necessarily resile from tempering the application of those demands according to local and regional needs and sensitivities. The hardening line by the UAE and Qatar in their respective stalled FTA negotiations should be a signal to the United States that there has been a diametric shift in the balance of negotiating power, dynamics and the former willingness to generally concur.

8.6 Concluding remarks

The substitution of imperial exploitation by economic and political exploitation does not change the exploitation, only its character. Regrettably, it is not easy to change local attitudes borne out of hard experience and reinforced over generations, and whose current-day justifications continue to be reinforced. Cloaking the exploitation with a transparent veneer of adopted moral superiority will only serve to exacerbate this ill-feeling and strengthen a determination to generate change when the opportunity arises.

The Gulf states may well accept without great demurral the demands of the United States and the other industrialised nations for the regional installation of the international frameworks of global intellectual property protection and the manner in which they are demanded. Arabic cultural mores and a fine appreciation of the relative bargaining strengths of the protagonists dictate that they do so. However, such acceptance does not necessarily mean that the matter is closed and its conditions no longer negotiable. Adoption of an agreement may well constitute the conclusion of a matter and the fixation of its conditions in western eyes, but in Arabic minds it represents the status quo at a particular point of time. And, as has already been demonstrated, installation of the legislative framework does not guarantee successful implementation of the strategy.

In the intellectual property context, the states will continue to operate within the US-dominated paradigm for the time being. They will work towards developing those elements that suit their needs and advance their public policy objectives, and accept for the time being those elements which they are presently unable to resist or change. However, most matters are always changeable in Arabic eyes and nothing is ever really concluded, even a formal agreement.[28] Conditions agreed to in one context or at one point in time may no longer be appropriate or tenable as circumstances change or time progresses. In any case, the hypocrisy of some industrialised nations in advocating the minimum (and maximum) mandatory protection standards of TRIPS, while virtually at the same time actively endeavouring to extend those standards in respect of, say, copyright, trademarks, patent and geographical indications, and seeking to prevent new or equitable standards of protection in respect of traditional knowledge and cultural heritage, and sharing of genetic resources, would not be lost on the states.

It would be a mistake to assume that the *Qur'an* and the *Shariah* are no longer relevant in the intellectual property context and thus will not have any influence on the future dynamics of the states' intellectual property regimes. Public order, morality and the dictates of the *Shariah* currently set protection parameters in the laws of the states in respect of copyright patent and trademark protection, and will continue to do so, and the possibility of their influence growing in the future should not be discounted. Recent demonstrations throughout the Muslim world against the publication in an obscure Danish newspaper of cartoons that insulted the Prophet Mohammed are a graphic illustration of the power of radical Islam as a catalyst for change, even in the short-term time frame. In the final analysis, the nature of the intellectual property protection regimes of the Gulf states will be subject to further change and development, and that change is likely to involve a greater degree of internal influence and direction than has been seen in the past – Insha'allah.[29]

Notes

1 'Infidels at the gates' – introduction and context

1 The Gulf Cooperation Council came into existence on 26 May 1981, in part as a response to perceived threats from an Islamic fundamentalist Iran, an imperialistic Ba'athist Iraq, the state of civil war in Yemen, and the recent Soviet intervention in Afghanistan – all of which threatened to destabilise the ruling dynasties in the Gulf region and to involve their states in wider conflicts.

2 Yemen has been seeking membership of the GCC since 1996. Its application for membership has been sponsored by Oman and Qatar, but has been vetoed by Saudi Arabia, the main obstacle being the difference between Yemen's and the GCC members' political and economic systems. In January 2002 Yemen was granted observer status at GCC-affiliated non-political bodies and agencies, and in October 2002 Yemen and the GCC signed a protocol defining the relationship between the two sides – considered to be the first step towards Yemen's full membership of the GCC. As recently as June 2008, Yemen was still seeking full membership of the GCC.

3 The Paris Convention for the Protection of Industrial Property, the Berne Convention for the Protection of Literary and Artistic Works, the International Convention for the Protection of Performers, Producers of Phonograms, adopted at Rome on 26 October 1961, and the Treaty on Intellectual Property in Respect of Integrated Circuits, adopted at Washington on 26 May 1989. Although the Washington Treaty never entered into force, its provisions nevertheless became enforceable through TRIPS arts. 35–8.

4 John Carroll, 'Intellectual Property Rights in the Middle East: A Cultural Perspective' (2000/2001), 11, *Fordham Intellectual Property Media and Entertainment Law Journal*, p. 555.

5 William M Ballantyne, *Commercial Law in the Arab Middle East: The Gulf States* (1986), pp. 1–2.

6 Oman has enjoyed independent status since it expelled the Portuguese in 1650. During the eighteenth century it established an empire encompassing Zanzibar, parts of East Africa and the southern Arabian Peninsula, and established effective trading control over parts of the Persian and Pakistan coasts. In 1800 Great Britain entered into a Friendship Treaty which recognised Oman's independence but which developed into Great Britain gaining effective control over Oman's foreign relations and over the affairs of non-Muslims in the Sultanate. Oman's regional influence and empire declined during the late nineteenth century as it retreated into a period of sustained isolationism until the 1970s.

7 Nicholas Angell, 'An Overview of Legal Structures in the GCC Countries', Legal 500 Research Paper No. 3 (March 2002), available at <http://www.legal500.com/devs/emirates/cc/uacc_010.htm>.
8 *UK Commission on Intellectual Property Rights*, 2001, pp. 1–2.
9 Ibid.
10 Ibid.
11 Ibid.
12 Peter Drahos, 'Developing Countries and International Intellectual Property Standard-Setting' (2002), 5, *Journal of World Intellectual Property*, p. 788.
13 See John Braithwaite and Peter Drahos, *Information Feudalism: Who Owns the Knowledge Economy?* (2002), 9–13; see also Jagdish Bhagwati, quoted in 'Integrating Intellectual Property Rights and Development Policy', *Report of the UK Commission on Intellectual Property Rights*, DFID, February 2003, p. 160.
14 In 2000, Oman became the fifth GCC state to join the WTO after Bahrain (1995), Kuwait (1995), Qatar (1996) and UAE (1996), but the first required to go through the WTO scrutiny process. Saudi Arabia, having sought membership since 1993, first of GATT and then the WTO, finally achieved membership in November 2005 and accordingly attended the WTO Ministerial Conference in Hong Kong in December 2005 as a full member. Yemen has been seeking membership since April 2000 and at the time of writing enjoys observer status as a precursor.
15 *Oman Observer*, 10 October 2000, p. 1.
16 Ibid.
17 Howard Stovall, 'Arab Commercial Laws – Into the Future' (2000), 34, *The International Lawyer*, p. 842.
18 Drahos, op. cit., p. 781.
19 Carroll, op. cit., p. 594.
20 These criticisms appear with regular frequency in the USTR's Annual Special 301 Reports. The Reports as they relate to the GCC states are discussed in greater detail in Chapter 6.
21 Mohammed Al-Said, 'From TRIPS-minus to TRIPS to TRIPS-plus: Implications of IPRs for the Arab World' (2005), 8, *Journal of World Intellectual Property*, p. 60.
22 The WIPO Internet Treaties are the WIPO Copyright Treaty (1966) (WCT), and the WIPO Performances and Phonograms Treaty (1996) (WPPT).
23 Carlos Correa, *Intellectual Property Rights, The WTO and Developing Countries: The TRIPS Agreement and Policy Options* (2000), p. 4.
24 See the Report of the Asian Regional Workshop on Bilateral Free Trade Agreements, Kuala Lumpur, August 2005, 8, available at <http://www.twnside.org.sg/title2/twninfo254.htm>, last accessed 30 November 2006.
25 Aziz Choudry, 'Bombarded by Bilateral Trade and Investment Agreements', *Bilaterals.org*, March 2004, p. 3, available at <http://www.bilaterals.org/IMG/pdf/Bombarded_by_Bilatera_92909-2.pdf>, last accessed 6 January 2006.
26 Aziz Choudry, 'Bilateral Trade and Investment Deals a Serious Challenge to Global Justice Movements', *GRAIN*, December 2003, p. 1, available at <http://www.grain.org/rights/tripsplus.cfm?id=2>, last accessed 30 September 2006.
27 Drahos, op. cit., pp. 781–2.
28 Ibid, p. 788.
29 USTR 2005 Special 301 Report, p. 2, available at <http://www.ustr.gov/assets/Document_Library/Reports_Publications/2005/2005_Special_301/assets_upload_file195_7636.pdf>, last accessed 20 December 2006.

2 'The golden thread that binds' – the *Shariah* and intellectual property protection

1 William M Ballantyne, *Commercial Law in the Arab Middle East: The Gulf States* (1986), pp. 1–2.
2 Susan Rayner, *The Theory of Contracts in Islamic Law* (1991), p. 372.
3 Mahda Zahraa, 'Characteristic Features of Islamic Law: Perceptions and Misconceptions' (2000), 15(2), *Arab Law Quarterly*, p. 169.
4 The *Shariah* or sacred law of Islam was developed and assembled during the first three centuries following the death of the Prophet Muhammad in 632 AD. While *Shariah* (literally the way) is translated as 'Islamic law', it is neither canonical nor secular law because no such concept exists in Islam; it is rather a whole system of social and personal morality, prescribing the way a man should live if he is to act according to God's Will. See Peter Mansfield, 'A History of the Middle East', 5, quoted by John Carroll, 'Intellectual Property Rights in the Middle East', (2000/2001), 11, *Fordham Intellectual Property, Media and Entertainment Journal*, p. 588.
5 Zahraa, op. cit., p. 174.
6 William Ballantyne, *Legal Development in Arabia* (1980), p. 121.
7 S H Amin, *Law of Intellectual and Industrial Property in Developing Countries: Muslim World* (1993), pp. 36–7.
8 Howard Stovall, 'Arab Commercial Laws – Into the Future' (2000), 34, *The International Lawyer*, pp. 841–2.
9 Rayner, op. cit., p. 372.
10 Ahmad Saif, 'Constitutionalism in the Arab Gulf States', *GCC Research Program – GCC Constitutions* (2004), Gulf Research Centre, p. 17.
Bahrain first adopted a constitution on 26 May 1973, which came into effect on 6 December 1973. It adopted a new constitution on 14 February 2001, which came into effect one year later.
Kuwait achieved its independence from the United Kingdom on 19 June 1961 and gained its original constitution on 16 November 1962. This constitution remains in place.
Oman did not establish a form of constitution until 6 November 1996. By Royal Decree No. 101/1996, it established the Basic Law of the State, as the Sultanate's constitutional equivalent.
Qatar was granted a provisional constitution by the United Kingdom on 2 April 1970 and gained its independence on 3 September 1971. A new and permanent constitution was approved by national referendum on 29 April 2003.
Saudi Arabia, like Oman, does not possess a formal constitution *per se*. It enacted, in March 1992, a Basic Statute of the Kingdom, which declares that the Holy *Qur'an* is the constitution of Saudi Arabia.
The UAE adopted a provisional constitution on 18 July 1971, which, with some minor amendments, was eventually confirmed on 2 December 1996 by the Constitutional Amendment Law No. 1 of 1996.
Yemen was established as a Republic in May 1990 on the unification of the Yemen Arab Republic (North Yemen) and the People's Democratic Republic of Yemen (South Yemen). A Unification Constitution was adopted in 1991 and amended in 1994 after the cessation of secessionist hostilities in the south and again in 2001.
11 Ballantyne, Legal Development in Arabia (1980), p. 27.
12 Bahrain, Constitution, art. 1; Kuwait, Constitution, art. 2; UAE, Constitution, art. 7.
13 Qatar, Constitution, art. 1.

14 Oman, Basic Law of the State, art. 2.
15 Yemen, Constitution, art. 3.
16 Saudi Arabia, Basic Law of the Kingdom, art. 1.
17 Qatar, Constitution, arts. 74, 92 and 119.
18 Oman, Basic Law of the State, art. 10.
19 Yemen, Constitution, art. 159.
20 Saudi Arabia, Basic Law of the Kingdom, art. 1.
21 Ibid, arts. 7–8.
22 Ibid, art. 23.
23 Ibid, art. 9.
24 Ibid, art. 67.
25 The Saudi King is first 'The Custodian of the Two Holy Mosques', a responsibility and title which is perhaps akin, in principle if not in practice, to the British Monarch's awful responsibility as 'Defender of the Faith'. The two holy mosques referred to above are the sacred Islamic sites in Makah and Madinah.
26 See Saudi Arabia, Basic Law of the Kingdom, art. 43, which establishes the right of every citizen to have a consultation with the King in his capacity as the final arbiter on any complaint. The Omani Basic Law has similar provision.
27 *Bahrain*: The government comprises the King as Head of State and separate executive and legislative branches. The executive branch consists of the Prime Minister (as head of government) and the Council of Ministers (Cabinet), all of whom are appointed by the King. The legislative arm consists of a bicameral National Assembly with a partially elected lower house and an appointed upper house. In general, all legislation passes through both bodies and Cabinet for recommendation for royal assent. The King and the Cabinet may also promulgate legislation directly through royal, prime ministerial and ministerial decrees, all of which carry the force of law.

Kuwait: The Constitution provides for the establishment of separate executive and legislative branches of government. Like Bahrain, the executive branch comprises the Amir (as head of state), the Prime Minister (as head of government) and a Council of Ministers which serves as the Cabinet. The Amir appoints the Prime Minister who in turn appoints the Council of Ministers, the appointments still subject to Amiri approval.

Oman: The Cabinet, deriving its authority solely from the Sultan, is the highest administrative authority, with its members all appointed directly by the Sultan. The Cabinet considers matters related to administrative functions of the State, internal policies and foreign relations and submits its recommendations to the Sultan for approval. A popularly elected Consultative Council provides advice to the Cabinet on state policy and reviews draft legislation prepared by the ministries.

Qatar: The Qatari Constitution stipulates that the system of governance shall be based on the separation of authority; the Emir as Ruler holds the executive authority assisted by his Cabinet, while an Advisory Council holds the legislative authority. Since the Emir appoints the Cabinet and one third of the Advisory Council, the division between the two branches of government is notional. The Constitution requires the Emir to rule in accordance with Islamic precepts.

Saudi Arabia: The Basic Law provides for a Council of Ministers as the executive arm of government and a Consultative Council as the legislative arm. The members of both bodies are appointed by the King. The Council of Ministers is led by the King in his capacity as Prime Minister. It is responsible for drafting and overseeing the implementation national policies and general affairs of state. The Consultative Council advises the King and Council of

Ministers. The King has the power to restructure and to dissolve the Consultative Council as he deems necessary.

The UAE: The Chairman of the Supreme Council and thereby the President of the Federation is elected from among their own number – by unchallenged convention since independence in 1971, the Presidency has been held by the ruler of Abu Dhabi, the largest and wealthiest of the emirates, and the Prime Ministership by the ruler of Dubai.

Yemen: Yemen is a republic with an executive arm and a bicameral legislature. The President is head of state and the Prime Minister is head of government. The executive arm consists of the President and the Vice-President, Prime Minister and the Council of Ministers, all of whom are appointed by the President. The legislative branch consists of a Shura Council appointed by the President and an elected House of Representatives. President Ali Abdullah Saleh has been head of state since unification in 1990, having previously been President of the Yemen Arab Republic (North Yemen) since 1978.

28 Saudi Arabia, Basic Law of the State, art. 46.

29 The Qatari Criminal Code, for example, stipulates that jurisdiction over certain crimes, such as intentional or unintentional homicide, and crimes of a sexual nature, such as sexual assault, homosexuality and prostitution, rests with the *Shariah* court if the accused is a Muslim and with the secular court in respect of non-Muslims.

30 Saif, op. cit., p. 14.

31 Kuwait, Law No. 19 of 1959, the Judicial Code, as amended by Law No. 19 of 1990.

32 Ibid, art. 1; see also S H Amin, The Legal System of Kuwait (1991), p. 77.

33 Bahrain, Legislative Decree No. 13 of 1971, the Law of the Judiciary.

34 Ballantyne, Legal Development in Arabia (1980), p. 25.

35 Qatar, Law No. 16 of 1971, the Civil and Commercial Code, arts. 1–4.

36 UAE, Law No. 10 of 1973, Establishing the Federal Supreme Court, art. 75.

37 UAE, Federal Law No. 6 of 1978, Establishing the Courts of First Instance, art. 8.

38 Law Forming the Dubai Courts of 1970, art. 4; Law Forming the Courts of Ras Al-Khaimah, art. 1.

39 Ballantyne, *Commercial Law in the Arab Middle East: The Gulf States* (1986), p. 58.

40 Saudi Arabia, Basic Law of the State, art. 49.

41 Ballantyne, *Commercial Law in the Arab Middle East: The Gulf States* (1986), p. 64.

42 Mufti Taqi Usmani, 'Copyright according to *Shariah*', available at *Al-Balagh Webzine,* <http://www.islamic-finance.net/research/taqi4.html>, last accessed 30 May 2008.

43 Ibid, p. 99.

44 Ida Abdul Ghani Azmi, 'Basis for the Recognition of Intellectual Property in the Light of the *Shariah*' (1996), 27, *International Review of Intellectual Property and Competition Law*, p. 650.

45 Usmani, op. cit., p. 98.

46 See S H Amin, *Law of Intellectual and Industrial Property in Developing Countries: Muslim World* (1993), pp. 36–7.

47 Steven Jamar, 'The Protection of Intellectual Property under Islamic Law' (1992), 21, *Capital University Law Review*, p. 1082.

48 Usmani, op. cit., p. 99.

49 According to the cardinal Islamic principle of *annasu musallatun als amwaliham*, 'People should be given recognition for the exclusive use of their property'. *Amwal* (labour) applies equally to intellectual property outputs; see S H Amin,

Law of Intellectual and Industrial Property in Developing Countries: Muslim World (1993), p. 36.

50 Ibid. See also Azmi, op. cit., p. 671.

51 See S H Amin, *Law of Intellectual and Industrial Property in Developing Countries: Muslim World* (1993), p. 37.

52 Amir Khoury, 'Ancient and Islamic Sources of Intellectual Property Protection in the Middle East' (2003), 43, IDEA, p. 151.

53 Ballantyne, *Commercial Law in the Arab Middle East: The Gulf States* (1986), pp. 121–2.

54 Khoury, op. cit., pp. 193–5.

55 Ibid.

56 S H Amin, *Law of Intellectual and Industrial Property in Developing Countries: Muslim World* (1993), p. 40.

57 Ibid.

58 Azmi, op. cit., pp. 655–6.

59 Ibid, p. 666.

60 Ibid, pp. 667–8.

61 Ballantyne, *Commercial Law in the Arab Middle East: The Gulf States* (1986), p. 66.

62 GCC, Unified Patent Regulation 2000, art. 2.

63 Saudi Arabia, Royal Decree No. M/27 of 1425 AH (2004), art. 4.

64 See United States, *Diamond v Chakrabarty*, 447 US 303 (1980).

65 Board of Grievances Decision No. 9/1424 of 23 August 2003. Reported in Abu-Setta & Co, Legal Attorneys Saudi Arabia, 'Letter to Clients', September 2003, available at <http://www.abu-setta.com>, last accessed 20 December 2006.

66 Ibid.

3 Pre-TRIPS and intellectual property protection in the Gulf states

1 Nicholas Angell, 'An Overview of Legal Structures in the Gulf States', Legal 500 Research Paper No. 3 (March 2002), p. 1; available at <http://www.legal500.com/devs/emirates/cc/uacc_010.htm>, last accessed 30 June 2005.

2 For an excellent background to the state of pre-TRIPS intellectual property protection in the Gulf region, see Alastair Hirst, 'Developing IPR in the Gulf: Current Coverage, Problems, Post-Uruguay Round Trends' (1994), 17(2), *Middle East Executive Reports*, pp. 9–14.

3 Strictly speaking, none of the then Trucial States (Bahrain, Kuwait, Qatar and the seven Emirates that subsequently became the UAE – Abu Dhabi, Dubai, Ras Al-Khaimah, Sharjah, Ajman, Fujeirah, Umm al Quwain) was ever a colony or even a protected territory of the UK, although they were on occasion referred to as such in some laws (see Bahrain's Patents, Designs and Trade Marks Regulation of 1955, for example). Instead, they were recognised by the UK as sovereign states which, by virtue of various Agreements of Friendship, sought the protection of the UK against unfriendly intentions or acts by other countries, and which were accordingly deemed by the UK to be 'Protected States'. However, since their foreign relations and disposal of their lands were subject to UK approval, since resident UK subjects, foreigners and non-Muslims were subject to English law and authority under British extra-territorial jurisdiction, the states were subject to effective UK control. Hence the use of the term 'independence' to describe their newly acquired status in 1961 (Kuwait) and 1971 (Bahrain, Qatar and the seven Emirates) is appropriate.

4 Bahrain, Patents, Designs and Trade Marks Regulation, No. 1 of 1955. The Regulation was derived from the British Indian patents statutes.
5 The Kuwaiti constitution and the secular civil and commercial codes were drawn up largely under the guidance and influence of the eminent Egyptian jurist Abdul al-Rizzaq Al-Sanhouri; see Susan Rayner, *The Theory of Contracts in Islamic Law* (1991), p. 51.
6 The Model Law for Arab Countries on Patents (1972) and the Model Law for Arab Countries on Trade Marks, Trade Names, Commercial Indications and Acts of Unfair Competition (1975) were devised by the Industrial Development Centre for Arab States (IDCAS), the organisation within the League of Arab States responsible for industrial property matters. The model laws were drafted with assistance from WIPO.
7 UAE, Court of Cassation Case No. 116/981 of 1981; the offending product being marketed as *Berylcream.*
8 Saudi Arabia, Board of Grievances Case No. 206/T/4 of 1992; the offending product being marketed as *Bettol.*
9 Saudi Arabia, Royal Decree No. 8762 of 1358 AH (1939), concerning Trade Marks.
10 See Husain Al-Baharna, *British Extra-Territorial Jurisdiction in the Gulf 1913–1971* (1998) for a concise analysis of British extra-territoriality and the pre-independence system of British courts in the British Protected States of the Persian Gulf.
11 The Political Resident was the senior representative of the British government in the Gulf region and was responsible for the implementation of British policy in the Gulf through a number of Political Agents resident in Bahrain, Qatar, Dubai and Abu Dhabi. The Political Resident enjoyed ambassadorial status. The British government appointed a Consul-General to Oman in recognition of its long-established sovereignty, but the Consul-General was administratively responsible to the Political Resident.
12 Bahrain, Patents, Designs and Trade Marks Regulation, No. 1 of 1955.
13 *Trade Marks Act 1938* (UK); *Registered Designs Act 1949* (UK).
14 Bahrain, Amiri Decree No. 22 of 1977, amending certain provisions of the Patents, Designs and Trade Marks Regulation of 1955.
15 Queen's Regulation No. 5 of 1958, the Patent, Industrial Designs and Trade Marks Regulation.
16 Kuwait, Law No. 2 of 1961, the Commercial Code (articles 54–61 for trade names, articles 62–67 for protection against unfair competition and articles 69–92 for trademarks).
17 Qatar, Amiri Law No. 3 of 1978, the Trade Marks and Commercial Indications Law.
18 The Ras Al-Khaimah statute appears to have been largely based on the trademark provisions of the Kuwaiti Commercial Code, since with a few exceptions the order of the articles and their wording is near identical. The Ras Al-Khaimah statute had some deterrent potential insofar as it prescribed a penalty of up to one year's imprisonment and/or a fine of not more than 3,000 Emirati dirhams for persons found guilty of unlawfully using a registered mark, forging or imitating a registered mark, or using a counterfeit or forged mark, or selling goods with a forged mark. Articles 24–25 of the statute provided for the issuance of precautionary orders.
19 *Situation of Industrial Property in the Arab States*, WIPO, Geneva, 1978, p. 34. The report warns that the absence of Saudi statistics in the report should be construed as a reflection on the difficulty of obtaining reliable statistical data from local Saudi sources and the paucity of local data-collection procedures rather than any indication of local trademark inactivity.

20 Ibid, p. 35.
21 Ras Al-Khaimah Chamber of Commerce and Agriculture Records, cited by Mohamed Al-Kamali, 'Development of Intellectual Property Law in the UAE', unpublished PhD thesis, University of Exeter, 1994, p. 151.
22 *Patents Act 1949* (UK).
23 Bahrain, Amiri Decree No. 22 of 1977 amending certain provisions of the Patents, Designs and Trade Marks Regulation of 1955.
24 Bahrain, Legislative Decree No. 1 of 2004 in respect of Patents and Utility Models.
25 Kuwait, Law No. 4 of 1962, governing Patents, Designs and Industrial Models.
26 Ibid, art. 12.
27 WIPO, op. cit., p. 36.
28 The US Patent and Trademark Office (USPTO) reports that, for the period 1977–1982, only four patent applications from the Gulf region were granted registration, all to applicants from Saudi Arabia. However, the USPTO determines the origin of a patent according to the place of residence of the first-named inventor, as distinct from nationality. In each of the four cases, the application claimed priority on the basis of a US-origin patent. USPTO, *Patent Counts by Country/State and Year, January 1 1997–December 31 2001,* February 2002, available at <http://www.uspto.gov/web/offices/ac/ido/oeip/taf/est_all.pdf>, last accessed 31 December 2005.
29 Saudi Arabia, Royal Decree M/11 of 1410 AH (1989) concerning the Protection of Copyrights.
30 Bahrain, Legislative Decree No. 20 of 1975 with respect to the Legal Deposit of Intellectual Works; Kuwait, Law No. 3 of 1961, the Press and Publications Law.
31 Saudi Arabia, Royal Decree No. M/17 of 1402 AH (1982), the Printing Matter and Publications Law, arts. 20–21.
32 The UK government envisaged the establishment of Joint Courts in Bahrain, Qatar and the Trucial States as part of the system of British extra-territorial jurisdiction to consider mixed cases, that is matters between nationals of the individual states concerned and non-nationals. While the jurisdiction of the Joint Court could encompass both civil and criminal cases, in practice it confined itself to civil matters only. The Joint Court was composed of a judge of the British Court in the Gulf states and the Ruler (Emir) or his representative. The system was only fully established in Bahrain, where the jurisdiction of the Joint Court was extended specifically to include matters under the Queen's Regulation and the Bahrain Regulation on Patents, Designs and Trade Marks Regulation of 1955. Joint Courts were not established for Kuwait; although they were planned for introduction in Qatar, they did not eventuate.
33 Bahrain, Patents, Designs and Trade Marks Regulation 1955, art. 1.
34 Ibid, art. 23.
35 Ibid, art. 17.
36 Ibid, art. 17.
37 Ibid, art. 31.
38 Ibid, art. 13.1. Pursuant to art. 3, the Registrar of Patents, Designs and Trade Marks was required to maintain three separate registers – one for patents, one for designs and a third in two parts for UK-dependent (Part II) and marks of local origin for local use (Part III).
39 The Registrar of Patents, Designs and Trade Marks was appointed by the Political Registrar and notionally the Emir and was an officer of HM government. It is interesting that the subordinate Supplementary Rules for the 1955 Regulation were issued by the Registrar on behalf of the Ruler of Bahrain and the UK's Political Resident in Bahrain jointly, instead of by a Bahraini government

minister, department or authorised local official. In a subtle display of cultural sensitivity, the Supplementary Rules stipulated in art. 2 that trademark applications in respect of all goods in classes 32 (beer and stout) and 33 (wines and spirits) were to be published separately from the main Official Gazette (in which trademark registrations were normally publicly notified) and posted concurrently on the Registry noticeboard at 'Her Britannic Majesty's Political Agency, Bahrain'.

40 Bahrain, Patents, Designs and Trade Marks Regulation 1955, art. 8.

41 Ibid, art. 9.

42 Ibid, art. 26.

43 Ibid, art. 22.

44 Ibid, art. 32.

45 Ibid, arts. 46–47.

46 Ibid, art. 56.

47 Ibid, arts. 55, 60. The use of Indian rupees as the legal tender for the purposes of the regulation was a legacy from British Indian patents and trademarks regulation, on which the Bahraini regulation and the 1958 Kuwaiti regulation were based, from the period when the administration of the British Persian Gulf interests was under the control of the British Indian Office until India's independence in 1947. Control then moved to the British Foreign and Commonwealth Office.

48 Bahrain, Amiri Decree No. 22 of 1977.

49 Ibid, art. 11.

50 Kuwait, Law No. 4 of 1962, the Law on the Control and Register of Trade Marks, art. 5.

51 Ibid, art. 1.

52 Ibid, art. 2.

53 Ibid, art. 12.

54 Ibid, art. 42.

55 Ibid, arts. 22 and 31–32, and Implementing Regulations, art. 66.

56 Ibid, arts. 29 and 30.

57 Ibid, art. 31.

58 Ibid, arts. 46–47. Article 47 provides that the owner is limited to seeking such relief 'during the hearing of a civil or criminal case . . .'.

59 The following represent just some of the laws enacted across the Gulf states from the 1970s onwards which included to a lesser or greater extent some degree of intellectual property rights protection. The list is by no means intended to be exhaustive, but does illustrate the range of laws then in force.

Bahrain: Law No. 12 of 1971, the Civil and Commercial Procedures Code; Law No. 20 of 1975, concerning the Legal Deposit of Intellectual works.

Kuwait: Law No. 2 of 1961, the Commercial Code; Law No. 3 of 1961, the Press and Publications Law; Law No. 67 of 1980, the Civil Code; Law No. 16 of 1960, the Penal Code; Law No. 56 of 1966, the Commercial Companies Code.

Oman: Royal Decree No. 7/1974, the Penal Code; Royal Decree No. 49/1984, concerning Printed Matter and Publications.

Qatar: Law No. 14 of 1971, the Criminal Code; Law No. 16 of 1971, Civil and Commercial Code; Law No. 8 of 1979 in respect of Printed Materials and Publications.

Saudi Arabia: Royal Decree No. M/17 of 1402 AH (1982), concerning the Control of Publications and Publishing; Royal Decree No. M/11 of 1404 AH (1984), for Combatting Commercial Deceit; Royal Decree No. M/49 of 1409 AH (1989), Law for Combatting Concealed Trading.

The UAE: Law No. 5 of 1973, concerning Press and Publications; Law No. 5 of 1985, the Civil Transactions Code; Law No. 3 of 1987, the Federal Penal Code; Law No. 18 of 1981, the Commercial Agencies Law; Law No. 4 of 1979, the Commercial Transactions Law.

Dubai: The Civil Wrongs Law of 1966 and Law No. 1 of 1970, the Penal Code.

60 UAE, Federal Law No. 5 of 1985, the Civil Transactions Code, art. 106.

61 UAE Federal Law No. 3 of 1978, the Penal Code, art. 423.

62 Oman Royal Decree No. 7/1974, the Penal Code, arts. 305–307.

63 Angell, op. cit., p. 4.

64 Ibid. See also Essam Al-Tamimi, *The Framework for Litigation in the United Arab Emirates,* pp. 1–2, available at <http://www.tamimi.com/site_1024/pdf/litigati.pdf>, last accessed 6 January 2006.

65 Dubai Court of First Instance, Civil Division, Case No. 1378/1977, decided 24 June 1978; discussed in Al-Kamali, above n 21, 212, and S H Amin, *Law of Intellectual and Industrial Property in Developing Countries: Muslim World* (1993), pp. 41–2.

66 See Maren Hansen, 'Taking a Realistic Approach to Trade Mark Protection in the Gulf Countries' (1993), 16, *Middle East Executive Reports*, p. 12.

67 Dubai Court of First Instance Case No. 3/1981, decided 10 January 1982; Dubai Court of Appeal Case No. 17/1982, decided 15 May 1982; discussed in Al-Kamali, op. cit., p. 180.

68 *McDonald's Corporation v Hassan Arzouni*, Abu Dhabi Court of Appeal, Case No. 240/1980, decided 18 March 1981; discussed in Al-Kamali, op. cit., pp. 143 and 177.

69 *McDonald's v Hassan Arzouni*, Sharjah Court of First Instance, Case No. 823/1985, decided 13 January 1986; discussed in Al-Kamali, op. cit., p. 143. In a landmark case in early 1996, McDonald's pursued six companies in Riyadh and Jeddah for violations of trademark legislation and filed suits against four of them. McDonald's had registered all its trademarks and promotional logos with the Ministry as soon as it entered into the Saudi market. McDonald's had settled its cases by the end of 1997 and is building further restaurants in Saudi Arabia, which suggests that it was satisfied with the outcome; *EIU Viewswire*, 15 June 2004, available at <http://www.proquest.umi.com.ae>, last accessed 11 February 2005.

70 *Reckitt and Colman v Al Jazirah*, Saudi Board of Grievances Case No. 206/T/M of 27 June 1992. This final decision came after four years of legal proceedings. Discussed in Amin, above n 65, 105–111. See also Amir Khoury, 'The Development of Modern Trademark Legislation and Protection in Arab Countries in the Middle East' (2000), 16, *Transnational Lawyer*, p. 325.

71 Hansen, op. cit., p. 8.

72 Ibid, 14–15.

73 Bahrain, Legislative Decree No. 10 of 1991 in respect of Trade Marks, promulgated 25 June 1991.

74 Kuwait, Law No. 67 of 1980, Law No. 68 of 1980 and Ministerial Order No. 8 of 1995, for example.

75 WIPO, op. cit., p. 38.

76 UAE, Federal Law No. 37 of 1992, in respect of Trade Marks. The law covered the seven Emirates of Abu Dhabi, Dubai, Sharjah, Ras Al-Khaimah, Ajman, Fujeirah and Umm al Quwain.

77 The GCC Unified Patent Regulations were approved by the GCC Supreme Council in September 1992 and issued in December 1992. At the same time the GCC Supreme Council approved the establishment of the GCC Patent Office, to be located in Riyadh, Saudi Arabia.

78 Kuwait, Law No. 4 of 1962 governing Patents, Designs and Industrial Models, as amended, arts. 2 and 15.

79 UAE, Federal Law No. 44 of 1992 concerning the Organisation and Protection of Patents, Industrial Drawings and Industrial Designs, arts. 6 and 14. See also USTR, 1995 National Trade Estimates, Gulf Cooperation Council Chapter, available at <http://www.ustr.gov/html/1995_gcc.html>, last accessed 21 April 2005.

80 See WTO, Working Party on the Accession of the Sultanate of Oman, *Accession of the Sultanate of Oman: Additional Questions and Replies*, Document WT/ACC/OMN/22 (01–0140), 13 January 2000, 18–19.

81 GCC Unified Patent Regulations, September 1992, art. 15.

82 Oman, Ministerial Regulation No. 219/1993, adopting the GCC Unified Patent Regulations as the Patents Law of Oman.

83 'Regional Update' (1989), 3, *World Intellectual Property Report*, p. 12.

84 Bahrain, Legislative Decree No. 10 of 1993; Saudi Arabia, Royal Decree No. M/11 of 1410 AH (1989); UAE, Federal Law No. 40 of 1992; Yemen, Law No. 19 of 1994.

85 See Reema Ali and Loubna Haddad, 'WTO Membership and Compliance in the Middle East Countries' (1999), 16(2), *Middle East Executive Reports*, p. 15; Rolf Meyer-Reumann, 'The Endeavours of Gulf Countries to Meet WTO Requirements' (2001), 16(1), *Arab Law Quarterly*, p. 49; Amin, op. cit., pp. 112, 126, 129.

86 The Universal Copyright Convention (UCC) comprises 25 articles, only 10 of which really address substantive issues of copyright protection, and two accompanying protocols and resolutions. The UCC was developed by UNESCO as an alternative to the Berne Convention for those states which disagreed with aspects of the Convention but still wished to participate in some form of multilateral copyright protection. These states included developing countries and the Soviet Union, which thought that the strong copyright protections granted by the Berne Convention overly benefited western copyright-exporting nations, the United States and most of Latin America. The United States and Latin America were already members of a Pan-American copyright convention, which was weaker than the Convention. The Berne Convention states also became party to the UCC, so that their copyrights would exist in non-Berne Convention states. Berne Convention states were concerned that the existence of the UCC would encourage parties to the Berne Convention to leave that convention and adopt the UCC instead. So the UCC included a clause stating that parties which were also Berne Convention parties need not apply the provisions of the Convention to any former Berne Convention state which renounced the Convention after 1951. Thus any state which adopts the Berne Convention is penalised if it then renounces it in favour of the UCC, since its copyrights might no longer exist in Berne Convention states (extracted from Wikipedia Encyclopaedia, available at <http//en.wikipedia.org/wiki/Universal_Copyright_Convention>).

87 Bahrain, Law No. 10 of 1993 concerning the Protection of Copyright, art. 35; Saudi Arabia, Royal Decree No. M/11 of 1410 AH (1989) Law on the Protection of Copyright, arts. 26 and 27; UAE, Federal Law No. 40 of 1992 concerning Copyright, arts. 33–36. The lodgement had to be made by the publisher and not by the author.

88 Hirst, op. cit., p. 10.

89 Ibid.

90 Oman, Royal Decree No. 7/1986. Qatar is listed by WIPO as having become a party to the Nairobi Treaty in July 1983, but Qatar does not appear to have issued any domestic decree or ministerial regulation, as it normally would have

done, authorising this action. Saudi Arabia enacted Royal Decree No. M/2 of 1406 AH (1986), approving accession to the Nairobi Treaty, but does not appear to have lodged the instruments of accession with WIPO, which does not record it as being party to the Treaty.

91 GCC Charter, 'The Concept and Foundations', p. 1, available at <http://www.gcc-sg.org/foundations.html>, last accessed 5 November 2005.

92 See R K Ramanazi, *The Gulf Cooperation Council: Record and Analysis* (1988).

93 GCC Charter, Preamble, p. 1, available at <http://www.gcc-sg,org/charter.html>, last accessed 5 November 2005.

94 Bahrain, Law No. 11 of 2006; Oman, Royal Decree No. 67/2008.

95 Interviews conducted by the author with officials from the Oman Ministry of Commerce and Industry and Bahrain Ministry of Commerce, December 2004.

96 Hansen, op. cit., p. 16.

97 WIPO Economic Development Sector, available at <http://www.wipo.int/eds/en>, last accessed 5 November 2005.

98 WIPO's current model laws (which it also describes as 'draft laws') address the major areas of intellectual property enshrined in TRIPS, namely, Copyright and Related Rights; Geographical Indications; Trademarks; Industrial Designs; Patents; Layout-Designs (Topographies) of Integrated Circuits; Protection Against Acts of Unfair Competition, including protection of secret information.

99 See WIPO document 'Legislative Assistance Provided by the World Intellectual Property Organization (WIPO) in Relation to the Implementation of the Agreement on Trade-Related Aspects of Intellectual Property Rights (the TRIPS Agreement) and the Doha Declaration', 8 July 2003, available at <http://www.wipo.int/info\CFD/legislativeassistance.htm>, last accessed 30 December 2004.

100 Interview by the author with officials of the Oman Ministry of Commerce and Industry, December 2004.

101 Article 63.2 of TRIPS requires members to notify the laws and regulations made effective by that member pertaining to the subject matter of TRIPS to the Council of TRIPS in order to assist the Council in its review of the operation of TRIPS. These notifications are the basis for the reviews carried out by the Council. Initially the reviews focused on those WTO members that were developed countries and not entitled to a transition period. In 2000 reviews began for countries that had delayed notifying their laws until 2000, and continued throughout 2001. The reviews encompassed some 70 countries, although many of these members put into effect national legislation to implement much of TRIPS before January 2000. The record of the submissions made by the interviewed states, including the questions posed to them and their responses, is available at WTO Document series IP/C/W and IP/N.

102 See WTO, 'Report of the Working Party on the Accession of Oman to the World Trade Organization', WTO Document WT/ACC/OMN/26, 28 September 2000 (00–3948), Annex 1, p. 11.

103 Interviews conducted by the author with officials from the Oman Ministry of Commerce and Industry, and Ministry of Heritage and Culture; Bahrain, Ministry of Commerce, and Ministry of Cabinet Affairs and Information; Qatar, Ministry of Finance, Economy and Commerce; UAE, Ministry of Information and Culture, and Ministry of Economy and Commerce. December 2004.

Interviews conducted by the author in November 2003 with WIPO officials in Geneva confirmed that WIPO Arab Bureau staff also viewed their relationship with the state ministries responsible for intellectual property matters as being both positive and reciprocal, and one which both sides have strived to foster.

104 See Peter Drahos, 'Developing Countries and International Intellectual Property Standard-setting' (2002), 5, *Journal of World Intellectual Property*, p. 777.
105 WIPO, *General Information*, 1 (WIPO Publication No. 400(E)).
106 Drahos, op. cit., p. 777.
107 Carlos Correa, 'Implementing the TRIPS Agreement' (1998), 1, *Journal of World Intellectual Property*, p. 75.
108 Ibid.
109 Ibid, p. 82.
110 As reported in 'USTR's Annual Report: GCC Trade and Investment Barriers' (1995), 18(5), *Middle East Executive Report*, pp. 13–17.
111 Hirst, op. cit., p. 12.

4 TRIPS and the nature of compliance by the Gulf states

1 Specifically, members are obliged to comply with:
- Articles 1–12 and 19 of the Paris Convention, generally in respect of TRIPS Parts II, III and IV and specifically in respect of TRIPS' provisions on trademarks, geographical indications and undisclosed information;
- Articles 1–21 (except Article 6bis) of the Berne Convention and its Appendix in respect of TRIPS Part II, Section 1, copyright and related rights;
- Articles 1–6, 10, 12–15 and 19 of the Rome Convention in respect of permitted exceptions to the rights of performers, producers and broadcast organisations;
- Articles 2–7 (other than Article 6.3), Article 12 and Article 16 of the Washington Treaty.

2 TRIPS Part II, Standards Concerning the Availability, Scope and Use of Intellectual Property Rights addresses the seven intellectual property rights of Copyright and Related Rights (Articles 9–14), Trademarks (Articles 15–21), Geographical Indications (Articles 22–24), Industrial Designs (Articles 25–26), Patents (Articles 27–34), Layout Designs of Integrated Circuits (Articles 35–38), Undisclosed Information (Article 39) and Anti-competitive Practices in Contractual Licences (Article 40).
3 Carlos Correa, 'Implementing the TRIPS Agreement in the Patent Field – Options for Developing Countries' (1998), 1, *Journal of World Intellectual Property*, p. 16.
4 Ibid, p. 3.
5 Kuwait, Law No. 64 of 1999, art. 43.
6 Kuwait, Law No. 4 of 1962, art. 5.
7 Qatar, Law No. 7 of 2002, art. 5; Law No. 9 of 2002, art. 2.
8 Saudi Arabia, Royal Decree No. M/211423 (2002), art. 4; Royal Decree No. M/41 of 1424 (2003), art. 18.
9 UAE, Federal Law No. 44 of 1992, art. 2; Federal Law No. 37 of 1992, art. 5.
10 Oman, Royal Decree No. 65/2008, art. 59.
11 WTO Council for Trade-Related Aspects of Intellectual Property Rights, *Review of Legislation: Oman*, WTO Document IP/Q/OMN/1 (03–1675), 24 March 2003.
12 Yemen, Law No. 19 of 1994, arts. 6, 64 and 120.
13 TRIPS art. 9.1. Article 2 of the Berne Convention lists the main group of artistic and literary works which is entitled to receive protection. This group includes the following:

'(1) The expression 'literary and artistic works' shall include every production in the literary, scientific and artistic domain, whatever may be the mode or form of its expression, such as books, pamphlets and other writings; lectures, addresses, sermons and other works of the same nature; dramatic or dramatico-musical works; choreographic works and entertainments in dumb show; musical compositions with or without words; cinematographic works to which are assimilated works expressed by a process analogous to cinematography; works of drawing, painting, architecture, sculpture, engraving and lithography; photographic works to which are assimilated works expressed by a process analogous to photography; works of applied art; illustrations, maps, plans, sketches and three-dimensional works relative to geography, topography, architecture or science.

----

(3) Translations, adaptations, arrangements of music and other alterations of a literary or artistic work shall be protected as original works without prejudice to the copyright in the original work.

----

(5) Collections of literary or artistic works such as encyclopaedias and anthologies which, by reason of the selection and arrangement of their contents, constitute intellectual creations shall be protected as such, without prejudice to the copyright in each of the works forming part of such collections.'

14 TRIPS, art. 10.1.
15 Ibid, art. 10.2.
16 The Berne Convention, art. 7 provides that a literary work shall be protected for the life of the author plus 50 years, while the minimum term of protection for a photograph or work of applied art shall be 25 years.
17 TRIPS, art. 12.
18 Ibid, art. 14.5.
19 Kuwait, Law No. 64 of 1999, art. 1 and UAE Federal Law No. 7 of 2002, both include almost identical definitions.
20 Bahrain, Legislative Decree No. 22 of 2006, art. 1; Oman, Royal Decree No. 65/2008, art. 1; Qatar, Law No. 7 of 2002, art. 1; Saudi Arabia, Royal Decree No. M/48 of 1424 (2003), art. 1.
21 Bahrain, Legislative Decree No. 22 of 2006, art. 2; Kuwait, Law No. 64 of 1999, art. 1; Oman, Royal Decree No. 65/2008, art. 2; Qatar Law No. 7 of 2002, art. 2; Saudi Arabia, Royal Decree No. M/41 of 1424 AH (2003), art. 2; UAE, Federal Law No.7 of 2002, art. 2.
22 As stipulated in Bahrain, Legislative Decree No. 22 of 2006, art. 2; Oman, Royal Decree No. 65/2008, sect. 2.
23 Bahrain, Legislative Decree No. 22 of 2006, art. 3; Oman, Royal Decree No. 65/2008, sect. 3.
24 Kuwait, by Law No. 64 of 1999, art. 2, still recognises computer works including software and databases or computer programs as entitled to protection, but does not take the additional steps of the other GCC member states.
25 Saudi Arabia, Royal Decree No. M/41 1424 AH (2003), art. 15(12).
26 UAE Federal Law No. 7 of 2002, art. 2(2).
27 Saudi Arabia, Royal Decree No. M/41 of 1424 AH (2003), art. 19(1)(6).
28 Bahrain, Legislative Decree No. 22 of 2006, Chapter 7, arts. 37–44.
29 Oman, Royal Decree No. 65/2008, arts. 26 and 27.
30 Ibid, arts. 28–33.
31 Yemen, Law No. 19 of 1994, arts. 23–27.
32 Bahrain, Legislative Decree No. 22 of 2006, art. 5; Kuwait, Law No. 64 of 1999, arts. 1, 2 and 5; Oman, Royal Decree No. 65/2008, art. 5; Qatar, Law No. 7 of 2002, arts. 7–14; Saudi Arabia, Royal Decree No. M/41 of 1424 AH (2003), arts. 8–9; UAE, Federal Law No. 7 of 2002, arts. 5, 7–8; Yemen, Law No. 19 of 1994, arts. 12–13 and 18–19.

33 Qatar, Law No. 7 of 2002, art. 29; Saudi Arabia, Royal Decree No. M/11 of 1410, art. 17.
34 Alastair Hirst, 'A Comprehensive Reform of the UAE Copyright Law' (2002), 1, *Middle East Executive Reports*, p. 17.
35 Bahrain, Legislative Decree No. 22 of 2006, arts. 14–15; Kuwait, Law No. 64 of 1999, art. 15; Oman, Royal Decree No. 65/2008, art. 15; Qatar, Law No. 7 of 2002, art. 40; UAE, Federal Law No. 7 of 2002, art. 16.
36 Bahrain, Legislative Decree No. 22 of 2006, arts. 16–17; Kuwait, Law No. 64 of 1999, art. 15; Oman, Royal Decree No. 65/2008, arts. 16–17; Qatar, Law No. 7 of 2002, arts. 41–42; UAE, Federal Law No. 7 of 2002, arts. 18–19.
37 Qatar, Law No. 7 of 2002, art. 40(2); UAE, Federal Law No.7 of 2002, art. 17.
38 Bahrain, Legislative Decree No. 22 of 2006, art. 32; Kuwait, Law No. 64 of 1999, art. 18; Oman, Royal Decree No. 65/2008, art. 21; Qatar, Law No. 7 of 2002, art. 46; UAE, Federal Law No. 7 of 2002, art. 25.
39 Bahrain, Legislative Decree No. 22 of 2006, arts. 31–32; Kuwait, Law No. 64 of 1999, arts 20–21; Oman, Royal Decree No. 65/2008, art. 25; Qatar, Law No. 7 of 2002, art. 35; Saudi Arabia, Royal Decree No. M/41 of 1424 AH (2003), art. 5(3); UAE, Federal Law No. 7 of 2002, art. 27.
40 Bahrain, Legislative Decree No. 22 of 2006, art. 35; Kuwait, Law No. 64 of 1999, art. 22; Oman, Royal Decree No. 65/2008, art. 24; Qatar, Law No. 7 of 2002, art. 36; Saudi Arabia, Royal Decree No. M/41 of 1424 AH (2003), art. 5; UAE, Federal Law No. 7 of 2002, art. 27.
41 Bahrain, Legislative Decree No. 22 of 2006, arts. 33 and 35; Kuwait, Law No. 4 of 1999, art. 26; Oman, Royal Decree No. 65/2008, arts. 22–23; Qatar, Law No. 7 of 2002 art. 34; Saudi Arabia, Royal Decree No. M/41 of 1424 AH (2003), art. 6(3); UAE, Federal Law No. 7 of 2002, art. 26.
42 Qatar, Law No. 7 of 2002, art. 27; Saudi Arabia, Royal Decree No. M/ 41 of 1424 AH (2003), art. 16; UAE, Federal Law No. 7 of 2002, art. 21.
43 Saudi Arabia, Royal Decree No. M/ 41 of 1424 AH (2003), art. 16.
44 Bahrain, Legislative Decree No. 22 of 2006, arts. 57–61; Oman, Royal Decree No. 65/2008, arts. 35–39; UAE, Federal Law No. 7 of 2002, arts 30–33.
45 Bahrain, Legislative Decree No. 22 of 2006, art. 45; Oman, Royal Decree No. 65/2008, art. 41; Qatar, Law No. 7 of 2002, art. 51; Saudi Arabia, Royal Decree No. M/41 of 1424 AH (2003), art. 21.
46 Bahrain, Legislative Decree No. 22 of 2006, arts. 48–49 and 51–54.
47 The nature of sanctions across all intellectual property laws of the Gulf states is discussed in greater detail in Section 5.2 in Chapter 5.
48 Oman, Royal Decree No. 67/2008, the Law on Industrial Property Rights, Title II, Part 1, ss 36–47.
49 Bahrain, Legislative Decree No. 11 of 2006, art. 2.
50 Oman, Royal Decree No. 67/2008, s 1.
51 Saudi Arabia, Royal Decree No. M/21 of 1423 AH (2002), art. 1.
52 Qatar, Law No. 9 of 1992, arts. 1 and 6.
53 Kuwait, Law No. 1 of 2001, art. 61; UAE, Federal Law No. 37 of 1992, art. 2.
54 As prescribed by UAE, Federal Law No. 37 of 1992, as amended by Federal Law No. 8 of 2002, art. 3.
55 Of which the six GCC member states and Yemen are also members. The boycott, which is still officially in force, operates on three levels: primary level, which prohibits direct business dealings with Israel; secondary level, which prohibits dealing with blacklisted firms which do business with Israel, which may include registering a trademark in Israel; and tertiary level, which prohibits dealing with firms which deal with blacklisted firms.

In 1994, the states decided to end the secondary and tertiary levels of the boycott, while notionally continuing with the primary level. The United States continues to pressure the states, particularly Saudi Arabia, to end the boycott. The pressure upon Saudi Arabia has been effective, since it has recently agreed to end its participation in the boycott as part of the package of conditions imposed upon it by the United States in return for US approval of Saudi Arabia's accession to the WTO.

56 Bahrain, Legislative Decree No. 11 of 2006, arts. 27 and 28; Kuwait, Law No. 1 of 2001, art. 62.5; Oman, Royal Decree No. 67/2008, sect. 36(2); Qatar, Law No. 9 of 2002, art. 2; Saudi Arabia, Royal Decree No. M/21 of 1424 AH (2002), art. 2(i); UAE, Federal Law No. 37 of 1992 as amended by Federal Law No. 8 of 2002, art. 4.

57 Qatar, Law No. 9 of 2002, art. 10; Oman, Royal Decree No. 67/2008, sect. 38(4); Saudi Arabia, Law No. M/21 of 1423 AH (2002), art. 9.

58 Bahrain, Legislative Decree No. 11 of 2006, art. 15; Oman, Royal Decree No. 67/2008, s 39; Qatar, Law No. 9 of 2002, art. 20; Saudi Arabia, Royal Decree No. M/21 of 1423 AH (2002), art. 21; UAE, Federal Law No. 37 of 1992 as amended by Federal Law No. 8 of 2002, art. 17.

59 Bahrain, Legislative Decree No. 11 of 2006, art. 6; Kuwait, Law No. 2 of 1961 as amended by Law No. 6 of 1980 and Law No. 3 of 1999, art. 65; Oman, Royal Decree No. 67/2008, s 36; Qatar, Law No. 9 of 2002, art. 7; Saudi Arabia, Royal Decree No. M/21 of 1423 AH (2002), art. 21; UAE, Federal Law No. 37 of 1992 as amended by Federal Law No. 8 of 2002, art. 17.

60 The Arabic or Hajri calendar is based on lunar months rather than the western Gregorian calendar, and is marginally shorter. Hence, ten Hajri years is approximately equivalent to nine years and eight months according to the Gregorian calendar. Saudi Arabia has removed reference to the Hajri calendar in its current trademark law.

61 Bahrain, Legislative Decree No. 11 of 2006, arts. 24–26; Oman, Royal Decree No. 67/2008, ss 24–26 and 45; Qatar, Law No. 9 of 2002, art. 22; Saudi Arabia, Royal Decree No. M/21 of 1423 AH (2002), art. 29; UAE, Federal Law No. 37 of 1992, arts. 30–32.

62 Oman, Royal Decree No. 67/2008, s 41(1), the responsible minister being the Minister for Commerce and Industry.

63 Bahrain, Legislative Decree No. 11 of 2006, art. 23; Kuwait, Law No. 2 of 1961 as amended by Law No. 6 of 1980 and Law No. 3 of 1999, arts. 68 and 83; Oman, Royal Decree No. 67/2008 s 45(3); Qatar, Law No. 9 of 2002, art. 21; Saudi Arabia, Royal Decree No. M/21 of 1423 AH (2002), art. 31; UAE, Federal Law No. 37 of 1992, art. 28.

64 Some commentators claim that the Kuwaiti, Qatari and Saudi trademark laws themselves prohibit the registration of marks for goods or services relating to alcoholic beverages; see Abu Ghazali Intellectual Property, *Intellectual Property Handbook 2007*, country entries for Kuwait, Qatar and Saudi Arabia, available at <http://www.agip.com/lAGIP_Handbook.pdf>, last accessed 30 June 2008; see also Amir Khoury, 'The Development of Modern Trademark Legislation and Protection in the Arab Countries of the Middle East' (2000), p. 16, *The Transnational Lawyer,* 278. This is not quite accurate, since the prohibition lies in the interpretation and application of the public order and public morals provision of the trademark law rather than an express prohibition in the law itself.

65 See Abu Ghazali Intellectual Property, *Intellectual Property Handbook 2007*, respective country entries, available at <http://www.agip.com/lAGIP_Handbook.pdf>, last accessed 30 June 2008.

66 Qatar, Implementing Regulations for Amiri Law No. 3 of 1978, art. 3, Appendix 1.

67 See Rawan Makram Sunna, 'Bridging the Gulf: Harmonisation of Trade Mark Laws in the Gulf Cooperation Council Countries' (2003), 1, *Trademark World*, Supplement, p. 29. See also the respective country entries in the following regional legal attorneys and trademark and patents agents: AGIP, op. cit.; ST&P, Attorneys and Agents at <http://www.stplegal.com>, last accessed 30 November 2005; NJQ 7 & Associates at <http://www.qumsieh.com>, last accessed 30 November 2005; Saba & Co Group at <http://www.sabaip.com>, last accessed 30 November 2005.

Kuwait has reported to the WTO Council of TRIPS, that 'since acquiring, marketing or importing wines and spirits is prohibited, protection of such marks may be rejected for resulting in a breach of morality and public order', WTO Document IP/Q4/KWT/1 (01–6322), 13 December 2001, 15. Saudi Arabia also reportedly prohibits registrations in class 28 for 'Christmas trees and related products' (reported by Saba & Co Group, above).

The rules of the GCC Customs Union, which entered into force on 1 January 2003, recognise and categorise pork, alcoholic products and tobacco products as 'special goods' and further recognise that the GCC states may import or prohibit them at their own discretion.

68 Reported in the Al-Tamimi Law Update April 2004, 31, available at <http://www.tamimi.com/catalog/1998_2004/pdf/april%20LU.pdf>, last accessed 6 January 2006.

69 Saudi Arabia, Royal Decree No. M/21 of 1423 AH (2002), arts. 43–44.

70 Kuwait, Law No. 2 of 1961 as amended by Law No. 6 of 1980 and Law No. 3 of 1999, art. 92.

71 Bahrain, Legislative Decree No. 11 of 2006, art. 47.

72 Oman, Royal Decree No. 67/2008, s 67.

73 See, for example, J Keon, 'Intellectual Property Rules for Trade Marks and Geographical Indications: Important Particles of the New World Order' in Correa and Abdulqawi (eds), *Intellectual Property and International Trade – The TRIPS Agreement* (1998), p. 178.

74 Ibid, p. 176.

75 Kuwait, Law No. 1 of 2001, art. 62(6) and (7); Saudi Arabia, Royal Decree M/21 of 1423 AH (2002), art. 2(f); UAE, Federal Law No. 37 of 1992, as amended by Federal Law No. 8 of 2002, art. 3(6).

76 As expressed by Qatar, Law No. 9 of 2002, art. 1; Oman, Royal Decree No. 67/2008, s 49.

77 As expressed by Bahrain, Legislative Decree No. 16 of 2004, art. 2.

78 See, for example, Oman, Royal Decree No. 67/2008, arts. 52 and 53.

79 As expressed by Qatar, Law No. 9 of 2002, art. 39.

80 Bahrain, Legislative Decree No. 16 of 2004, art. 9; Oman, Royal Decree No. 67/2008, sect. 51.

81 Qatar, Law No. 9 of 2002, art. 38.

82 Non-Muslim expatriates who earn above a prescribed minimum monthly wage, may buy a licence fee and registration book from the Muscat police headquarters enabling them to purchase specified amounts of alcohol at specially designated (and discreetly disguised) shops.

83 WTO Council for Trade-Related Aspects of Intellectual Property Rights, *Review of Legislation: Oman*, Document IP/Q/OMN/1 (03–1675), 24 March 2003, p. 6.

84 J Phillips, 'Protecting Values in Industrial Designs', in Correa and Abdulqawi (eds), *Intellectual Property and International Trade – The TRIPS Agreement* (1998), p. 179.

85 Originally, Kuwait, Law No. 4 of 1962, the Law of Patents, Designs and Industrial Models, as amended by Law No. 4 of 1999 and Law No. 3 of 2001.

86 Ibid, arts. 42–45.

87 UAE, Law No. 17 of 2002, specifically arts. 43–53; Saudi Arabia, Royal Decree M/27 of 1425 (AH) (2004), arts. 59–60. Prior to the introduction in mid 2004 of this omnibus law on patents, layout-designs of integrated circuits, new plant varieties and industrial models, industrial designs were not protectable or registrable in Saudi Arabia, due to the absence of a dedicated design statute or any provision in its other intellectual property legislation.

88 Oman, Royal Decree No. 67/2008, art. 1.

89 UAE, Federal Law No. 17 of 2002, art. 1.

90 Kuwait, Law No. 4 of 1962 as amended by Law No. 4 of 1999 and Law No. 3 of 2001, art. 35.

91 Saudi Arabia, Royal Decree No. M/27 of 1425 AH (2004), art. 4.

92 Oman, Royal Decree No. 67/2008, s 20; Saudi Arabia, Royal Decree No. M/27 of 1425 AH (2004) arts. 2, 59; UAE, Federal Law No. 17 of 2002, arts. 1 and 4.

93 Qatar, Law No. 9 of 2002, art. 44.

94 Saudi Arabia, Royal Decree No. M/27 of 1425 AH (2004) art. 1; UAE, Federal Law No. 17 of 2002, art. 2.

95 Oman, Royal Decree No. 67/2008, s 68; Saudi Arabia, Royal Decree No. M/27 of 1425 AH (2004) art. 34.

96 Qatar, Law 9 of 2002, art. 12; UAE, Federal Law No. 17 of 2002, arts. 51 and 62.

97 Bahrain, Legislative Decree No. 6 of 2006, art. 30; Kuwait, Law No. 4 of 1962 as amended by Law No. 4 of 1999 and Law No. 3 of 2001, art. 46; Yemen, Law No. 19 of 1994, art. 114.

98 TRIPS, art. 28.1.

99 Ibid, art. 33.

100 Ibid, art. 30.

101 The term 'compulsory licence' does not appear in TRIPS, although it is used in the Paris Convention. The term used is 'other use without authorisation'.

102 TRIPS, art. 31.

103 For example, the USTR's Special 301 Report for 2008 makes little comment on the status (parlous or otherwise) of patent protection in the GCC member states. The only remarks expressing concern were directed towards Kuwait over undue delays in upgrading its outdated intellectual property laws, including its patent law. See USTR, *2008 Special 301 Report*, available at <http://www.ustr.gov/assets/Document_Library/Reports_Publications/2008/2008_Special_301_Report/asset_upload_file553_14869.pdf?ht=>, last accessed 30 June 2008.

104 See United States Patent and Trademark Office Statistical Report, 'Patents By Country, State, and Year – All Patent Types, Granted: 01/01/1977 – 12/31/2007', available at <http://www.uspto.gov/web/offices/ac/ido/oeip/taf/cst_all.htm>, last accessed 30 June 2008. The report displays the number of US patents by country of origin, which is determined by the place of residence (as distinct from country of nationality) of the first-named inventor. The report includes utility patents, design patents, plant patents, reissue patents, statutory invention registrations and defensive publications. On the assumption that any patent for which protection was sought beyond the country of origin would, as a first priority, seek protection in the United States, the report is a fairly accurate indication of the extent of patent activity in the Gulf region. The report indicates that, over the 30 years from 1977 to 2004, patents were granted to residents in the Arab Gulf states as follows: Bahrain – 5; Kuwait – 96; Oman – 2; Qatar – 5; Saudi Arabia – 270; UAE – 58.

105 Under the 1992 GCC Regulations, duplication of application or registration with the GCC Patent Office and with any GCC state national patent office was not permitted. The GCC Patent Office would not accept any patent application

if a separate application had already been lodged or a patent granted in a member state, unless the applicant undertook to first relinquish the national application or patent or as soon as a patent was provisionally granted by the GCC Patent Office (GCC Unified Patent Regulations, art. 29; Patent Office Guidelines, para 11). The force of this cumbersome restriction was never effectively tested, since none of the member states issued a patent in its own right and originating from its own nationals (as distinct from an international patent) by the time this restriction was deleted by the year 2000 amendments.

106 Bahrain, Legislative Decree No. 1 of 2004, art. 1; Kuwait, Law No. 4 of 1962 as amended by Law No. 4 of 1999, art. 1; Oman, Royal Decree No. 67/2008, s 2; Qatar, Law No. 30 of 2006, art. 2; Saudi Arabia, Royal Decree No. M/27 of 1425 AH (2004), art. 43; UAE, Federal Law No. 17 of 2002, art. 4; Yemen, Law No. 19 of 1994, arts. 59–60.

107 Oman, Royal Decree No. 67/2008, s 3.

108 Bahrain, Legislative Decree No. 1 of 2004, art. 30; Oman, Royal Decree No. 65/2008, ss 1 and 15; Kuwait, Law No. 4 of 1962 as amended by Law No. 4 of 1999, art. 34bis; UAE, Federal Law No. 17 of 2002, art. 1.

109 Reported in AGIP News, June 2004, 2, at <http://www.agip.com/bulletin_sub.aspx?year=2004&month=6&lang=en>, last accessed 30 June 2007.

110 Saudi Arabia, Royal Decree No. M/27 of 1425 AH (2004), art. 4(a); GCC Unified Patent Regulations, art. 2.

111 UAE, Federal Law No. 17 of 2002, art. 6.2.

112 Oman, Royal Decree No. 67/2008, s 2(1)(c) and 2(2).

113 Bahrain, Legislative Decree No. 1 of 2004 as amended by Law No. 14 of 2006, art. 3(a).

114 Kuwait, Law No. 4 of 1962, art. 2(2); UAE, Federal Law No. 44 of 1992, art. 6(ii).

115 Yemen, Law No. 19 of 1994, art. 65.

116 Bahrain, Legislative Decree No. 1 of 2004, art. 11.2; Oman, Royal Decree No. 67/2008, s 11; UAE, Federal Law No. 17 of 2002, art. 15.

117 Kuwait, Law No. 4 of 1962, art. 10.

118 Bahrain, Legislative Decree No. 1 of 2004, art. 14; Kuwait, Law No. 4 of 1962 as amended by Law No. 4 of 1999, art. 12; Oman, Royal Decree No. 67/2008, s 12(1); Qatar, Law No. 30 of 2006, art. 11; Saudi Arabia, Royal Decree No. M/27 of 1425 AH (2004), art. 19; UAE, Federal Law No. 17 of 2002, art. 14.

119 Kuwait, Law No. 4 of 1999, art. 34bis (a).

120 Bahrain, Legislative Decree No. 1 of 2004, as amended by Legislative Decree No. 14 of 2006, art. 14(b)–(c); Oman, Royal Decree No. 67/2008, s 12.

121 Yemen, Law No. 19 of 1994, art. 77.

122 Oman, Royal Decree No. 67/2008, s 74(3); Saudi Arabia Royal Decree No. M/27 of 1424 AH (2004), art. 48.

123 Bahrain, Legislative Decree No. 1 of 2004, as amended by Legislative Decree No. 14 of 2006, art. 12.

124 In June 2002, the UAE reported to the WTO Council of TRIPS, in a response to questions from members, that the draft amendments to its patent law provided that 'in the case of litigation concerning process patents, the court shall have the authority to order a defendant to prove the manufacturing process which he has used is different from the process protected by the Patent'. However, this provision does not appear in the settled law, which was enacted later that year. See WTO Document IP/C/W/291/Add.2 (02–1093), 5 March 2002, p. 3.

125 Fred Warshovsky, as quoted by Carlos Correa in Correa and Abdulqawi (eds), *Intellectual Property and International Trade – The TRIPS Agreement* (1998), p. 217.

126 Bahrain, Legislative Decree No. 1 of 2004, art. 25; Kuwait, Law No. 4 of 1962 as amended by Law No. 4 of 1999, art. 29; Oman, Royal Decree No. 67/2008, s 13; Qatar, Law No. 30 of 2006, art. 15; Saudi Arabia, Royal Decree No. M/27 of 1425 AH (2004), art. 24; UAE, Federal Law No. 17 of 2002, art. 24.

127 Bahrain, Legislative Decree No. 1 of 2004, art. 25; Oman, Royal Decree No. 67/2008, s 13(9); Saudi Arabia, Royal Decree No. M/27 of 1425 AH (2004), art. 24(b); UAE, Federal Law No. 17 of 2002, art. 24.1(h).

128 Qatar, Law No. 30 of 2006, art. 15; UAE, Federal Law No. 17 of 2000, art. 24.2.

129 In the case of the UAE, WTO Council for Trade-Related Aspects of Intellectual Property Rights, *Review of Legislation: the United Arab Emirates*, Document IP/C/W/291 (01–3419), 10 July 2001, 5. The UAE has also clouded the issue on importation. It originally advised the Council of TRIPS that 'in defending his position, the owner of the patent cannot introduce imported product as a valid ground. It does not present a legitimate reason for avoiding compulsory licensing if one or more of the reasons referred to in the above-mentioned Article 23 of the Patent Law are met'. When the UAE was further questioned on this point, it advised that 'the approved amendment of the Article 23 of the Patent and Designs Law doesn't stipulate any more that the importation of the product is not considered legal justification for the owner to avoid compulsory licence. Therefore, the Patent law related provisions are now in conformity with Article 27 and 31 of the TRIPS Agreement' (WTO Document IP/C/W/291/Add. 3 (02–3461), 24 June 2002). However, when the settled law was issued a few months later, it retained the provision of the earlier law that excluded importation as working the patent.

130 WTO Council for Trade-Related Aspects of Intellectual Property Rights, *Review of Legislation: Oman*, Document IP/Q/OMN/1 (03–1675), 24 March 2003.

131 WTO Council for Trade-Related Aspects of Intellectual Property Rights, *Checklist of Issues on Enforcement: Responses from Qatar*, Document IP/C/W/291/Add 3 (02–3461), 24 June 2002.

132 There would have been little point in the United States bringing such a dispute to the WTO's Dispute Settlement Body (DSB), since it had already 'covered the ground' on this issue with its dispute against Brazil in May 2000 (DS199 of 30 May 2000) in respect of the provisions on the local working of a patent in Article 68 of Brazil's industrial property law. The position already taken by Brazil was very similar to that adopted by Bahrain, Oman and the UAE. In what was more or less a face-saving win for both sides, the US agreed to withdraw the dispute and settle its differences with Brazil outside the formal WTO DSB forum. It also acknowledged that its dispute related to the potential use by Brazil of its Article 68 rather than any actual application. In return, Brazil, while asserting that its patent law did not contravene TRIPS Article 27, agreed to hold prior consultation with the US if it ever decided to impose a compulsory licence on a US-held patent in Brazil. See WTO Dispute Settlement: *Dispute DS199: Brazil – Measure Affecting Patent Protection* and WTO Dispute Settlement: *Dispute DS224: United States – US Patent Code*, Documents WT/DS199/1 and 3 (01–0093 and 01–3506), both available at <http://www.wto.org/english/tratop_e/dispu_e/>, last accessed 25 July 2005.

133 Namely, the President of the King Abdul Aziz City for Science and Technology (KACST), the national centre responsible for patents, and all other industrial property, policy and administration. See Royal Decree No. M/27 of 1425 AH (2004), arts. 27–28.

134 UAE, Federal Law No. 17 of 2002, arts. 28, 29.1.

135 Kuwait, Law No. 4 of 1962 as amended by Law No. 4 of 1999, art. 29.

136 Bahrain, Legislative Decree No. 1 of 2004, as amended by Law No. 14 of 2006, art. 36; Oman, Royal Decree No. 67/2008, s 14; UAE, Federal Law No. 17 of 2002, art. 29.2.
137 GCC Unified Patent Regulations as amended 2000, art. 20.3.
138 See GCC Patent Office news, available at <http://www.gulf-patent-office.org.sa/Regulationframe.htm>, last accessed 30 November 2004.
139 As stipulated by Saudi Royal Decree No. M/27 of 1425 AH (2004), art. 34.
140 Oman, Royal Decree No. 67/2008, s 66(1); UAE, Federal Law No. 17 of 2002, art. 62.
141 Bahrain, Legislative Decree No. 1 of 2004, as amended by Legislative Decree No. 14 of 2006, art. 41; Kuwait, Law No. 4 of 1999, art. 46.
142 See Yemen, Law No. 19 of 1994, arts 49–57.
143 Washington Treaty on Intellectual Property in Respect of Integrated Circuits, arts. 2–7 (except art. 6(3)), art. 12 and art. 16(3). The Washington Treaty was opened for signature in May 1989, but has never come into force. Articles 2 (i) and (ii) of the Treaty define an integrated circuit and layout-design (topography) as follows:
– 'an 'integrated circuit' means a product, in its final form or an intermediate form, in which the elements, at least one of which is an active element, and some or all of the interconnections are integrally formed in and/or on a piece of material and which is intended to perform an electronic function;
– a 'layout-design (topography)' is defined as the three-dimensional disposition, however expressed, of the elements, at least one of which is an active element, and of some or all of the interconnections of an integrated circuit, or such a three-dimensional disposition prepared for an integrated circuit intended for manufacture.'
144 Carlos Correa, 'Layout Designs of Integrated Circuits', in Correa and Abdulqawi (eds), *Intellectual Property and International Trade – The TRIPS Agreement* (1998), pp. 234–5.
145 TRIPS, art. 35 and Rome Convention, art. 3.2.
146 TRIPS, art. 36.
147 Ibid, art. 38.2–3.
148 Carlos Correa, 'Layout Designs of Integrated Circuits', in Correa and Abdulqawi (eds), *Intellectual Property and International Trade – The TRIPS Agreement* (1998), p. 234.
149 See Bahrain, Legislative Decree No. 5 of 2006, arts. 7–9.
150 See WTO Council for Trade-Related Aspects of Intellectual Property Rights, *Review of Legislation: Kuwait*, Document IP/Q4/KWT/1 (01–6332), 13 December 2001, p. 28.
151 Kuwait, Law No. 4 of 1999, art. 1.
152 Oman, Royal Decree No. 67/2008, ss 27–35.
153 Saudi Arabia, Royal Decree No. M/27 of 1425 AH (2004), arts. 49–53.
154 WTO Council for Trade-Related Aspects of Intellectual Property Rights, *Review of Legislation: the United Arab Emirates*, Document IP/C/W/291 (01–3419), 10 July 2001. UAE Federal Law No. 44 of 1992, arts. 43–51, applied specifically to industrial designs and models and does not make any reference to layout-designs.
155 WTO Council for Trade-Related Aspects of Intellectual Property Rights, *Review of Legislation: the United Arab Emirates*, Document IP/C/W/291.Add.2 (02–1093), 3 March 2002, p. 3.
156 See WIPO, 'Draft Act on the Protection of Layout-Designs (Topographies) of Integrated Circuits', available at <http://www.wipo.int/cfdiplaw/en/trips/doc/integrated_circuits.doc>, last accessed 20 January 2006.

157 Bahrain, Legislative Decree No. 5 of 2006, art. 1; Oman, Royal Decree No. 67/2008, s 1; Qatar, Law No. 6 of 2005, art. 1; Saudi Arabia, Royal Decree No. M/27 of 1425 AH (2004), art. 2.

158 Bahrain, Legislative Decree No. 5 of 2006, art. 2; Oman, Royal Decree No. 67/2008, s 27; Qatar, Law No. 6 of 2005, art. 6; Saudi Arabia, Royal Decree No. M/27 of 1425 AH (2004), art. 49.

159 Bahrain, Legislative Decree No. 5 of 2006, arts. 6, 10, 12 and 15; Oman, Royal Decree No. 67/2008, s 29; Qatar, Law No. 6 of 2005, arts. 3–4; Saudi Arabia, Royal Decree No. M/27 of 1425 AH (2004), arts. 49–53.

160 Bahrain, Legislative Decree No. 5 of 2006, art. 13; Qatar, Law No. 6 of 2005, art. 8; Saudi Arabia, Royal Decree No. M/27 of 1425 AH (2004), art. 19(b).

161 Oman, Royal Decree No. 67/2008, s 31.

162 Bahrain, Legislative Decree No. 1 of 2004, art. 23; Saudi Arabia, Royal Decree No. M/27 of 1425 AH (2004), art. 24.

163 Bahrain, Legislative Decree No. 5 of 2006, art. 10; Oman, Royal Decree No. 67/2008, art. 29(1); Saudi Arabia, Royal Decree No. M/27 of 1425 AH (2004), art. 51.

164 The Paris Convention, art. 10bis, requires countries to provide effective protection against unfair competition. Any act of competition contrary to honest practices in commercial or industrial matters is an act of unfair competition. In particular, the following are prohibited:

- all acts which create confusion by any means in respect of the establishment, goods, or activities of a competitor;
- false allegations in the course of trade which discredit the establishment, goods or activities of a competitor;
- indications or allegations the use of which is liable to mislead the public in respect of the nature, manufacturing process, characteristics, suitability of purpose, or quantity of goods.

165 A note to TRIPS Article 39 describes 'a manner contrary to honest commercial practices' as at least: 'practices such as breach of contract, breach of confidence and inducement to breach, and includes the acquisition of undisclosed information by third parties which knew, or were grossly negligent in failing to know, that such practices were involved in the acquisition.'

166 WTO Council for Trade-Related Aspects of Intellectual Property Rights, *Review of Legislation: Kuwait*, Document IP/Q4/KWT/1 (01–6322), 13 December 2001.

167 WTO Working Party on the Accession of the Kingdom of Saudi Arabia, *Additional Questions and Replies*, Document WT/ACC/SAU/6/Add.3 (96–4561), 30 October 1996. The Saudi Companies Law, Article 22, for example, provides for sanctions against any government official who improperly or without authorisation divulges company secrets to which he has, or has had, access by reason of his duties.

168 Bahrain, Legislative Decree No. 12 of 2006, arts. 2bis, 2Abis, and 2Bbis.

169 Oman, Royal Decree No. 67/2008, ss 60–65.

170 WTO Council for Trade-Related Aspects of Intellectual Property Rights, *Minutes of Meeting*, 27–28 November 2001, Document IP/C/M/34 (01–6407), 20 December 2001.

171 Bahrain, Legislative Decree No. 7 of 2003, art. 2; Oman, Royal Decree No. 67/2008, s 65(2) 34; Qatar, Law No. 5 of 2005, art. 7; UAE, Federal Law No. 17 of 2002, arts. 39–40.

172 Bahrain, Legislative Decree No. 7 of 2003, art. 2; Oman, Royal Decree No. 67/2008, s 65(3).

173 UAE, Federal Law No. 17 of 2002, arts. 70–71.

174 Oman, Royal Decree No. 67/2008, ss 61–64.
175 Bahrain, Legislative Decree No. 7 of 2003, art. 4.
176 Ibid, art. 6.
177 Carlos Correa, 'Patent Rights', in Correa and Abdulqawi (eds), *Intellectual Property and International Trade – The TRIPS Agreement* (1998), p. 197.
178 'UPOV Convention' being the Act of the International Convention for the Protection of New Varieties of Plants of 2 December 1961, as revised at Geneva on 19 March 1991. Although UPOV is an autonomous international body, its association with the WTO and WIPO in particular is close, with the WIPO Director-General being *ex-officio* UPOV Secretary-General. WIPO has prepared a Plant Breeder's Rights Bill, which serves as its *sui generis* alternative to the TRIPS patent-protection approach. The Bill is based on the 1991 UPOV Convention.
179 UPOV Convention, arts. 5–9.
180 Ibid, arts. 14–15.
181 See the discussion on patentability in Sections 4.7.2 and 4.7.3 above.
182 In June 2002, Qatar was advising the WTO Council for TRIPS that the GCC Council was currently examining a separate form of regulation on plant-variety protection and that this legislation, once approved, would apply in Qatar. However, the GCC Council has yet to draft, let alone issue, such a law. See WTO Council for Trade-Related Aspects of Intellectual Property Rights, *Review of Legislation: Responses from Qatar to the questions posed by Australia, Canada, the European Communities and their member States, Switzerland and the United States*, IP/C/W/346 (02–3101), 5 June 2002, pp. 1, 6.
183 The UPOV Convention came into effect in December 2005 in Bahrain and in October 2007 in Oman.
184 The Ministry of Commerce and Industry has responsibility for Royal Decree No. 67/2008, while the Ministry of Agriculture has responsibility for Royal Decree No. 92/2000.
185 Oman, Royal Decree No. 92/2000, art. 8; Oman, Royal Decree No. 67/2008, s 11(2); Saudi Arabia, Royal Decree No. 1425 AH (2004) arts. 54–55.
186 Oman, Royal Decree No. 92/2000, arts. 10–14; Oman, Royal Decree No. 67/2008, s 11(2); Saudi Arabia, Royal Decree No. 1425 AH (2004), art. 56.
187 Saudi Arabia, Royal Decree No. M/27 of 1425 AH (2004), arts. 56(a) and (b). These provisions in essence replicate the breeder's rights as detailed in the WIPO Model Law, art. 14.
188 Oman, Royal Decree No. 67/2008, s 11(4)(b).
189 Oman Royal Decree No. 92/2000, arts. 21–22 and Royal Decree No. 67/2008, s 13; Saudi Arabia, Royal Decree No. M/27 of 1425 AH (2004), arts. 24–31.
190 See WTO Council for Trade-Related Aspects of Intellectual Property Rights, *Review of Legislation: Oman*, Document IP/Q4/OMN/1 (03–1675), 24 March 2003.
191 WTO Council for Trade-Related Aspects of Intellectual Property Rights, *Minutes of Meeting*, 27–28 November 2001, Document IP/CM/34 (01–6407), 20 December 2001, p. 3.
192 Ibid, p. 6.
193 WTO Council for Trade-Related Aspects of Intellectual Property Rights, *Minutes of Meeting*, 25–27 June 2002, Document IP/C/M/36/Add.1 (02–4741), 10 September 2002, pp. 3–4.
194 WTO Council for Trade-Related Aspects of Intellectual Property Rights, *Minutes of Meeting*, 17–19 September 2002, Document IP/C/M/37/Add.1 (02–6169), 8 November 2002, pp. 2–3.
195 Ibid, pp. 4–5.

5 Post-TRIPS and the enforcement dichotomy

1 The following summaries of the salient features of TRIPS Part III are taken from the WTO website description, available at <http://www.wto.int/english/tratop_e/trips_e/intel2_e.htm>, last accessed 1 December 2005.

2 TRIPS, art. 42.

3 Ibid, arts. 43 and 47–48.

4 Some of the major codifications relating to the Gulf legal and judicial systems and procedures, and which address in part the above requirements of TRIPS, include the following:
Bahrain: Decree No. 13 of 1971, the Judiciary Act; Civil Procedures Code (1971, as amended 1990), Law of Commerce (1971, as amended 1990), Criminal Code (1987), Code of Criminal Procedure (1966).
Kuwait: Law No. 19 of 1959, the Judiciary Law, as amended by Law No. 19 of 1990; Law No. 16 of 1960, the Penal Code; Law No. 17 of 1960, the Criminal Procedure Code; Law No. 38 of 1980, the Code of Civil Procedure, as amended by Law No. 47 of 1994; Law No. 67 of 1980, the Civil Code; Law No. 68 of 1980, the Commercial Code, as amended by Law No. 45 of 1989.
Oman: Law No. 7/1974, the Penal Code; Commercial Code (1990); Royal Decree 90/99 the Judicial Structure of Oman; Royal Decree No. 91/1999 establishing the Administrative Court; Royal Decree No. 92/1999, the Public Prosecution Authority; Royal Decree No. 93/1999 establishing the Supreme Judicial Council.
Qatar: Law No. 14 of 1972, the Criminal Code; Law No. 16 of 1971, the Civil and Commercial Code; Law No. 6 of 1999, the Law of the Judiciary.
Saudi Arabia: Royal Decree No. M/64 of 1395 AH (1975), regulating the Judiciary; Ministerial Ordinance No. 109 of 1332 AH (1959), the Administrative Rules of Procedure of Judicial Bodies.
UAE: Federal Law No. 10 of 1973, establishing the Federal Supreme Court; Federal Law No. 6 of 1978, establishing the Courts of First Instance; Federal Law No. 3 of 1987, the Penal Code; Law No. 11 of 1992, the Code of Civil Procedure; Federal Law No. 35 of 1992, the Code of Criminal Procedure.
Yemen: Law No. 1 of 1990, the Judicial Authority Act, Law No. 1 of 1991, the Judicature Act, Law No. 19 of 1992, the Civil Code, Law No. 12 of 1994, the Penal Code.

5 See, for example, Bahrain, Legislative Decree No. 11 of 2006 (trademark law), art. 51, and Law No. 14 of 2006 (patent and utility model law), art. 36; Oman, Royal Decree No. 67/2008 s 98.

6 UAE, Law No. 17 of 2002, art. 66.

7 The Saudi Board of Grievances was established in 1955 by Royal Decree No. 17/13/8759 of 1374 AH, as a quasi-judicial review body for government and administrative decision-making. It has been restructured a number of times over the years, to now become an independent entity directly responsible to the Saudi Council of Ministers. The Board consists of a president with the rank of minister, deputy president and two directors, legal advisers on *Shariah* law and other legal matters, and an unspecified number of magistrates according to specific need. Members of the Board are statutory appointments; the president is appointed by the King on the recommendation of the Council of Ministers.

8 GCC Unified Patent Regulations, 2000, arts. 25 and 28. The Committee comprises 12 members, two drawn from each state, and maintains a balance between legal and technical expertise.

9 Kuwait, Law No. 64 of 1999 (copyright), arts. 14, 18, 36–38; Saudi Arabia, Royal Decree No. M/41 of 1424 AH (2003) (copyright), arts. 16, 23.

10 Yemen, Law No. 19 of 1994, arts. 84, 102, 113 and 115.
11 See, for example, Bahrain, Legislative Decree No. 22/2006, arts. 62–63, and Legislative Decree No. 11 of 2006, art. 45; Oman, Royal Decree No. 67/2008, s 73.
12 Oman, Royal Decree No. 92/2000, art. 5.
13 Saudi Arabia, Royal Decree No. M/27 of 1425 AH (2004) arts. 34–35. The relevant Saudi committee in this case being a committee established by the King Abdul Aziz City for Science and Technology (KACST) as the statutory authority responsible for the oversight of patents and related areas.
14 Saudi Arabia, Royal Decree No. M/41 of 1424 AH (2003), art. 23.6.
15 TRIPS, art. 51. As a footnote to this article, the term 'counterfeit trademark goods' is defined as 'any goods, including packaging, bearing without authorization a trademark which is identical to the trademark validly registered in respect of such goods, or which cannot be distinguished in its essential aspects from such a trademark, and which thereby infringes the rights of the owner of the trademark in question under the law of the country of importation'. The term 'pirated copyright goods' is defined as 'any goods which are copies made without consent of the rights holder in the country of production and which are made directly or indirectly from any article where the making of that copy would have constituted an infringement of a copyright or a related right under the law of the country of importation'.
16 Paris Convention, art. 9(1).
17 TRIPS, art. 51.
18 Ibid, art. 59.
19 Ibid, art. 53.
20 Ibid, arts. 55–56.
21 WTO Council for Trade-Related Aspects of Intellectual Property Rights, *Review of Legislation: Oman*, 16; Document IP/Q4/OMN/1 (03–1675), 24 March 2003.
22 Ibid, 25.
23 UAE, Federal Law No. 7 of 2002, art. 36.
24 Saudi Arabia, Ministerial Decision No. 1277 of 1425 AH (2004), Regulations for Border Procedures for Protection of Intellectual Property Rights of Trademarks and Copyright.
25 Kuwait, Law No. 1 of 2001 (trademarks), art. 95; Law No. 4 of 1999 (patents), art. 48; Law No. 64 of 1999 (copyright), art. 42.
26 Kuwait, Law No. 64 of 1999, art. 38, and Explanatory Memorandum.
27 Oman, Royal Decree No. 65/2008 (copyright), arts. 42–43; Royal Decree No. 67/2008 ss 75–78.
28 Oman, Royal Decree No. 92/2000, art. 6.
29 UAE, Federal Law No. 7 of 2002 (copyright), arts. 38 and 40; Federal Law No. 8 of 2002 (trademarks), arts. 39–40; Federal Law No. 17 of 2002 (patents), art. 63.
30 UAE, Federal Law No. 8 of 2002 (trademarks), art. 41.2.
31 Bahrain, Legislative Decree No. 16 of 2004 (geographical indications), art. 6; Legislative Decree No. 7 of 2003 (trade secrets), art. 7.
32 Bahrain, Legislative Decree No. 14 of 2006 (patents), art. 41, Legislative Decree No. 11 of 2006 (trademarks), art. 48, Legislative Decree No. 6 of 2006 (designs), art. 30, Legislative Decree No. 5 of 2006 (integrated circuits) art. 35. The standard Bahraini, Kuwaiti and Omani currency unit is worth just under ten Qatari, Saudi and Emirati units. The currencies of all the GCC states are linked, formally or effectively, to the US dollar. The exchange rates (as at 30/06/08) are as follows:

BD (Bahraini dinar)	= US$2.65;	US$1.00	= BD0.377
KD (Kuwaiti dinar)	= US$3.760	US$1.00	= KD0.2659
OR (Omani rial)	= US$2.598	US1$.00	= OR0.3848
QR (Qatari riyal)	= US$0.2748	US$1.00	= QR3.640
SR (Saudi riyal)	= US$0.2666	US$1.00	= SR3.750
AED (UAE dirham)	= US$0.2724	US$1.00	= AED3.672
YER (Yemeni rial)	= US$0.005	US$1.00	= YER200.00

33 Bahrain, Legislative Decree No. 22 of 2006, art. 65.
34 Kuwait, Law No. 64 of 1999, art. 42.
35 Kuwait, Law No. 68 of 1980, art. 92.
36 Kuwait, Law No. 3 of 2001, art. 46.
37 Qatar, Law No. 7 of 2002 (copyright), arts. 50–51; Law No. 30 of 2006 (patents), art. 24.
38 Qatar, Law No. 7 of 2002, art. 51.
39 UAE, Federal Law No. 17 of 2002 (patents), art. 62; Federal Law No. 7 of 2002 (copyright), arts. 38–39.
40 UAE, Federal Law No. 8 of 2002 (trademarks), arts. 37–38.
41 Saudi Arabia, Royal Decree No. M/ 27 of 1425 AH (2004) (patents), art. 34; Royal Decree No. M/41 of 1424 AH (2003) (copyright), art. 22.
42 Saudi Arabia, Royal Decree No. 21 of 1423 AH (2002), art. 43.
43 Oman, Royal Decree No. 65/2008 (copyright) art. 43, Royal Decree No. 67/2008 s 93.
44 Interviews conducted by the author with officials of the Oman Ministry of Commerce and Industry, January 2003 and December 2004.
45 Ibid.
46 Yemen, Law No. 19 of 1994, art. 124.
47 UAE, Federal Law No. 7 of 2002, arts. 37.2 and 38–39.
48 The proposed increased penalties were first reported in *The Peninsula* (Qatar) on 24 August 2004, but some four years later amendments to the Kuwaiti copyright law have yet to appear.
49 As enunciated in a survey conducted in 2002 by WIPO amongst its member states and reported in WIPO Document WIPO/CME/3, pp. 4–5. The Report is discussed in Michael Blakeney, 'Enforcement of Intellectual Property Rights: Challenges, Remedies and Public Awareness', WIPO National Seminar on Intellectual Property for Faculty Members of Ajman University, Ajman, May 2004, p. 25; WIPO Document WIPO/IP/UNI/DUB/04/7.
50 The survey was addressed to all WIPO member countries, including the Gulf states. None of the states, nor any other Arab country, responded to the survey, which in itself can be construed as an indicator of deep-seated systemic deficiencies and infrastructural shortcomings in intellectual property enforcement in the region. It also illustrates the difficulty that faces any researcher in obtaining reliable, periodic and comparative data for any of the Gulf states on intellectual property enforcement practices and performance.
51 The Saudi Minister of Commerce and Industry, Hashim Bin Abdullah Yamani, when interviewed on Saudi Arabia's admission to the WTO in December 2005, suggested that the Kingdom had little choice: 'The idea of seeing Saudi Arabia outside the WTO, isolated from the developments in international trade, would result in it being unable to compete internationally . . . if Saudi Arabia did not join the WTO it would lose any chance to defend its important economic and trade interests' (as quoted in the *Gulf News*, 30 October 2005, available at <http://www.gulf-news.com/articles/articleid=189356>, last accessed 1 November 2005.

52 Interviews conducted by the author with officials, Oman Ministry of Commerce and Industry, and Qatar Ministry of Economy and Trade, December 2004. See also Maren Hansen, 'Taking a Realistic Approach to Trademark Protection in the Gulf Countries' (1993), 5, *Middle East Executive Reports*, p. 15; *Times of Oman*, 27 August 2002, available at <http://www.timesofoman.com/archives.asp>, last accessed 1 November 2005.
53 S H Amin, *Law of Intellectual and Industrial Property in Developing Countries: Muslim World* (1993), pp. 1–2.
54 *Times of Oman*, op. cit., 27 August 2002.
55 Alastair Hirst, 'Developing IPR in the Gulf' (1994), 17(2), *Middle East Executive Reports*, pp. 9–11.
56 John Carroll, 'Intellectual Property Rights in the Middle East: A Cultural Perspective' (2000–2001), 11, *Fordham Intellectual Property, Media and Entertainment Journal*, p. 590.
57 'A Window into the World of Anti-Piracy', *Arab News*, 11 October 2005, available at <http://www.arabnews.com/services/print/print.asp?artid=71540&d=11&m=1=&d=2005>, last accessed 30 January 2008.
58 *Gulf News*, op. cit., 16 July 1998, p. 3. The local reaction in some quarters to the offers reported above is also based on the author's own experiences and discussions with some regional educational institutions.
59 Carroll, op. cit., pp. 596–7.
60 Ibid, p. 594.
61 Saudi legal advocate quoted in 'WIPO Examines ADR to Resolve IP Disputes' (1996), 10, *World Intellectual Property Report*, p. 144.
62 These semi-official processes of alternative dispute resolution (ADR) may often result in satisfactory outcomes, but little other than the outcome is recorded. Use of the ADR approach is officially supported, with all states having mediation and arbitration legislation in place. Oman and the UAE, for example, require all civil cases to be offered the arbitration and mediation process associated with the courts before the cases come before the courts.
63 Howard Stovall, 'Arab Commercial Laws – Into the Future' (2000), 34, *The International Lawyer*, p. 844.
64 The impact of the youth culture and expatriate populations has generally been overlooked by the few commentators on intellectual property in the Gulf region, but is worth further study, unfortunately beyond the scope of this work. However, three points of significance need to be borne in mind. All the Gulf states have very young populations, with more than half of the indigenous population in each state being under 21 years of age. Further, except for Saudi Arabia and Oman, the expatriates make up the majority of the total populations, comprising over 80 per cent thereof in the case of the UAE. In Oman and Saudi Arabia the expatriate numbers are considerably lower, but still comprise 20–25 per cent of the total population (see www.grc.ae and search on GCC country profiles). Expatriates are predominately at either end of the socio-economic spectrum – the lower end comprising low-paid workers from the Indian and Asian sub-continents and the upper end mainly comprising very well-paid (certainly by local indigenous standards) western expatriates from the developed countries. Caught between these two groups are the local youth – amongst whom high unemployment is endemic – being unwilling to undertake the menial, lowly paid jobs carried out by the former expatriate group and unable to secure the highly paid executive contracts enjoyed by the latter expatriate group. These three elements create a regional environment in which the demand for 'best-price' latest fashion consumer goods and cheapest entertainment through pirated audio and video items is high and the market for illegal goods flourishes.

65 Interview conducted by the author with officials in the Bahrain Ministry of Cabinet Affairs and Information, December 2004.
66 Ibid. See also 'Shadowy Traders, Shady Deals . . . the Piracy Business Continues', *Bahrain Tribune,* 16 October 2003, p. 2, available at <http://www.bahrain tribune.com/archives>, last accessed 16 October 2004.
67 *Kuwait News Agency* (KUNA), 4 July 2002, p. 1, available at <http://www.kuna.net.kw/home/Story.aspx?Language=en&DSNO=432029>, last accessed 1 December 2005.
68 For reports on similar illicit street operations in the Bahraini capital Manama, and Jeddah in Saudi Arabia, see the *Bahrain Tribune*, op. cit., pp. 1–2, and *Arab News*, 'Designer Product Dealers Angry at Flood of Fakes', 1 October 2007, available at <http://www.arabnews.com/?m=10&d=1&y=2007>, last accessed 3 June 2008.
69 1000 fils = 1 Kuwaiti dinar (= US$2.91).
70 The *Arab News* reported on 31 August 2004 that regular raids by Kuwaiti Ministry of Information officials on suspect shops and businesses had failed to deter the flourishing piracy business, available at <http://www.arabnews.com/?page=4&section=0&article=50758>, last accessed 13 September 2005.
71 International Intellectual Property Alliance (IIPA) Submission on Kuwait to the USTR for the USTR 2005 Special 301 Report, p. 3, available at <http://www.iipa.com/rbc/2005/2005special301Kuwait.pdf>, last accessed 10 December 2006. According to its own website, IIPA is a private-sector coalition formed in 1984 to represent the US copyright-based industries in bilateral and multilateral efforts to improve international protection of copyrighted materials. IIPA is composed of seven member associations: the Association of American Publishers (AAP), the Business Software Alliance (BSA), the Entertainment Software Association (ESA), the Independent Film & Television Alliance (IFTA), the Motion Picture Association of America (MPAA), the National Music Publishers' Association (NMPA) and the Recording Industry Association of America (RIAA). These associations represent approximately 1,900 US companies producing and distributing materials protected by copyright laws throughout the world:

> 'IIPA works closely with the US Trade Representative in the annual 'Special 301' reviews on whether acts, policies or practices of any foreign country deny adequate and effective protection of intellectual property rights or fair and equitable market access for US persons relying on intellectual property protection. . . . In the multilateral arena, IIPA is involved with the implementation of the WTO TRIPS (Trade-Related Aspects of Intellectual Property Rights) Agreement. IIPA works on IPR developments in bilateral initiatives such as free trade agreement (FTA) negotiations. IIPA also participates in policy developments in copyright and enforcement issues in regional initiatives.'

72 IIPA, Submission on Kuwait to the USTR for the USTR 2008 Special 301 Report, p. 248, available at <http://www.iipa.com/rbc/2008/2008special301 Kuwait.pdf>, last accessed 10 June 2008.
73 Interview conducted by the author with officials, Oman Ministry of Commerce and Industry, December 2004.
74 Interview conducted by the author with officials, Oman Ministry of Commerce and Industry, January 2003, and Qatar Ministry of Economy and Trade, December 2004. See also Maren Hansen, op. cit., p. 14; see further *Arab News,* op. cit.
75 See, for example, *Times of Oman,* 5 October 2005, p. 1, in which it was reported that a number of Asian nationals were arrested in a raid in which thousands of

pirated classified arts and pornographic CDs were confiscated. The report mentioned more than once that the 'culprits' were Asian nationals. A subsequent report of further raids in which those arrested were all expatriates appeared in the *Times of Oman*, 5 December 2005, available at <http://www.timesofoman.com/newsdetails.asp?newsid=15491>, accessed 5 December 2005.

76 Al-Tamimi & Co, Legal Advocates (UAE), *Law Update*, Issue No. 136, July 2002, p. 9, available at <http://www.tamimi.com/catalog/1998_2004/pdf/issue136july2002>, last accessed 1 December 2005.

77 The President of the Qatari Chamber of Commerce claimed that 'a number of traders . . . have imported and distributed pirated products in the domestic markets . . . the perpetrators are few in number and have never represented Qatari businessmen . . . Such acts are new and peculiar to the Qatari business community, and hence it is necessary that the culprits should be duly prosecuted to protect the image and reputation of Qatari businessmen'. The report continued that QR250,000 of counterfeit products were seized and destroyed in a recent campaign in Doha (the Qatari capital); *The Peninsula* (Qatar), 27 July 2002, p. 3.

78 *Arab News*, 8 June 2004, available at <http://www.arabnews.com/?page=1&section=0&article=46470>, last accessed 20 January 2006.

79 Al-Tamimi, op. cit., Issue No. 131, February 2002, p. 1.

80 *Arab News* (Saudi Arabia), 12 July 2004, available at <http://www.arabnews.com/?page=1&section=0&article=48229&d=12&m=7&y=2004>, last accessed 30 November 2005.

81 As reported in Saba & Co, Trademark & Patent Agents & Attorneys (Saudi Arabia), *Bulletin*, September 2007, available at <http://www.sabaip.com/bulletin>, last accessed 30 March 2008.

82 Ibid, April 2005.

83 Ibid.

84 UK Commission on Intellectual Property Rights, *Integrating Intellectual Property Rights and Development Policy* (2002), p. 147. The Preamble to TRIPS recognises that intellectual property rights are private rights.

85 Ibid.

86 Michael Blakeney, 'Enforcement of Intellectual Property Rights: Challenges, Remedies and Public Awareness', WIPO National Seminar on Intellectual Property for Faculty Members and Students of Ajman University, May 2004, p. 32, WIPO Document WIPO/IP/UNI/DUB/04/7. See also Alastair Hirst, 'The Role of the Government Authorities in the Enforcement of Intellectual Property Rights', WIPO Workshop on the Enforcement of Intellectual Property Rights for Judges, Beirut, December 1999, p. 3; WIPO Document WIPO/IPR/JU/BEY/99/5B.

87 Alastair Hirst, ibid.

88 Ibid.

89 IIPA, Submission on Saudi Arabia to the USTR for the USTR 2005 Special 301 Report, p. 3, available at <http://www.iipa.com/rbc/2005/2005special301SaudiArabia.pdf>, last accessed 10 December 2005.

90 IIPA, Submission on Kuwait to the USTR for the USTR 2004 Special 301 Report, pp. 3–4, available at <http://www.iipa.com/rbc/20042004special301Kuwait.pdf>, last accessed 10 December 2005. It should be noted that KD500 (US$1,880) is the maximum financial penalty permitted under Kuwait's copyright law, Law No. 64 of 1999, art. 42. The report continues that 'one case against one of the largest commercial groups in Kuwait for unlicenced software usage remains pending after three years . . . the MOI [Ministry of Information] . . . sent 79 cases for prosecution [since 2001], but the results for these cases were quite disappointing, with four acquittals, four non-deterrent

fines, only seven cases in which materials were confiscated in addition to a fine, and an overwhelming 64 cases still being considered by the prosecutor or awaiting decision or sentencing.'

91 Qatar, Law No. 6 of 1999 and Law No. 10 of 2003, the Law of Judicial Authority; see Al-Tamimi, op. cit., Issue 165, December 2004, p. 18.

92 Hirst, 'The Role of the Government Authorities in the Enforcement of Intellectual Property Rights', op. cit., p. 2.

93 Alastair Hirst, 'Enforcement of Intellectual Property Rights', WIPO Arab Regional Consultation Meeting on the Implementation of the TRIPS Agreement, Cairo, Egypt, March 1998, p. 4. WIPO Document WIPO/IP/CAI/98/3.

94 *Times of Oman*, 5 October 2005, available at <http://www.timesofoman.com/newsdetails.asp?newsid=14167>, last accessed 7 October 2005.

95 Al-Tamimi, *The Framework for Litigation in the United Arab Emirates*, pp. 2–3, available at <http://www.tamimi.com/site_1024/pdf/litigati.pdf>, last accessed 1 December 2005.

96 Ibid.

97 United Nations Development Programme, *Programme on Governance in the Arab Region: Bahrain*, available at <http://www.undp-pogar.org/countries/judiciary.asp?cid=2>, last accessed 1 August 2006.

98 United Nations Development Programme, *Programme on Governance in the Arab Region: Kuwait*, available at <http://www.undp-pogar.org/countries/judiciary.asp?cid=8>, last accessed 1 August 2006.

99 Interviews conducted by the author with officials in the Bahrain Ministry of Commerce, Qatar Ministry of Economy and Trade, and Oman Ministry of Commerce and Industry, December 2004.

100 UAE Federal Law No. 4 of 2001 provides for the appointment by the Minister of Justice of one or more reconciliation committees at the federal courts of first instance. This law is not applicable in Dubai or Ras Al-Khaimah.

101 Interviews conducted by the author with officials in the Oman Ministry of Commerce and Industry, December 2004.

102 Ibid. See also *The Economist Intelligence Unit*, Viewswire, 15 June 2004, at <http://www.proquest.umi.com.ae>, last accessed 11 February 2005.

103 Interviews conducted by the author with officials in the Oman Ministry of Commerce and Industry, December 2004.

104 N Khasawneh and J Steinhardt, 'Enforcing Copyright under TRIPS: The Future of Digital Copyright Industries in the Middle East and North Africa' (1999), p. 4; quoted by Yahya Al-Riami, 'Intellectual Property Protection and Enforcement in the Gulf States, and Copyright Protection in the Middle East', unpublished LLM thesis, Franklin Pierce Law Centre (2002), NH, USA, p. 42.

105 Yahya Al-Riami, 'Intellectual Property Protection and Enforcement in the Gulf States, and Copyright Protection in the Middle East', unpublished LLM thesis, Franklin Pierce Law Centre (2002), p. 43.

106 Al-Tamimi & Co, Legal Advocates (UAE), Law Update, Issue No. 163, October 2004, p. 22; available at <http://www.tamimi.com/downloads/lawupdates/lu-163oct04.pdf>, last accessed 1 June 2008.

107 As reported in the *Gulf News*, 24 January 2008, at <http://archive.gulfnews.com/articles/08/01/23/10184360.html>, last accessed 30 January 2008.

108 As reported in the IIPA Submission to the USTR, Saudi Arabia: Special 301 Out-of-Cycle Review, August 2006, Appendix C, available at <http://www.11pa.com/rbc/2006/2006SPEC301SAUDIARABIA.pdf> last accessed 17 July 2007.

109 See USTR 2005 Special 301 Report, p. 5, available at <http://www.ustr.gov/assets/Document_Library/Reports_Publications/2005/2005_Special_301/assets_upload_file195_7636.pdf>, last accessed 15 January 2006.

110 Dubai Court of First Instance Judgment No. 6106 of 26 February 2001; discussed in Al-Tamimi & Co, Legal Advocates (UAE), Law Update, Issue No. 120, March 2001, p. 9; available at <http://www.tamimi.com/downloads/law updates/lu-120mar01.pdf>, last accessed 1 June 2008.
111 Al-Tamimi & Co, Legal Advocates (UAE), Law Update, Issue No. 133, April 2002, p. 3; available at <http://www.tamimi.com/downloads/lawupdates/lu-133apr02.pdf>, last accessed 1 June 2008. In both the Dubai and the Ajman case, penalties were reportedly imposed pursuant to UAE Federal Law No. 40 of 1992, the Copyright Law, arts. 42 and 45.
112 Jawad al-Redha, co-Chair BSA Middle East, quoted in *The Peninsula* (Qatar), 8 July 2004, available at <http://www.thepeninsulaqatar.com/display_news. asp?section=local_news&month=july2004>, last accessed 7 February 2005.
113 Interview conducted by the author at Al-Tamimi & Co, Legal Advocates, Dubai, UAE, December 2004.
114 Abu Dhabi Court of Appeal, Case No. 874/2004, 6 June 2004; discussed in Al-Tamimi, op. cit., No. 162, September 2004, pp. 20–1.
115 UAE Federal Law No. 3 of 1987, the Penal Code. Article 83 allows a court to order a stay of execution of a jail sentence and a non-proportional fine.
116 As reported in Saba & Co, op. cit., December 2007.
117 Ibid, July 2007.
118 As reported by Al-Tamimi & Co, Legal Advocates (UAE), Law Update, Issue No. 194, May 2007, p.20; available at <http://www.tamimi.com/downloads/lawupdates/lu-194may07.pdf>, last accessed 1 June 2008.
119 As reported in Saba & Co, op. cit., April 2007.
120 As reported by Al-Tamimi & Co, Legal Advocates (UAE), Law Update, Issue No. 178, January 2006, p.17; available at <http://www.tamimi.com/downloads/lawupdates/lu-178jan06.pdf>, last accessed 1 June 2008.
121 UK Commission on Intellectual Property Rights, op. cit., pp. 138–9.
122 Hirst, 'The Role of the Government Authorities in the Enforcement of Intellectual Property Rights', op. cit., p. 2.
123 Ibid.
124 See, for example, Kuwait, Law No. 64 of 1999 (copyright), art. 45; Oman, Royal Decree No. 38/2000 (trademarks), art. 44; Qatar, Law No. 7 of 2002 (copyright), art. 55; Saudi Arabia, Royal Decree No. M/41 of 1424 (copyright), art. 24; UAE, Federal Law No. 17 of 2002 (patents), art. 65.
125 The first implementing regulations to appear, in May 2004, were those for Royal Decree No. 92/2000, the Law on the Protection of New Plant Varieties. The implementing regulations for Royal Decree No. 38/2000, the Law on Trade Marks, Indications and Secrets and Protection from Unfair Competition, appeared in July 2005, and those for Royal Decree No. 82/2000, the Patents Law, appeared in September 2005. On 17 December 2005, the Ministry announced that it was then able to start accepting patent applications for filing purposes only, since the fees and charges for such filing had just been issued – more than five years after the patents law had been gazetted.
126 However, this is not to say that, on occasion, the issuance of laws and subordinate regulation cannot be effectively coordinated and occur in rapid succession. Saudi Arabia, for example, issued implementing regulations for its new law on Patents, Layout-designs of Integrated Circuits, Plant Varieties and Industrial Models on 26 December 2004, within the prescribed three-month period since the law's promulgation and within two months of the law coming into effect.
127 Reported in Abu Ghazaleh Intellectual Property (AGIP), *AGIP Newsletter*, May, 2004, available at <http://www.agip.com/bulletin_news.aspx?id=200&month =5&year=2004>, last accessed 1 December 2005.

128 By Ministerial Decision No. 54 of 2006, published in Official Gazette No. 2783 of 10 May 2006.
129 AGIP, op. cit., June 2006, last accessed 30 June 2007.
130 Interviews conducted by the author with the Bahrain Ministry of Commerce, December 2004, and subsequent personal correspondence, June 2005.
131 Interviews conducted by the author with Bahrain Ministry of Information, December 2004.
132 Qatar, Ministerial Regulation No. 47 of 2005. Reported in Saba & Co, op. cit., June 2005.
133 According to its own website (<http://www.kacst.edu.sa/en/about.asp>), the King Abdul Aziz City for Science and Technology is an independent scientific organisation of the Saudi Arabian government, established in 1977 as the Saudi Arabian National Center for Science & Technology (SANCST) and later in 1985 renamed as King Abdul Aziz City for Science and Technology. KACST is governed by a Supreme Committee, which is chaired by the Prime Minister (the King) and is composed of the ministers of the major ministries to which science and technology are of greatest relevance, the President of KACST, and three other members nominated by the Prime Minister. KACST is responsible for promoting the developmental sciences and technology in the Kingdom.
134 See WTO Working Party on the Accession of the Sultanate of Oman, *Accession of the Sultanate of Oman: Communication from the Sultanate of Oman*, Document WT/ACC/SPEC/OMN/5 (98–0272), 26 January 1998; see also WTO Working Party on the Accession of the Sultanate of Oman, *Accession of the Sultanate of Oman: Additional Questions and Replies*, document WT/ACC/OMN/9 (98–3054), 3 August 1998.
135 UK Commission on Intellectual Property Rights, op. cit., pp. 151–2. See also Mart Leesti and Tom Pengelly, 'Institutional Issues for Developing Countries in Intellectual Property Policymaking, Administration and Enforcement', UK Commission on Intellectual Property Rights Study Paper 9, pp. 32–4. The developed countries have also suggested to some GCC member states on occasion that specialist intellectual property courts should be established for the civil and criminal prosecution of intellectual property rights infringements. All suggestions have so far been resisted or simply not acted upon by the states concerned.
136 IIPA, Submission on Kuwait to the USTR for the USTR 2005 Special 301 Report, op. cit., p. 2.
137 Ibid.
138 *The Economist* Intelligence Unit, Country Briefing: Kuwait, 14 October 2005, quoting the IIPA Report to the USTR, 2001, available at <http://www.eiu.com/index.asp?_id=1919491577>, last accessed 10 November 2005.
139 Saba & Co, op. cit., April 2005.
140 Ibid, June 2005.
141 The Business Software Alliance (BSA) is an international organisation representing the leading software and e-commerce developers in 65 countries around the world. Promoting itself as the voice of the international software industry, BSA interacts with governments and consumers on the promotion of the role of software in global development and in relation to its fight against software piracy and internet theft. The following description is taken directly from BSA's website, at <http://www.bsa.org/about>, last accessed 20 October 2006:

> 'The Business Software Alliance (www.bsa.org) is the foremost organisation dedicated to promoting a safe and legal digital world. BSA is the voice of the world's commercial software industry and its hardware partners before

governments and in the international marketplace. Its members represent one of the fastest growing industries in the world. BSA programs foster technology innovation through education and policy initiatives that promote copyright protection, cyber security, trade and e-commerce. . . . Since 1995, the Business Software Alliance (BSA) has commissioned an annual study on global trends in computer software piracy, the studies since 2004 having been conducted by International Data Corporation (IDC), on behalf of BSA. IDC and previous studies conducted for BSA used the following basic research architecture to measure piracy rates and dollar losses:

- determine how much packaged software was put into use in 2004.
- determine how much packaged software has been paid for during the year.
- then subtract one from the other to get the amount of pirated software.

Once the amount of pirated software is known, the piracy rate is determined as the percentage of total software installed that was pirated.'

142 Business Software Alliance, *Fifth Annual BSA and IDC Global Software Piracy Study*, p. 4, available at <http://www.global.bsa.org/idcglobalstudy2007/studies/2007_global_piracy_study.pdf>, last accessed 30 June 2008.

143 See *Mena Report,* 14 April 2004, quoted in Al-Tamimi, op. cit., No. 128, November 2001.

144 Business Software Alliance, *Second Annual BSA and IDC Global Software Piracy Study*, p. 4, available at <http://www.bsa.org/globalstudy/upload/2005-Global-Study-Software-Piracy-Study.pdf>, last accessed 30 June 2006.

6 TRIPS-plus and 'raising the bar'

1 David Vivas, 'Regional and Bilateral Agreements and a TRIPS-plus World: The Free Trade Area of the Americas', TRIPS Issues Papers No. 1, p. 4, available at <http://www.iprsonline.org/icstd/docs/WIPO_Vivas.pdf>, last accessed 20 December 2006. Sisule Musungu and Graham Dutfield, for example, also describe post-TRIPS as a 'concept which refers to the adoption of multilateral, plurilateral, regional and/or national IP rules and practices which have the effect of reducing the ability of developing countries to protect the public interest'. See Sisule Musungu and Graham Dutfield, 'Multilateral Agreements and a TRIPS-plus World: The World Intellectual Property Organisation', TRIPS Issues Papers No. 3, p. 3, available at <http://www.iprsonline.org/ictsd/docs/WIPO_Musungu_Dutfield.pdf>, last accessed 20 December 2006.

2 The international conventions which commonly form part of the US bilateral treaty negotiating agenda include WIPO's Copyright Treaty (WCT) and Performances and Phonograms Treaty (WPPT) in particular, but also generally include the:

- Patent Cooperation Treaty (PCT);
- Convention Relating to the Distribution of Programme-Carrying Signals Transmitted by Satellite (1974) (Brussels Convention);
- Protocol Relating to the Madrid Agreement Concerning the International Registration of Marks (1989) (Madrid Protocol);
- Budapest Treaty on the International Recognition of the Deposit of Micro-organisms for the Purposes of Patent Procedure (1980);
- Hague Agreement Concerning the International Registration of Industrial Designs (1999);

- International Convention for the Protection of New Varieties of Plants (1991) (UPOV Convention);
- Trademark Law Treaty (TLT);
- Patent Law Treaty (PLT).

3 See Report of the Asian Regional Workshop on Bilateral Free Trade Agreements, Kuala Lumpur, August 2005, p. 8, available at <http://www.twnside.org.sg/title2/twninfo254.htm>, last accessed 30 November 2005.

4 Peter Drahos, 'BITs and BIPs – Bilateralism in Intellectual Property' (2001), 4, *Journal of World Intellectual Property*, 6, pp. 798–9.

5 USTR, *2005 Special 301 Report*, p. 2, available at <http://www.ustr.gov/assets/Document_Library/Reports_Publications/2005/2005_Special_301/assets_upload_file195_7636.pdf>, last accessed 20 December 2005.

6 Aziz Choudry, 'Bombarded by Bilateral Trade and Investment Agreements', *Bilaterals.org*, March 2004, p. 3, available at <http://www.bilaterals.org/IMG/pdf/Bombarded_by_Bilatera_92909-2.pdf>, last accessed 6 January 2006. See also Peter Drahos and John Braithwaite, *Information Feudalism: Who Owns the Global Economy?* (2002) and Carlos Correa, 'Bilateral Investment Agreements: Agents of new global standards for the protection of intellectual property rights?', *GRAIN*, August 2004, available at <http://www.grain.org/briefings/?id=186>, last accessed 6 January 2006.

7 Ibid.

8 See Drahos, 'BITs and BIPs – Bilateralism in Intellectual Property', op. cit., p. 798.

9 Aziz Choudry, 'Bilateral Trade and Investment Deals a Serious Challenge to Global Justice Movements', *GRAIN*, December 2003, p. 1. Available at <http://www.grain.org/rights/tripsplus.cfm?id=2>, last accessed 30 September 2006.

10 Drahos and Braithwaite, op. cit., p. 194.

11 Peter Drahos, 'Developing Countries and International Intellectual Property Standard-Setting' (2002), 5, *Journal of World Intellectual Property*, p. 781.

12 See UNCTAD, 'Investment Provisions in Economic Integration Agreements', 114–6, Document UNCTAD/ITE/IIT/2005/10, available at <http://www.unctad.org/en/docs/iteiit200510_en.pdf>. The Pan-Arab Free Trade Area Agreement, sponsored by the Arab League and signed at the League's Economic and Social Council Meeting on 19 February 1997, included provisions on trade, investments, intellectual property rights and dispute settlement, available at <http://www.bilaterals.org/article-print.php3?id_article=2309>, last accessed 19 July 2006. For examples of South–South agreements involving the GCC states, and with similar investment and intellectual property provisions, see the agreements between Bahrain–Jordan, Kuwait–Pakistan, Oman–India, Qatar–Turkey, Saudi Arabia–Korea and UAE–Lebanon, all available at <http://www.unctadxi.org/templates/DocSearch>.

13 USTR Robert Zoellick, 'Global Trade and the Middle East: Reawakening a Vibrant Past', Address delivered at the World Economic Forum, Dead Sea, Jordan, 23 June 2003, pp. 7–9, available at <http://www.ustr.gov/speech_test/zoellick/2003-06-23-jordan.pdf>, last accessed 30 September 2006. See also USTR Fact Sheet, 'Middle East Free Trade Initiative', 23 June 2004, available at <http://www.ustr.gov/Document_Library/Fact_Sheets/2003/Middle_East_Free_Trade_Initiative.html>, last accessed 30 September 2006.

14 USTR Trade Facts, 'Middle East Free Trade Initiative: US Regional Plan to Spur Economic Growth', 2 March 2004, available at <http://www.ustr.gov/Fact_Sheets/2004/middle_east_free_trade_initiative.html>, last accessed 20 December 2006.

15 Report of the Industry Trade Advisory Committee on Intellectual Property Rights (ITAC-15), 'U.S.–Bahrain Free Trade Agreement: the Intellectual Property Provisions', p. 4, available at <http://www.ustr.gov/assets/Trade_Agreements/Bilateral/Bahrain_FTA/Reports/assets_upload_file822_5528.pdf>, last accessed 20 December 2006.

16 In this case, Saudi Arabia, Yemen and Lebanon. Saudi Arabia applied for accession to GATT (1947) on 23 June 1993 and reaffirmed its intention to accede to the WTO in December 1995. The original GATT Working Party on Saudi Arabia's accession continued as the WTO Accession Working Party. It is worth noting that the United States is currently sponsoring an application from Iraq for accession, but opposes applications from Iran and Syria.

17 The USTR describes 'technical assistance' as including the review of, and drafting assistance on, laws concerning intellectual property and enforcement. 'Training' usually covers the substantive provisions of TRIPS, including enforcement. Such assistance is provided by a number of US government agencies, including the US Patent and Trademark Office, the Copyright Office, Department of State, the US Agency for International Development, Customs and Border Protection, Department of Justice and Department of Commerce. US industry is also actively involved in providing specific enforcement-oriented training in key markets. The United States expects progress in the near term, but where this is not achieved, it will consider other means of encouraging implementation, including the possibility of dispute-settlement consultations. See USTR, *2005 Special 301 Report*, op. cit., p. 6.

18 Bahrain BIT, art. 1(d)(5), available at <http://www.tcc.mac.doc.gov/cgi-bin/doit.cgi?>, last accessed 12 January 2006.

19 The investor may choose among the International Centre for Settlement of Investment Disputes (ICSID), ad hoc arbitration using the Arbitration Rules of the United Nations Commission on International Trade Law (UNCITRAL), or any other mutually agreed arbitral institution or rules. An investor may still seek, without affecting its right to pursue international arbitration, interim injunctive relief from local courts or administrative tribunals for the preservation of its rights and interests.

20 US Secretary of State Albright, 'Letter of Submittal to The President on an Investment Treaty with Bahrain', 23 March 2000, p. IX, available at <http://www.tcc.mac.doc.gov/cgi-bin/doit.cgi?204:64>, last accessed 12 January 2006.

21 See Carlos Correa, 'Bilateral Investment Agreements: Agents of new global standards for the protection of intellectual property rights?', op. cit., p. 16.

22 The TIFAs which the United States signed with each of the Gulf states are identical in terms of subject matter and structure, and virtually identical in terms of actual text. Bahrain, being the first to sign, set the tone and character for the following TIFAs. See Bahrain TIFA, Preamble, paragraph 13, at <http://www.ustr.gov/assets/Trade_Agreements/Regional/MEFTA/asset_upload_file168_3538.pdf>, last accessed 20 December 2006.

23 Drahos, 'BITs and BIPs – Bilateralism in Intellectual Property', op. cit., p. 798.

24 USTR, *2003 Special 301 Report*, 'Statutory Authority', p. 9, available at <http://www.ustr.gov/assets/Document_Library/Reports_Publications/2003/2003_Special_301/assets_upload_file665_6124.pdf>, last accessed 20 December 2005.

25 Douglas Rosenthal, 'A Comment on the Special 301 Annual Review' (1998), 1, *Journal of World Intellectual Property*, p. 743.

26 Drahos, 'BITs and BIPs – Bilateralism in Intellectual Property', op. cit., p. 798. However, such a flurry of enforcement activity does not necessarily achieve the desired results. Kuwait's Ministry of Commerce and Customs Directorate

conducted a number of raids in November and December 2004 and April 2005 which included more than 45 stores and establishments. The raids netted approximately 250,000 pirated DVDs and CDs and caused the closure of a huge DVS-R production operation, the first discovered in the Middle East. The series of raids was even acknowledged in the 2005 Special 301 Report. Despite these enforcement successes, Kuwait still did not succeed in being removed from the Priority Watch List in the 2005 Report. Similarly, in March 2005, Saudi authorities seized over US$1.2 million of pirated audio-visual material in the Riyadh area, but Saudi Arabia was retained on the Watch List. See USTR, *2005 Special 301 Report*, op. cit., p. 6, Appendix on Positive Developments 2004–2005.

27 Deputy USTR Richard Fisher before the Subcommittee on International Economic Policy and Trade, House Committee on International Relations, Washington, USA, 3 October 1999; quoted by Drahos, above n 4, p. 792.

28 Perhaps not entirely coincidental in this regard was Bahrain's removal from the Special 301 Listing in 1999 and the completion of the transfer of the command base for the US Navy Fifth Fleet from Saudi Arabia to the southern part of Bahrain. In August 2001, the United States designated Bahrain as a 'major non-NATO ally', an indication not only of a strong desire by the United States to strengthen military ties with Bahrain but also the importance of Bahrain in the US global military strategy. Similarly, Qatar's removal from a Special 301 Listing in 2003 coincided with the transfer in early 2003 of the US Combined Air Operations Centre from the Prince Sultan air base in Saudi Arabia to Qatar, after Saudi Arabia directed that a strong US air force presence on Saudi air bases was no longer necessary following the lifting of the no-fly zones in southern Iraq and the Saudi refusal to allow the bases to be used for possible air strikes against Iraq after 9/11. *BBC News*, 29 April 2003, available at <http://www.news.bbc.co.uk/1/hi/world/middle_east/2984547.stm>, last accessed 30 April 2005.

29 See, for example, Assafa Endeshaw, 'The Paradox of Intellectual Property Lawmaking in the New Millennium: Universal Templates as Terms of Surrender for Non-industrial Nations; Piracy as an Offshoot', available at <http://www.papers.ssrn.com/sol3/papers.cfm?abstract_id=291692>, last accessed 7 March 2007. See also Sangeeta Shashikant, 'The Politics of United States Free Trade Agreements', Third World Network, available at <http://www.twnside.org.sg/title2/twr167-168.htm>, last accessed 6 January 2006.
However, the most telling illustration of the degree of influence of these industry lobby groups is their submissions to USTR when examined in the context of the USTR reports.

30 According to its website, the Pharmaceutical Researchers and Manufacturers of America (PhRMA) 'comprises the US' leading research-based pharmaceutical and biotechnology companies, which are devoted to inventing medicines that allow patients to live longer, healthier, and more productive lives . . .'. Its members include the world's leading pharmaceutical companies. It represents the interests of both US and other pharmaceutical multinationals from the UK, Switzerland and France in the Gulf. See <http://www.phrma.org/whoweare/>, last accessed 6 January 2006.

31 IIPA submission on Saudi Arabia to the USTR for the *2004 Special 301 Report*, available at <http://www.iipa.com/rbc/2004/2004SPEC301SAUDIARABIA.pdf>, last accessed 20 December 2006.

32 PhRMA Submission on the USTR *2004 Special 301 Report*, available at <http://www.phrma.org/international/resources/13.02.2004.600.cfm>, last accessed 20 December 2006.

33 USTR, *2008 Special 301 Report*, Executive Summary, p. 2, available at <http://www.ustr.gov/assets/Document_Library/Reports_Publications/2008/2008_Special_301_Report/asset_upload_file553_14869.pdf>, last accessed 30 June 2008.

34 The data for the 1998 year are available in the BSA, *Eighth Annual Global Piracy Study*, June 2003, available at <http://www.bsa.org/globalstudy2003/upload/2003-Global-Software-Piracy-Study.pdf>, last accessed 30 June 2008, p. 7.

35 See WTO, Document IP/Q4/BHR/1 (01–6218), 6 December 2001, 2.

36 USTR, *1999 Special 301 Report*, as quoted in IIPA, '2005 Special 301 Report on Global Copyright Protection and Enforcement', Appendix E, p. 28, available at <http://www.iipa.com/special301_appendixE/2005_SPEC301_appendixE.html>, last accessed 12 December 2005. Also reported in 'Results of 1999 'Special 301' Provisions of 1974 Trade Act Regarding Intellectual Property Protection' (1999), 13, *World Intellectual Property Report*, p. 216.

37 USTR, *2005 Annual Special 301 Report*, op. cit., p. 29.

38 USTR, *2008 Special 301 Report*, op. cit., p. 42.

39 See IIPA, '2005 Special 301 Report on Global Copyright Protection and Enforcement', Appendix E, op. cit., p. 36.

40 As reported in 'Results of 1998 'Special 301' Provisions of 1974 Trade Act Regarding Intellectual Property Protection' (1998), 12, *World Intellectual Property Report*, p. 201.

41 BSA, First Annual BSA and IDC Global Software Piracy Study, July 2004, op. cit., p. 8.

42 See IIPA, '2005 Special 301 Report on Global Copyright Protection and Enforcement', Appendix E, op. cit., p. 37.

43 See BSA, *Eighth Annual BSA Global Piracy Study*, June 2003, op. cit., p. 7.

44 USTR, *2003 Special 301 Report*, op. cit., Saudi Arabia Appendix.

45 USTR, *2005 Special 301 Report*, op. cit., p. 46. In fact, the Saudi Copyright Law art. 22.1(4) provides for confiscation of all copies of the infringing work as well as all materials used or intended to be used in the infringements, while art. 22.4 provides for the award of financial compensation. The Saudi authorities have also shown their willingness to seize and destroy infringing material, as evidenced by a series of publicised destruction events in late 2004 and early 2005.

46 The significance of this particular concern lies in the fact that the great majority of Saudi patents, that is, where the country of residence of the applicant is Saudi Arabia, emanate from within the Saudi oil industry, have been generated by expatriate residents rather than Saudi nationals and rely on a priority claim on the basis of an original patent lodgement in either the United States, the UK or the Netherlands. See <http://www.wipo.int/pctdb/en/search.jsp>, searching on ARE=SA; last accessed 14 September 2006.

47 See USTR, *2008 Special 301 Report*, op. cit., p. 42.

48 As quoted in IIPA, '2005 Special 301 Report on Global Copyright Protection and Enforcement', Appendix E, op. cit., p. 50.

49 Ibid.

50 Reported in Al-Tamimi & Co, Legal Advocates (UAE), 'UAE's Progress in Pharmaceutical Protection Recognised', *Newsletter*, No. 110, May 2000, p. 6, available at <http://www.tamimi.com/catalog/1998_2004/catalog.htm>, last accessed 1 December 2005.

51 Ibid.

52 Ibid, 'Pharma Group Again Putting Pressure on UAE for IP Violations', *Newsletter*, 117, December 2000, p. 20.

53 UAE, Ministerial Order No. 404 of 2000, arts. 1 and 2.
54 USTR, *2001 Special 301 Report*, p. 18, available at <http://ottawa.usembassy.gov/content/can_usa/pdfs/special301_2001.pdf>, last accessed 1 June 2008. Also reported in Al-Tamimi & Co, Legal Advocates (UAE), 'USTR 2001 Special 301 Report Released', *Newsletter*, No. 123, June 2001, 9; op. cit., p. 66. By 'unauthorised', the USTR meant generic pharmaceuticals.
55 UAE, Federal Law No. 17 of 2002, art. 71.
56 USTR, *2008 Special 301 Report*, op. cit., pp. 4–5. Abu Dhabi, Dubai, Sharjah and Ras Al-Khaimah are all in the process of establishing free trade zones, Dubai's Jebel Ali zone in particular being on an enormous scale.
57 See Drahos, 'BITs and BIPs – Bilateralism in Intellectual Property', op. cit., p. 800; Shashikant, op. cit., p. 1; Aziz Choudry, 'Corporate Conquest, Global Geopolitics, *Seedling*, January 2005, p. 1, available at <http://www.grain.org/seedling/?id=314> , last accessed 3 January 2006.
58 USTR, *2005 Special 301 Report*, op. cit., p. 7.
59 Peter Drahos and John Braithwaite, *Global Business Regulation* (2000), p. 64.
60 USTR, *2002 Special 301 Report*, Executive Summary, pp. 2 and 6. Available at <http://www.ustr.gov/assets/Document_Library/Reports_Publications/2002/2002_Special_301/assets_upload_file628_6354.pdf>, last accessed 20 December 2005.
61 See WIPO, 'Contracting Parties to Treaties Administered by WIPO', 15 July 2008, available at <http://www.wipo.int/treaties/en/general/parties>, last accessed 20 July 2008. The WCT came into force on 6 March 2002 and the WPPT on 20 May 2002, coincidentally the same dates on which the US acceded to the respective treaties.
62 USTR, *2008 Special 301 Report,* op. cit., p. 10.
63 Interview conducted by the author with officials of the Bahrain Ministry of Information, Directorate of Publications, December 2004. See also WIPO Document, IP/Q/4/BHR/1 (01–6218), 6 December 2001, p. 2.
64 See Kenneth Katzman, 'The Persian Gulf States: Post-War Issues for US Policy', *CRS Report for Congress*, No. RL31533, The Library of Congress, 21 December 2005, Executive Summary.
65 USTR Zoellick, reported in 'Sultanate, US Hold Joint Meeting on Free Trade Pact', *Times of Oman*, 15 October 2004, available at <http://www.timesofoman.com/archives/newsdetails.asp?newsid=2954&archdate=10/15/2004>, last accessed 12 January 2007.
66 See Choudry, 'Bilateral Trade and Investment Deals a Serious Challenge to Global Justice Movements', op. cit., p. 1.
67 'FTA with EU looks more imminent than ever', *Gulf News,* 9 April 2005, available at <http://www.archive.gulfnews.com/articles/05/04/09/160040.html>, last accessed 12 January 2007.
68 See Christian Koch, 'GCC–EU Free Trade Agreement Must Be Saved', 10 July 2008, *Gulf Research Centre,* available at <http://www.grc.ae/?frm_action=view_newsletter_web&sec_code=grcanalysis&frm_module=contents&show_web_list_link=1&int_content_id=52076&PHPSESSID=cfd763ec478ed20680a08ff12636c6ad>, last accessed 12 July 2008.
69 Secretary of State Albright, Letter of Transmittal to the US President on the Bahrain BIT, op. cit., p. 1.
70 Ibid.
71 Ibid, art. 2.3(a).
72 Presidential Letter of Transmittal to the US Congress on the Bahrain BIT, 24 March 2000, op. cit., p. 3.
73 The Bahrain FTA consists of 21 chapters incorporating market access, textiles and apparel, rules of origin, customs administration, sanitary and phytosanitary

measures, technical barriers to trade, safeguards, government procurement, cross-border trade in services, financial services, telecommunications, electronic commerce, intellectual property rights, labour, environment, transparency, agreement administration and dispute settlement. Chapter 14 addresses intellectual property rights and represents a significant component of the FTA. The final version of the FTA text is available at <http://www.ustr.gov/Trade_Agreements/Bilateral/Bahrain_FTA/final_Texts>, last accessed 21 October 2005. To come into effect, the FTA needs to be approved by both the Bahraini and US governments. The Bahraini King issued a decree ratifying the FTA on 21 July 2005, after it was passed by the Bahraini parliament and the Shura Council earlier that month. The US President signed the FTA into law on 11 January 2006, after Congress passed the Agreement by an overwhelming majority in December 2005.

74 As quoted in the *Bahrain Tribune*, 30 May 2004, available at <http://www.bahraintribune.com/ArticleDetail.asp>, last accessed 12 January 2006.

75 Ibid, 28 May 2004.

76 USTR Press Release, 'US and Bahrain Conclude Free Trade Agreement', 27 May 2004, at <http://www.ustr.gov/new/fta/Bahrain/2004-05-27>, last accessed 30 June 2006.

77 'Bahrain FTA, USTR Notification of Initiation of Negotiations', US Senate, 4 August 2003, pp. 3–4, available at <http://www.ustr.gov/new/fta/2003-08-4-notification-senate>, last accessed 30 June 2006.

78 As part of the consultative process with US industry and stakeholders, the USTR has established a group of industry advisory committees to advise and recommend on each chapter of an FTA. The advisory group overall is made up of more than 700 carefully selected stakeholders, comprising senior members of major US industries or their legal counsel, government officials and business, academic experts and consumer groups. The advisory group provides advice on both proposed and ongoing USTR activities and is kept informed on developments in both agreement negotiations and Special 301 reviews. See <http://www.ustr.gov/document_library/press_releases/2005/november/trade_advisory_committee>, last accessed 14 December 2006. For a concise description of the modus operandi of the USTR's expert advisory committee structure, see also 'Mission of the USTR', at <http://www.ustr.gov/Who_We_Are/Mission_of_the_USTR>, last accessed 14 December 2006.

The members of ITAC-15, the committee responsible for advising on the intellectual property provisions of the Bahrain FTA, include persons who have a particular vested interest in ensuring that the highest possible standards of intellectual property protection for US rights holders are incorporated into any FTA. They include the President of IIPA, as chairman of ITAC-15, and representatives of PhRMA, as well as very senior executives from Pfizer, Lilly & Co, Merck & Co, Time Warner Inc., Anheuser-Busch Companies, the Recording Industry Association of America, and John Wiley & Sons Inc. See ITAC-15 Report on the Bahrain FTA, available at <http://www.ustr.gov/assets/Trade_Agreements/Bilateral/Bahrain_FTA/Reports/asset_upload_file822_5528.pdf>, last accessed 30 November 2006, pp. 2, 22.

79 USTR Trade Facts, 'Free Trade with Bahrain: A Model for Trade in the Persian Gulf Region', 27 May 2004, available at <http://www.ustr.gov/fta/bahrain/2004–05–27/factsheet>, last accessed 1 June 2005.

80 The US joined the above-mentioned treaties on the following dates: WCT (6 March 2002), WPPT (20 May 2002), PCT (24 January 1978), Brussels Convention (7 March 1985), Madrid Protocol (2 November 2003), Budapest

Treaty (19 August 1980), UPOV (8 November 1981), TLT (12 August 2000). At the time of writing it has not yet acceded to the Hague Agreement. See WIPO, 'Contracting Parties to Treaties Administered by WIPO', 15 July 2008, op. cit.

81 Bahrain FTA, arts. 14.2.1 and 14.2.6.
82 Ibid, arts. 14.2.4 and 14.2.4.13.
83 Ibid, arts. 14.3.1 and 14.3.2.
84 Ibid, art.14.4.1.
85 Ibid, art. 14.4.10(b), art. 14.5 and art. 14.6.2.
86 Ibid, art. 14.4.4.
87 ITAC-15 Report on the Bahrain FTA, op. cit., p. 11.
88 Ibid.
89 Ibid.
90 Bahrain FTA, art. 14.4.7(a)–(b).
91 Ibid, art. 14.4.8–9.
92 Ibid, art. 14.7.
93 Ibid, art. 14.8 (a). By article 14.8(a), the 'wilfulness' requirement as contained in TRIPS is reduced to 'knowing' or 'having reason to know'.
94 ITAC-15 Report on the Bahrain FTA, op. cit., p. 12.
95 Bahrain FTA, art. 14.8.2. TRIPS art. 27.3(b) grants a member state discretion to exclude from patentability plants and animals other than micro-organisms and essentially biological processes for the production of plants or animals other than non-biological and microbiological processes.
96 UPOV Convention, art. 15(1).
97 Somesh Mathur, 'TRIPS and Copyright Provisions – Some Issues for Developing Countries' (2003), 6, *Journal of World Intellectual Property*, 1, p. 81.
98 Bahrain FTA, art. 14.8.4.
99 Ibid, art. 14.8.3.
100 ITAC-15 Report on the Bahrain FTA, op. cit., p. 15.
101 Carlos Correa, 'Bilateral Investment Agreements: Agents of new global standards for the protection of intellectual property rights?', op. cit., p. 16.
102 Bahrain FTA, arts. 14.9.1 and 14.9.2(c)–(d).
103 Ibid, arts. 14.9.3 and 14.9.4.
104 ITAC-15 Report on the Bahrain FTA, op. cit., p. 18.
105 Bahrain FTA, art. 14.10.6–7.
106 Ibid, art. 14.10.10(a).
107 Ibid, art. 14.10.11.
108 Ibid, art. 14.10.26–7.
109 ITAC-15 Report on the Bahrain FTA, op. cit., pp. 19–20.
110 Bahrain FTA, art. 14.10.29. The two exceptions are adherence to the Brussels Satellite Convention and the Budapest Treaty on the International Recognition of Micro-organisms, both of which require adherence within one year of the FTA coming into force.
111 Ibid, art. 14.11.
112 USTR Trade Facts, 'Free Trade with Bahrain', op. cit., p. 91.
113 Acting USTR Allgeier, 'United States to Begin Free Trade Negotiations This Week with the United Arab Emirates and Oman', USTR Press Release, 8 March 2005, p. 2, available at <http://www.ustr.gov/Trade_Agreements/Bilateral/Oman_FTAPress_ReleasesSection_Index.html?ht=oman520oman>, last accessed 17 December 2005. See also 'Oman–US FTA: What's the Deal?', *Oman Economic Review Online*, March 2005, available at <www.oeronline.com/php/2005_march/cover.php>, last accessed 6 January 2006.

114 'Oman Cautious on US Trade Talks', *Arab News*, 30 November 2004, available at <http://www.arabnews.com/?page=68&section=0&article=5539&d=30&m=11&y=2004&pix=business.jpg>, last accessed 1 December 2005.

115 The Oman FTA consists of 21 chapters covering the same subject areas as the Bahrain FTA. Chapter 15 addresses intellectual property rights and again represents a significant component of the FTA. The FTA text is available at <http//www.ustr.gov/Trade_Agreements/Bilateral/Oman_FTA/Final_Texts>, last accessed 6 January 2006.

116 'Washington Seals Trade Agreement with Oman', *Financial Times* (London), 4 October 2005.

117 Ibid.

118 Report of the Industry Trade Advisory Committee on Intellectual Property Rights (ITAC-15), 'The U.S.–Oman Free Trade Agreement (FTA): The Intellectual Property Provisions', 15 November 2005, p. 8, available at <http://www.ustr.gov/assets/Trade_Agreements/Bilateral/Oman_FTA/Reports/asset_upload_file124_8402.pdf>, last accessed 6 January 2006.

119 Oman FTA, art. 15.2.13(a).

120 The footnote to art. 15.2.4 of the FTA describes geographical indications for the purpose of Chapter 15 as 'indications that identify a good as originating in the territory of a Party, or a region or locality in that territory, where a given quality, reputation, or other characteristic of the good is essentially attributable to its geographical origin. Any sign or combination of signs (such as words – including geographical and personal names, as well as letters, numerals, figurative elements and colors, including single colors), in any form whatsoever, shall be eligible to be a geographical indication.'

121 Oman FTA, art. 15.4.4.

122 IIPA testimony before the 'Public Hearing Concerning Proposed United States – Oman Free Trade Agreement, Friday January 14, 2005, Before the Trade Policy Staff Committee', Washington DC, pp. 5–6. Testimony is available at <http://www.iipa.com/pdf/2004_SIWEK_FULL.pdf>, last accessed 1 December 2005.

123 Oman FTA, art. 15.8.1.

124 ITAC-15 Report on the Oman FTA, op. cit., p. 15.

125 Ibid, p. 19.

126 Oman FTA, art. 15.10.27(d).

127 Ibid, art. 15.10.27(d). See also ITAC-15 Report on the Oman FTA, op. cit., p. 22.

128 'The U.S.–Oman Free Trade Agreement (FTA): Report of the Advisory Committee for Trade and Policy Negotiations (ACTPN)', 15 November 2005, pp. 1–4, available at <http://www.ustr.gov/assets/trade_agreements/bilateral/Oman FTA/Reports/assets_upload/file604_8376.pdf>, last accessed 15 December 2006.

129 Ibid, Covering Letter.

130 Interview conducted by the author with the UAE Ministry of Information, Abu Dhabi, December 2004.

131 The former Minister also criticised the UAE delegation for the FTA negotiations, claiming that it was not sufficiently qualified and had no experience in legal and negotiating matters. Quoted in 'GCC States Urges to Avoid Free Trade Deals with US', *Arab News*, 9 December 2004, available at <http://www.arabnews.com/?page=6&section=0&article=55810&d=9&m=12&y=2004&pix=business.jpg>, last accessed 1 December 2006.

132 As reported in the *Gulf News*, 12 May 2006, available at <http://archive.gulfnews.com/articles/06/05/12/10039365>, last accessed 7 March 2007.

133 Ibid.
134 As reported in the *Gulf News*, 12 March 2007, available at <http://archive.gulfnews.com/articles/07/03/12/10110486.html>, last accessed 2 April 2007.
135 As quoted by *Kuwait News Agency*, 14 June 2006, at <http://www.kuna.net.kw>, last accessed 7 March 2008.
136 Zoellick, op. cit., p. 6.
137 HE Abdullah Hassan Saif, Bahraini Minister for Finance and National Economy, quoted in the *Bahrain Daily News*, 28 January 2004, available at <http://www.gulf-daily-news.com/arc_home.asp?date=28-1-2004>, last accessed 30 June 2005.
138 USTR Press Release, 'US and Bahrain Conclude Free Trade Agreement', op. cit.
139 ITAC-15 Report on the Bahrain FTA, op. cit., pp. 16–17.
140 *Khaleej Times* (UAE), 20 December 2004, available at <http://www.khaleejtimes.com/Displayarticle.asp?section=middleeast&xfile=data/middleeast/2004/december/middleeast_december743.xml>, last accessed 7 March 2007. See also Emilie Rutledge and Dr Janardhan, 'Bahrain–US FTA Exposes GCC Chinks', *Gulf Research Centre*, December 2004, available at <http://www.grx.ae/data/contents/uploads/GCC_6533.pdf>, last accessed 7 March 2007; see also Editorial, *Saudi Gazette*, 21 December 2005.
141 The Unified Economic Agreement Between the Countries of the Gulf Co-operation Council, art. 25, available at <http://www.gcc-sg.org/Economic.html>, last accessed 30 November 2005.
142 Statement by GCC Secretary-General Abdurrahman al-Attiya, reported in the *Arab News*, 25 April 2005.
143 'GCC States Agree to Except US from Bilateral Free Trade Agreements', *Kuwait News Agency* (KUNA), 24 May 2005, available at <http://www.kuna.net.kw/printaspx?DSNO=736022>, last accessed 3 June 2005.
144 See 'Ports Deal: A UAE Perspective', *Gulf News*, 17 March 2006, available at <http://archive.gulfnews.com/articles>, last accessed 7 March 2007.

7 TRIPS-minus and protection still pending

1 Kamal Puri, 'How Intellectual Property Rights Could Work Better for Developing Countries and Poor People', *UK Commission on Intellectual Property Rights*, Conference Transcript, Session 3: Traditional Knowledge and Folklore (2002), p. 2.
2 WIPO International Bureau, 'Intellectual Property and Traditional Knowledge: Our Identity, Our Future', WIPO International Forum on Matters Concerning Intellectual Property and Genetic Resources, Traditional Knowledge and Folklore, Oman, 21–2 January 2002, WIPO Document IPTK/MCT/02/INF.11 November 2002.
3 WIPO, *Intellectual Property and Traditional Cultural Expressions/Folklore*, WIPO Publication No. 913(E), p. 6, available at <http://www.wipo.int/ebookshop>, last accessed 20 May 2008.
4 Ibid.
5 Kamal Puri, op. cit., p. 2; see also Report of the UK Commission on Intellectual Property Rights (2002), pp. 78–9.
6 See Surinder Verma, 'Protecting Intellectual Property: Is a Sui Generis System an Answer?' (2004), 7, *Journal of World Intellectual Property*, p. 770; see also Kamal Puri, 'Is Traditional Knowledge or Cultural Knowledge a Form of Intellectual Property?', *Oxford Electronic Journal of Intellectual Property Rights*, 18 January 2000, available at <http://www.oiprc.ox.ac.uk/EJWP0100.pdf>, last accessed 30 December 2005.

7 WIPO, 'Intellectual Property Needs and Expectations of Traditional Knowledge Holders', *WIPO Report on Fact-Finding Missions on Intellectual Property and Traditional Knowledge (1998–9)*, Geneva (2001), p. 5. The fact-finding missions were carried out in the following areas: South Pacific (Australia, New Zealand, Fiji and Papua New Guinea), South Asia (Bangladesh, India and Sri Lanka), Southern and Eastern Africa (Uganda, United Republic of Tanzania, Namibia and South Africa), North America (United States of America and Canada), West Africa (Nigeria, Ghana, Mali and Senegal), the Arab countries (Oman, Qatar, Egypt and Tunisia), South America (Peru and Bolivia), Central America (Guatemala and Panama) and the Caribbean (Trinidad and Tobago, Guyana and Jamaica). The reports of the missions are available at <http://www.wipo.int/globalissues/tk/report/final>, last accessed 31 December 2006.
8 WIPO International Bureau, op. cit., p. 2.
9 WIPO, 'Intellectual Property Needs and Expectations of Traditional Knowledge Holders', op. cit., Part III, Annex 5, pp. 83–4.
10 Yemen, Law No. 19 of 1994, art 4.
11 Ibid, art 38.
12 Kuwait, Law No. 64 of 1999, art 41.
13 UAE, Federal Law No. 7 of 2002, art 1.
14 Ibid, art. 42.
15 Saudi Arabia, Royal Decree No. M/41 of 1424 AH (2003), art. 1.
16 Ibid, art. 7(1)–(2).
17 Oman, Royal Decree No. 65/2008, art. 1.10.
18 Ibid, art. 1.8.
19 Ibid, art. 1.17.
20 Ibid, art. 5. The competent authority in this context is the Minister of Commerce and Industry, with whom most intellectual property protection responsibility resides, notwithstanding the existence of the Ministry of Heritage and Culture and an independent Public Authority for Craft Industries.
21 Bahrain, Legislative Decree No. 22 of 2006, art. 1.
22 Ibid.
23 Ibid, art. 65(1)(g) and art. 68.
24 Ibid, arts. 58–60.
25 Qatar, Law No. 7 of 2002, art. 1.
26 Ibid, art. 32.
27 Bahrain FTA, art. 14.6.5; Oman FTA, art. 15.6.5.
28 Bahrain FTA, art. 14.4.1; Oman FTA, art. 15.1.
29 Examples of national heritage-type laws introduced by each state include the following:

Bahrain – Legislative Decree No. 5 of 1986, the National Council for Culture, Arts and Literature;
Kuwait – Law No. 11 of 1960, the Law of Antiquities, as amended by Law No. 9 of 1994;
Oman – National Heritage Protection Law, 1976;
Qatar – Law No. 2 of 1980 on Antiquities;
Saudi Arabia – Law No. M/26 of 23/6/1392 AH (1972), the Law on Antiquities;
UAE – Law No. 8 of 1970 on Archaeological Heritage;
Yemen – Archaeology Protection Law of 1994, amended in 1997.

30 Jaber bin Marhun Fleyfel al-Wahabi, 'Intellectual Property System in the Sultanate of Oman', WIPO Introductory Seminar on Intellectual Property,

Muscat, Oman, 19 April 2004, p. 3; WIPO Document WIPO/IP/MCT/APR/04/3, April 2004.

31 'Chattels of cultural property' are defined as including archaeological fossils, rare archetypes of flora and fauna, fragments of manuscripts, ancient books, documents and printed matter of special historical, artistic, scientific or literary value or interest, as well as traditional-style furniture items, painted earthenware, musical instruments, jewellery, precious stones and weapons.

32 *Oman*: the Archaeological Sites of Bat, Al-Khutm and Al-Ayn (1988), Bahla Fort (1987), Land of Frankincense in Dhofar governerate (2000) and the aflaj irrigation system of Oman (2006).
Yemen: Old Walled City of Shibam (1982), Old City of Sana'a (1986), Historic Town of Zabid (1993), Socotra Archipelago (2008).

33 See Verma, op. cit., p. 780.

34 WTO Ministerial Declaration, Doha, November 2001, para 18, available at <www.wto.org/english/thewto_e/minist_e/min01_e/mindecl_e.htm>

35 Convention on Biological Diversity, art. 1; available at <http://www.biodiv.org/convention/articles.asp>, last accessed 30 January 2006.

36 Ibid, art. 15.

37 Article 8j of the CDB provides that 'Members should respect, preserve and maintain knowledge, innovations and practices of indigenous and local communities embodying traditional lifestyles relevant for the conservation and sustainable use of biological diversity and promote their wider application with the approval and involvement of the holders of such knowledge, innovations and practices and encourage the equitable sharing of the benefits arising from the utilization of such knowledge, innovations and practices'.

38 See WTO, 'TRIPS Article 27.3(b) and Related Issues: Background and the Current Situation', at <http://www.wto.org/english/tratop_e/trips_e/art27_3b_background_e.htm>, last accessed 20 May 2008.

39 Ibid.

40 See Verma, op. cit., pp. 779 and 804–5.

41 Saudi Arabia, Royal Decree No. M/27 of 1425 AH (2004), art. 20.

42 Bahrain, draft plant-varieties protection law, provided by officials of the Ministry of Commerce, December 2004.

43 Oman, Royal Decree No. 92/2000, art. 7.

44 Bahrain FTA, art. 14.8.4; Oman FTA, art. 15.8.4.

45 See *Gulf News*, 11 April 2002, available at <http://www.gulfnews.com/search/Advance_search_result.jsp?d=11&m=04&y=2002>, last accessed 25 June 2006.

46 Ibid, 3 May 2002, available at <http://www.gulfnews.com/search/Advance_search_result.jsp?d=103m=05&y=2002>, last accessed 25 June 2006.

47 See *OMAN: Years of Achievement*, Ministry of Information, Sultanate of Oman (2001), pp. 74–5.

48 See UAE Ministry of Culture, cultural heritage website, at <http://82.195.132.90/history/trad/trd10.asp>, last accessed 30 January 2006.

49 Paragraph 18 of the Doha Declaration notes that the Council of TRIPS will handle work on extension under the Declaration's paragraph 12 on implementation issues. Paragraph 12 states that 'negotiations on outstanding implementation issues shall be an integral part' of the Doha work programme and that implementation issues 'shall be addressed as a matter of priority by the relevant WTO bodies . . .'. Many developing and European countries argue that the outstanding implementation issues are already part of the negotiation and its package of results (the 'single undertaking'). Others argue that these issues can become negotiating subjects only if the Trade Negotiations Committee decides to include them in the talks.

50 The three proposals on the multilateral register issue are all available together in WTO Document TN/IP/W/12 (05–4018) of 14 September 2005, available at <http://docsonline.wto.org>, last accessed 30 December 2005.
51 Bahrain, Legislative Decree No. 16 of 2004, art 3.
52 Oman, Royal Decree No. 40/2000, art. 4; Qatar, Law No. 9 of 2002, arts. 38 and 40.
53 Interviews conducted by the author with officials in the Bahrain Ministry of Commerce, Oman Ministry of Commerce and Industry, and Qatar Ministry of Economy and Trade, December 2004.

8 TRIPS anew, Insha'allah

1 Assafa Endeshaw, 'The Paradox of Intellectual Property Lawmaking in the New Millennium: Universal Templates as Terms of Surrender for Non-industrial Nations; Piracy as an Offshoot', p. 24, available at <http://www.papers.ssrn.com/sol3/papers.cfm?abstract_id=2916912>, last accessed 7 March 2007.
2 Ibid.
3 USTR, *2008 Special 301 Report*, p. 42, available at <http://www.ustr.gov/assets/Document_Library/Reports_Publications/2008/2008_Special_301/assets_upload_file553_14869.pdf>, last accessed 30 June 2008.
4 Jawad al-Redha, co-Chairman Middle East, Business Software Alliance, Quoted in the *Gulf News*, Dubai, 5 February 2005, available at <http://archive.gulfnews.com/articles/05/02/05/150680.htm>, last accessed 30 June 2005; see also 'Kuwait to Stiffen Penalties for Copyright Violations', *Arab News*, 31 August 2004, available at <http://www.arabnews.com/?page=4&section=0&art=50758&d=31&m=8&y=2004&pix=world.jpg&category=World>, last accessed 20 January 2006.
5 USTR, op. cit., p. 44.
6 See Zayed bin Qami, 'Saudi Arabia and the U.S. Sign Bilateral Free Trade Agreement', *Bilaterals.Org*, posted 5 September 2005, available at <http://www.bilaterals.org>, last accessed 25 January 2006.
7 Working Party on the Accession of the Kingdom of Saudi Arabia, *Report of the Working Party on the Accession of the Kingdom of Saudi Arabia to the World Trade Organisation*, 84; WTO Document WT/ACC/ SAU/61 (05–5141), 1 November 2005.
8 Endeshaw, op. cit., p. 31.
9 Ibid.
10 Ibid, p. 34.
11 Ahmed Abdel Latif, 'Current Developments and Trends in the Field of Intellectual Property: Implications for Arab Countries', *Bilaterals.Org*, 28 June 2005, p. 6, available at <http://www.bilaterals.org>, last accessed 20 January 2006.
12 Mohammed Al-Said, 'From TRIPS-minus to TRIPS to TRIPS-plus: Implications of IPRs for the Arab World' (2005), 8, *Journal of World Intellectual Property*, p. 60.
13 ARIPO – African Regional Industrial Property Organisation. Member states are: Botswana, Gambia, Ghana, Kenya, Lesotho, Malawi, Mozambique, Sierra Leone, Somalia, Sudan, Swaziland, Uganda, United Republic of Tanzania, Zambia and Zimbabwe.
14 The 'Group of the Friends of Development' comprises Argentina, Brazil, Bolivia, Cuba, Dominican Republic, Ecuador, Egypt, Iran, Kenya, Peru, Sierra Leone, South Africa, United Republic of Tanzania and Venezuela.

15 WIPO General Assembly, Thirty-First Session, 27 September–5 October 2004, *Proposal by Argentina and Brazil for the Establishment of a Development Agenda for WIPO*, Document WO/GA/31/11 Add., 4 October 2004.

16 WIPO, Inter-sessional Intergovernmental Meeting on a Development Agenda for WIPO, *Proposal by the Kingdom of Bahrain on the Importance of Intellectual Property in Social and Economic Development and National Development Programs*, 20–22 June 2005, WIPO Document IIM/2/2, 14 June 2005.

17 'US, Oman Feud Over Patents in WTO Accession Agreement' (2000), 14, *World Intellectual Property Report*, 117. Report details confirmed in interviews conducted by the author with officials, Oman Ministry of Commerce and Industry, December 2004. The United States called on Oman to include a specific commitment in the draft Report of the Working Party on Oman's accession, which sets out the terms and conditions of Oman's WTO membership, to extend patent protection under Omani law to 25 years – notwithstanding the TRIPS benchmark of 20 years.

18 Gulf Research Centre, Regional Seminar on Future GCC–US Relations Post the US Presidential Elections, Dubai, January 2005, pp. 3–4. Available at <http://www.grc.ae>, last accessed 29 May 2005.

19 Ibid.

20 Ibid.

21 USTR Robert Zoellick, 'Global Trade and the Middle East: Reawakening a Vibrant Past', Address delivered at the World Economic Forum, Dead Sea, Jordan, 23 June 2003, p. 2, available at <http://www.ustr.gov/speech_test/zoellick/2003-06-23-jordan.pdf>, last accessed 30 November 2005.

22 Ibid, p. 7.

23 'Bilateral FTAs are Tools to Serve US Interests', *Arab News*, 11 November 2005, available at <http://www.arabnews.com/services/print/print.asp?artid=73044&d=11&m=11&y=2005>, accessed 14 November 2005.

24 Ibid. The Jordanian Minister also acknowledged that, while the US–Jordanian FTA, signed in October 2000, had greatly enhanced Jordanian exports to the United States and created many local job opportunities, it had failed to deliver know-how and knowledge to Jordanian industry.

25 Ibid.

26 'Ports Deal: A US Perspective', *Gulf News*, 17 March 2006, available at <http://archive.gulfnews.com>, last accessed 20 December 2007.

27 Christian Koch, 'The US Should Pay Attention to Arab Gulf Interests', *Gulf Research Centre*, 23 October 2007, available at <http://www/grc.ae/index.php?sec=GRC+analysissec_type=h>, last accessed 20 December 2007.

28 See Jeremy Williams, *Don't They Know It's Friday? Cross-cultural Considerations for Business in the Gulf* (1998), pp. 72–9.

29 Insha'allah – literally, if the will of Allah. The Muslim believes that the hand of Allah is present in every event that occurs, or indeed does not occur, in the mortal world. Nothing can happen without Allah ordaining it; by the same token, an event or action will not, or did not, occur if Allah so ordains. Hence, conversations on future actions or events are invariably qualified by the phrase 'Insha'allah'.

Appendix

1 As would otherwise be customary practice, there does not appear to be any record, either in Ballantyne's Register of Laws of the Arabian Gulf, or other

national registers, of Qatar having issued a decree or other law ratifying accession to the Nairobi Treaty.

2 Saudi Arabia still issues its decrees and regulations according to the Hajri, or Islamic, Calendar. Hence this form of yearly notation (with the Gregorian calendar equivalent in brackets) is maintained above.

3 As would otherwise be customary practice, there does not appear to be any record, either in Ballantyne's Register of Laws of the Arabian Gulf or other national registers, of Saudi Arabia having issued a decree or other regulation ratifying accession to the Nairobi Treaty.

4 WIPO does not record Saudi Arabia as having lodged Instruments of Accession to the Treaty.

5 WIPO does not record the UAE as having lodged Instruments of Accession to the Agreement.

Appendix

Dedicated intellectual property laws, regulations and orders in the Arab Gulf states

Bahrain

Main current dedicated intellectual property laws, regulations and orders

1. Legislative Decree No. 22 of 2006 concerning Copyright and Neighbouring Rights (issued 25 June 2006, and published in Official Gazette No. 2754 of 28 June 2006).
2. Legislative Decree No. 18 of 2006 ratifying Bahrain's accession to the Trademark Law Treaty (Instrument of Accession lodged 18 December 2006, and treaty entered into force in Bahrain on 18 March 2007).
3. Legislative Decree No. 16 of 2006 amending Law No. 16 of 2004 concerning Geographical Indications (issued 28 May 2006, and published in Official Gazette No. 2741 of 31 May 2006).
4. Legislative Decree No. 14 of 2006 amending Law No. 1 of 2004 concerning Patents and Utility Models (issued 28 May 2006, and published in Official Gazette No. 2741 of 31 May 2006).
5. Legislative Decree No. 12 of 2006 amending Law No. 7 of 2003 concerning Trade Secrets (issued 28 May 2006, and published in Official Gazette No. 2741 of 31 May 2006).
6. Legislative Decree No. 11 of 2006 concerning Trademarks (issued 28 May 2006, and published in Official Gazette No. 2741 of 31 May 2006).
7. Ministerial Decree No. 54 of 2006, the Implementing Regulations for Law No. 1 of 2004 in respect of Patents and Utility Models (issued 8 May 2006, and published in Official Gazette No. 2738 of 10 May 2006).
8. Legislative Decree No. 6 of 2006 concerning Industrial Designs (issued 29 April 2006, and published in Official Gazette No. 2737 of 3 May 2006).

9. Legislative Decree No. 5 of 2006 concerning Layout Designs of Integrated Circuits (issued 29 April 2006, and published in Official Gazette No. 2737 of 3 May 2006).
10. Legislative Decree No. 44 of 2005 ratifying Bahrain's accession to the Patent Cooperation Treaty (published in Official Gazette No. 2722 of 18 January 2006) (Instruments of Accession lodged 18 December 2006, and treaty entered into force in Bahrain on 18 March 2007).
11. Legislative Decree No. 23 of 2005 ratifying the Free Trade Agreement between Bahrain and the United States.
12. Legislative Decree No. 19 of 2005 ratifying Bahrain's accession to the WIPO Patent Law Treaty (PLT) (issued 10 July 2005 and published in Official Gazette No. 2695 of 13 July 2005) (Instrument of Accession lodged 15 September 2005, and treaty entered into force in Bahrain on 15 December 2005).
13. Legislative Decree No. 18 of 2005 ratifying Bahrain's accession to the Protocol Relating to the Madrid Agreement Concerning the International Registration of Marks (1989) (issued 10 July 2005 and promulgated in Official Gazette No. 2695 of 13 July 2005) (Instrument of Accession lodged 15 September 2005, and Protocol entered into force in Bahrain on 15 December 2005).
14. Legislative Decree No. 17 of 2005 acceding to the Nice Agreement Concerning the International Classification of Goods and Services for the Purpose of the Registration of Marks (8th edition) (issued February 2005) (Instrument of Accession lodged 15 September 2005, and Agreement entered into force in Bahrain 15 December 2005).
15. Legislative Decree No. 12 of 2005 ratifying Bahrain's accession to the International Convention for the Protection of New Plant Varieties (UPOV) (issued 4 June 2005 and promulgated in Official Gazette No. 2690 of 8 June 2005) (Instrument of Accession lodged 15 September 2005, and Convention entered into force in Bahrain 15 December 2005).
16. Legislative Decree No. 16 of 2004 in respect of Geographical Indications (issued 14 August 2004 and published in Official Gazette No. 2648 of 18 August 2004).
17. Legislative Decree No. 15 of 2004 approving the accession of Bahrain to the WIPO Performances and Phonograms Treaty (Instrument of Accession lodged 15 September 2005, and treaty entered into force in Bahrain on 15 December 2005).
18. Legislative Decree No. 14 of 2004 approving the accession of Bahrain to the WIPO Copyright Treaty (Instrument of Accession lodged 15 September 2005, and treaty entered into force in Bahrain on 15 December 2005).

19. Legislative Decree No. 13 of 2004 acceding to the Nice Agreement Concerning the International Classification of Goods and Services for the Purpose of the Registration of Marks.
20. Legislative Decree No. 12 of 2004 adopting the GCC Unified Patent Regulation in Bahrain (issued 22 June 2004, and published in Official Gazette No. 2640 of 2004).
21. Legislative Decree No. 1 of 2004 in respect of Patents and Utility Models (issued 24 January 2004 and published in Official Gazette No. 2619 of 28 January 2004).
22. Legislative Decree No. 7 of 2003 in respect of Trade Secrets (issued 13 June 2003, and published in Official Gazette No. 2587 of 18 June 2003).
23. Legislative Decree No. 47 of 2002 in respect of the Organization of the Press, Printing and Publication.
24. Legislative Decree No. 31 of 1996 ratifying Bahrain's accession to the Paris Convention for the Protection of Industrial Property (issued 29 October 1996 and published in Official Gazette No. 2240 of 1996) (Instrument of Accession lodged on 2 December 1996, and Convention entered into force in Bahrain on 2 March 1997).
25. Legislative Decree No. 30 of 1996 ratifying Bahrain's accession to the Berne Convention for the Protection of Literary and Artistic Works (issued 29 October 1996, and published in Official Gazette No. 2240 of 1996) (Instrument of Accession lodged 2 December 1996, and Convention entered into force in Bahrain on 2 March 1997).
26. Legislative Decree No. 1 of 1995 ratifying Bahrain's accession to the Convention Establishing the World Intellectual Property Organisation (issued 11 February 1995 and published in Official Gazette No. 2151 of 1995) (Instrument of Accession lodged 22 March 1995, and Convention entered into force in Bahrain 22 June 1995).
27. Legislative Decree No. 7 of 1994 ratifying Bahrain's accession to the Protocol Establishing the World Trade Organisation (issued 12 June 1994, and published in Official Gazette No. 2120 of 1994) (Protocol entered into force in Bahrain on 1 January 1995).
28. Ministerial Order No. 12 of 1993, the Implementing Regulations for Amiri Decree No. 10 of 1991 concerning Trade Marks (issued 17 May 1993, and published in Official Gazette No. 2060 of 19 May 1993).

Subordinate, associated and superseded legislation

29. Ministerial Order No. 1 of 1994 on the System of Deposit at the Copyright Protection Office (issued 15 May 1994, and published in Official Gazette No. 2112 of 1994).

30. Legislative Decree No. 10 of 1993 with respect to the Protection of Copyright (issued 7 June 1993, and published in Official Gazette No. 2063 of 9 June 1993).

31. Ministerial Order No. 4 of 1993, with respect to the establishment of the Copyright Protection Office in the Ministry of Information (issued 14 November 1993, and published in Official Gazette No. 2086 of 1993).

32. Amiri Decree No. 10 of 1991, concerning Trade Marks (issued 25 June 1991, and published in Official Gazette No. 1961 of 26 June 1991).

33. Amiri Decree No. 7 of 1987, the Law of Commerce (published in Official Gazette No. 1739 of 1987).

34. Amiri Decree No. 5 of 1986, establishing the National Council for Culture, Arts and Literature (published in Official Gazette No. 1720 of 1986).

35. Ministerial Order No. 10 of 1981, amending the Implementing Regulations for Decree No. 22 of 1977 concerning Trade Marks (published in Official Gazette No. 1436 of 1981).

36. Amiri Decree No. 14 of 1979, the Law on Printed Matter and Publishing (published in Official Gazette No. 1344 of 1979).

37. Ministerial Order No. 13 of 1978 amending Ministerial Order No. 2 of 1978, the Implementing Regulations for Amiri Decree No. 22 of 1977 (issued 18 June 1978, and published in Official Gazette No. 1285 of 1978).

38. Ministerial Order No. 2 of 1978, the Implementing Regulations for the Patents, Design and Trade Marks Regulation of 1955 as amended by Amiri Decree No. 22 of 1977 (issued 1 February 1978, and promulgated in Official Gazette No. 1266 of 9 February 1978).

39. Amiri Decree No. 22 of 1977 amending certain provisions of the Patents, Designs and Trade Marks Regulation of 1955 (issued 9 November 1977, and published in Official Gazette No. 1253 of 10 November 1977).

40. Amiri Decree No. 20 of 1975 with respect to the Legal Deposit of Intellectual Works (published in Official Gazette No. 114 of 1975).

41. Amiri Decree No. 12 of 1971, the Civil and Commercial Procedures Code (published in Official Gazette No. 926 of 1971).

42. Patents, Designs and Trade Marks Regulation, No. 1 of 1955 (promulgated 15 June 1955).

Kuwait

Main current dedicated intellectual property laws, regulations and orders

1. Law No. 3 of 2001 amending certain provisions of Law No. 4 of 1962, concerning Patents, Designs and Industrial Models.
2. Law No. 1 of 2001 amending certain provisions relating to Trademarks and Trade Indications of Law No. 68 of 1980, the Commercial Code.
3. Law No. 64 of 1999, governing Copyrights and Related Rights (issued as Law No. 5 of 1999 on 6 June 1999, during the period of dissolution of Parliament. Reissued by the new Parliament as Law No. 64 of 1999 on 29 December 1999, and published in Official Gazette No. 445 of 9 January 2000).
4. Law No. 4 of 1999, amending certain provisions of Law No. 4 of 1962 concerning Patents, Designs and Industrial Models (issued 25 May 1999, and published in Official Gazette No. 414 of 1999).
5. Law No. 3 of 1999, amending certain provisions of Law No. 68 of 1980, the Commercial Code (issued 25 May 1999).
6. Law No. 2 of 1998 ratifying Kuwait's accession to the Convention Establishing the World Intellectual Property Organization (Instrument of Accession lodged 14 April 1998, and Convention entered into force in Kuwait on 14 July 1998).
7. Law No. 16 of 1986, ratifying the Arab Agreement for the Protection of Authors' Rights (published in Official Gazette No. 1657 of 1986).

Subordinate, associated and superseded legislation

8. Ministerial Order No. 127 of 2000, establishing the Directorate of Intellectual Property in the Ministry of Information.
9. Ministerial Order No. 106 of 2000, granting judicial authority to designated Ministry of Information Officials.
10. Ministerial Order No. 8 of 1995, establishing the Trade Mark Register (issued 8 January 1995, and published in Official Gazette No. 190 of 15 January 1995).
11. Law No. 68 of 1980, the Commercial Code (published in Official Gazette No. 1338 of 1980).
12. Law No. 67 of 1980, the Civil Code (promulgated in Official Gazette No. 1335 of 1981).

13. Ministerial Order No. 15 of 1965, the Implementing Regulations for Law No. 4 of 1962 governing Patents, Designs and Industrial Models (published in Official Gazette No. 555 of 5 December 1965).
14. Law No. 4 of 1962 governing Patents, Designs and Industrial Models (issued 9 April 1962, and published in Official Gazette No. 373 of 15 April 1962).
15. Law No. 3 of 1961, the Printed Matter and Publications Law (published in Official Gazette No. 312 of 1961).
16. Implementing Regulations for Law No. 2 of 1961, for the Control and Register of Trade Marks (published in Official Gazette No. 317 of 5 March 1961).
17. Law No. 2 of 1961, the Commercial Law (published in Official Gazette No. 311 of 1961).

Oman

Main current dedicated intellectual property laws, regulations and orders

1. Royal Decree No. 67/2008, the Law on Industrial Property Rights (issued 12 May 2008, and published in the Official Gazette of 15 May 2008).
2. Royal Decree No. 65/2008, the Law on Copyright and Related Rights (issued 4 May 2008, and published in the Official Gazette of 15 May 2008).
3. Royal Decree No. 37/2007 ratifying the Sultanate's accession to the Convention Relating to the Distribution of Programme-Carrying Signals Transmitted by Satellite (Brussels Convention), the Budapest Treaty on the International Recognition of the Deposit of Microorganism for the Purposes of Patent Procedure, the Protocol Relating to the Madrid Agreement Concerning the International Registration of Marks (Madrid Protocol), International Convention for the Protection of New Varieties of Plants (UPOV Convention), the Patent Law Treaty, and the Trademark Law Treaty (issued 23 April 2007) (Instrument of Accession lodged on 16 July 2007, and Treaties entered into force in Oman on 16 October 2007).
4. Ministerial Decision No. 73/2005, the Implementing Regulations for Royal Decree No. 82/2000, the Patents Law (issued 10 September 2005, and published in Official Gazette No. 799 of 17 September 2005).
5. Royal Decree No. 53/2006 ratifying the Sultanate's accession to the WIPO Copyright Treaty (WCT) and the WIPO Performances and

Phonograms Treaty (WPPT) (Instrument of Accession lodged 20 June 2005, and Treaties entered into force in Oman 20 September 2005).

6. Ministerial Decision No. 62/2005, the Implementing Regulations for Royal Decree No. 38/2000 on the Protection of Trademarks (issued 25 June 2005, and published in Official Gazette No. 795 of 16 July 2005 or No. 798).
7. Royal Decree No. 56/2005 endorsing the Agreement on the Preservation of non-materialist Cultural Heritage (Paris 2003) (issued 22 June 2005).
8. Royal Decree No. 24/2005 establishing the Functions of the Ministry of Heritage and Culture and its organisational structure (issued 26 February 2005).
9. Ministerial Decision No. 35/2004, the Implementing Regulations for Royal Decree 92/2000 on the Protection of New Plant Varieties (issued 10 May 2004 and published in Official Gazette No. 768 of 2004).
10. Royal Decree No. 37/2001 ratifying the Sultanate's accession to the WIPO Patent Cooperation Treaty (PCT) (issued 24 April 2001 and published in Official Gazette No. 694 of 1 May 2001) (Instrument of Accession lodged on 27 July 2001, and Convention entered into force in Oman on 27 October 2001).
11. Royal Decree No. 112/2000 ratifying the Sultanate's accession to the Protocol Establishing the World Trade Organisation (issued 15 November 2000) (Protocol entered into force in Oman 20 November 2000).
12. Royal Decree No. 92/2000, the Law on the Protection of New Plant Varieties (issued 8 October 2000).
13. Ministerial Decision No. 14/2000 recognising the GCC Unified Patent Regulation as amended (1999) as the Patent Law of Oman (issued 23 February 2000, and published on 20 March 2000).
14. Royal Decree No. 63/1998 ratifying the Sultanate's accession to the Paris Convention for the Protection of Industrial Property and the Berne Convention for the Protection of Literary and Artistic Works (issued 28 July 1998, and published in Official Gazette No. 632 of 3 October 1998) (Instrument of Accession lodged 14 April 1999, and Conventions entered into force in Oman on 14 July 1999).
15. Royal Decree No. 74/1996, ratifying the Sultanate's accession to the Convention establishing the World Intellectual Property Organization (issued November 1996) (Instrument of Accession lodged 19 February 1997, and Convention entered into force in Oman on 14 April 1997).

Subordinate, associated and superseded legislation

16. Royal Decree No. 82/2000, the Patents Law (issued 23 September 2000).
17. Royal Decree No. 41/2000, the Law on the Topographies Rights of Integrated Circuits (issued 21 May 2000, and published in Official Gazette No. 672 of 3 June 2000).
18. Royal Decree No. 40/2000, the Law on the Protection of Geographical Indications (issued 21 May 2000, and published in Official Gazette No. 672 of 3 June 2000).
19. Royal Decree No. 39/2000, the Law on the Protection of Industrial Designs (issued 21 May 2000, and published in Official Gazette No. 672 of 3 June 2000).
20. Royal Decree No. 38/2000, the Law on Trade Marks, Indications and Secrets and Protection from Unfair Competition (issued 21 May 2000, and published in Official Gazette No. 672 of 3 June 2000).
21. Royal Decree No. 37/2000, the Law on the Protection of Copyrights and Neighbouring Right, and cancelling Royal Decree 47/96 (issued 21 May 2000, and published in Official Gazette No. 672 of 3 June 2000).
22. Ministerial Regulations Nos. 43/1998 and No. 170/1998, implementing Royal Decree No. 47/1996 concerning copyright.
23. Royal Decree No. 65/1997, the Artistic Works Control Law (issued 5 October 1997, and published in Official Gazette No. 209 of 1997).
24. Royal Decree No. 47/1996, promulgating the Law on Copyright (issued 8 June 1996, and published on 15 June 1996).
25. Ministerial Resolution No. 219/1993, adopting the GCC Unified Patent Regulations as the Patents Law of Oman (issued September 1993, and published in Official Gazette No. 514 of 1993).
26. Royal Decree No. 33/1991, amending Royal Decree No. 68/1987, the Trade Mark Law (issued 6 April 1991, and published in Official Gazette No. 453 of 1991).
27. Ministerial Decision No. 103/1988, the Implementing Regulations for Royal Decree No. 68/1987 (issued 24 November 1988, and published in Official Gazette No. of 1988).
28. Royal Decree No. 68/1987, the Law of Trade Marks and Commercial Data (issued 5 October 1987, and published in Official Gazette No. 369 of 15 October 1987).
29. Royal Decree No. 7/1986 ratifying Oman's accession to the Nairobi Treaty on the Protection of the Olympic Symbol (published in Official

Gazette No. 328 of 1986) (Instrument of Accession lodged 26 February 1986, and Treaty entered into force in Oman on 26 March 1986).

30. Royal Decree No. 49/1984, the Law on Printed Matter and Publications (issued 26 May 1984, and published in Official Gazette No. 289 of 1984).
31. Royal Decree No. 6/1980, the National Heritage Protection Law (issued 10 February 1980, and published in Official Gazette No. 188 of 1980).
32. Royal Decree No. 70/1977, the Law on the Protection of Manuscripts (published in Official Gazette No. 137 of 1977).
33. Royal Decree No. 3/1975, the Law on Printed Matter (published in Official Gazette No. 83 of 1975).
34. Royal Decree No. 7/74, the Oman Penal Code (published in Official Gazette No. 52 of 1974).

Qatar

Main current dedicated intellectual property laws, regulations and orders

1. Law No. 18 of 2007, adopting the GCC Unified Trade Marks Regulation in Qatar (issued July 2007).
2. Law No. 30 of 2006, issuing the Patents Law (issued 6 August 2006).
3. Law of 2005 approving Qatar's accession to the WIPO Copyright Treaty (WCT) (Instrument of Accession lodged 28 July 2005, and Treaty entered into force in Qatar on 28 October 2005).
4. Law of 2005 ratifying Qatar's accession to the WIPO Performances and Phonograms Treaty (WPPT) (Instrument of Accession lodged on 28 July 2005, and Convention entered into force in Qatar on 28 October 2005).
5. Law No. 6 of 2005 on the Protection of Layout Designs of Integrated Circuits (issued 2 March 2005).
6. Law No. 5 of 2005 concerning Trade Secrets (issued 2 March 2005).
7. Law No. 12 of 2003, adopting the GCC Unified Patent Regulation as the Patent Law of Qatar (issued 19 February 2003).
8. Law No. 9 of 2002, the Law of Trade Marks, Business Names and Data, Industrial Designs and Geographical Indications (issued 15 June 2002).
9. Law No. 7 of 2002, the Law of Copyrights and Neighbouring Rights (issued 8 June 2002).
10. Decree No. 33 of 2001 ratifying Qatar's Accession to the Berne Convention for the Protection of Literary and Artistic Works (issued

4 July 2001) (Instrument of Accession lodged 5 April 2000, and Convention entered into force in Qatar on 5 July 2000).

11. Decree No. 31 of 2001 ratifying Qatar's Accession to the Paris Convention for the Protection of Industrial Property (issued 4 July 2001) (Instrument of Accession lodged on 5 April 2000, and Convention entered into force in Qatar on 5 July 2000).
12. Decree No. 24 of 1995 in respect of Qatar's Accession to the Protocol establishing the World Trade Organisation (published in Official Gazette No. 2 of 1995).
13. Decree No. 50 of 1986 in respect of Qatar's Accession to the Arab League Agreement for the Protection of Authors' Rights (published in Official Gazette No. 11 of 1986).

Subordinate, associated and superseded legislation

14. Law No. 25 of 1995 in respect of the Protection of Intellectual Works and Copyrights (issued 22 July 1995, and published in Official Gazette No. 14 of 12 August 1995).
15. Ministerial Order No. 8 of 1995, Executive Regulations for the Trademark Register (published in Official Gazette No. 190 of 15 January 1995).
16. Law No. 16 of 1993 in respect of Public Relations, Artistic Production and Artistic Works (published in Official Gazette No. 13 of 1993).
17. Law No. 37 of 1988 amending Law No. 2 of 1978, the Trade Marks and Descriptions Law (published in Official Gazette No. 11 of 1988).
18. Accession to the Nairobi Treaty on the Protection of the Olympic Symbol (Instrument of Accession lodged on 23 June 1983, and Treaty entered into force in Qatar on 23 July 1983).[1]
19. Law No. 5 of 1983, the Law on Combatting Fraud in Commercial Transactions (published in Official Register No. 2 of 1983).
20. Law No. 14 of 1982 in respect of the Deposit of Works with the Qatar National Library (published in Official Gazette No. 8 of 1982).
21. Ministerial Decision No. 30 of 1980, the Implementing Regulations for Law No. 3 of 1978 the Trade Marks and Commercial Indications Law (issued 11 June 1980, and published in Official Gazette No. 7 of 1980).
22. Amiri Law No. 8 of 1979 in respect of Printed Materials and Publication (published in Official Gazette No. 7 of 1979).
23. Amiri Law No. 3 of 1978, the Trade Marks and Commercial Indications Law (issued 18 April 1978, and published in Official Gazette No. 3 of 20 May 1978).

24. Amiri Law No. 16 of 1971, the Law of Civil and Commercial Matters (published in Official Gazette No. 7 of 1971).
25. Amiri Law No. 11 of 1966, the Law on the Control of Printed Matter (published in Official Gazette No. 4 of 1966).

Saudi Arabia[2]

Main current dedicated intellectual property laws, regulations and orders

1. Ministerial Decision No. 50 of 1426 AH (2005), the Regulations for the Protection of Confidential Commercial Data (issued 4 April 2005), as amended by Ministerial Decision No. 3218 and Ministerial Decision No. 431 of 1426 AH (2005).
2. Ministerial Decision No. 118828/M/10 of 1425 AH (2005) Issuing the Implementing Regulations for Royal Decree No. M/27 of 1425 AH (2004) (issued 26 December 2004).
3. Royal Decree No. M/27 of 1425 AH (2004), the Law of Patents, Layout Designs of Integrated Circuits, Plant Varieties, and Industrial Models (issued 17 July 2004, and promulgated in Official Gazette No. 4004 of 6 August 2004).
4. Ministerial Decision No. 1277 of 1425 AH (2004), Regulations for Border Procedures for the Protection of Intellectual Property Rights of Trademarks and Copyrights (issued 3 July 2004).
5. Ministerial Decision No. 1688/1 of 1425 AH (2004) issuing the Implementing Regulations for Royal Decree No. M/41 of 2003, the Law of Copyright (issued 29 May 2004, and promulgated in Official Gazette No. 3995 of 4 June 2004).
6. Royal Decree No. M/48 of 1424 AH (2003), ratifying the Kingdom's accession to the Paris Convention for the Protection of Industrial Property and the Berne Convention for the Protection of Literary and Artistic Works (issued 9 September 2003) (Instrument of Accession lodged 11 December 2003, and Conventions entered into force in the Kingdom on 11 March 2004).
7. Royal Decree No. M/41 of 1424 AH (2003), the Law of Copyright (issued 30 August 2003, published in Official Gazette No. 3959 of 19 September 2003).
8. Ministerial Decision No. 1723 Issuing the Implementing Regulations for Royal Decree No. M/21 of 1423 AH (2002), (published in the Official Gazette of 18 October 2002).

9. Royal Decree No. M/21 of 1423 AH (2002), the Law of Trademarks (issued 7 August 2002, and published in Official Gazette No. 3907 of 6 September 2002).
10. Royal Decree No. M/15 of 1423 AH (2002), the Law of Commercial Data (issued 25 June 2002).
11. Ministerial Decision No. 1641 of 1422 AH (2001), amending the Implementing Regulations of the Trade Mark Law in respect of the International Classification of Goods and Services (issued 9 July 2001).
12. Implementing Regulations for Royal Decree No. M/15 of 1420 AH (1999), the Law of Trade Names (date uncertain).
13. Royal Decree No. M/15 of 1420 AH (1999), the Law of Trade Names (issued 20 November 1999).
14. Ministerial Order No. 1339 of 1416 AH (1994), establishing the Permanent Committee for IP rights in the Ministry of Trade and Commerce.
15. Royal Decree No. M/12 of 1414 AH (1994), ratifying the Kingdom's assent to the Universal Copyright Convention (issued 29 December 1993, and published in Official Gazette No. 3489 of 21 January 1994) (Instrument of assent lodged with UNESCO on 13 April 1994, and Convention came into effect in Saudi Arabia on 13 July 1994).
16. Royal Decree No. M/6 of 1406 AH (1985), ratifying the Arab Agreement for the Protection of Authors' Rights (issued 22 December 1985, and published in Official Gazette No. 3096 of January 1986).
17. Accession to the Convention Establishing the World Intellectual Property Organisation (Instrument of Accession lodged with WIPO on 22 February 1982, and Convention came into effect in Saudi Arabia on 22 May 1982).[3]

Subordinate, associated and superseded legislation

18. Ministerial Order M/O/158 of 1412 AH (1992), amending the Implementing Regulations for Royal Decree No. M/11 of 1410 AH (issued 9 September 1992).
19. Royal Decree No. M/26 of 1412 AH (1992), the Regulations for the Deposit of Literary Manuscripts (published in Official Gazette No. 3401 of April 1992).
20. Ministerial Resolution No. 35187/M/10, the Implementing Regulations for Royal Decree No. M/38 of 1409 AH, the Patent Regulations (issued 18 June 1990).

21. Ministerial Resolution No. 699 of 1410 AH (1990), the Implementing Regulations for Royal Decree No. M/61 of 1409 AH) (published in Official Gazette No. 3299 of March 1990).
22. Royal Decree No. M/11 of 1410 AH (1989), the Regulation for the Protection of Copyrights (issued 17 December 1989 and published in Official Gazette No. 3291 of 12 January 1990).
23. Royal Decree No. M/61 of 1409 AH (1989), the Commercial Books Regulation (published in Official Gazette No. 3269 of August 1989).
24. Ministerial Resolution No. 473/DS of 1409 AH (1989), the Implementing Regulations for Royal Decree M/17 of 1402 AH (issued 6 June 1989, and published in Official Gazette No. 3266 of July 1989).
25. Royal Decree No. M/38 of 1409 AH (1989), in respect of Patents (issued 17 January 1989, and published in Official Gazette No. 3248 of 17 February 1989).
26. Royal Decree No. M/5 of 1406 AH (1985), ratifying the Kingdom's accession to the Nairobi Treaty on the Protection of the Olympic Symbol (published in Official Gazette No. 3091 of December 1985).[4]
27. Ministerial Resolution No. 94 of 1404 AH (1984), the Implementing Regulations for Royal Decree No. M/5 concerning Trade Marks (issued 6 May 1984, and published in Official Gazette No. 3016 of 25 May 1984).
28. Royal Decree No. M/5 of 1404 AH (1984) concerning Trade Marks (issued 5 February 1984, and published in Official Gazette No. 3004 of 2 March 1984).
29. Royal Decree No. 28 of 1382 AH (1982), the Boycott of Israel Law (issued July 1982).
30. Royal Decree No. M/17 of 1402 AH (1982) concerning the Control of Publications and Publishing (issued 7 February 1982, and published in Official Gazette No. 2904 of 12 February 1982).
31. Royal Decree No. 8762 of 1358 AH (1938) ratifying Rules for the Registration of Trade Marks (also referred to as Royal Decree No. 33/1/4) (issued 10 August 1938).

United Arab Emirates

Main current dedicated intellectual property laws, regulations and orders

1. Federal Decree No. 52 of 2007, adopting the GCC Unified Trade Mark Regulation in the UAE (issued 25 July 2007, and published in Official Gazette No. 466 of 28 June 2007).

2. Federal Decree No. 10 of 2005, ratifying the UAE's accession to the WIPO Performances and Phonograms Treaty (WPPT) (published in Official Gazette No. 425 of 28 February 2005) (Instrument of Accession lodged on 9 March 2005, and Treaty came into effect in the UAE on 9 June 2005).
3. Federal Decree of 2005, ratifying the UAE's accession to the International Convention for the Protection of Performers, Producers of Phonograms and Broadcasting Organizations (Rome Convention) (Instrument of Accession lodged on 14 October 2004, and Convention came into effect in the UAE on 14 January 2005).
4. Ministerial Decision No. 121 of 2004 concerning the Issuance of Five Patents (issued 19 September 2004 and published in Official Gazette No. 420 of 13 October 2004).
5. Federal Law of 2004 ratifying the UAE's accession to the WIPO Copyright Treaty (WCT) (Instrument of Accession lodged on 14 April 2004, and Treaty entered into force in the UAE on 14 July 2004).
6. Federal Decree No. 10 of 2004, acceding to the Berne Convention for the Protection of Literary and Artistic works (issued and published in Official Gazette No, 408 of February 2004) (Instrument of accession lodged with WIPO on 14 April 2004, and Convention entered into force in the UAE on 14 July 2004).
7. Ministerial Decision No. 134 of 2004 on the Mandatory Licencing for Copying or Translating Copyright Works (issued 22 March 2004).
8. Ministerial Decision No. 133 of 2004 on the Collective Management of Copyrights and Neighbouring Rights (issued 22 March 2004).
9. Ministerial Decision No. 132 of 2004 on the Registration of Importers and Distributors of Published Works (issued 22 March 2004).
10. Ministerial Decision No. 131 of 2004 on the Registration of Published Works (issued 22 March 2004).
11. Federal Law No. 17 of 2002 for the Industrial Regulation and Protection of Patents, Industrial Drawings, and Designs, (issued 19 November 2002, and published in Official Gazette No. 390 of 30 November 2002).
12. Federal Law No. 8 of 2002 amending Law No. 37 of 1992 concerning Trademarks (issued 24 July, and published in Official Gazette No. 384 of 31 July 2002).
13. Federal Law No. 7 of 2002 concerning Copyright and Neighbouring Rights, (issued 1 July 2002, and published in Official Gazette No. 383 of 14 July 2002).
14. Ministerial Decision No. 165 of 2001 adopting the Nice Agreement Concerning the International Classification of Goods and Services for the Purpose of the Registration of Marks (issued 24 November 2001).[5]

15. Ministerial Decision No. 61/16 of 2000, adopting the GCC Unified Patent Regulations as amended (1999) in the UAE (issued April 2000).
16. Ministerial Decree No. 404 of 2000 Regarding Pharmaceutical Patents (issued 28 April 2000).
17. Federal Decree No. 84 of 1998, ratifying the accession of the UAE to the Patent Cooperation Treaty (PCT) (issued 18 August 1998) (Instrument of accession lodged with WIPO on 10 December 1998, and Treaty entered into force in the UAE on 10 March 1999).
18. Federal Decree No. 21 of 1997, ratifying the accession of the UAE to the Protocol establishing the World Trade Organization (issued 10 April 1996) (Protocol entered into force in the UAE on 10 April 1996).
19. Federal Decree No. 20 of 1996, ratifying the accession of the UAE to the Paris Convention for the Protection of Industrial Property (issued 18 March 1996 and published in Official Gazette No. 291 of 11 March 1996) (Instrument of accession lodged with WIPO on 19 September 1996, and Convention entered into force in the UAE on 19 December 1996).
20. Federal Law No. 37 of 1992 Governing Trade Marks (issued 28 September 1992, and published in Official Gazette No. 243 of 12 October 1992).
21. Federal Law No. 21 of 1975, ratifying the UAE's accession to the Convention establishing the World Intellectual Property Organization (published in Official Gazette No. 27 of 1975) (Instrument of accession lodged with WIPO on 24 June 1974, and Convention entered into force in the UAE on 24 September 1974).

Subordinate, associated and superseded legislation

22. Ministerial Decree No. 165 of 2001 concerning the reclassification of services in accordance with WIPO classifications.
23. Ministerial Decree No. 68 of 2001 Amending some of the Provisions of Ministerial Decree No. (6) of 1993 concerning the Implementing Regulations of the Trademark Law (issued on 2 May 2001).
24. Federal Law No. 19 for 2000 Amending Some Provisions of Federal Law No. 37 for 1992 with regard to Trademarks (issued 16 September 2000).
25. Ministerial Decision No. 412 of 1993, concerning Regulations for the Deposit of Protected Works (issued 1 September 1993, and published in Official Gazette No. 256 of 1993).
26. Ministerial Decision No. 411 of 1993, concerning the Deposit of Protected Intellectual Works (issued 1 September 1993, and published in Official Gazette No. 256 of 1993).

27. Federal Law No. 18 of 1993, the Commercial Transactions Code (published in Official Gazette No. 255 of 1993).
28. Ministerial Decision No. 11 of 1993, the Implementing Regulations for Federal Law No. 44 of 1992 (issued 12 May 1993, and published in Official Gazette No. 251 of 1993).
29. Ministerial Decision No. 6 of 1993, being the Executive Regulations for Federal Law No. 37 of 1992 (issued 2 February 1993).
30. Federal Law No. 44 of 1992, concerning the Organization and Protection of Patents, Industrial Drawings and Industrial Models (issued 12 October 1992, and published in Official Gazette No. 243 of 12 October 1992).
31. Federal Law No. 40 of 1992 concerning the Protection of Intellectual Compilations and Author's Rights (issued 28 September 1992, and published in Official Gazette No. 243 of 12 October 1992).
32. Federal Law No. 11 of 1992, the Civil Procedures Code (published in Official Gazette No. 235 of 1992).
33. Federal Law No. 3 of 1987, the Penal Code (published in Official Gazette No. 182, 1987).
34. Federal Law No. 5 of 1985, the Civil Transactions Code (published in Official Gazette No. 158 of December 1985).
35. Federal Law No. 28 of 1984, ratifying the Arab Agreement for the Protection of Authors' Rights (published in Official Gazette No. 139 of 1984).
36. Federal Law No. 18 of 1981, the Commercial Agencies Law (published in Official Gazette No. 94 of 1981).
37. Federal Law No. 15 of 1980, the Control of Press and Publications (issued 16 November 1980, and published in Official Gazette No. 85 of 1980).
38. Federal Law No. 4 of 1979, on the Suppression of Fraud and Deceit in Commercial Transactions (published in Official Gazette No. 67 of 1979).
39. Federal Law No. 5 of 1973, the Law on Printed Matter and Publishing (published in Official Gazette No. 12 of August 1993).

Yemen

Main current dedicated intellectual property laws, regulations and orders

1. Accession to the Berne Convention (Instrument of Accession lodged 14 April 2008, and Agreement entered into force in Yemen on 14 July 2008).

2. Implementing Regulations for Law No. 19 of 1994 (entered into force on 2 July 2007).
3. Accession to the Paris Convention (Instrument of Accession lodged 15 November 2006, and Agreement entered into force in Yemen on 15 February 2007).
4. Law of 2006 amending Law No. 19 of 1994 concerning Copyright and Industrial Property.
5. Law No. 19 of 1994 concerning Copyright and Industrial Property (issued 29 October 1994, and published in Official Gazette No. 20 of 31 October 1994).
6. Law No. 25 of 1990, on Press and Publications (issued 23 December 1990).
7. Accession to the WIPO Convention (December 1990).
8. Trademarks Law 1976 (Yemen Arab Republic, entered into force 1982).

Regional legislation

1. GCC Unified Trade Mark Law (issued by the 27th GCC Supreme Council on 10 December 2006).
2. Implementing By-laws for the GCC Patent Regulations of 2000 (issued by the GCC Ministerial Council at its 74th session on 8–9 April 2000).
3. GCC Unified Patent Regulations, amending the 1992 Regulations (issued by the GCC Supreme Council on 29 November, 1999, and published in the GCC Patents Gazette No. 1 of 15 May 2000).
4. Implementing By-Laws for the GCC Unified Patent Regulations (issued by the GCC Ministerial Council in October 1996).
5. GCC Unified Patent Regulations (issued by GCC Supreme Council 22 September 1992).
6. Arab Agreement for the Protection of Author's Rights, adopted at the meeting of member states of the Arab Organization for Education, Culture, and Science, Baghdad, 5 November 1981.

Bibliography

Books

Abu-Ghazali, Talal, *Intellectual Property Laws of the Arab Countries*, Kluwer Law International, London, 2000

Amin, S H, *The Legal System of Kuwait*, Royston Publishers, Glasgow, 1991

—— *Law of Intellectual and Industrial Property in Developing Countries: Muslim World*, Scottish Institute of International and Comparative Law, Edinburgh, 1993

Al-Baharna, Husain, *British Extra-Territorial Jurisdiction in the Gulf 1913–1971*, Archive Editions, Slough, 1998

Ballantyne, William M, *Legal Development in Arabia,* Graham & Trotman, London, 1980

—— *Commercial Law in the Arab Middle East: The Gulf States*, Lloyd's of London, London, 1986

—— *Essays and Addresses on Arab Laws,* Curzon Press, Richmond, 2000

Blakeney, Michael, *Legal Aspects of the Transfer of Technology to Developing Countries*, ESC, Oxford, 1989

—— *Trade Related Aspects of Intellectual Property Rights: A Concise Guide to the TRIPS Agreement*, Sweet & Maxwell, London, 1996

Correa, Carlos M and Abdulqawi, Yusuf, *Intellectual Property and International Trade – The TRIPS Agreement*, Kluwer Law International, London, 1998

Correa, Carlos M, *Intellectual Property Rights, The WTO and Developing Countries: The TRIPS Agreement and Policy Options*, Third World Network, Penang, 2000

D'Amato, A and Long, D E (eds) *International Intellectual Property Law*, Kluwer Law International, London, 1997

Doi, Abdur Rahman, *Shariah: The Islamic Law,* A S Nordeen, Kuala Lumpur, 2002

Drahos, Peter and Braithwaite, John, *Global Business Regulation*, CUP, Cambridge, 2000

—— *Information Feudalism: Who Owns the Knowledge Economy?*, Earthscan, London, 2002

Edge, Ian, *Islamic Law and Theory*, Dartmouth, London, 1996

Gutterman, A S and Anderson, B J, *Intellectual Property in Global Markets*, Kluwer Law International, London, 1997

Hall, Marjorie and Moxon, Richard, *Business Laws of the United Arab Emirates*, Graham & Trotman, London, 1979

Hussain, Jamilla, *Islam: Its Law and Society*, Federation Press, Sydney, 2004

Kamoonpuri, Hasan, *Oman's Best Brands,* Oman Daily Observer, Muscat, 2008

Lawrence, Robert, *A US–Middle East Trade Agreement: A Circle of Opportunity?*, Peterson Institute for International Economics, Washington DC, 2006

May, Christopher, *The World Intellectual Property Organization: Resurgence and the Development Agenda*, Routledge, Oxford, 2007

Ramanazi, Rouhoulla K, *The Gulf Cooperation Council: Record and Analysis*, University Press of Virginia, Charlottesville, 1988

Rayner, Susan E, *The Theory of Contracts in Islamic Law*, Graham & Trotman, London, 1991

Williams, Jeremy, *Don't They Know It's Friday? Cross-cultural Considerations for Business in the Gulf*, Motivate Publishing, Dubai, 1998

Monographs, reports and theses

Abu-Ghazali Intellectual Property (AGIP), *Intellectual Property Handbook 2007*, available at <http://www.agip.com/AGIP_Handbook.pdf?lang=en>

'Arab comparative and commercial law: the international approach', *Proceedings of the International Bar Association First Arab Regional Conference*, Cairo, February 1987, Graham & Trotman and International Bar Association, London, 1987

Business Software Alliance (BSA), *Sixth Annual BSA Global Software Piracy Study*, May 2001, available at <http://www.bsa.org/resources/upload/2001-Global-Software-Piracy-Study.pdf>

—— *Seventh Annual BSA Global Software Piracy Study*, June 2002, available at <http://www.bsa.org/resources/upload/2002-Global-Software-Piracy-Study.pdf>

—— *Eighth Annual BSA Global Software Piracy Study: Trends in Software Piracy 1994–2002*, June 2003, available at <http://www.bsa.org/globalstudy2003/ upload/2003-Global-Software-Piracy-Study.pdf>

—— *First Annual BSA and IDC Global Software Piracy Study*, May 2004, available at <http://www.bsa.org/globalstudy/upload/Global-Software-Piracy-Study.pdf>

—— *Second Annual BSA and IDC Global Software Piracy Study*, May 2005, available at <http://www.bsa.org/globalstudy/upload/2005-Global-Software-Piracy-Study.pdf>

—— *Third Annual BSA and IDC Global Software Piracy Study*, May 2006, available at <http://www.bsa.org/globalstudy/upload/2006-Global-Software-Piracy-Study.pdf>

—— *Fourth Annual BSA and IDC Global Software Piracy Study*, May 2007, available at <http://www.bsa.org/globalstudy/upload/2007-Global-Software-Piracy-Study.pdf>

—— *Fifth Annual BSA and IDC Global Software Piracy Study*, May 2008, available at <http://www.bsa.org/globalstudy/upload/2008-Global-Software-Piracy-Study.pdf>

Gulf Cooperation Council, *GCC Charter*, available at <http://www.gcc-sg,org/charter.html>

—— *The Unified Economic Agreement Between the Countries of the Gulf Co-operation Council*, available at <http://www.gcc-sg.org/Economic.html>

Convention on Biological Diversity, available at <http://www.biodiv.org/convention/articles.asp>

Al-Kamali, Mohamed Mahmoud, 'The Development of Intellectual Property law in the United Arab Emirates', unpublished PhD Thesis, University of Exeter, UK, 1994

Al-Riyami, Yahya, 'Intellectual Property Protection, Enforcement in the Gulf States and Copyright Protection in the Middle East', unpublished Master of Laws Thesis, Franklin Pierce Law Centre, Concord NH, USA, 2002

OMAN: Years of Achievement, Ministry of Information, Sultanate of Oman, 2001

Report of the Asian Regional Workshop on Bilateral Free Trade Agreements, Kuala Lumpur, August 2005, available at <http://www.twnside.org.sg/title2/twninfo254.htm>

Al-Tamimi, Essam, *The Framework for Litigation in the United Arab Emirates*, Tamimi & Co, Dubai UAE (undated), available at <http://www.tamimi.com/site_1024/pdf/litigati.pdf>

United Nations Commission for Trade and Development (UNCTAD), *Investment Provisions in Economic Integration Agreements*, Document UNCTAD/ITE/IIT/2005/10, available at <http://www.unctad.org/en/docs/iteiit200510_en.pdf>

United Nations Development Programme (UNDP), *Programme on Governance in the Arab Region: Bahrain,* available at <http://www.undp-pogar.org/countries/judiciary.asp?cid=2>

—— *Programme on Strengthening the Rule of Law in the Arab States,* Regional Conference on Intellectual Property Crimes, Bahrain, 13–14 April 2008, available at <http://www.arab-niaba.org/publications/crime/bahrain/background-e.pdf>

United States Patent and Trademark Office (USPTO), *Patent Counts by Country/State and Year, January 1 1997–December 31 2001*, February 2002, available at <http://www.uspto.gov/web/offices/ac/ido/oeip/taf/est_all.pdf>

Articles in journals and periodicals

Abdel Latif, Ahmed, 'Current developments and Trends in the Field of Intellectual Property: Implications for Arab Countries', *Bilaterals.Org*, at <http://www.bilaterals.org>, posted 28 June 2005

Abdul Ghani Azmi, Ida Madieha bt, 'Basis for the Recognition of Intellectual Property in the Light of the Shariah', 1996, 27, *International Review of Industrial Property and Copyright Law*, 649

—— 'The Philosophy of Intellectual Property Rights over Ideas in Cyberspace: A Comparative Analysis between the Western Jurisprudence and the Shariah', 2004, 19(1–2) *Arab Law Quarterly*, 191

Addor, Felix and Grazioli, Alexandra, 'Geographical Indications Beyond Wines and Spirits – A Roadmap for Better Protection for Geographical Indications in the WTO TRIPS Agreement', 2002, 5, *Journal of World Intellectual Property*, 865

Ali, Reema and Haddad, Loubna, 'WTO Membership and Compliance in the Middle East Countries: Extensive Efforts Still Needed', 1999, 22(9), *Middle East Executive Reports*, 11

Alsamdan, Ahmad, 'Development of Copyright Law in Kuwait', 2006 20(3), *Arab Law Quarterly*, 211

Amin, S H, 'Trade Mark Protection: Recent Case May Affect Saudi Law's Credibility', 1989, 12(1), *Middle East Executive Reports*, 10

Angell, Nicholas, 'An Overview of Legal Structures in the GCC Countries', Legal 500 Research Paper No. 3 (March 2002), available at <http://www.legal500.com/devs/emirates/cc/uacc_010.htm>

Ashour, Mona and Barakat, Hoda, 'Judgment for International Company in Pharmaceutical Trademark Case', 1999, 22(4), *Middle East Executive Reports*, 9

Bahgat, Gawdat, 'Military Security and Political Stability in the Gulf', 1995, Fall, *Arab Studies Quarterly*, 55

Blakeney, Michael, 'Proposals for the International Regulation of Geographical Indications', 2001, 4, *Journal of World Intellectual Property*, 629

Buckingham, Simon, 'In Search of Copyright Protection in the Kingdom', 1988, 11(5), *Middle East Executive Reports*, 11

Carroll, John, 'Intellectual Property Rights in the Middle East', 2000/2001, 11, *Fordham Intellectual Property Media and Entertainment Law Journal*, 555

Choudry, Aziz, 'Bilateral Trade and Investment Deals: A Serious Challenge to Global Justice Movements', *GRAIN,* December 2003, available at <http://www.grain.org/rights/tripsplus.cfm?id=2>

—— 'Bombarded by Bilateral Trade and Investment Agreements', *Bilaterals.org*, March 2004, available at <http://www.bilaterals.org/IMG/pdf/Bombarded_by_Bilatera_92909–2.pdf>

—— 'Corporate Conquest, Global Geopolitics: Intellectual property rights and bilateral investment agreements', *Seedling,* January 2005, available at <http://www.grain.org/seedling/?id=314>

Correa, Carlos M, 'Implementing the TRIPS Agreement in the Patent Field – Options for Developing Countries', 1998, 1, *Journal of World Intellectual Property*, 75

—— 'The WTO Dispute Settlement Mechanism: TRIPS Rulings and the Developing Countries', 2001, 4, *Journal of World Intellectual Property*, 257

—— 'Bilateral Investment Agreements: Agents of new global standards for the protection of intellectual property rights?', *GRAIN*, August 2004, available at <http://www.grain.org/briefings/?id=186>

Drahos, Peter, 'BITS and BIPS – Bilateralism in Intellectual Property', 2001, 4, *Journal of World Intellectual Property*, 791

—— 'Developing Countries and International Intellectual Property Standard-Setting', 2002, 5, *Journal of World Intellectual Property*, 765

—— 'Expanding Intellectual Property's Empire: The Role of FTAs', *GRAIN,* November 2003, available at <http://www.grain.org/TRIPS-plus>

Dutfield, Graham, 'Thinking Aloud on Disclosure of Origin', *Quaker International Affairs Programme/Quaker United Nations Office,* Occasional Paper 18, October 2005

Endeshaw, Assafa, 'The Paradox of Intellectual Property Lawmaking in the New Millennium: Universal templates as terms of surrender for non-industrial nations, piracy as an offshoot', available at <http://www.papers.ssrn.com/sol3/papers.cfm?abstract_id=291692>

Fink, Carsten and Reichenmiller, Patrick, 'Tightening TRIPS: The Intellectual Property Provisions of Recent US Free Trade Agreements', *World Bank Group International Trade Department,* Trade Note 20, 7 February 2005, available at <http://www.worldbank.org/INTRANETTRADE/Resources/Pubs/TradeNote20.pdf>

'Future of GCC–US Relations Post–US Presidential Elections', *Gulf Research Centre,* Symposium, Dubai UAE, 5–6 January 2005

Garoub, Majed, 'Protection of Trademarks in the Kingdom of Saudi Arabia', 1999, 14, *Arab Law Quarterly*, 66

Gervais, Daniel, 'TRIPS, Doha and Traditional Knowledge', 2003, 6, *Journal of World Intellectual Property*, 40

Ghadyan, Mohammad Hashim Kamali, 'The Judiciary in Saudi Arabia', 1998, 13, *Arab Law Quarterly*, 235

Hansen, Maren, 'Intellectual Property in the Kingdom', 1990, 13(12), *Middle East Executive Reports*, 8

—— 'Taking a Realistic Approach to Trade Mark Protection in the Gulf Countries', 1993, 16(5), *Middle East Executive Reports*, 8

Hirst, Alastair, 'Developing IPR in the Gulf: Current Coverage, Problems, Post-Uruguay Round Trends', 1994, 17(2), *Middle East Executive Reports*, 9

—— 'Restructuring Oman's Court System and Judiciary', 1999, 22(9), *Middle East Executive Reports*, 11

—— 'Oman: Comprehensive Reform, Extension of Intellectual Property Legislation', 2000, 23(10), *Middle East Executive Reports*, 9

—— 'A Comprehensive Reform of the UAE Copyright Law', 2002, 25(1), *Middle East Executive Reports*, 17

ICTSD and IISD, 'Doha Round Briefing Series: Intellectual Property', November 2005, available at <http://www.ictsd.or/pubs/dohabriefings/Hong_Kong_Update/5-IPRs.pdf>

Jackson, David, 'The Kingdom Enacts a New Patents Law', 1989, 12(4), *Middle East Executive Reports*, 9

Jamar, Stephen, 'The Protection of Intellectual Property Under Islamic Law', 1992, 21, *Capital University Law Review*, 1079

Johnson, Neal and Cassin J J, 'New Saudi Copyright Law', 1990, 13(2), *Middle East Executive Reports*, 9

Joyce, Miriam, 'On the Road towards Unity: The Trucial States from a British Perspective, 1960–66', 1999, 35(2), *Middle Eastern Studies*, 35

Al-Kandari, Mahmoud, 'Infringement of Copyright and Trade Marks in Electronic Commerce: A Kuwaiti and Comparative Approach', 2002, 17, *Arab Law Quarterly*, 3

Khoury, Amir, 'Ancient and Islamic Sources of Intellectual Property Protection in the Middle East: A Focus on Trademarks', 2003, 43, *IDEA*, 151

—— 'The Development of Modern Trademark Legislation and Protection in Arab Countries of the Middle East', 2000, 16, *Transnational Lawyer*, 249

Katzman, Kenneth, 'The Persian Gulf States: Post-War Issues for US Policy', *CRS Report for Congress*, No. RL31533, The Library of Congress, 21 December 2005

King, Henry, 'The WTO: What it Does and Doesn't Do, and How it Affects US Business', 1999, 22(10), *Middle East Executive Reports*, 8

Koch, Christian, 'GCC–EU Free Trade Agreement Must Be Saved', *Gulf Research Centre,* 10 July 2008, available at<http://www.grc.ae/print.php,last>

—— 'The US Should Pay Attention to Arab Gulf Interests', *Gulf Research Centre*, 23 October 2007, available at http://www/grc.ae/index.php?sec=GRC+analysis sec_type=h,

Kongolo, Tshimanga and Shyllon, Folarin, 'Panorama of the Most Controversial IP Issues in Developing Countries', 2004, 6, *European Intellectual Property Review*, 258

Laubach, Charles and Wolfson, Herbert, 'WIPO Suggestions to Bring New UAE Copyright Law into International Standards', 2003, 16(7), *Middle East Executive Reports*, 8

Malkawi, Bashar H, 'Anatomy of the Case of Arab Countries and the WTO', 2006, 20(2), *Arab Law Quarterly*, 110

Markheim, Daniella, 'America's Free Trade Agenda: The State of Bilateral and Multilateral Trade Negotiations', *Bilaterals.Org*, 2 November 2005, available at <http://www.bilaterals.org/article-print.php?id_article=3032>

Mathur, Somesh, 'Trade-related Aspects of Intellectual Property Rights and Copyright Provisions – Some Issues with Special Reference to Developing Countries', 2003, 6, *Journal of World Intellectual Property*, 65

Meyer-Reumann, Rolf, 'The Endeavours of Gulf Countries to Meet WTO Requirements', 2001, 16, *Arab Law Quarterly*, 49

Al-Muhairi, Butti Sultan Butti Ali, 'The Development of the UAE Legal System and Unification with the Judicial System', 1996, 11, *Arab Law Quarterly*, 116

Musungu, Sisule and Dutfield, Graham, 'Multilateral Agreements and a TRIPS-plus World: The World Intellectual Property Organization', TRIPS Issues Papers No. 3, available at <http://www.iprsonline.org/ictsd/docs/WIPO_Musungu_Dutfield.pdf>

El-Nafie, Abdelrahman Mohamed, 'Oman Reforms its Judicial System', 1997, 20(3), *Middle East Executive Reports*, 8

O'Connor, Bernard, 'Protecting Traditional Knowledge – An Overview of a Developing Property Law', 2003, 6, *Journal of World Intellectual Property*, 677

'Office of the U.S. Trade Representative's Fact Sheet on Special 301 Intellectual Property Lists', 1997, 11, *World Intellectual Property Report*, 207

Prados, Alfred, 'Saudi Arabia: Current Issues and US Relations', *CRS Report for Congress*, No. IB93113, The Library of Congress, 15 September 2003

Price, David, 'Intellectual Property Protection in the Gulf Region', 2004, 35, *International Review of Industrial Property and Copyright Law*, 281

Price, David, 'The US–Bahrain Free Trade Agreement and Intellectual Property Protection', 2004, 7, *Journal of World Intellectual Property*, 829

Puri, Kamal, 'Is Traditional Knowledge or Cultural Knowledge a Form of Intellectual Property?', *Oxford Electronic Journal of Intellectual Property Rights*, 18 January 2000, available at <http://www.oiprc.ox.ac.uk/EJWP0100.pdf>

Qami, Zayid bin, 'Saudi Arabia and the US Sign Bilateral Free Trade Agreement', *Bilaterals.Org*, at <http://www.bilaterals.org>, posted 5 September 2005

Regional Seminar on Future GCC–US Relations Post the US Presidential Elections, Gulf Research Centre, Dubai, January 2005, available at <http://www.grc.ae>

'Regional Update', 1989, 3, *World Intellectual Property Report*, 12

'Results of 1998 "Special 301" Provisions of 1974 Trade Act Regarding Intellectual Property Protection', 1998, 12, *World Intellectual Property Report*, 195

'Results of 1999 "Special 301" Provisions of 1974 Trade Act Regarding Intellectual Property Protection', 1999, 13, *World Intellectual Property Report*, 216

Rosenthal, Douglas, 'A Comment on the 1998 "Special 301 Annual Review" of the U.S. Trade Representative', 1998, 1, *Journal of World Intellectual Property*, 743

El-Said, Mohammed, 'From TRIPS-minus to TRIPS to TRIPS-plus: Implications of IPRs for the Arab World', 2005, 8, *Journal of World Intellectual Property*, 53

Saif, Ahmed, 'Constitutionalism in the Arab Gulf States', *GCC Research Program – GCC Constitutions*, Gulf Research Centre, Dubai, UAE, December 2002

—— 'Arab Gulf Judicial Systems and Structures', *GCC Research Program – GCC Judiciaries*, Gulf Research Centre, Dubai, UAE, December 2004

Samahon, Tuan N, 'TRIPS Copyright Dispute Settlement after the Transition and Moratorium: Nonviolation and Situation Complaints against Developing Countries (Agreement on Trade-Related Aspects of Intellectual Property)', 2000, 31, *Law and Policy in International Business*, 1051

Schackel, Torsten and Meyer-Reumann, Rolf, 'The Trademark Law of the United Arab Emirates', 1994, 6, *European Intellectual Property Review*, 250

Shashikant, Sangeeta, 'The Politics of United States Free Trade Agreements', 2004, 167–168, *Third World Resurgence*, Third World Network, available at <http://www.twnside.org.sg/title2/twr167–168.htm>

Stovall, Howard L, 'Arab Commercial Laws – Into the Future', 2000, 34, *The International Lawyer*, 839

Su, Evelyn, 'The Winners and the Losers: The Agreement on Trade-Related Aspects of Intellectual Property: Rights and its Effects on Developing Countries', 2000, 23, *Houston Journal of International Law*, 169

Subedi, Surya, 'The Road from Doha: The Issues for the Development Round of the WTO and the Future of International Trade', 2003, 52, *International and Comparative Law Quarterly*, 425

Sunna, Rawan Mkaram, 'Bridging the Gulf: Harmonisation of Trade Mark Laws in the Gulf Cooperation Council Countries', 2003, 1, *Trade Mark World*, Supplement No. 1

'The TRIPS review at a turning point?', *GRAIN,* July 2003, available at <http://www.grain.org/briefings/?id=122>, last accessed 18 January 2006

Thomas, John R, 'Intellectual Property and Free Trade Agreements: Innovation Policy Issues', *CRS Report for Congress*, The Library of Congress, 21 December 2005, available at <http://www.bilaterals.org/IMG/pdf/RL33205_20051221.pdf>

'Trips-plus Through the Back Door: How Bilateral Treaties Impose Much Stronger Rules for PIRS on Life than the WTO', *GRAIN,* July 2001, available at <http://www.grain.org/briefings/index.cfm?id=6>

Usmani, Mufti Taqi, 'Copyright according to *Shariah*', available at *Al-Balagh Webzine*, <http://www.islamic-finance.net/research/taqi4.htm>

'U.S. Report Spotlights Egyptian and Saudi Copyright Problems', 1989, 12(6), *Middle East Executive Reports*, 9

'USTR's Annual Report: GCC Trade and Investment Barriers', 1995, 18(5), *Middle East Executive Reports*, 13

'USTR Names 16 to Priority List, 32 to Watch List in Special 301 Process', 2001, 16, *World Intellectual Property Report*, 11

Vandoren, Paul, 'The TRIPS Agreement – A Rising Star', 2001, 4, *Journal of World Intellectual Property*, 307

Verma, Surinder, 'Protecting Traditional Knowledge: Is a Sui Generis System an Answer?', 2004, 7, *Journal of World Intellectual Property*, 765

Vivas, David, 'Regional and Bilateral Agreements and a TRIPS-plus World: The Free Trade Area of the Americas', TRIPS Issues Papers No. 1, available at <http://www.iprsonline.org/icstd/docs/WIPO_Vivas.pdf>, last accessed 20 December 2005

Watal, Jayashree, 'The TRIPS Agreement and Developing Countries – Strong, Weak or Balanced Protection?', 1998, 1, *Journal of World Intellectual Property*, 281

Weiss, B, 'Interpretation in Islamic Law: The Theory of "Ijtihad"', 1978, 26, *American Journal of Comparative Law*, 199

'WIPO Examines ADR to Resolve IP Disputes', 1996, 10, *World Intellectual Property Report*, 144

Zahraa, Mahdi, 'Characteristic Features of Islamic Law: Perceptions and Misconceptions', 2000, 15, *Arab Law Quarterly*, 168

World Intellectual Property Organisation (WIPO), Documents, Reports and Publications

(at <http://www.wipo.int>)

Blakeney, Michael, 'Proposals for the Disclosure of Origin of Genetic Resources in Plant Applications', WIPO Document WIPO/IP/GR/05/01, Annex

'Contracting Parties to Treaties Administered by WIPO', 15 July 2008, available at <http://www.wipo.int/treaties/en/general/parties>

Consultation Meeting on Enforcement, *Existing Needs for Training and for Development of Enforcement Strategies,* 11–13 September 2002, WIPO Document WIPO/C/ME/2 Rev., 10 September 2002

'Draft Act on the Protection of Layout-Designs (Topographies) of Integrated Circuits', available at <http://www.wipo.int/cfdiplaw/en/trips/doc/integrated_circuits.doc>

Intellectual Property and Traditional Cultural Expressions/Folklore, WIPO Publication No. 913(E), available at <http://www.wipo.int/ebookshop>

'Intellectual Property Needs and Expectations of Traditional Knowledge Holders', *Report of the Fact-Finding Missions on Intellectual Property and Traditional Knowledge*, WIPO, Geneva, 2002

Inter-sessional Intergovernmental Meeting on a Development Agenda for WIPO, *Proposal by the United States of America for the Establishment of a Partnership Program in WIPO,* 11–13 April 2005, WIPO Document IIM/1/2, 18 March 2005

—— *Proposal by the Kingdom of Bahrain on the Importance of Intellectual Property in Social and Economic Development and National Development Programs,* 20–22 June 2005, WIPO Document IIM/2/2, 14 June 2005

'Legislative Assistance provided by WIPO in Relation to the Implementation of the Agreement on Trade-related Aspects of Intellectual Property Rights (the TRIPS Agreement) and the Doha Declaration', 8 July 2003, available at <http://www.wipo.int/info\CFD/legislativeassistance.htm>

Lesser, W, 'The Effects of TRIPS-Mandated IP Rights on Economic Activity in Developing Countries', 17 April 2001, at <http://www.wipo.int/about-ip/en/studies/pdf/ssa_lesser_trips>

WIPO General Assembly, Thirty-First Session, 27 September–5 October 2004, *Proposal by Argentina and Brazil for the Establishment of a Development Agenda for WIPO,* WIPO Document WO/GA/31/11 Add., 4 October 2004

'Situation of Industrial Property in the Arab States', *WIPO Occasional Report*, Geneva, 1978

'WIPO Economic Development Sector', available at <http://www.wipo.int/eds/en>

World Intellectual Property Organisation (WIPO), National and Regional Seminars

Blakeney, Michael, 'Enforcement of Intellectual Property Rights: Challenges, Remedies and Public Awareness', WIPO National Seminar on Intellectual Property for Faculty Members of Ajman University, United Arab Emirates, 5–6 May 2004, WIPO Document WIPO/IP/UNI/DUB/04/7

—— 'International Protection of Industrial Property: From the Paris Convention to the TRIPS Agreement', WIPO National Seminar on Intellectual Property, Cairo, 17–19 February 2003, WIPO Document WIPO/IP/CAI/1/03/02

—— 'Intellectual Property, Traditional Knowledge and Genetic Resources: Policy, Law and Current Trends', WIPO National Seminar on Intellectual Property for Faculty Members and Students of Ajman University, United Arab Emirates, 5–6 May 2004, WIPO Document, WIPO/IP/UNI/DUB/04/10.

Ghafale, Roya, 'Unlocking the Hidden Potential of Traditional Knowledge: Building Up a Phytopharmaka Market', WIPO National Seminar on Omani Traditional Values in a Globalised World, Muscat, 13 February 2005, WIPO Document WIPO/IP/MCT/05/4

Hirst, Alastair, 'Enforcement of Intellectual Property Rights', WIPO Arab Regional Consultation Meeting on the Implementation of the TRIPS Agreement, Cairo, Egypt, March 1998, WIPO Document WIPO/IP/CAI/98/3

—— 'The Role of the Government Authorities in the Enforcement of Intellectual Property Rights', WIPO Workshop on the Enforcement of Intellectual Property Rights for Judges, Beirut, December 1999, WIPO Document WIPO/IPR/JU/BEY/99/5B

International Bureau of WIPO, 'Intellectual Property and Traditional Knowledge: Our Identity, Our Future', WIPO International Forum on Matters Concerning Intellectual Property and Genetic Resources, Traditional Knowledge and Folklore, Muscat, Oman, 21–22 January 2002, WIPO Document WIPO/IPTK/MCT/02/INF.11, November 2002

International Bureau of WIPO, 'Introduction to the Protection of Plant Varieties', WIPO National Seminar on Innovation Services and Their Management, Muscat, Oman, 20 April 2004, WIPO Document WIPO/INN/MCT/04/INF.3, April 2004

Olssen, Henry, 'Difficulties in the Enforcement of Intellectual Property Rights and Possible Solutions', WIPO National Workshop for Judges, Riyadh, Saudi Arabia, 13–15 December 2004, WIPO Document WIPO/IP/JU/RYD/04/5

—— 'Policy Considerations and Practical Measures for the Effective Enforcement of Intellectual Property Rights (Copyright), Role of the Public and Private Sector', WIPO National Workshop for Judges, Riyadh, Saudi Arabia, 13–15 December 2004, WIPO Document WIPO/IP/JU/RYD/04/3, May 2004

Suthersanen, Uma, 'Copyright on the Internet: Risks and Opportunities for Authors and Composers', WIPO National Seminar on Copyright and Collective Management, Muscat, Oman, 3 December 2003, WIPO Document WIPO/CCM/MCT/03/1, 28 November 2003

Al-Wahabi, Jaber bin Marhun Fleyfel, 'Intellectual Property System in the Sultanate of Oman', WIPO Introductory Seminar on Intellectual Property, Muscat, Oman, 19 April 2004, WIPO Document WIPO/IP/MCT/APR/04/3, April 2004

World Trade Organisation (WTO) Documents

(at <http://www.wto.org>)

Accession of the Sultanate of Oman, Document WT/ACC/OMN/2 (96–4520), 29 October 1996

Working Party on the Accession of the Sultanate of Oman, *Accession of the Sultanate of Oman: Communication from the Sultanate of Oman*, Document WT/ACC/SPEC/OMN/5 (98–0272), 26 January 1998

Accession of the Sultanate of Oman: Communication from the Sultanate of Oman, WT/ACC/OMN/9 (98–3054), 3 August 1998

Accession of the Sultanate of Oman: Additional Questions and Replies to the Memorandum on the Foreign Trade Regime, Document WT/ACC/OMN/22 (00–0140), 13 January 2000

Report of the Working Party on the Accession of Oman to the World Trade Organisation, Document WT/ACC/OMN/26 (00–3948), 28 September 2000

Working Party on the Accession of the Kingdom of Saudi Arabia, *Accession of Saudi Arabia: Additional Questions and Replies*, Document WT/ACC/SAU/6/Add.3 (96–4561), 30 October 1996

Additional Questions and Replies, Document WT/ACC/SAU/8 96–4635), 4 November 1996

Report of the Working Party on the Accession of the Kingdom of Saudi Arabia to the World Trade Organization, Document WT/ACC/SAU/61 (05–5141), 1 November 2005

Council for Trade-related Aspects of Intellectual Property Rights, *Checklist of Issues on Enforcement: Responses from Bahrain*, Document IP/N/6/BHR/1 (01–3100), 21 June 2001

Review of Legislation: Bahrain, Document IP/Q4/BHR/1 (01–6218), 6 December 2001

Review of Legislation: Kuwait, Document IP/Q4/KWT/1 (01–6332), 13 December 2001

Review of Legislation: Oman, WTO Document IP/Q4/OMN/1 (03–1675), 24 March 2003

Review of Legislation: Responses from Qatar to the Questions Posed by Australia, Canada, the European Communities and Their Member States, Switzerland and the United States, Document IP/C/W/346 (02–3101), 5 June 2002

Checklist of Issues on Enforcement: Responses from Qatar, Document IP/N/6/QAT/1 (02–3467), 24 June 2002

Review of Legislation: Qatar, Document IP/Q4/QAT/1 (04–2460), 8 June 2004

Review of Legislation: the United Arab Emirates, Document IP/C/W/291 (01–3419), 10 July 2001

Review of Legislation: the United Arab Emirates, Document IP/C/W/291/Add. 3 (02–3461), 24 June 2002

Review of Legislation: Responses from the United Arab Emirates, Document IP/Q4/ARE/1 (04–0364), 2 February 2004

Minutes of Meeting, 27–30 November 2000, Document IP/C/M/29 (01–1088), 6 March 2001

Annual Report 2000, Document IP/C/22 (00–5308), 6 December 2000

Minutes of Meeting, 27–28 November 2001, Document IP/C/M/34 (01–6407), 20 December 2001

Minutes of Meeting, 25–27 June 2002, Document IP/C/M/36/Add.1 (02–4741), 10 September 2002

Minutes of Meeting, 17–19 September 2002, Document IP/C/M/37/Add.1 (02–6169), 8 November 2002

WTO Ministerial Declaration, Doha, November 2001, available at <http://www.wto.org/english/thewto_e/minist_e/min01_e/mindecl_e.htm>

WTO Dispute Settlement: *Dispute DS199: Brazil – Measures Affecting Patent Protection*: Request for Consultations by the United States, WT/DS199/1, Document No. 00–2254, 8 June 2000

—— *Brazil – Measures Affecting Patent Protection*: Request for the Establishment of a Panel by the United States, WT/DS1993/4, Document No. 01–0093, 9 January 2001

—— *Brazil – Measures Affecting Patent Protection*: Notification of Mutually Agreed Solution, WT/DSI994/4, Document No. 01–3506, 19 July 2001

—— United States – *US Patents Code*: Request for Consultations by Brazil, WT/DS224/1 G/L/437 Document No. 01–0597, 7 February 2001

Press Release Press No. 420 of 11 November 2005, available at <http://www.wto.org/news_e/pres05_e/pr420_e.htm>

'TRIPS Article 27.3(b) and Related Issues: Background and the Current Situation', available at <http://www.wto.org/english/tratop_e/trips_e/art27_3b_background_e.htm>

UK Commission on Intellectual Property Rights

'Integrating Intellectual Property Rights and Development Policy', *Report of the UK Commission on Intellectual Property Rights*, DFID, February 2003

Blakeney, Michael, 'Access to Genetic Resources, Gene-based Inventions and Agriculture', Study Paper 3b, UK Commission on Intellectual Property Rights, 2002

Drahos, Peter, 'Developing Countries and International Intellectual Property Standard-setting', Study Paper 8, UK Commission on Intellectual Property Rights, 2002

'How Intellectual Property Rights Could Work Better for Developing Countries and Poor People', Conference Transcript, Session 3: Traditional Knowledge and Folklore, UK Commission on Intellectual Property Rights, 2002

Leesti, Marti, and Pengelly, Tom, 'Institutional Issues for Developing Countries in Intellectual Property Policymaking, Administration and Enforcement', Study Paper 9, UK Commission on Intellectual Property Rights, 2002

Leesti, Marti, 'Institutional Issues for Developing Countries in IP Policymaking, Administration and Enforcement', Background Paper for Study Paper 9, UK Commission on Intellectual Property Rights, 2002

Puri, Kamal, 'How Intellectual Property Rights Could Work Better for Developing Countries and Poor People', *UK Commission on Intellectual Property Rights*, Conference Transcript, Session 3: Traditional Knowledge and Folklore, 2002

Thorpe, Phillip, 'Study on the Implementation of the TRIPS Agreement by Developing Countries', Study Paper 7, UK Commission on Intellectual Property Rights, 2002

Office of the United States Trade Representative (USTR)

Agreement Between the United States of America and the Government of the Kingdom of Bahrain Concerning the Development of Trade and Investment Relations, available at <http://www.ustr.gov/assets/Trade_Agreements/Regional/MEFTA/asset_upload_file168_353>

'Facts on Global Reform', *Doha Development Agenda Policy Brief*, December 2005, available at <http://www.ustr.gov/assets/Document_Library/Fact_Sheets/2005/asset_upload_file850_8542>

'Free Trade With Bahrain: A Model for Trade in the Persian Gulf Region', *USTR Trade Facts*, 27 May 2004, available at <http://www.ustr.gov/fta/bahrain/2004-05-27/factsheet>

International Intellectual Property Alliance (IIPA), '2005 Special 301 Report on Global Copyright Protection and Enforcement', available at <http://www.iipa.com/special301.html>

—— Submission on Kuwait to the USTR for the USTR 2004 Special 301 Report, available at <http://www.iipa.com/rbc/20042004pecial301Kuwait.pdf>

—— Submission on Kuwait to the USTR for the USTR 2005 Special 301 Report, available at <http://www.iipa.com/rbc/2005/2005special301Kuwait.pdf>

—— Submission on Kuwait to the USTR for the USTR 2008 Special 301 Report, available at <http://www.iipa.com/rbc/2008/2008special301Kuwait.pdf>

—— Submission on Saudi Arabia to the USTR for the USTR 2004 Special 301 Report, available at <http://www.iipa.com/rbc/2004/2004spec301Saudiarabia.pdf>

—— Submission on Saudi Arabia to the USTR for the USTR 2005 Special 301 Report, available at <http://www.iipa.com/rbc/2005/2005special301SaudiArabia.pdf>

—— Submission on Saudi Arabia to the USTR for the USTR 2008 Special 301 Report, available at <http://www.iipa.com/rbc/2008/2008special301Saudiarabia.pdf>

—— Testimony before the Public Hearing Concerning Proposed United States–Oman Free Trade Agreement Before the Trade Policy Staff Committee, 14 January 2005, available at <http://www.iipa.com/pdf/2004_SIWEK_FULL.pdf>

Message of Transmittal from the President of the United States Transmitting Treaty Between the Government of the United States of America and the Government of the State of Bahrain Concerning the Encouragement and Reciprocal Protection of Investment, with Annex, Signed at Washington on September 29, 1999, available at <http://www.tcc.mac.doc.gov/cgi-bin/doit.cgi?204:64>

Memorandum of Understanding on Issues Related to the Protection of Intellectual Property Rights Under the Agreement Between the United States and Jordan on the Establishment of a Free Trade Area, available at <http://www.ustr.gov/assets/Trade_Agreements/Bilateral/Jordan/asset_upload_file250_5112>

'Middle East Free Trade Initiative', *USTR Fact Sheet*, 23 June 2004, available at <http://www.ustr.gov/Document_Library/Fact_Sheets/2003/Middle_East_Free_Trade_Initiative.html>

'Middle East Free Trade Initiative: US Regional Plan to Spur Economic Growth', *USTR Trade Facts*, 2 March 2004, at <http://www.ustr.gov/Fact_Sheets/2004/middle_east_free_trade_initiative.html>

'Mission of the USTR', at <http://www.ustr.gov/Who_We_Are/Mission_of_the_USTR>

Pharmaceutical Research and Manufacturers of America (PhRMA), *Submission to the National Trade Estimate Report on Foreign Trade Barriers (NTE)*, 12 December 2003, available at <http://www.phrma.org/international/resources/2003_12_18_459.pdf>

—— Submission on the USTR 2004 Special 301 Report, available at <http://www.phrma.org/international/resources/13.02.2004.600.cfm>

The US–Bahrain Bilateral Investment Treaty, available at <http://www.tcc.mac.doc.gov/cgi-bin/doit.cgi?>

The US–Bahrain Free Trade Agreement (FTA), available at <http://www.ustr.gov/Trade_Agreements/Bilateral/Bahrain_FTA/Final_Texts>

The US–Bahrain Free Trade Agreement (FTA): USTR Notification of Initiation of Negotiations, US Senate, 4 August 2003, available at <http://www.ustr.gov/new/fta/2003–08–4-notification-senate>

The US–Bahrain Free Trade Agreement (FTA): Report of the Advisory Committee for Trade Policy and Negotiations (ACTPN), 14 July 2004, available at <http://www.ustr.gov/assets/Trade_Agreements/Bilateral/Bahrain_FTA/Reports/asset_upload_file 713_5503.pdf>

The US–Bahrain Free Trade Agreement (FTA): Report of the Industry Trade Advisory Committee on Intellectual Property Rights (ITAC-15), 14 July 2004, available at <http://www.ustr.gov/assets/Trade_Agreements/Bilateral/Bahrain_FTA/Reports/assets_upload_file822_5528.pdf>

The US–Bahrain Trade and Investment Framework Agreement, available at <http://www.ustr.gov/assets/Trade_Agreements/Regional/MEFTA/asset_upload_file168_3538.pdf>

The US–Oman Free Trade Agreement (FTA), available at <http://www.ustr.gov/Trade_Agreements/Bilateral/Oman_FTA/Draft_Texts>

The US–Oman Free Trade Agreement: Report of the Advisory Committee for Trade Policy and Negotiations (ACTPN), 15 November 2005, available at <http://www.ustr.gov/assets/Trade_Agreements/Bilateral/Oman_FTA/Reports/asset_upload_file 604_8376.pdf>

The US–Oman Free Trade Agreement (FTA): Report of the Industry Trade Advisory Committee on Intellectual Property Rights (ITAC-15), 15 November 2005, available at <http://www.ustr.gov/assets/Trade_Agreements/Bilateral/Oman_FTA/Reports/asset_upload_file 124_8402.pdf>

'United States to begin Free Trade Negotiations this Week with the United Arab Emirates and Oman', *USTR Press Release*, 8 March 2005, available at <http://www.ustr.gov/Trade_Agreements/Bilateral/Oman_FTAPress_ReleasesSection_Index.html>

'US and Bahrain Conclude Free Trade Agreement', *USTR Press Release*, 27 May 2004, available at <http://www.ustr.gov/new/fta/Bahrain/2004–05–27>

USTR, 1995 National Trade Estimates on Foreign Trade Barriers, available at <http://www.ustr.gov/html/1995_gcc.html>

USTR, 2005 National Trade Estimates on Foreign Trade Barriers, available at <http://www.ustr.gov/Document_Library/Reports_Publications/2005/2005_NTE_Report/Section_Index.html>

USTR, 2001 Special 301 Report, available at <http://ottawa.usembassy.gov/content/can_usa/pdfs/special301_2001.pdf>

USTR, 2002 Special 301 Report, available at <http://www.ustr.gov/assets/Document_Library/Reports_Publications/2002/2002_Special_301/assets_upload_file628_6354.pdf>

USTR, 2003 Special 301 Report, available at <http://www.ustr.gov/assets/Document_Library/Reports_Publications/2003/2003_Special_301/assets_upload_file665_6124.pdf>

USTR, 2004 Special 301 Report, available at <http://www.ustr.gov/assets/Document_Library/Reports_Publications/2004/2004_Special_301/assets_upload_file16_5995.pdf>

USTR, 2005 Special 301 Report, available at <http://www.ustr.gov/assets/Document_Library/Reports_Publications/2005/2005_Special_301/assets_upload_file195_7636.pdf>

USTR, 2008 Special 301 Report, Executive Summary, available at <http://www.ustr.gov/assets/Document_Library/Reports_Publications/2008/2008_Special_301_Report/asset_upload_file553_14869.pdf>

USTR Robert Zoellick, 'Global Trade and the Middle East: Reawakening a Vibrant Past', Address delivered at the World Economic Forum, Dead Sea, Jordan, 23 June 2003, 7–9, available at <http://www.ustr.gov/speech_test/zoellick/2003-06-23-jordan.pdf>

USTR Robert Zoellick, Letter to United States Senator Ted Stevens, notifying Congress of the President's intention to commence negotiations for a Free Trade Agreement with Bahrain, 4 August 2003, available at <http://www.ustr.gov/new/fta/2003–08–4-notification-senate>

Selected media sources

Arab News (Middle East), available at <http://www.arabnews.com>

Bahrain Gulf Daily News, available at <http://www.gulf-daily-news.com/arc_home.asp>

Bahrain Tribune, available at <http://www.bahraintribune.com/archives>

BBC News, 29 April 2003, available at <http://www.news.bbc.co.uk/1/hi/world/middle_east/2984547.stm>

GCC Patent Office News, available at <http://www.gulf-patent-office.org.sa/Regulationframe.htm>

Gulf in the Media (Gulf region), available at <http://www.gulfinthemedia.com>

Gulf News (Saudi Arabia, UAE, Kuwait, Bahrain, Qatar, Oman), available at <http://www.arabnews.com>

Khaleej Times (UAE), available at <http://www.khaleejtimes.com>

Kuwait News Agency (KUNA), available at <http://www.kuna.net.kw>

Middle East and North Africa News Agency (MENA), available at <http://www.menareport.com>

Oman Economic Review Online, available at <http://www.oeronline.com/php/2005_march/cover.php>

Oman Observer, available at <http://www.omanobserver.net>

Saudi Gazette, available at <http://www.saudigazette.com.sa>

The Economist (UK), Economist Intelligence Unit, Viewswire, available at <http://www.proquest.umi.com.ae>

The Financial Times (London)

The Peninsula (Qatar), available at <http://www.thepeninsulaqatar.com>

Times of Oman, available at <http://www.timesofoman.com>

Yemen Observer, available at <http://www.yobserver.com>

Yemen Times, available at <http://yementimes.com/index.shtml>

Regional legal advocate websites and newsletters

Abu Ghazaleh Intellectual Property (AGIP), *AGIP Newsletter*, series 1999–current, available at <http://www.agip.com/bulletin_news.aspx>

Saud M.A. Shawwaf and Abu-Setta and Partners, *New Updates*, available at <http://www.abu-setta.com>

NJQ 7 & Associates, *Newsletter*, August 2000–present, available at <http://www.qumsieh.com/newsletters.html>

Rouse & Co. International, *MEISCA Express IP*, No. 1 (July 2002) to present, available at <http://www.iprights.com/publications/meiscaipexpress.asp>

Saba & Co, Trademark and Patent Agents and Attorneys, *Bulletin*, January 2002–present, available at <http://www.sabaip.com/bulletinwww.sabaip.com>

ST&P, Attorneys and Agents, *Newsletter*, available at <http://www.stplegal.com>

Al-Tamimi & Co, Legal Advocates, *Law Updates*, Issue No. 1 (April 1991) to present, available at <http://www.tamimi.com/catalog/htm>

Trowers & Hamlins, *Publications* (Bahrain, Oman, UAE), available at <http://www.trowers.com/site/default.asp?=10>

Index

An environmentally friendly book printed and bound in England by www.printondemand-worldwide.com

PEFC Certified

This product is from sustainably managed forests and controlled sources

www.pefc.org

PEFC/16-33-415

FSC www.fsc.org

MIX

Paper from responsible sources

FSC® C004959

This book is made entirely of chain-of-custody materials

#0105 - 110612 - C0 - 234/156/20 - CB